War Lives

Judaic Traditions in Literature, Music, and Art
Ken Frieden, *Series Editor*

Select Titles in Judaic Traditions in Literature, Music, and Art

Café Shira: A Novel
David Ehrlich; Michael Swirsky, trans.

From a Distant Relation
Mikhah Yosef Berdichevsky; James Adam Redfield, ed. and trans.

*From Our Springtime: Literary Memoirs
and Portraits of Yiddish New York*
Reuben Iceland; Gerald Marcus, trans.

Once There Was Warsaw: A Memoir
Ber Kutsher; Gerald Marcus, trans.

*The People of the Book and the Camera:
Photography in the Hebrew Novel*
Ofra Amihay

A Plague of Cholera and Other Stories
Jonah Rosenfeld; Rachel Mines, trans.

A Provincial Newspaper and Other Stories
Miriam Karpilove; Jessica Kirzane, trans.

The Tears and Prayers of Fools: A Novel
Grigory Kanovich; Mary Ann Szporluk, trans.

For a full list of titles in this series, visit:
https://press.syr.edu/supressbook-series
/judaic-traditions-in-literature-music-and-art/.

War Lives

Revenge, Grief, and Conflict in Israeli Fiction

Nitza Ben-Dov
Translated from the Hebrew

Syracuse University Press

The Hebrew version of this book won the
Yitzhak Sadeh Prize for Military Literature in Israel.

Copyright © by Schocken Publishing House Ltd., Tel-Aviv, Israel
Syracuse, New York 13244-5290

All Rights Reserved

First Edition 2024

24 25 26 27 28 29   6 5 4 3 2 1

∞ The paper used in this publication meets the minimum requirements
of the American National Standard for Information Sciences—Permanence
of Paper for Printed Library Materials, ANSI Z39.48-1992.

For a listing of books published and distributed by Syracuse University Press,
visit https://press.syr.edu.

ISBN: 9780815637981(paperback)
9780815655831 (e-book)

Library of Congress Cataloging-in-Publication Data
Names: Ben-Dov, Nitza, author.
Title: War lives : revenge, grief, and conflict in Israeli fiction / Nitza Ben-Dov.
Other titles: Ḥaye milḥamah. English
Description: Syracuse, New York : Syracuse University Press, 2024. |
Series: Judaic traditions in literature, music, and art | "Translated from the Hebrew". |
Includes bibliographical references and index.
Identifiers: LCCN 2024029532 (print) | LCCN 2024029533 (ebook) |
ISBN 9780815637981 (paperback) | ISBN 9780815655831 (ebook)
Subjects: LCSH: War in literature. | Israeli fiction—History and criticism.
Classification: LCC PJ5012.W37 B4613 2024 (print) | LCC PJ5012.W37 (ebook) |
DDC 892.43/6093581—dc23/eng/20240827
LC record available at https://lccn.loc.gov/2024029532
LC ebook record available at https://lccn.loc.gov/2024029533

Manufactured in the United States of America

Contents

Introduction · 1

1. Only Sons and Bereavement in S. Y. Agnon's *To This Day*
   A Novel of the First World War · 71

2. Vengeance or Salvation? The Tragic Dilemma in Hanoch Bartov's *The Brigade*
   A Novel of the Jewish Brigade · 82

3. The Vengeance of the Skull in Yehuda Amichai's *Not of This Time, Not of This Place*
   A Novel of Two Wars · 109

4. Abjection, Camaraderie, and Passion in Yehoshua Kenaz's *Infiltration*
   A Novel of IDF Basic Training in the Early 1950s · 136

5. Dream and Illness in Amos Oz's *My Michael*
   A Novel of the Sinai War in 1956 · 174

6. Language Barriers, Roadblocks, and Frustrated Love in Eli Amir's *Yasmine*
   A Novel of the Six-Day War · 183

7. The Human Voice in Inhumane Wars in David Grossman's *To the End of the Land*
   The Yom Kippur War in Israeli Prose · 220

8. Brothers in Blood in Sami Michael's *Pigeons at Trafalgar Square*
   A Novel of the First Intifada · 240

9. Soldiers in a Bubble in Ron Leshem's *Beaufort*
   A Novel about an Outpost in the "Mud of Lebanon" · 269

10. The Bereaved Family in A. B. Yehoshua's *Friendly Fire*
A Novel of the Second Intifada • 285

11. Fighting Men, Adored by Women. Really?
The Examined Corpus through the Lens of Gender • 310

Conclusion • 334

Appendix
Novels Analyzed in War Lives • 343

Notes • 345

Bibliography • 365

War Lives

Introduction

Will They Know Nothing of War Anymore?

Since its inception, Israel has lived in a state of almost perpetual warfare. Despite this historical fact, Hebrew novels that deal with the experience of war itself are surprisingly rare. Ron Leshem's best-seller *Beaufort*[1] is an exception to the rule: The novel depicts the daily routine and personal lives of a team of warriors in a single outpost in South Lebanon just before the Israeli withdrawal of May 2000. The platoon, stationed in a modern forward-operating base adjacent to the historic crusader fort, Beaufort, consists of fifteen soldiers. The platoon members deal, personally and collectively, with the reality of guard duty and improvised explosive devices (IEDs), incoming fire and the whistle of mortar shells—"purple rain" in the outpost's vernacular. The ever-present danger is exacerbated by an inherent tension: Stationed on enemy soil, hounded by constant fear, charged with shielding Israeli towns from Hezbollah militiamen, the soldiers are also acutely aware of the agitation on the home front, the roiling sentiment, rapidly reaching a boil, against Israel's—that is, their—ongoing, eighteen-year presence in Lebanon. In 2006, the novel won Israel's annual Sapir Prize for the best work of literature; it was later adapted into a movie, and was successful in Israel and abroad, serving as a strong contender for the best foreign film award at the February 2008 Academy Awards ceremony. Leshem had this to say about the palpable reality portrayed in his novel:

> It can't be that all of our canonic writers pen their coming of age novels about the Holocaust, and then remain rooted in 1948 or the fifties in Nahalal or Jerusalem. How little has been written of the Yom

Kippur War. How little has been written of the Lebanon War. Those are immense traumas, open wounds . . . We are fearful of dealing with true traumas. This is the duty of our intellectuals and in my opinion, it is being shirked.[2]

The reasons why Hebrew literature does not faithfully reflect the traumas of war and its lingering, unhealed wounds—one of the most significant and basic experiences in the lives of young Israelis—is to be found in extra-literary realms. Perhaps it is escapism, enabling young Israelis to deny in order to live, to dream. But there are those who will say that the assertion itself is incorrect, for many classic and canonic Hebrew novels have dealt with the wars of Israel and the effects of those wars on the protagonists. *War Lives* takes such novels and their unique negotiation of war and its aftermath as its subject, exploring war narratives that, taken together, trace the full course of Israel's history. Hanoch Bartov's *The Brigade* (1965) describes the experiences of the soldiers in the Jewish Brigade at the end of World War II, some three years shy of the founding of the modern State of Israel; S. Yizhar's *Days of Ziklag* (1958) is considered the opus of Israel's 1948 War of Independence; Yehoshua Kenaz's *Infiltration* (1986), set in the period between the War of Independence and the 1956 War, depicts the traumatic encounter of Israeli youths and the discipline of the military, which was then, during the state's formative years, far more severe than the tolerant and understanding norms adopted by the Israel Defense Forces (IDF) several decades later; the 1956 Sinai War trickles into Amos Oz's *My Michael* (1968); Eli Amir's *Yasmine* (2004) revolves around the 1967 Six-Day War; and Sami Michael's *Refuge* (1977) deals with the first three days of the Yom Kippur War. David Grossman's *To the End of the Land* stretches between Israel's Six-Day War of 1967 and the wave of terror attacks in the early 2000s known as the Second Intifada, with the Yom Kippur War lying heavy in between. Grossman's aforementioned novel was published one year after Ron Leshem's statement. Eshkol Nevo's *Neuland* (2011), a novel about a post-traumatic veteran, also touches on the Yom Kippur War and seems ex post facto to contradict Leshem's assertion—"How little has been written of the Yom Kippur War."[3]

However, despite this impressive and inconclusive list, it would seem that most of the aforementioned works do not deal head-on with warfare—with the blood, the sweat, the tears of soldiers, the annihilating fear of being wounded, the boundless camaraderie and friendship between the men, along with the concern that ideology might weaken the resolve of the soldier beside you at the moment of truth. As *War Lives* demonstrates, indirection is perhaps the most salient feature of Israeli war narratives. The reluctance to deal directly with the experience of war is perhaps partly explained by the wishful thought that closes David Grossman's Holocaust novel, *See Under: Love* (1986):[4] "All of us prayed for one thing: that one person might live in this world an entire lifetime, from beginning to end, knowing nothing of war." Perhaps to face the realities of Israel's wars would mean to acknowledge that this characteristic post–World War II wish has not been fulfilled in the course of Israel's existence. Grossman's more recent novel, *To the End of the Land* (2008), spans more than a quarter of a century of Middle East violence. This contemporary novel relegates the yearning for a warless life to the realm of redemptive dreams. What is more, the desire for a life free of war, which in Grossman's earlier novel encompasses "an entire lifetime, from beginning to end," is supplanted in the later novel by the tragic-ironic realization that the escape of one person, or one family from war's lethal clutches, even for a limited time—is a blessing. "We had twenty good years. In our country, that's almost chutzpah," Ora, the novel's female protagonist, reflects in a nocturnal writing ritual that forms part of the monologue she reads out to Avram, her friend since adolescence, who had been severely injured in the Yom Kippur War.

> Twenty years we had. A long time. And don't forget that six of those years covered the two boys' army service . . . And they both served in the territories, in the lousiest places. The fact that we somehow managed to walk between the raindrops without really getting splattered even once, from any war or terrorist attack, from any rocket, grenade, bullet, shell, explosive device, sniper, suicide bomber, metal marbles, slingstone, knife, nails. The fact that we just lived out a quiet, private life.

Ora concludes her description of twenty years' "repose" with a reference to Avram's war injury three decades earlier: "Do you get it? A small, unheroic life, one that deals as little as possible with the situation, God damn it, because as you know, we already paid our price" (298–99).

The fact that Israeli literature seems averse to contending with the direct experience of war may therefore also be the result of a reality of omnipresent war, as Israeli historical time itself becomes trapped between war and the interim periods between wars. War becomes the paradoxical condition of Israeli normalcy. How do the traumas of past wars and the fear of future wars bleed into one another and shape the temporality of major Israeli novels? In his book *A Soldier Returns Home*,[5] a documentary novel of injury and illness, Yoram Eshet-Alkalai describes the atmosphere at home long after his return as a rehabilitated veteran of the Yom Kippur War: "The war dwelled in our home for decades, present yet absent, hovering over the anger and the fear, among helplessness and hopefulness, between limping and blindness . . . We all felt its presence" (9). Undoubtedly, war casualties will carry the burden of its memory for the rest of their lives, as will their families. This insight forms the crux of Eshet-Alkalai's autobiographical book as much as it does David Grossman's work. Both authors stress that the anxiety of war also dominates peacetime, in a modified form. Indeed, most of the narrative trajectories mentioned in this book take place on the home front, not the battle front.

In his novel *Pigeons at Trafalgar Square*,[6] Sami Michael expresses another possible theory for why Israeli prose seems to scrupulously avoid touching this red-hot "third rail" through the protagonist Ze'ev, his attraction to Hebrew literature, and his reservations about it—because it avoids contending with local traumas:

> From a young age, Ze'ev eagerly read Israeli literature that was tied to the human context of the Middle East very loosely, almost accidentally. On the one hand, this literature despised the cold, cruel Europe. But on the other hand, it idolized the restrained Europe, which—like a British gentleman, like a Prussian general—is always careful to avoid being swept by emotions. (Hebrew, 85)

Michael migrated from Iraq at the age of twenty-three. His protagonist sees major Israeli authors' reluctance to directly confront the region's historical realities as a European bequest: Seeking to emulate Prussian decorum, the authors (primarily Ashkenazi men), who defined for Michael the mainstream of Israeli prose fiction, sought to distance their texts from the emotional turbulence of war. Whether for cultural reasons, as a form of escapism, as a response to trauma, or for other reasons entirely, it is clear that the subject of war is an absent presence at the center of many Israeli novels.

Despite the complexity in tackling the subject of war, army life and military conflicts are present in countless works, either as an explicit theme (main or secondary) or as an analogy, a platform for the development of ideas, or a potent allusion. For Israeli authors, the army experience and wars form an inseparable part of reality. As Israelis, we, and our sons, and our sons' sons, join the army in perpetual preparation for war, guided by the adage of Publius Flavius Vegetius, the late fourth-century Roman author: "He who desires peace, should prepare for war." In addition, the wars of the past, particularly the Second World War (and especially the events of the Holocaust) and the War of Independence (customarily perceived as a direct response to the Holocaust), are the defining historical experiences that continue to echo in the psyches of Israeli Jews, of diverse ages and ethnicities. In Yehuda Amichai's voluminous novel, *Not of This Time, Not of This Place* (1963),[7] these two wars (which are not directly mentioned by their official names) are alive in the protagonist's soul as he laments: "Oh, my sad and stricken generation, the generation of two wars per capita, at least" (416). This follows his all-too-true epigrammatic observation: "People always live in between two wars" (412). War bookends the lives of Israeli Jews of all generations, sustaining an indelible link to both their past and future—how, then, does it characterize their literature?

The different chapters of this book explore the often paradoxical ways in which Israeli authors deal with Israel's troubled history. If Michael and Leshem correctly diagnose a literary escape from the traumas of history, such an escape can never be complete. By offering close readings of a wide range of texts, the book foregrounds war as a coordinate which Israeli novels are driven, with equal force, to flee from and return to. I propose such recursive textual movement as characteristic of Israeli military and war literature. While each chapter focuses on a different theme—from mourning, to battleground camaraderie, to vengeance—in their totality, the different chapters point to the historical reality of war as a defining framework of the Israeli condition. In the prose works under discussion, the individual living in the constant shadow of war is prevented the escapism of peacetime narrative structures, of simple love stories or family histories. In all the works I discuss, protagonists are more or less helpless in the face of the events that intrude into their lives with the outbreak of war.

In order to trace the charged counterpoint between the subjective and collective experience of war in Israeli texts, *War Lives* adheres to textual analysis as a critical paradigm, taking the words of the novels themselves as a point of departure. In its reliance on close readings, the book differs from most recent scholarly accounts addressing the topic of war in Israeli literature and culture. These contemporary studies tend to adopt a historicist critical perspective, aiming to unearth previously silenced or repressed aspects of the Israeli national ethos by reading major prose texts as they participate in (or undermine) this ethos. Such is Dana Olmert's impressive study of the figure of the "mother of soldiers" in Hebrew literature.[8] Like *War Lives*, Olmert's work foregrounds military life and war as defining characteristics of Israeli culture and literature. *Barricade of Mothers* is also similarly interested in the ways war permeates the everyday, the familiar and intimate spaces of Israeli family life. Olmert specifically examines the position of mothers in the Israeli national narrative, especially as they are faced with the contradictory expectation that they protect their sons, even as they offer them up in sacrifice, as soldiers, to the state. Olmert traces a historical continuum of literary and extra-literary representations of Jewish women, from pre-statehood times to the present day, to ask how Israeli literature positions mothers vis-à-vis its prevailing ideologies, whether overtly or implicitly stated. She suggests that whether they adhere to the patriotic role they are expected to play or diverge from it, mothers must always pay a heavy price for war's presence in their lives, and can never successfully protect the space of their private home from the charged and gendered spaces of collective Israeli national experience.

Olmert's study shares a central literary-historical assumption with most recent scholarship on Israeli war narratives—that a turning point in the Israeli ethos of war and public sentiment regarding military service occurred in the 1980s, following several key events. First, the signing of a peace treaty with Egypt in 1979 offered a new horizon of hope for normalization with surrounding Arab states. Secondly, the Lebanon War, which broke out in June 1982, sparked a wave of mass protests in Israel, and was the first conflict to be perceived by many Israelis as a "war of choice," a conflict which is not necessary or unavoidable.[9] Finally, the Intifada (Palestinian uprising) of 1987 brought the reality of Israel's military presence in the Palestinian territories into Israeli public discourse, which began to acknowledge, however partially, the ethical problems resulting from the continued occupation of Palestinian land. All of these events altered Israeli perceptions of war. As Olmert suggests, the literary representation of soldiers and their mothers also changed around this time. If war and military service began to be perceived as morally ambivalent, mothers were now expected not only to offer up their sons for the protection of the national project, but also, paradoxically, to protect their sons from this project and its potentially destructive consequences. The contradictory claims leveled at mothers following the Israeli public's crisis of faith in its political leadership in the 1980s led to a wave of portrayals of mothers on the verge of mental breakdown. Olmert links such portrayals of maternal madness to women's real or perceived divergence from their normative role in the national order, especially in their opposition to their sons' enlistment. Thus, Grossman's Ora, when taking a critical stance toward her son's military service, is struck with fear that she may contract "leftist Tourette's Syndrome," which she associates with women's activist groups, and worries that this condition would prevent her from occupying her "proper," familiar family role of protector.

Several other recent studies of Israeli war narratives hinge on the same fundamental literary-historical argument, positioning the 1980s as a kind of Archimedean point from which to survey Israeli cultural perceptions of war. Adia Mendelson-Maoz's *Borders, Territories, Ethics*[10] and Ranen Omer-Sherman and Rachel Harris's *Narratives of Dissent*[11] share Olmert's interest in this cultural-historical timeline. However, Mendelson-Maoz's book chooses to focus on the aftermath of this watershed decade by examining how the literary representation of Israeli public consciousness changed between the two intifadas, given the return of the repressed knowledge of the occupation of the Palestinian territories. Focusing her analysis on the trope of borders, Mendelson-Maoz examines how Israelis' belated discovery of the country's borderless condition dictated an "overriding theme of a society's sickness"[12] in the literature of this period. She is particularly interested in the manner in which this "sickness" corresponds with questions of ethics. Mendelson-Maoz argues that the representations of soldiers and war in this period tend to portray a state of ethical chaos and disorientation. Whereas Olmert is interested in changes in the representation of mothers, Mendelson-Maoz's book is closer in its concerns to *War Lives*, focusing on soldiers and on the spaces of everyday life. Mendelson-Maoz suggests that if in earlier Israeli narratives soldiers are admirable, self-sacrificing heroes, in this later period they become agents of a greater evil or victims of the national war machine. The civilian spaces of Israeli life likewise become permeated by ethical uncertainty. Omer-Sherman and Harris's collection of essays examines the same post-Lebanon shift in the Israeli representation of war in diverse artistic media and traces the increasing public alienation from militarization with far-reaching effects on every avenue of Israeli culture. *War Lives* shares part of the impetus of these recent scholarly works in its endeavor to demonstrate that Israeli war narratives complicate some of the mythologies of Israeli history. However, whereas existing scholarship takes as its point of departure a certain literary historical claim, which is shared by all of the aforementioned studies, and grounds this claim in readings of varied cultural texts, *War Lives* first addresses the literary text in order to arrive at certain overarching themes. Taken together, these themes tell the story of Israeli literature and its ambivalent relationship with war and military life.

The chapters of the book trace several key ways in which Israeli writers employ the freedoms granted by fiction to challenge the heroic myth of war. *War Lives* suggests that these writers do so not only by turning inward, toward the home front and the psyches of individuals marked by post-trauma, but also by unsettling the relationship between historical fact and fiction, and between diegetic and metadiegetic time. In these ways, Israeli war narratives show a basic tendency to question the reliability of stories and storytellers. While they often rely on the autobiographical voice, these narratives tend to cast doubt on the authenticity of their own testimonies. Their temporalities are disjunctive, jumping surprisingly from one timeline to another, each frame of reference relativizing and recontextualizing the events as they are transmitted to the potential reader. In this manner, the events of war refuse to be relegated to a completed past: They are unrepresentable, yet become a center of gravity for the texts, exerting a pull on their surroundings. If the events of war, for all their emotional intensity and ethical complexity, seem to demand an authentic and accurate retelling, *War Lives* shows that they also render such a retelling problematic—indeed, perhaps impossible.

Testimony as Literary Ploy:
History and Memory in the Shadow of War

It is worthwhile surveying some key structural tensions that are broadly characteristic of Western war literature in order to examine their presence in Israeli literature. The first of these is the tension between testimony and fiction. Literary works containing a representation of historical events in some form or other are, of course, not scientific-historiographical studies. They are a personal reworking of the historical experiences that percolated into artists' lives, or the lives of their protagonists. Novelists allow themselves to amplify a real-life event, motif, or element and to suppress others, while weaving together incidents, utterances, personae, and voices with analogical, symbolic, mythical, or associative threads, compromising the tale's "truthful," earthly proportions and "real" chronological sequence, to offer in return an emotional-artistic response to the events in question. That is, in the work of fiction, the premise of objective testimony is always replaced with personal, psychological testimony that is nonetheless commensurate with its external-factual counterpart. The subjective dimension of the description of reality, which allows authors to recast the events according to their taste, needs, and free imagination, sometimes to the point of conjuring up a narrator-protagonist who is completely distinct from the author, complements the external documentation of events and presents them in a different light. The author observes reality and creates a parallel imaginary world that bears certain similarities to and yet differs from real-life happenings, thanks to the unique proportions between incidents, objects, characters, and conversations related in the characters' own language. As authors creatively tweak reality, they refine the text's literary quality. The deeper they penetrate into their protagonists' minds, the more they enrich the text's psychological dimension. Both aspects correspond with reality.

And yet, despite their declared subjectivity, literary texts are relevant not only for scholars researching culture but also for scholars studying the past. Historiography borrows from literary models of representation and writing; that is, literature helps historians describe the scenes and landscapes, conjure up picturesque descriptions, and select the materials they deem fit to emphasize. What is more, literature provides historiographers with materials that are useful and even essential to their analyses and assumptions. Writing a cultural, spiritual, or geopolitical history without taking into consideration belles-lettres is almost inconceivable. Many of the literary texts about war are autobiographical by nature. This observation equally holds for world literature and Hebrew literature. It is customary to think that literary devices—recurring patterns, allusions, analogies, powerful metaphors, imaginary worlds—primarily serve the artwork. But in war literature, which draws its materials from life on the verge of annihilation, the figurativeness of the text serves both genres—fiction and documentary—and blurs the boundaries between them.

While purporting to offer an authentic description of the military experience, some works invite readers to wonder what is historically true and what is fictional—that is, which events were retained in the author's mind as genuine and which events were reconstructed with the help of the author's craft. Sometimes authors and storytellers confess, either in extra-literary testimonies or in the literary works themselves, that things did not actually occur as depicted, since memories are elusive and often correspond with historical events in oblique ways, especially in contexts of violence and trauma. In some works about war, military service, or vengeance against enemies, readers are aware that the text does reflect an historical reality even though many of the details sprang from the author's imagination. The literary imagination, in turn, is informed by first-person accounts, rumors, and actual experiences that underwent literary adaptation. Hence, while fantasy and fiction figure in war literature like in any other genre, in many cases they reflect true autobiographical details.

Let us consider how individual war experiences can be simultaneously autobiographical and fictional, and how an author's choice not to self-identify as the protagonist may conceal autobiographical accuracy, even as first-person narratives mask a writer's imaginative liberty.

Throughout Erich Maria Remarque's *All Quiet on the Western Front*,[13] the sober and reliable voice of a twenty-year-old German soldier relates a first-person account in the present tense, giving the impression that the events related are taking place in the here-and-now, and that the accounts are authentic, as they detail the unfathomable experiences on the battlefront and the home front, in the trenches, on trains and in hospitals. This leads the reader to think that the author is telling his personal story with documentary precision.

In the novel's final paragraph, however, the author abruptly and unexpectedly separates himself from his protagonist. Remarque replaces the first-person, present tense with a distant and cold report in the third-person past tense about the protagonist's death. Paul, the narrator-protagonist, who spent about four years on the western front, dug in, assaulted, feared death, endured starvation, was injured, and then returned to the front, tells how over the years his close friends, who became like family to him, die horrid deaths one after the other. In October 1918, shortly before the war ends, expectedly as much as unexpectedly, he joins the fallen. Expectedly, because it is hard to believe that death, so omnipresent throughout the novel, would skip over its protagonist; unexpectedly, because Paul, the narrator-protagonist, tells the novel's story, which means he must be alive! Yet the reader learns that Paul was killed, while Erich Maria Remarque survived to tell his story, and the two separated. Or did they? Both of them died. One physically, the other spiritually:

> He fell in October 1918, on a day that was so quiet and still on the whole front, that the army report confined itself to the single sentence: All quiet on the Western Front.

> He had fallen forward and lay on the earth as though sleeping. Turning him over one saw that he could not have suffered long; his face had an expression of calm, as though almost glad the end had come. (320)

In *Avigdor Hameiri and War Literature* (1986), Avner Holtzman reflects on the physical death of the first-person narrator, which undermines "the authenticity of the descriptions," and by that increases the work's literary quality. There are many parallels between Erich Maria Remarque's *All Quiet on the Western Front* and Avigdor Hameiri's *The Great Madness: The Notes of a Hebraic Officer in the Great War*.[14] Both novels were published in the same year (1929), and both deal with the First World War. They share a well-known literary pattern that Holtzman calls "elimination" (or "ten little Indians").[15] This pattern follows a group of people who lose one member at a time, until the last to survive, who tells its story, is left all alone. Remarque's narrator tells the story of seven school friends killed in the war, before ultimately losing his own life. Hameiri's book relates the story of the narrator's four friends who die one after another by disease and torture. But contrary to Remarque's literary ploy that transforms his protagonist from subject to object in the novel's final paragraph, Hameiri's protagonist survives, retaining the book's documentary nature and keeping at bay elements of literary fiction.

Nonetheless, literary elements are found in each and every work written about war and army life. Even in a self-declared autobiography such as Yoram Eshet-Alkalai's *A Man Walks Home*, the author makes clear: "This is not a historical document. Rather, it is the story that I tell myself today with the hindsight of close to forty years about my war experience—and mostly about what took place after it ended" (11). Moreover, the book offers accounts told by family members, friends, and other injured soldiers who stayed with the narrator in hospitals and in rehabilitation, which on first reading appear reliable contributions to its Rashomon effect. Later in the book it emerges that those testimonies were invented by the narrator in order to gain an outside perspective on himself.

The problematizing of the status of testimony, so characteristic of war narratives, is closely associated with another key feature of Israeli war literature: the destabilization of the relationship between diegetic and metadiegetic time. The question of whether it is preferable to write about war in real time or in hindsight can be answered either way. Real-time eyewitness accounts offer detailed and accurate descriptions, as well as a record of the failure to fully grasp the reality of war as it unfolds. More poetry is written than prose in wartime, as it enables the soldier-poet to express instant, emotional, and spontaneous responses to the experiences he undergoes. Requiring a broad context, a plot of some sort, and a chronology of events, the soldier-author usually engages in prose writing at a later time, more conducive to the task.

Unlike real-time accounts, retrospection enables authors to approach a past reality more conclusively. Armed with the wisdom of hindsight, the author or historiographer may offer an ironic presentation of those who were deluded to think that war would skip them over, or alternatively, to admire their foresight if they prepared for what was to come. The historical perspective allows authors to decry the reality they write about, either empathetically or with the arrogance of the all-knowing. In his book on Avigdor Hameiri's war literature, Holtzman describes at length two waves of literary writing on the First World War: a patriotic wave during the war and a pacifist wave a decade after its conclusion. "Critics agree," Holtzman writes, "on the merits of the perspective that enabled authors to observe the war from a distance, to process their experiences, and turn them into literary works of value."[16]

Suite Française, a novel describing Parisians' en masse escape from the threat of Nazi air raids in June 1940, was written by Irène Némirovski in real time.[17] That is, although the novel was first published in France in 2004, more than sixty years after it was written, its narrative time is close to its story time. The novel's strength lies in the absence of perspective between the time in which the events took place (story time) and the time of their narration (narrative time). The novel's first part, entitled "Storm in June," is a powerful, lucid fresco of France and the French in the summer of 1940. Chapter 31, which concludes this part, is centered on the winter of 1940–41, as war and winter coalesced into an inexorable nightmare. The terrible predicament of families, individuals, captives, prostitutes, and romantics, who all run head-on to the war without fathoming its nature (while maintaining class differences even under horrendous living conditions), form a credible jigsaw puzzle of the French and of Paris and its surrounding villages, to which millions of Parisians fled. The protagonist of "Storm in June" is the multitude of road travelers, some of whom decide at a certain point in their onerous and futile journey to return to Paris. The potency of the novel's first part lies in its collectivist camera-like depiction of war life in real time.

Another real-time camera-like documentation of the Parisian exodus is offered in Antoine de Saint-Exupéry's novel *Flight to Arras*,[18] which he began writing in the summer of 1940. "As a pilot," writes Giddon Ticotsky in his afterword to the Hebrew translation of the work (published together with *Letter to a Hostage*), "[Saint-Exupéry] had the privilege of observing the war from a unique vantage point: witnessing the events simultaneously on the battlefront and the home front—at the central command headquarters of the exasperated, deteriorating French army; and in the convoys of tens of thousands of uprooted citizens flowing from France's north southward."[19] From his aerial viewpoint, Saint-Exupéry likens the masses inching their way on the roads to "interminable syrup flowing endless to the horizon" (67). The lively and detailed expression of the collective experience should also be credited to the narrative time's proximity to the story time. *Suite Française* and *Flight to Arras* belong to a French genre called "the literature of defeat" (*la littérature de la défaite et de la collaboration*) (194).

In her comparison between soldiers' attitudes toward the First World War and the "current" war (the Second World War), Irène Némirovski praises the merits of real-time description: "They were all former soldiers . . . They had had time to filter the past, to decant it, to get rid of the dregs, the poison, to make it bearable for their souls; but recent events remained confusing and laced with venom" (178). More insights on the advantages of real-time description may be found in the work of Nitza Priluk, who studied some 170 letters written by Hermann Weil (1893–1916), a German-Jewish soldier in the First World War, who sent them to his family from the Eastern Front. In her article, Priluk writes: "Reading a text written by a young, unknown author, who gradually becomes a close, almost intimate figure, resembles the process one undergoes when one reads good literature. We fear for his fate, we are impressed by his courage, and wish to console him." Priluk later comments on the benefits of the proximity of narrative time and story time, "which draws the reader into a first-hand, authentic experience."[20] In *Suite Française* and *Flight to Arras*, narrative time and story time are exceptionally close. Usually, many years separate the author's war experiences from the time they are committed to the page, while the written outcome does not necessarily lose its "dregs, the poison," as Irène Némirovski observes. Sometimes, they even grow more intense. What is more, good novels succeed in "drawing the reader into an authentic-primary experience" (in Nitza Priluk's words), even if the narrative time is distant from the story time. Erich Maria Remarque began writing *All Quiet on the Western Front* in 1927, and published it in 1929. Some ten years separate his discharge from military service and the writing of the novel, an exemplary anti-war work due to its detailed, precise, and nauseatingly vivid depictions of the horrors of war, thanks to which it became one of the most popular novels in world literature.[21]

In Hebrew literature, story time and narrative time can sometimes be decades apart. S. Y. Agnon recorded his wartime experiences in *To This Day* (1950)[22] more than thirty years after they took place. Hanoch Bartov wrote about his service in the British Army in *The Brigade* (1965) twenty years after the fact. Yoram Kaniuk's *1948*[23] was published in Hebrew in 2010, nearly six decades after the battles it describes had ended. On the book's back cover, Kaniuk confesses that time has probably undermined the authenticity of his descriptions:

> For fifty-nine years, I have been trying to write this . . . I am not sure what I truly remember, as I do not trust memory; it is cunning and does not preserve a single truth. You think, and a moment later you remember what you choose to remember. I was seventeen and a half, a goodie-two-shoes Tel Avivian amid a bloodbath . . . and maybe it was all just a dream.[24]

Many Israeli novels refer simultaneously to several wars in a single work, clearly requiring a broad time perspective. At the heart of Agnon's posthumously published novella "The Covering of the Blood, or At the Same Time" (1975), a panhandler with a wooden leg is standing on a Jerusalem street in the 1960s. His life had been impacted, directly and indirectly, by the First World War, the Second World War, and the War of Independence (dubbed in the novella, "The War between the Jews and the Arabs"), as well as by the Syrian provocations before the Six-Day War. Agnon presents these military clashes, which had pointlessly claimed countless Jewish and Arab victims, as a single mass that makes it impossible to draw a rationale, structure, or insight from their chronological sequence. The founding of the Jewish state forms an integral part of this mass, which has neither beginning nor end.[25]

Several wars and an obsessive back-of-mind preoccupation with them haunt the three main characters of David Grossman's *To the End of the Land*. The novel opens with the Six-Day War and ends with the terrorist attacks of the early 2000s, yet both are overshadowed by the Yom Kippur War. It took Grossman thirty-three years to write about that war, in a novel that merges documentary reality with literary reality. Eli Amir's *Yasmine* (2005) is a novel about the Six-Day War. After depicting the nerve-wracking anticipation that led up to the war and the battles that were waged, *Yasmine* dwells on the transformation in the perception of the two peoples: the triumphant Israelis and the defeated Palestinians. Written with the hindsight of forty years about the war that changed the face of the Middle East, the novel also accommodates other wars. On a night before the war begins, guarding on the outskirts of Gaza City and consumed by anxiety, the protagonist counts the wars that have surrounded him since childhood, knowing that the war about to break is not the last:

> At night the choking sensations came back, as if a vampire had me in a stranglehold. Come on then, how much longer do we have to wait? Memories were flooding in threatening to engulf me. I was two when **World War II** broke out and we fled from the house where I'd been born in the Muslim al-Muadham quarter of Baghdad, but the rioters had caught up with us in the Jewish quarter, where they killed and raped and robbed. I was ten when Israel's **War of Independence** began in Palestine. The Iraqis had arrested my Uncle Hizkel and we abandoned Baghdad like refugees fleeing for their lives. I was nineteen when the **Suez War** broke out, and my mother miscarried from anxiety.

Now I'm approaching thirty and there is no end in sight! (*Yasmine*, 34; emphasis added)

An endless sequence of wars is also treated to a chilling effect in Yehudit Hendel's *The Mountain of Losses* (1991).[26] A bereaved father, Shmulik Ron, comes with a bereaved couple, Meira and Ariel, to tend the graves of their fallen sons, both killed in 1973. Shmulik surveys the cemetery divided into plots, each dedicated to a different war: "His eyes shift from the War of Independence to the Six-Day War to the War of Attrition to the Yom Kippur War to the Lebanon War to the large, empty plot that lies in wait" (*The Mountain of Losses*, 34). Later on in the work, the relentless sequence of wars is only denoted by their year. Accompanying a bereaved couple to the cemetery, the narrator is reminded of her Aunt Pessya, whose son was killed in March 1948 in an ambush on a convoy that made its way to Kibbutz Yehi'am. Forty-six men lost their lives in the attack (the novel mistakenly cites forty-two fatalities). Using years as codes, she reflects on the ongoing loss of lives: "Like I said, that was in '48. Then there was '56. Then '73. And then '82. And there was the War of Attrition. And my Uncle Simchah used to say: The War of Attrition takes them in stride" (60).

Israeli novels that center on families, rather than wars, also measure time with the chronology of the country's wars. Chronicles of individuals and the collective are related by using military draft, service, and conflicts as milestones. For example, the prologue to the first dialogue in A. B. Yehoshua's *Mr. Mani* (1990), a dialogue between two female interlocutors, revolves around the army, Israel's reprisal operations, and military clashes. *Mr. Mani* is a dynastic novel spanning five generations of the Mani family, whose members (the novel's characters) are impacted by wars and army life in the course of two centuries, beginning with the Janissary armies of the Ottoman Empire that bought horse fodder from a family ancestor, and ending with the First Lebanon War. The prologue describes war orphan Hagar Shiloh by emphasizing the central role that war, army, and orphanhood have played in her young life:

Hagar attended a regional high school in the nearby kibbutz, Revivim . . . She began her army service in August 1980 and served as a noncommissioned counseling officer with a paratroop unit stationed in central Israel . . . upon finishing her military service, the last months of which were highly eventful because of the outbreak of the war in Lebanon in 1982 . . . she persuaded a general meeting of the kibbutz to allow her to continue her studies. This decision was facilitated by the fact that, as the daughter of a fallen soldier, Hagar stood to have her tuition fully paid for by the Ministry of Defense (*Mr. Mani*, 5–6).[27]

The description of Hagar's mother, war widow Yael Shiloh, in the same prologue intertwines her military service, the reprisal operations, the Sinai War, and the Six-Day War with her own biography:

Ya'el Shiloh, née Kramer. Born in a suburb of Haifa in 1936 . . . In 1954, she began her army duty, serving with a group from her movement in Kibbutz Rosh Hanikra near the Lebanese border. It was there that she met her future husband Roni Shiloh, a movement member from Tel Aviv. Trained as a paratrooper like the other boys in the group, he saw action in a number of border raids and in the 1956 Sinai Campaign. In their final months in the army, Ya'el and Roni were stationed in Mash'abei Sadeh, a young kibbutz in the Negev desert . . . Roni was killed in the Six-Day War along the Kuneitra-Damascus road. (7)

Ronnie's death in the Six-Day War is mentioned as part of a natural, self-evident chronicle.

Like her other novels, Zeruya Shalev's *Pain* (2015) grapples with archetypal family relationships. Uncharacteristically of the author, however, army and war form an integral part of the work. Iris, the protagonist, is a war orphan injured in a terror attack in the 2000s. These two facts trigger long years of physical and mental pain, as well as nightmares and anxiety. When her son Omer is about to join the army, she is supposed to process this bitter fact in the short timespan between his first conscription letter and the day he joins the army: "Don't worry, it's a first draft notice, you'll have time to get used to the idea" (285),[28] his father tells him. Traumatized by her own military service, his sister soothes the young man by saying: "I'm so glad that's all behind me! Don't worry. Believe me, if I survived it, you will too" (286). In the second decade of the twenty-first century, young Israeli men and women no longer join the army with enthusiasm, but rather with painful acceptance.

Israel's unique national story itself may be legitimately likened to a gripping literary work. Its upheavals, dramatic turns, and tense anticipation for what is to come confirm the cliché: The Israeli story exceeds the imagination. In this country, the predicament of individuals is inextricably bound up with the story of the nation as a whole. The biography of every Israeli, personal and intimate as it might be, is inseparable from the political reality. Yet the local dimension of the stories based on these wars does not necessarily overlap with the universal dimension. War, after all, confronts humans with radical situations in which they learn about themselves and the limits of their abilities and endurance. Melding together the personal with the national in the Jewish-Israeli experience on every step and turn, *Mr. Mani* states in its opening paragraph:

> Hagar Shiloh [notice the charged, multivalent name of the young woman, born in the Negev desert]. Born in 1962 in Mash'abei Sadeh, a kibbutz thirty kilometers south of Beersheba that was founded in **1949**. Her parents, Roni and Ya'el Shiloh, first arrived there in **1956** in the course of their army service. Hagar's father **Roni was killed on the last day of the Six-Day War** as a reservist on the Golan Heights. As Hagar was five at the time, her claim to have clear memories of her father may well have been correct. (5; emphasis added)

Other than Hagar's date of birth, her personal chronology is measured according to Israel's wars. The year her kibbutz was founded, 1949, was the aftermath of the War of Independence; 1956, the year of her parents' arrival in the desert community, is concurrent with the Sinai War; 1967, the year of her father's death, is tragically linked to the brief and fateful war of the same year. The novel drily reports that Roni, a kibbutznik from the Negev, is killed on the Golan Heights on the sixth and last day of the war, a tragedy that need not even be spelled out. The events are described with a cold and precise tone of transcendent objectivity, by an authoritative, omniscient voice; yet every first name, date, or place bears meaning and memories that resonate in the mind of every Israeli who hears them, triggering an onrush of both personal and collective memories. Brimming with nostalgia, the details of time and place form sweeping yet ambiguous statements, which lend themselves to divergent and sometimes contradictory interpretations. One statement, however, remains beyond dispute: War is central to the lives of all Israelis, and uncannily entwines the most private and personal to the historical. War subtends private and collective memories that may be broken down to precise dates and times, as well as accurate geographical locations, even as it eludes precise representation.

War (*Milhamah*), Dream (*Halom*), Illness (*Mahalah*), Bread (*Lehem*), Folly (*Helma'ut*)

The Israeli ethos concerning armies and war has its deeper roots in Jewish tradition. Many of the narratives of war we find in modern Hebrew literature are elaborated in an explicit or implicit relationship to biblical archetypes—the myth of the few against the many; the counsel of the Book of Proverbs (24:6), "For through designs you shall make war";[29] the advantage of having a small and smart army; the importance of reliable intelligence; feelings of fear versus acts of daring; the power of psychological warfare (in which the appearance of power produces power); the commander as the spearhead of the forces and role model (Gideon's "look to me and do the same," "after me"); and the thematic link between war (*milhamah*), illness (*mahalah*), dream (*halom*), and bread (*lehem*) in the way the sound of these Hebrew words carries meaning. Each of the works of prose discussed in *War Lives* brings this aspect to light, most of all David Grossman's focus on acoustics in *To the End of the Land*. I will therefore survey some of the biblical themes that echo in the modern texts under discussion.

The account of Gideon's war against the Midianites (Judges 7:1–25) is one of the stories that combines almost all these features in a few verses.[30] "The troops are still too many" (verse 4), God says to Gideon after 20,000 men, two-thirds of those assembled for war, have already turned back in response to the pronouncement, "Whoever is fearful and trembling, let him turn round from Mount Gilead" (verse 3). The ten thousand who remain undergo a "water test"—"whoever laps water with his tongue, as a dog laps, set him apart" (verse 5). Only three hundred warriors pass the test: "And the number of those lapping from their hands to their mouth came to three hundred men. And all the rest of the troops kneeled on their knees to drink water" (verse 6). God's promise—"With the three hundred men who lapped I shall make you victorious and give Midian into your hand" (verse 7)—does not reassure Gideon, and he goes down at night with his servant Purah to eavesdrop in order to ascertain the mood prevailing in the Midianite camp, which fills the valley, stretching out from north of the Hill of Moreh "like locusts in multitude, and their camels were beyond numbering, like the sand that is on the shore of the sea in multitude" (verse 12). Under the cover of darkness, Gideon slips into the vast enemy encampment, where, by means of a dream and its interpretation, he comes to understand the mood pervading the camp:

> And Gideon came, and, look, a man was recounting a dream to his fellow, and he said, "Look, I dreamed a dream, and, look, a loaf of barley bread was rolling over through the camp of Midian and came up to the tent and struck it and overturned it, and the tent fell." And his fellow answered and said, "That could only be the sword of Gideon, son of Joash, man of Israel. God has given into his hand Midian and all its camp." (verses 13–14)

From this point, the way is clear to the sweeping and certain victory. Gideon knows that the enemy is mortally fearful, and by exploiting this fear, using psychological warfare through sound and baffling light with a handful of men, he sows confusion and terror that leave the enemy with no recourse.

> And he split the three hundred men into three columns and put ram's horns in everyone's hand and empty pitchers with torches inside the pitchers. And he said to them, "Look to me and do the same, and just as I come to the edge of the camp, so as I do, do the same. And when I blast on the ram's horn, and all those by me, you too shall blast on the ram's horns all round the camp and say, "For the LORD and for Gideon." (verses 16–18)

Panic and confusion overtake the enemy's camp, each man kills his comrade, and the survivors run for their lives. Gideon, who discounted his own capacity as a rescuer of the people when he was summoned to the mission of saving them—"My clan is poor in Manasseh, and I am the youngest in my father's house" (Judges 6:15)—marshals the neighboring tribes to finish the job, to seize the water sources and the fords of the Jordan and to capture the two Midianite commanders. The war (*milhamah*) thus is decided by virtue of a dream (*halom*) of barley bread (*lehem*) that the Israelite leader hears when he dares to penetrate the very heart of the enemy's camp, or, more precisely, to the very heart of the solitary soldier in the camp of the adversary.

Gideon's war against the Midianites belongs to a long series of wars, described either in detail or in passing in Joshua and Judges. Deceiving the enemy with contrived sounds and sights aimed to create the illusion of a mighty army, as in the conquest of Jericho and Ai, and terrorizing the Midianite army, are part of the legacy of Israel's modern-day army, the IDF. These wars are often invoked in Israeli literature in a variety of contexts. Here is an example of an analogy that one of A. B. Yehoshua's protagonists draws between the Bible and our time:

> And then I read a little of Joshua and mainly Judges. Those little wars are quite amusing, breaking out all the time in all sorts of places in the Land of Israel, just like today; and accordingly, in some remote town there pops up a homegrown judge—Ehud, Gideon, Deborah, Jephthah, Samson—to do battle for a while and then disappear. True democratic rotation (*Friendly Fire*, 327).[31]

In her foreword to Flavius Josephus's *The Jewish War*,[32] the latest Hebrew translator of this unique historiographical-literary work, Lisa Ullmann,[33] notes, "We find numerous times this combination of war-hunger-plague in *The Jewish War*."[34] Hunger is of course a reference to bread, or more precisely to the lack thereof, while the plague is a disease. Hence, the combination of war (*milhamah*), bread (*lehem*), and illness (*mahalah*) also figures in Josephus's chronicle, the only eyewitness account we have of the brutal war that led to the sacking of Jerusalem and the destruction of the Second Temple.

And what about "dream" (*halom*)? It fits in with the chronicler's objection to the Jewish rebellion against the Romans: Josef son of Matityahu understood the rebellion to be an illusion, a nightmare that would bring the Jewish polity to an end.[35] Before relating his speech at the cave of Jotapata (Yodfat), Josephus mentions that suddenly "He called to mind the dreams which he had dreamed in the night time, whereby God had signified to him beforehand both the future calamities of the Jews, and the events that concerned the Roman emperors" (book 3, chapter 8, 351). That is, dreams (the dream in question is prophetic), have a substantial role in shaping the course of war. Moreover, Jonathan Price writes in his introduction to the new Hebrew translation of *The Jewish War*,

> It could be that Josephus also identified with the biblical Joseph, whose story is related in Genesis; like Joseph, Josephus had heard God's Word in a dream, rather than in direct revelation, and redeemed himself from prison and perhaps from death row as well by interpreting dreams and predicting the future; although unlike Joseph the dreamer, Josephus failed to save his people.[36]

Dream and war, *halom* and *milhamah*, whose Hebrew roots share the same consonants (*hlm*—dream; *lhm*—war), resonate with the dark side of being: dream with the dark side of the individual and war with the dark side of society, each shadow feeding into the other; war is an amplified, externalized expression of dreams. Freud, whose German did not render itself to the same alliterative connection of the Hebrew words with the thematic and semantic connotations of war and dream, recognized this bond nonetheless in his chapter on censorship in dreams in his *Introduction to Psychoanalysis*. "Psychoanalysis," Freud says, "confirm[s] Plato's old saying that the good are those who are content to dream of what the others, the bad, really do." Venturing from this observation to the First World War, which was raging at the very time he was lecturing, Freud goes on to say:

And now turn your eyes away from individuals and consider the Great War which is still laying Europe to waste. Think of the vast amount of brutality, cruelty, and lies which are able to spread over the civilized world. Do you really believe that a handful of ambitious and deluding men without conscience could have succeeded in unleashing all these evil spirits if their millions of followers did not share their guilt? Do you venture, in such circumstances, to break a lance on behalf of the exclusion of evil from the mental constitution of mankind?[37]

In his prose, S. Y. Agnon treated the First World War carefully and extensively. In the short novel *To This Day* (1950),[38] (explored here in chapter 1 in the context of German Jews' involvement in the war), Agnon emphasizes the alliterative connection between dream and war. A dream of the protagonist-narrator invokes another war story from the Book of Judges, Jephthah the Giladite's war against the Amonites, which ends with the sacrifice of his daughter (Judges 11). The protagonist-narrator's dream in *To This Day* bespeaks the dread of war that ancient sources inspire:

Somehow I managed to fall asleep. The reason I know I did is that I had a **dream**. What did I **dream**? I **dreamed** that a great **war** had broken out and that I was called up to fight in the **war** and took a solemn oath that if God brought me home safe and sound from the **war**, I would sacrifice to Him whatever came forth from my house to greet me. I returned home safe and sound and behold, coming forth to greet me was myself. (8; emphasis added)

In this terse dream-story, the words *dream* and *war* occupy a central role, as each is mentioned three times. Later in the novel, the protagonist-narrator unfurls a more elaborate play on words. At a certain point in his sojourn in search of a home and perhaps also a woman, he goes to bed hungry, and in an attempt to fall asleep he chooses "different combinations that could be made from the letters of Hebrew roots." This original "counting sheep" technique ends as follows: "Little by little my eyes grew heavy until, thinking of **dream**, I fell asleep and **dreamed** of **war**" (39; emphasis added).[39] To demonstrate the madness, anomaly, and inhumanity that war brings into the world, Agnon repeats the word "war" at both the protasis and apodosis—a rhetorical effect known in poetry as an anaphora—without joining them with the words "dream" and "bread." Another word, *me-hamat*, which means "because of" or "due to," provides a similar alternative:

> **War** here and **war** there, **war** everywhere. **Because of the war** [*me-hamat ha-milhamah*] you weren't allowed to pity or talk to a poor boy taken from his mother. **Because of the war** there were no longer human beings, just soldiers and officers and casualties and prisoners and enemies. (51; emphasis added)

Play on words and alliteration that blend sound and meaning, phonetics and semantics, with linguistic manipulations conveying sophisticated, ambiguous yet memorable messages—together form a cluster of elements that transforms a documentary text into a work of literature.

The successive appearance of war-dream-disease-bread in Hebrew literature seeks to bind them together in order to either hint or stress that war is a disease, a nocturnal terror. This bond also serves as a reminder that its constituents are the bread and butter of history, as military conflicts sustain an infinite cycle of war and peace, triumph and failure, dreaming and waking, hunger and satiety, life and death. The literature about armies and war enriches this cyclical, life-regulating pattern with its evocative depiction of the denial of privacy and loss of identity, the scarcity of physical and spiritual sustenance, and the intricate links between dreams, wishful thoughts, and the specter of death, among other themes. In Hebrew, with the stroke of a few verbal gestures, one can weave a unique onomatopoeic alliteration, which is not necessarily mimetic, into a Gordian knot that fastens together related words. In Erich Maria Remarque's (1898–1970) masterpiece *All Quiet on the Western Front* (1929), the dispassionate depiction of the horrors of the Great War melds dream, war, and bread into a single mass:

> We stir a bit as the door opens and Kat appears. I think I must be **dreaming**; he has two loaves of **bread** under his arm and a blood-stained sandbag full of horse flesh in his hand. The artilleryman's pipe drops from

his mouth. He feels the **bread**. "Real **bread**, by God! And it is still hot, too!" Kat gives no explanation. He has the **bread**, and the rest doesn't matter (47; emphasis added).[40]

The vitality offered by bread to the combat soldier reappears in many and varied contexts in this pacifist novel on the lost generation that spent four years in the trenches under torrents of fire, starving for want of bread until cruel death arrived:

> [The search for food] miscarries. A second party goes out, and it also turns back. Finally Kat tries, and even he reappears without accomplishing anything. No one gets through, not even a fly is small enough to get through such a barrage. We pull in our belts tighter and chew every mouthful three times as long. Still the food does not last out; we are damnably hungry. I take out a scrap of bread, eat the white and put the crust back in my knapsack; from time to time I nibble at it. (120)

In the novel's final pages, the bond between war and disease crescendos in recounting the events of summer–autumn 1918, the war's final (and most devastating) months. Horror, lack of hope, and ghostlike existence—"Our hands are earth, our bodies clay and our eyes pools of rain. We do not know whether we still live" (311)—take over the souls of the few men who survive. War, the narrator decries, is the deadliest, most pluriform of diseases: "War is a cause of death like cancer and tuberculosis, like influenza and dysentery. The deaths here are merely more frequent, more varied and terrible" (294). Let us take a look at a spine-chilling catalogue of the war's ailments and the inescapable causes of death that it spreads:

> Shells, gas clouds, and flotillas of tanks—shattering, starvation, death.
> Dysentery, influenza, typhus—murder, burning, death.
> Trenches, hospitals, the common grave—there are no other possibilities. (306–7)

In Israeli war fiction, Hebrew's rich phonetic and semantic interplay between war, dream, disease, and also bread appears in endless variations. This context brings to mind two novels that *War Lives* does not treat extensively, which are nonetheless defined by the bond between war, dream, and illness.

A. B. Yehoshua's *The Lover* (1977),[41] a novel set in the aftermath of the Yom Kippur War, is preoccupied with "sleep culture"—insomnia, and alternatively, heavy sleep and the detailed dreams of its female protagonists. Yehudit Hendel's *The Mountain of Losses* is suffused with surrealism and fantasy, as made evident in her depiction of its setting (cemetery), the bereaved parents meandering through it as though moonstruck, and the sons laid to rest underneath the pillow-shaped headstones. The visitors of the "well-tended garden," the cemetery, who have been living with death and disease since their loved-ones' demise, used to believe in "a life cleansed of illness and war."[42] Finally, the familiar alliteration of war, dream, disease as well as bread takes an ironic turn in Ron Leshem's *Beaufort* (2005),[43] set in the final year (1999–2000) of the IDF's presence in the "Security Zone" in South Lebanon. A bereaved father shouts at his son's funeral, "This wasn't really war [*milhamah*], but folly [*helma'ut*]" (*Beaufort*, 215, translation altered), projecting the novel's implicit pacifism by using the alliterative link between *milhamah* (war) and *helma'ut* (folly), so characteristic of Israeli literary representations of the First Lebanon War.

From the Great War to the Second Intifada—War Lives: Overview

The Great War—S. Y. Agnon's To This Day

In the Great War, that is, the First World War (1914–18), famous for its trench warfare, Jews fought on both sides of the frontline. Close to 1.25 million Jews served in combat under the flags of the armies that fought this war, but few of them gave literary expression to their battle experiences in prose. "Avigdor Hameiri," writes Avner Holtzman in the foreword of his monograph, "is the only [Hebrew] author whose work focuses on his experiences as a combat soldier in the First World War. His travails on the battlefront and in captivity yielded two autobiographical novels, a play, twenty-seven short stories, and more than fifty poems."[44] He began writing those pieces in Odessa immediately after his release from captivity, and completed them in 1930s Tel Aviv.[45] A large portion of this corpus appears to have been written even earlier, during the war and close to the occurrence of the events described. There were, of course, many Jewish authors who wrote about their war experiences: British poets Isaac Rosenberg and Siegfried Sassoon, to name but two. Hameiri is exceptional for turning to prose, where he was able to conjure an extensive linear plot that breathes life into a wartime microcosm.

Although the major battles of the war were fought far from the Land of Israel, its impact on the Jewish Yishuv was immense as it had to endure the Ottoman tyranny triggered by Turkey's joining the war. A subversive literary account of Zionism during the Second Aliyah and life in Jerusalem during the First World War is offered in Aharon Reuveni's *All the Way to Jerusalem: A First World War Trilogy* (1932, reprinted 1954 and 1987).[46]

In the absence of more comprehensive literary reflections on the First World War by Jewish soldiers, we must suffice with other written testimonies, such as letters sent from the battlefront. Nitza Priluk's fine article portrays Hermann Weil by using his correspondence to present a firsthand account of the war. Weil, a combat paramedic with the soul of an artist, volunteered for the medical corps and lost his life in a war that was not his to fight. He died at twenty-three. His short life, as well as his emotional and intellectual potential and futile death, serves as a monument to the many other soldiers who shared a similar fate. By volunteering for the Kaiser's army, showing courage and sacrifice, Jewish youngsters—including some Jews who had already moved to Palestine and chose to return to their "German fatherland" to join the army (like Arthur Biram, founder of the Hebrew Reali School in Haifa)—hoped to be acknowledged with gratitude as German citizens with equal rights; they could not have imagined the future that awaited them and their families in post–World War I Germany.

Jews' expressions of German patriotism during the First World War are amply represented in Agnon's *To This Day*, published several years after the Holocaust (1950). From the piece's late vantage point, the patriotism of "Germans of mosaic faith" is read with bitter irony. Agnon's somewhat estranged perspective on fellow German Jews was prompted by his *Ostjude* descent (Galicia) and his halfhearted involvement in their affairs.

From a safe distance, guided by a mixture of criticism and compassion, he weaves an inimitable historical tapestry of the German-Jewish mindset and its divided existence in that era.

Agnon was very different from Avigdor Hameiri, who saw combat action in the Great War, and whose novel *The Great Madness: Notes of a Hebrew Officer in the Great War* (1929) is considered by some to be the Hebrew counterpart of *All Quiet on the Western Front*.[47] *To This Day* tells the tale of its narrator-protagonist, who is none other than Agnon, on the German home front. Though not a combat soldier, the novel's protagonist is nonetheless haunted by the prospect of military draft, overtaken by dread that consumes him both physically and mentally. What is more, his encounters with Germans (Jews and non-Jews alike) whose sons went to the war and either never returned or came back maimed, infuses the novel with the melancholy and bereavement that permeated Berlin and other parts of Germany throughout the war. In my book *Agnon's Art of Indirection* (1993), I dedicated three consecutive chapters to this essentially autobiographical, rich, and enigmatic novel. Here, in *War Lives*, I focus on a different aspect of the novel: the motif of an only son sent out to the war and a prophetic dream of a mother, or a vague notion of a father, which anticipate his fate. The narrator-protagonist, a seemingly uninvolved civilian, becomes involved in the lives of the bereaved families. Through Agnon's art of storytelling, their stories become interlaced with his own to form a rich and multilayered work of fiction.

The Yishuv Joins the British Army in the Second World War—Hanoch Bartov's The Brigade

The majority of literary works (past and present) written about the Second World War tell their story in retrospect. In this sense, *Suite Française* is an anomaly. In Jewish consciousness, the Second World War is bound up with the Holocaust, partisan resistance, the heroic uprising of the Warsaw Ghetto and the impossible mission behind Nazi lines of Hannah Szenes, the Jewish female paratrooper. The fact that 1.5 million Jewish soldiers, male and female, fought against the Germans in the Allied Forces—from the Soviet Union, the United States, the United Kingdom, South Africa, and other countries—has remained outside of Israeli collective memory. Perhaps this is so because Israeli literature about the Jewish fighting in the war begins with the enlistment of 40,000 members of the Yishuv to the British Army, including active and future authors and poets. Paradoxically, the fighters of the Jewish Brigade, whose ranks numbered no more than 5,000 troops who joined the fighting as late as September 1944, are remembered more than the 60,000 Jewish combat soldiers—from the Land of Israel and elsewhere—who joined the greater British Army. The Jewish Brigade comprised volunteers from the Yishuv, with a Hebraic lifestyle, Zionist symbols, and the wish to contribute to the formation of the future Jewish state's military force. Hanoch Bartov's autobiographical novel on his personal experiences in the Brigade offers an important contribution to our knowledge about this unit.

While Israelis do not know much about the Jewish Brigade, it has hardly been heard of in other countries. Famous comic artist Mark Van Oppen (known as Marvano) has called it "the most secret unit in the British Army," having written a trilogy about the Brigade (*La Brigade Juive*) seventy years after its dismantlement. The Flemish artist was inspired by an Israeli documentary about the Brigade, researched the subject, and decided to create a visual plot celebrating its nameless heroes in order to bring its story to a broad audience of both young and old readers.[48]

As noted, *The Brigade* (1965)[49] was written some twenty years after the events it describes. The novel is a personal-literary account of the warriors of the Jewish Brigade, who came from the Land of Israel to Europe as the Second World War was reaching its final stages. Motivated by two goals—to save Jews and to wreak vengeance upon the Nazis—they came to realize that their task was nigh impossible. Jewish revenge, which does not line up with the goals of the British Army, comes up in Marvano's graphic novel as well: Ari and Leslie, the heroes of the trilogy's first part, are members of the Jewish Brigade who come to Poland in 1945 and avenge the deaths of Jews by killing SS officers. They carry out their deeds as acts of personal revenge unbeknownst to the high British command.

As we have already emphasized, literary texts are important for our understanding of the past. Their added value compared to historical texts is their ability to plumb the depths of the human psyche in extreme situations of war, far from home. This is the premise that I set out to prove in the chapter on Bartov's novel, by focusing on the dilemma faced by a platoon and its individual soldiers: whether to engage in rescue actions or acts of vengeance. An expression of the vindictive impulse shared by Jewish Brigade troops may be found in a poem by Amir Gilboa (1917–84), "Dew of Vengeance" (*Tal Nekamot*). The Hebrew word *hyl* has a dual function in the poem: It denotes the Hebrew acronym for the Jewish Brigade (*Hativa Yehudit Lohemet*), in which the soldier in the poem serves and through which he is expected to carry out his revenge; and to express the pain and fear (*hyl* means in Hebrew deep anxiety, as in "fear and trembling") that possesses the warrior-cum-poet when he goes out to face the Germans who had murdered his family and take revenge:

> I am walking towards you
> fearful (*be-hyl*).
> I am walking towards you
> knowingly.
> I am about to curse you with wrath
> and with tears . . . I am walking towards your fire that has gone cold
> to rip the robes of your ancestors
> and to bury
> your dying hardness
> in the profanity of your cities' flames.[50]

The Holocaust and the War of Independence—
Yehuda Amichai's Not of This Time, Not of This Place

The Holocaust and the Israeli War of Independence are at the center of the voluminous novel by Yehuda Amichai (1924–2000), *Not of This Time, Not of This Place* (1963). Like all the works considered in this study, this is a novel that incorporates autobiographical elements. Nevertheless, more than all the other novels we are considering, it reflects the difference between history and literature. Amichai is a poet, and like his collection of short stories *In this Terrible Wind* (1973), the novel deploys poetic prose rich in surprising images and disparate fields of meaning. This prose abounds in symbols, to the point where it is difficult to distinguish between the symbolic and the concrete layers; it is suffused with biblical and other literary allusions that compel the reader to work through the bidirectional intertextual links that are a constant resource in literature; and, most essentially, fantasy, hallucination, and confusion mark every step of the way in the novel. In historical writing, of course, the dosage of all these is measured and limited.

Not of This Time, Not of This Place bears the stamp of Amichai's antiwar poems, the most famous of which—"Rain Falls on the Faces of My Friends," "God Takes Pity on Kindergarten Children," and "God Full of Mercy"—have achieved the status of anthems. The central literary device of the novel is splitting the protagonist in two: one who goes back to Germany, to the regions of his childhood he left just a few years before the Holocaust, and one who stays in Jerusalem to plunge into a great love that will constitute a counterweight to his adult experiences in the War of Independence. The unfathomable historical juncture between the nadir of destruction and the zenith of independence is expressed in the physical and spiritual split of the protagonist, who undergoes simultaneously, in close parallel, in two different places, two different sets of personal experiences that derive from the two large historical and national experiences.

Yehuda Amichai arrived in Palestine with his family from Würzburg, Germany, in 1935 at age eleven. The Nazi assumption of power in January 1933 brought to the Land of Israel the fifth wave of Zionist immigration (1932–36), largely comprising Jews from Germany. The fact that Amichai's father decided "one day" to sell his house and business and to take his family to the Land of Israel recurs again and again in this novel rich in repetitions and troubling thoughts. The repetition of this fateful autobiographical detail bears witness to the complex understanding of it in Amichai's consciousness. A sense of gratitude to the resourceful and farsighted father is mingled with a sense of guilt toward those who remained there, especially toward Ruth, his childhood friend. This dualism is repeatedly and variously manifested in the novel.

Yehuda Amichai fought against the Nazis in the Jewish Brigade that was part of the British Army. Afterward, in the War of Independence, as a combat soldier in the Palmach's Negev Brigade, he took part in several fierce battles, in which many of his friends were killed. All of this has a strong resonance in the novel, but anyone looking for documentation of a particular battle in the novel will be disappointed. An inward, chaotic, associative, allusive reality is intertwined with every concrete description of a battle or any other event. This is a novel that documents the fateful psychological impact of the Holocaust and the War of Independence on the protagonist and on his generation. The Eichmann trial (1961) helped Amichai turn the Holocaust into such a central subject and to link it with the War of Independence.

Two years before the Eichmann trial, in the summer of 1959, Amichai visited his native city, Würzburg, and became a kind of "wayfarer stopped for the night" there. The childhood memories triggered by this visit, the Eichmann trial's "legitimation" of delving into the Holocaust, and the permissive culture of the late 1950s and early 1960s are all in the background for the gestation of this novel.

The post-war experience of the divided protagonist, simultaneously in two different places, testifies to the experimental possibilities of imaginative literature as opposed to historiography. In this case, they enable a double location for the protagonist, in decadent Jerusalem after the War of Independence and after the Sinai War, and in Weinburg (the fictional name for Würzburg in northern Bavaria). The fantasies of vengeance of Amichai's protagonist, who comes to Weinburg in order to avenge his childhood friend, Ruth, a victim of the Holocaust, are absurd, clownish, and grotesque, much more so than the vengeance fantasies of Hanoch Bartov's characters, which are based on actual experiences and are historically grounded. In Bartov's case, it is the vengeance of the collective; for Amichai, it is the vengeance of an individual. Both efforts are doomed to fail.

The chapter here on Amichai's "schizophrenic" novel concentrates both on the awareness of the Holocaust and on the impact of the War of Independence on a lost generation searching for identity. Amichai's Jerusalem alter ego, named Joel, and the unnamed "I" in Weinburg constitute a single entity that represents both itself and its generation.

Thirty-five years after the publication of *Not of This Time, Not of This Place*, Amichai wrote a short newspaper article in honor of the jubilee celebration of the State of Israel. The article was entitled "A Divided Soul," a clear allusion to his novel, which places a divided protagonist at its center. The article begins as follows:

> A week ago, we veterans of the Palmach stood by the fresh grave of Uzi Narkiss. We stood in pounding rain beneath umbrellas on Mount Herzl. I recalled a man from the Negev Brigade, Dicky from Givat Brenner, who was killed and to whom I dedicated one of my first poems. Rain falls on the faces of my friends; on the faces of my living friends who cover their heads with a blanket—and on the faces of my dead friends, who cover no more.[51]

The split in this poem is between the living and dead friends who make up a single human entity that fights and fought, while a rain of water and of bullets showers down on their faces. It is noteworthy that in Remarque's novel, too, rain plays this sort of role, indifferently leveling the living and the dead, who both are also indifferent:

> Monotonously falls the rain. It falls on our heads and on the heads of the dead up in the line, on the body of the little recruit with the wound that is so much too big for his hip; it falls on Kammerich's grave; it falls in our hearts." (*All Quiet on the Western Front*, 85)

Amichai, after quoting "Rain Falls on the Faces of My Friends," goes on to say, "Yitzhak Rabin was the last among us to die in combat for the State of Israel. . . . To our sorrow, death in battle is still almost a natural death, until perhaps real peace will come about." Thus Amichai in 1997.[52]

In his introduction to the translated collection, *The Poetry of Yehuda Amichai* (2015), Robert (Uri) Alter, the book's editor and the English translator of a substantial portion of Amichai's poems, reports that once, in 1970, during an evening when Amichai was reading at the University of California at Berkeley, someone in the audience, a belligerent character, wanted to know whether Amichai had seen God on the battlefield. No, Amichai answered softly, he saw only men dying, and that is the task of the poet, to describe things as they are and not to envelope them in the pseudo-theological rhetoric of politicians and generals.[53]

Boot Camp 1955—Yehoshua Kenaz's Infiltration

More than thirty years after his conscription to the IDF in 1955, Yehoshua Kenaz wrote his novel *Infiltration* (1986) about the distressing mental, social, and physical vicissitudes undergone by new recruits in basic training. In other words, the novel engages the trauma of young Israelis who join military service, mandatory in Israel, immediately after graduating from high school. *Infiltration* is a masterpiece on ignominy and friendship, abuse, and fortitude. It is about the elite Unit 101, about Israeli myths and patriotism, and about the rise and fall of the Israeli melting pot in which the IDF played a major role.

The novel is set in the alleged "peacetime" between the War of Independence and the Sinai War. Peacetimes, however, are mere seams between wars; in these seams, which can be either coarse or fine, military conflict lives on. In the years 1953–56, thousands of terrorist infiltrations into Israel from Egypt and Jordan were carried out for robbery, murder, and sabotage, triggering daring retaliatory operations carried out by Unit 101. The legacy of men who became living myths—Meir Har-Zion, Yitzhak Jibli, and others—forms part of the novel's backdrop and resonates throughout it.

Yet the novel employs this glorious military heritage of rare courage, camaraderie, and creativity as the antithesis to the work's antiheroes: unfit new recruits who arrive petrified in the army's least-demanding boot camp; they are unmotivated, spineless, and suspicious individuals who are prepared to use their ailments to their own advantage. The wave of massive immigration to Israel between 1948 and 1956 had brought over "weak elements," primarily made up of Holocaust survivors and members of North African and Middle Eastern communities, who were foreign to the regnant culture of the Zionist founders of the state.[54]

They all meet in Yehoshua Kenaz's basic training. Each of the recruits, individually and as a group, is transformed by the experience. With thirty years' hindsight, Kenaz reflects on the era of his conscription, positing a contrarian epos to the classic narrative of the IDF's courage, resilience, and intrepidness.

Ostensibly, any attempt to compare the horrific war story of eighteen-year-olds on the battlefield in *All Quiet on the Western Front* to the story of eighteen-year-olds struggling to find their place in the military system in *Infiltration* would be absurd. And yet, despite the great distance between the time, place, and mode of the two novels, there are certain similarities between them. In both novels, the young men leave high school to join a system that deprives them of their identity, privacy, and singularity. The young soldiers in both works suffer unwarranted abuse from their sergeant. In the German novel, as in the Israeli one, on leave the young soldiers become aware of the changes that have occurred in their childhood home and bedroom, realizing that anyone who has not experienced the hell they are in has no way of understanding them. Both works express passion for the earth—which is the soldier's mother, his lover, the only one prepared to accept him into her bosom.

In this book, the chapter on *Infiltration* addresses, among other things, earth's physical and mental function in the novel and in the life of one of its protagonists. The myth of blood and soil that has the soil take precedence over everything else, including human lives, has a long literary history. It did not begin in Hebrew literature with Moshe Shamir's groundbreaking novels, *He Walked Through the Fields* and *With His Own Hands*.[55] As an introduction to the soil theme in the Israeli novel under discussion, I cite a passage from *All Quiet on the Western Front*, the work that guides me throughout *War Lives*:

> To no man does the earth mean so much as to the soldier. When he presses himself down upon her long and powerfully, when he buries his face and his limbs deep in her from the fear of death by shellfire, then she is his only friend, his brother, his mother; she stifles his terror and shelters him and gives him a new lease of ten seconds of life, receives him again and often forever.
> Earth! Earth! Earth!
> Earth with thy folds, and hollows and holes, into which a man may fling himself and crouch down! (*All Quiet on the Western Front*, 64–65)

Remarque's view of the earth also resonates in Alan Paton's famous call in his 1948 novella *Cry, the Beloved Country* to parents and educators of the yet-unborn infant: "Let him not love the earth too deeply."[56] In *Infiltration*, Yehoshua Kenaz demonstrates what happens to a young man, a new recruit, who has been educated to love the earth too much.

The Sinai War—Amos Oz's My Michael

The Sinai War, also known as Operation Kadesh (names denoting the location of Israel's first war after its War of Independence), is represented in *War Lives* by Amos Oz's *My Michael* (1968).[57] In the novel, the 1956 war serves as a backdrop for, and an analogy to, the illness of its female protagonist Hannah Gonen. War and disease (*milhamah* and *mahala* in Hebrew) are synonymous with abnormality and loss of control—the former in the public sphere, the latter in the private sphere. Although the Sinai War is not central to the novel, and though it is presented from the supposedly distorted perspective of its ill protagonist, the novel contains quite a few insights regarding the events that triggered the war, the atmosphere on the home front at the time, the war's duration and scope, and the role of the individual soldier.

The plot of *My Michael* begins in Jerusalem in 1950, while the Sinai War actually breaks out at a later point in the novel. Hence, the work contains palpable traces of the 1948 war, starting with the way Michael chooses to present himself to Hannah when they first meet: "'Tell me about yourself,' I said. Michael said: 'I didn't fight in the Palmach. I was in the Signal Corps. I was a wireless operator in the Carmeli Brigade" (*My Michael*, 6)—and ending with a depiction of postwar Jerusalem: "Many of the street lamps of the British Mandate period were destroyed by shellfire during the War of Independence. In 1950, most of them were still shattered" (*My Michael*, 19).

In an article written in memory of legendary commando Meir Har-Zion, Amir Oren claimed that Israel's leadership at the time—that is, Prime Minister and Defense Minister David Ben-Gurion and IDF Chief of Staff Moshe Dayan—made cynical use of war heroes to escalate the retaliatory attacks of Unit 101 and the IDF's Paratroops Corps in the early 1950s. This led "to a second round [of warfare], believed to be inevitable due to Arab animosity." And since another war was seen as inevitable, the thinking was that "Israel had better initiate its timing and circumstances."[58] The fact that it was not Egypt that initiated the war but the diplomatic triumvirate of Israel, France, and Britain, as well as the fact that the Israeli narrative attempted to ascribe to the war weighty considerations, are made present in the novel by radio broadcasts that are intermittently registered in the mind of the bedridden, self-absorbed protagonist, Hannah Gonen. Though irregular and faint, the news reports conveying Israel's shaky rationale for justifying the war's outbreak are a constant presence. One of the many examples of the radio's brainwashing of the young state's citizens concerns the causes for the war: "A military commentator explains. While from the political point of view. Repeated provocations. Flagrant violation of freedom of navigation. The moral justification. Terrorism and sabotage. Defenseless women and children. Mounting tension. Innocent civilians. Enlightened public opinion at home and abroad. Essentially a defensive operation" (*My Michael*, 157). The code words that Hannah sifts from the radio broadcasts are employed in order to ridicule the self-evident, overstated facts that the radio continually repeats.

My Michael's plot spans a decade in the life of its protagonist. She meets "her" Michael in the winter of 1950, at the age of twenty, and begins writing her fictitious confession—the narrative time—in January 1960. "I am thirty years of age and a married woman" is her way to present herself in the novel's second paragraph, after noting in handwriting on the top left-hand side of the page, "Jerusalem, January 1960," in order to endow her confession with a supposedly authentic, precise validity of a diary.[59] Interestingly, Michael presents himself by mentioning his unheroic military affiliation, while Hannah presents herself by referring to her unhappy family affiliation. The gender-based affiliation—army for the man, family for the woman—and the ironic light that Oz sheds on the traditional male and female roles through the eyes and voice of his female protagonist, call for further reflection.[60]

As noted, Hannah Gonen started writing the story about "her" Michael in January 1960. Amos Oz finished writing his novel in May 1967. This date, cited at the novel's end, is extra-literary information that the author offers to his readers, which may be seen as either clashing or complementing the fictive or semi-fictive dating by the novel's protagonist. Either way,

Oz finished writing *My Michael* as Israel marked the nineteenth anniversary of its independence, at which time it became known that Egypt was sending military forces to the demilitarized Sinai Peninsula, in breach of the agreements signed after the 1956 war. Later that month (on the twenty-third), the Straits of Tiran were closed off to Israeli vessels and the winds of war began to blow in the region. That is, as the author was finishing a novel set against the backdrop of the Sinai War, the Six-Day War was about to break out.

The tense anticipation of a fateful, all-out war may have helped give shape to the express wish of one of the novel's protagonists, called Kadishman (echoing the war's second name, Operation Kadesh). Of the 1956 war, Kadishman says: "There is going to be a great war, and the Holy Places will once again be ours." The reticent, cautious, and rational Michael replies: "Since the day the Temple was destroyed, the power of prophecy has been granted to men like you or me. If you want to know my opinion, the war we are about to fight will not be over Hebron or Nablus but over Gaza and Rafah" (*My Michael*, 143).

Michael's delineation of the war's setting and length is correct. To his wife Hannah he promises that the war will be very brief: "No war was likely to last longer than three weeks. 'The talk is of a limited, local war, of course. Times have changed. There won't be another 1948'" (155). That is, the perspective of Private Michael Ganz—a self-confessed antihero, neither fighter pilot nor paratrooper but a radio operator, who opines that this is what transpired in the War of Independence and what will transpire now, in the Sinai War—reinstates the true, moderate dimensions of Operation Kadesh. The multiple warfronts, as well as the messianic yearning to expand the country's borders and reach the holy sites that lie beyond them, are common to the two wars around the 1956 war—the one preceding it and, most of all, the one that will follow it.

The Six-Day War—Eli Amir's Yasmine

The Sinai War is named after its site of battles, whereas the Six-Day War is named for its brief duration. It was two days shorter than Operation Kadesh and its scope was more than three times greater: The IDF took over not only the Sinai Peninsula, but captured the West Bank and the Golan Heights as well. Kadishman's prediction in *My Michael* regarding Operation Kadesh was actualized in full.

The confusing days of military strife—Israel's mobilization of reserves forces, the nerve-wracking anticipation for the war to begin, the battle at the gates of Gaza City, the conquest of Jerusalem, and most of all, the new geopolitical reality that took shape in the war's aftermath—are comprehensively portrayed in Eli Amir's *Yasmine* (2005).[61] The multiple perspectives that the novel provides (including those on the defeated side) stand out as unique in the vast literature on the Israeli-Arab wars. Yet the novel offers more than a panorama of manifold viewpoints; it contains a whole range of symbols, motifs, and languages—spoken and whispered, bodily and cultural. *Yasmine* was written close to forty years after the war, which is why its retrospective depiction of events is fraught with criticism and irony. The Arabs' loud, fantastic ostentation before the war ("Throw them in the sea! Throw the Jews into the sea! . . . Go on, Jews, pack your belongings and leave!" [27]) and the Israelis' delusions of grandeur ("So, we went to sleep as a state and woke up as an empire!" [54]) are treated with equal irony and critical distance. One of the foremost representatives of the postwar euphoria was poet Natan Alterman, who, lacking the perspective of time, penned a mere few days after the war's end an article entitled, "Unparalleled Reality," which opens as follows: "Let us not say we are 'without words' to describe what has transpired in the past few days. The words are there, and words remain the primary means of expression and reflection, only that they, too, appear to be blinking and pinching themselves in order to be sure that they are awake and not dreaming."[62]

Words, language, and multilingualism are a central focus of my analysis of *Yasmine*, which shows that relations between conqueror and the conquered, man and woman, can become equivocal when the two sides share a language, both practically and metaphorically. Indeed, the two protagonists—Nuri Amari, a literary personification of Eli Amir, and Yasmine, a Palestinian Christian woman from East Jerusalem—fall in love (the phrase "make love, not war" keeps coming through the novel's intertextual, binary structure), but communicate in English, a neutral linguistic middle ground, the lingua franca of the modern era. The language that Yasmine chooses to speak with Nuri cannot overcome Hebrew, and certainly not Arabic—two languages the protagonists know well and which serve as the substructure of their love affair; moreover, Arabic is the mother tongue of both lovers. The novel proves that language does not consist of straightforward communication alone; it is a repository of memories, images, and cultural values, which function as a meta-language (that Benjamin Harshav terms "cultural semiotics"). In the novel, the borderline between linguistic semantics and cultural semiotics is far from clear: Multilingualism slides over to multiculturalism, which in turn facilitates the communication and liaison between the two protagonists of *Yasmine*. The English language, which the protagonists purportedly use in order to communicate, has no tangible representation in the novel. Their country appears to speak Hebrew and Arabic, primarily.

Knowledge of Arabic dictates the fate of *Yasmine*'s narrator-protagonist, both before the war and after it. After the war he is appointed to be an aide to the minister of Arab affairs thanks to his knowledge of the language; in this role, he learns of Israelis' disrespect for the language he shares with the defeated enemy. Nuri's hybrid identity receives authentic and extensive treatment in the novel. In response to an assessment by a scientific advisor to the minister, who claims that the Arabic language is "petrified, inferior, lacking theoretical literature or any modern scientific and cultural terminology, that Arabic culture as a whole lacked the tools for abstract thought," the narrator-protagonist responds: "Our great lexicographer Eliezer Ben-Yehuda considered Arabic to be a language that was engaged in a process of revival, dealing successfully with the modern world. He even introduced Arabic words into Hebrew" (60). He then goes on to say: "We need Arabic speakers as much as speakers of English and French. We live in the Middle East and our future is here. We still have Iraqi and Egyptian immigrants who know the language, but if we don't take care there won't be any in the next generation" (61). Therefore, it is for the sake of the state's future that he sides with Arabic, his mother tongue, which Israelis reject as they set their eyes on the West. Blinded by the cloud of euphoria, they fail to grasp that the victory in the Six-Day War does not mark the end to all wars.

Yom Kippur War Literature and David Grossman's To the End of the Land

The Yom Kippur War in 1973 took Israel by surprise merely six years after the Six-Day War. Voluminous studies such as Gideon Avital-Eppstein's *The Yom Kippur War, 1973: A Battle Over the Collective Memory—A Never-Ending War*, commemorative newspaper supplements, and radio and television broadcasts, among other sources, describe the war as "the breaking point," "an earthquake," "an eclipse," "a fog that refuses to disperse," "a heavy shadow over our hearts," "a lightning strike." These and a host of other images are used to convey the deep impact that this war has had on Israelis' lives.

The literature that this war has yielded, both documentary and fictional (two genres that tend to blend when it comes to wars), initially tackled the element of surprise. While the Six-Day War was preceded by long, anxious anticipation, the Yom Kippur War seemed to have come out of nowhere: "There was a war. That's right. It came upon us as a complete surprise," states the opening page of one of the first novels to deal with the 1973 war, A. B. Yehoshua's *The Lover* (1977).[63] The siren that went off at noon on the Sabbath of Yom Kippur, 1973, startling Israelis from the rest of the holiest day of the Jewish year, defined the question that guided the literature about the war: Was it really a surprise? Wasn't the writing already on the wall but conveniently ignored?

"Just so they won't get hysterical if some Egyptian lets out a fart," a brigade commander says, dismissing the prediction of war by an intelligence officer in Yitzhak Ben-Ner's short story "Nicole"[64] (166); while Amos Oz mentions "the praises that were heaped on Le Patron because he was one of the few who gave warning in time of the attack of Yom Kippur 1973"[65] (Oz, *To Know a Woman*, 116). These are but two passages testifying that there were indeed people who warned against the impending military meltdown.

The unnerving alarm that marked its dramatic opening heightens the element of surprise in several works of fiction about the war. The jarring siren could just as well have come out of a book or a play. In Yehoshua's

The Lover, it affects the bizarre behavior of Gabriel, the strange lover. Like the siren sound that penetrated into every Israeli household, he enters the home of Adam and Asia, the main characters of the novel, robbing them of their peaceful and quiet life. His sudden appearance and disappearance—two contradictory gestures—underscore the panic, confusion, and fear that were sown in a flash across the entire nation:

> Two hours after the alarm was sounded he was already with us. Apparently we didn't hear his knock and instead of waiting he opened the door ... [I] just watched him as he came into the room, confused, agitated, talking in a loud voice. As if the war that was breaking out was directed personally against him. He asked for explanations, and when it became clear that we had nothing to tell him he seized the radio and began frantically searching for news, for information, going from station to station, French, English, even pausing for a while over a Greek or a Turkish broadcast in his attempt to put some facts together. (*The Lover*, 16)

The famous siren also wails in Yehudit Hendel's *The Mountain of Losses*. This novel presents a slow, detailed portrayal of three bereaved parents (a couple and another father) who set out one summer morning in 1989 from their homes to the Kiryat Shaul cemetery, referred to in their inner code language as "The Garden." They tend to the plants they grow on the tombstones of their sons killed in the Yom Kippur War. In fact, until the novel's midpoint, the reader is not even sure whether the sons were killed specifically in that war, since "The Garden" houses victims of all wars, and is divided into plots, one for each war. But the discordant acoustics accompanying the departure for the cemetery are an implicit reference to the alarm sound that remains forever sudden: "'Someone must have touched a parking car and set off the alarm, which started emitting long and convulsive sounds. It's that screaming car again,' said Meira. The car kept on screaming for a long time and when it ceased a scooter drove by with heavy motor drone, then the phone rang" (14). "Even at this hour, off-peak traffic, the usual impatient honking kept resounding" (27).

The novel's readers ultimately learn that the war in question is the Yom Kippur War, thanks to an explicit reference to the unremitting siren sound that went off at 14:00 on that fateful day:

> A woman who walked past me was talking to herself half-whispering and I heard her say: "The war started at two in the afternoon." Yes, at two in the afternoon the war started, I repeated after her but the woman kept talking to herself: "At two in the afternoon the war started at two in the afternoon the war started," and once again I heard myself repeating after her: "Yes, at two in the afternoon the war started." Her muttering was now reaching me from the far end of the path: "At two in the afternoon the war started at two in the afternoon the war started" . . . The woman, who in the meantime walked away, kept talking to herself, turning her head around as if she were speaking to someone else . . . yet although she walked farther away I kept hearing her constant muttering, "at two in the afternoon the war started at two in the afternoon the war started." (85–86)

The 14:00 siren trope opens my discussion of the voice motif in David Grossman's *To the End of the Land* (2008). In his extensive article, "Inferno: Forty Years of Writing on the Yom Kippur War,"[66] Avner Holtzman argues that "the restraint practiced by literary authors to avoid reaching for the flames, i.e., writing explicitly about the battlefields, becomes all the more poignant when contrasted with the forthrightness of the documentary prose published after the Yom Kippur War, which continues to be written today."[67] In the opening to my reading of *To the End of the Land*, a late novel that boldly reaches for the flames, I cite documentary works such as Hanoch Bartov's *Dado* (1978) and documentary novels like Yuval Neria's *Fire* (1979). Among other things, these novels are characterized by the loud, explosive timing of the war's opening on the 6th of October: Like the mantra of the bereaved mother in Hendel's *The Mountain of Losses*, the literature about this war obstinately counts days and hours. Bartov's two-volume chronicle, *Dado: 48 Years and Twenty More Days*, is emblematic of this approach, while the 6th of October also serves as an important point of reference in Yitzhak Ben-Ner's "Nicole" and in Yuval Neria's *Fire*.

The plot of Haim Be'er's *Feathers*, which the opening of chapter 7 also discusses, provides a metaphorical supplement to our research question: Late in the war, a soldier dies an unnecessary death after refusing to heed warnings to guard himself, symbolizing the complacent, indulgent State of Israel that did not regard the warning signs that came its way.

The war refuted the axioms regarding Israel's invincibility and the Arabs' eternal defeat. The breach in Israel's defense lines along the Suez Canal also marked the collapse of a constellation of concepts and misguided notions. For many, the war was marked by frustrating isolation, as soldiers faced up to their fate all alone. My reading of David Grossman's great novel, *To the End of the Land*, focuses on the literary embodiment of this experience.

Thousands of men caught unprepared were left to their own devices, taken captive, injured, or lost in the Yom Kippur War. Uniquely, Grossman stages the fate of one of his protagonists, Avram, by surrounding him with two close friends, Ora and Ilan. The three of them form a love triangle that the war irreparably maims.

"The private experience of war is constitutive of the story of the Yom Kippur War," writes Gideon Avital-Eppstein in *The Yom Kippur War, 1973: A Battle over the Collective Memory—A Never-Ending War,*

> and finds its way to a variety of discourses. In many cases, a private war experience confronts the members of a squad, a pilot, a tank crew, a seaman, sometimes an entire platoon or a battalion, which find themselves fighting an utterly unplanned private war, a war to the death. There is no guiding hand, no support, no backup, no communication with nearby units, sometimes even the radio is mute.[68]

But at the outpost where Avram, Grossman's protagonist, is deployed, the radio does not die; this enables the author to transmit a rare record of a soldier at the height of his dramatic war experience. Avram, an artist at heart who had always been fascinated with the human voice, is convinced that he is about to die. Goaded by this sense of urgency, he brings up thoughts he had buried deep down and "fires" them, so to speak, on the radio. Miraculously, in this mayhem there is someone on the other end who receives, listens, and records Avram's outburst. These apocalyptic moments, which (tragically) trigger Avram's artistic use of his voice on the army radio network, form one of the high points of Grossman's novel.[69]

We Israelis—those who experienced it and those who were born after it ended—are haunted by the Yom Kippur War. We keep talking about it in countless forums, create works of art and historiographical studies, pry and explore this open wound to retrieve yet more discoveries. In Gideon Avital-Eppstein's words, it is "a past that does not pass, a ghost that refuses to relent, a memory that does not fade away with death."[70]

Two distinctions that Avital-Eppstein makes about the war—that combat soldiers were left to their own devices and that for decades the war has tenaciously remained at the center of Israeli public discourse—as well as the fact that Grossman's *To the End of the Land* provides literary expression to the historian's observations, lead me to pause here and tell a personal story.

In 2015–16, I initiated a lectures series at the University of Haifa entitled, "Following Her Path: Feminine Legacies." One of the speakers was Professor Gabriela Shalev, former Israeli ambassador to the United Nations. Her lecture was entitled "An Israeli at the UN: One against Many." Before the event, I asked her somewhat hesitantly if she would agree to say that she is a war widow. "Certainly," she replied, mentioning a stipend that the University of Haifa offers students in memory of her late husband, Shaul Shalev, who was killed in the Yom Kippur War.

As I walked Shalev to her car after her lecture, she urged me to read page 565 in *To the End of the Land*, because at that point the novel, she claimed, tells her late husband's war story. I rushed home, grabbed the book and turned to page 565, and found the story that brings to life the solitary fighting experience of the Yom Kippur War, where each man was forced to rely on the resilience, courage, and ability he was able to muster in the chaos that took the battlefields and the IDF by storm.

On pages 564–65 of the novel's Hebrew edition, Ilan tells his wife Ora about a war experience, which forms part of a longer and more elaborate story he tells her. In the passage in question, Ilan talks about himself, and more so about Avram, precisely as Ora suffers labor pains before giving birth to Ofer, Avram's biological son who is actually the son of the three of them. The following passage from Ilan's account to Ora is what Gabriela Shalev wanted me to read in order to learn about her husband's war experience:

> On the radio they told us they couldn't reach us. We had to wait some more. We waited. After a few hours they told us to try to reach this mountain range. They gave us a code map. We walked until we could see the range straight ahead. But see, the Egyptians are shooting at us all the time, from all the hilltops . . .
>
> They yelled at us over the radio to shoot up flares so they could see where we were. We shot a flare and they found us. One tank came down from the range, and it's a steep incline, a wall. It came all the way to us. An M60 Patton. An officer sticks his head out of the turret and motions for us to come quickly and get in the tank. We shout at him: "What should we do? How?" And he gestures: Climb up, there's not time. "You mean, all of us?" "Get up. Get up!" Where? "Get up already!" And there's thirty-three of us . . . We climbed up the tank, every guy grabbed onto something, people glued themselves to the MAG hatches, ten guys crowded into the turret basket, I jumped up on the back and grabbed onto the leg of the guy above me, someone else took hold of my shoes, and the tank rolled. Not just rolled but barreled, in zigzags, to get away from the Saggers, and we barely held on. And the whole time I just kept thinking: Don't fall, don't fall . . . The tank is jumping around like crazy . . . Your bones are breaking, you can barely breathe, dust everywhere, stones flying, you just stop up all your holes and just stay alive. (578–79)

"Indeed so," Shalev confirmed when I asked her if the officer that rescued thirty-three soldiers who had lost their way was indeed her husband, Shaul. Then she explained:

> A few hours before he was killed in the battle at the *Televizya* outpost, standing on the tank's turret, leading his forces, Shaul managed to save the lives of 33 reservists from the *Porkan* outpost, who had tried rejoining Israeli forces after evacuating the stronghold. He loaded all of them on the single tank after managing to reach them, and then drove this monster (with 33 soldiers hanging from the tank) toward our forces.[71]

In a letter David Grossman sent me, dated December 20, 2014, he confirms that he heard the unbelievable story of the rescue of the thirty-three soldiers from one of the survivors of the incident whom he knew well, and waited thirty-three years before committing this story to the page. This act of bravery also appears in a book entitled *Shaul*, which Shalev published in memory of her husband. She used a line from Haim Nahman Bialik's famous poem, "The Dead of the Desert," to describe the morning of Yom Kippur, 1973: "For the wilderness hath eternally muffled the roar of stronghold dwellers."[72]

The tank commander's act of bravery follows Ilan's story about Avram before his capture by the Egyptians, at which point he thought he was the last surviving human on the planet. Grossman conjured up by the power of his imagination (until proven otherwise) the story of Avram using the radio to say his final piece, in order to give voice to the sense of doom that so many soldiers shared in the war that still refuses to let us be.

The First Intifada—Sami Michael's Pigeons at Trafalgar Square

Although the chapter on *To the End of the Land* focuses on the Yom Kippur War, it is not the only war present in the novel. Grossman's opus begins with the first meeting of its three protagonists in the 1967 war during a blackout. The novel's present time is the early 2000s, as a wave of terrorist attacks (the Second Intifada) washes over the country. The Yom Kippur War is therefore placed in between: It is both an antithesis to and result of the Six-Day War, as well as the formative event that shapes the protagonists' perspective on wars. *To the End of the Land* stretches across some thirty-five years, during which war seethes in its protagonists' lives also in warless times.

In the same way that several wars "live" in Grossman's novel, there are several wars that are "alive" in Sami Michael's *Pigeons at Trafalgar Square*,[73] set in the late 1980s against the backdrop of the First Intifada. Just as Grossman refrains from naming the terror attacks in his novel's present as the "second intifada," Sami Michael chooses not to name the attacks of the late 1980s as the "first intifada," opting instead for "this Palestinian uprising" (124). As Michael's novel was published after the

Second Intifada, and assuming that he wrote it as the conflict was still roiling, it would be safe to suggest that he absorbed some of the gloom and violence of the latter wave of clashes in his portrayal of the First Intifada. The armed conflict between the two nations, which reached a boiling point in late 1987, raged throughout 1988–89, then slightly subsided, but ended only in 1991. *Pigeons at Trafalgar Square* attempts to foreground the Palestinian experience of this ongoing conflict.

Three wars preceding the First Intifada underlie and give shape to present events in Michael's novel. The stormy war of 1948 triggers the escape of the novel's Arab protagonists from Haifa and forces them to abandon their baby in his cradle, prompting each of the three family members to form a new identity. The Sinai War of 1956, in which the baby's adoptive father is killed, allegedly impacts only the novel's Jewish protagonists. But in fact, it has an analogous effect on the main character's dual identity: Some two decades after the death of his Jewish adoptive father, his Palestinian biological father is killed by Israelis in an Athens hotel, turning the protagonist into a war orphan on both sides. The 1967 war also has a prominent function in the plot, as a counterpoint to the 1948 war. While the earlier war had compelled the Arab parents to flee from Haifa and abandon their young baby, the 1967 war, which obliterated the Green Line separating Israel proper from the occupied territories, enables child and family to reunite. That is, nineteen or twenty years later, the parents come from Ramallah to Haifa to meet their abandoned son at the house he lives in, which used to be their home. Like any late homecoming, the visit holds certain surprises. The parents learn that their baby son grew up to be Ze'ev Epstein, a true-blue Jewish Israeli clad in IDF uniform. The protagonist learns that he is not only the Jewish Ze'ev Epstein, but also the Arab Badir. Shocked to see his progeny wearing Israeli army uniform, the Palestinian father, a political activist, harshly rebukes him, and father and son become sworn enemies. The father's prophetic curse at the end of their conversation concludes their relationship, and the two will never meet again. At the same time, the mother and her son form a clandestine bond.

Sami Michael borrowed parts of this biographical background from the work of Palestinian author Ghassan Kanafani: the Palestinian flight from Haifa in 1948, the adoptive father's death in the 1956 war, and the meeting between the biological parents and their abandoned son in 1967 that led to a bitter altercation between the Jewish-Israeli son and his Arab-Palestinian father. That is, the events depicted in Ghassan Kanafani's novella *Return to Haifa* form the basis for the events of the turbulent present of *Pigeons at Trafalgar Square* which, as mentioned, culminate in the First Intifada. The first part of chapter 8 of *War Lives* focuses on this unique intertextuality, which Michael calls in the opening of his novel "Dialogue with author Ghassan Kanafani." The chapter's second part is dedicated to the protagonist's (Ze'ev Epstein/Badir) hybrid existence, which is the prism through which Sami Michael, an author with a dual identity of his own, evaluates Israeli-Palestinian relations, during the First Intifada and at large. And since we are concerned with war and dreaming (*milhamah* and *halom*), let us consider what the Jewish protagonist has to say after learning that he is also Arab, about the dream of the two peoples fighting against one another:

> Sometimes I don't know how to put into words the way I feel, but both peoples have the same dream—each wants to get up in the morning and discover that the other one is gone, extirpated. The difference is that many of us feel ashamed of this, and even rebuke the ones who talk about it publicly. But on Nabila's side [his Arab mother], the majority is actually proud of this dream and is prepared to die for its sake." (*Pigeons at Trafalgar Square*, 109–10)

If this is the dream that the two peoples harbor, one secretly and the other openly, and the protagonist belongs to both of them, how will he resolve the test of identity and affiliation they impose? Leaving this question unanswered, Sami Michael's pessimistic view on the Israeli-Palestinian conflict takes shape in a captivating plot line that displays flashes of optimism.

The First Lebanon War—Ron Leshem's Beaufort

Ron Leshem's *Beaufort* (2005) chronicles the final year of a group of soldiers' service in South Lebanon, where they held the forward outpost in the center of the Lebanese quagmire, in the Israeli-held Security Zone, and from which the Israel Defense Forces (IDF) withdrew, after nearly two decades of occupation, late one night in May 2000. *Beaufort*, more than all of the other works discussed here, is a war-torn and martial tale, perhaps more than any other Israeli novel; in its potency, it is reminiscent of Erich Maria Remarque's *All Quiet on the Western Front* and Avigdor Hameiri's *The Great Madness*. Paradoxically, perhaps, it is also the least autobiographical of the novels discussed here. The narrative thrust of the two works of the Great War by Remarque and Hameiri owes a debt, to a certain extent, to the autobiographical nature of the tales. Likewise, many of the works discussed in *War Lives* are autobiographical in nature: *To This Day* is based on Agnon's experiences on the German home front during the First World War; *The Brigade* offers a literary account of Hanoch Bartov's experiences while serving in the Jewish Brigade during the Second World War; *Not of This Time, Not of This Place* gives voice to the two wars swirling in Yehuda Amichai's soul: the War of Independence, in which he fought in the Negev Brigade, and the Holocaust (though he did not experience the latter firsthand, as a child of Germany he was continually haunted by both the colossal murder of his peers and the personal murder of a childhood friend); *Infiltration* is based on Yehoshua Kenaz's experience in basic training in 1955; and *Yasmine*, by Eli Amir, reflects an important chapter in his biography before and after the Six-Day War. Unlike the aforementioned works, *Beaufort* has nothing to do with the author's personal life. The novel's narrator-protagonist, Liraz Liberti, nicknamed Erez, is not Ron Leshem. The author included an afterword at the close of the novel. It is entitled "Between Truth and Fiction," and it opens as follows:

> No, I wasn't familiar with the game that everyone plays when a friend is killed, "What He Can't Do Anymore." How could I, when no friends of mine have been killed? I wasn't there, I didn't know what they were doing. On the radio there would be reports on exchanges of fire, even heavy ones, and for eighteen years people came and went and talked about outposts and ambushes. But I stayed in Israel. (*Beaufort*, 353)

Leshem, it emerges, was never a combat soldier. He served in the IDF Military Intelligence Directorate in Tel Aviv and was not even required to wear a uniform. Contrary to the confessional-autobiographical impulses of many authors whose personal experiences inform their writing, Leshem confesses that he has no interest in writing about his natural habitat, the Tel Aviv media scene. His interest in writing lies in "entering a world I do not know, reaching people I do not know and living vicariously through them a life that I will probably not have an opportunity to live. I will never be a real combat soldier."[74]

Therefore, the game "What He Can't Do Anymore," which serves as the grave and irresistibly compelling opening of the novel, a kind of introduction that Leshem also uses in his afterword, is a game he never played. The game, so to speak, is a coping mechanism employed by young men of eighteen or nineteen, helping them come to terms with their bereavement and the fact that they remained alive. Resorting to macabre humor, the fallen soldier's friends compile a list of the things the deceased will no longer be able to do. Interestingly, a similar approach to bereavement appears in Grossman's *To the End of the Land*, where Ilan laments the imminent death of his close friend Avram, the talented poet and radio play writer, as the two of them are convinced that these are his final moments, stationed at an outpost along the Suez Canal: "There would be no more quotes from the sacred poetry of David Avidan and Yona Wallach or from *Catch-22* or *Under Milk Wood*—a song of praise for the human voice, from which Avram could recite entire pages by heart" (*To the End of the Land*, 540). A. B. Yehoshua's *Friendly Fire* also echoes this elegiac motif. Yirmi, the bereaved father of Eyal, cries upon reading the Song of Songs, as it makes him realize that his son will no longer enjoy the light this biblical text shines upon life: "It was actually in the Song of Songs that Eyal's death suddenly overwhelmed me and I read this poetry drowning in tears . . . the beauty overwhelmed me. The love . . . the wondrous eroticism, the descriptions of nature. And then it hit me hard what Eyal would never be able to enjoy" (*Friendly Fire*, 330).

In Ron Leshem's intriguing opening of the novel, the darkly therapeutic exercise of "What He Can't Do Anymore" ends with the words: "Yonatan can't sniff that sweet sweat mixed with the faint smell of shampoo during a long night of wild sex and cuddling, like the week we all had after we left Lebanon, when everything ended. Yonatan will never even know we left Lebanon" (*Beaufort*, 3). This sentence tells the reader that the events recorded in the diary are told in retrospect. That is, the narrative is put to paper after the Israeli withdrawal from South Lebanon and Beaufort, that highly symbolic Crusader fort, and Yonatan was killed before the withdrawal.

But who is Yonatan? Only when readers reach chapter 18 do they realize that the soldier in question is Yonatan Spitzer, a dainty "Ashkenazi," a talented musician, who dared to quote to his friends from *Henry V*; he was planning, promptly upon discharge from the army, to audition for acting school. Yonatan Spitzer, whom Ron Leshem chose as a symbol for "What He Can't Do Anymore," comes to represent all of the horror and the face of those, among the fifteen-strong detail at Beaufort, who were "wasted." In the novel, which for the most part is written in military slang but occasionally rises to rare heights of lyricism and poetry, the verb to be "wasted" denotes being a victim of a meaningless and random death—by missile, improvised explosive device, or mortar shell.

In what is today referred to as the First Lebanon War (1982–2000), 1,306 Israeli soldiers were killed; 654 died in combat during the initial months of the military operation (from June 6, 1982, through September 29, 1982), and another 652 over the course of the next eighteen years. If the game "What He Can't Do Anymore" was indeed a part of army life during those years, then it was played on a nearly weekly basis.

Like the First World War, which was initially called the Great War and acquired its official historical name only with the hindsight of the Second World War, the conflict in Lebanon was initially dubbed with the oxymoronic moniker "Operation Peace for Galilee," and was later engraved in Israeli minds as the "Lebanese quagmire" and then morphed back into the First Lebanon War only in the wake of the Second Lebanon War in 2006. Until then, the First Lebanon War was a war without name and without an official memorial; it devolved into a prolonged guerilla skirmish in and around the Security Zone (established in 1985) that really had very little to do with the initial IDF operation. That traumatic and prolonged conflict received impressive cinematic treatments, but few if any literary adaptations. The novel *Beaufort*—entitled "If Paradise Exists" or "If There's a Heaven" in the original Hebrew—was adapted into a film and a play, both of which were entitled *Beaufort*, after the site of the story's radical human drama. The site, the fortress, in which the members of the platoon experience the intensity of small-scale warfare, drove me to compare *Beaufort* with S. Yizhar's *Days of Ziklag*, which in literary historiography is considered the most important epos of the War of Independence. In Yizhar's novel, too, the site, possibly the biblical city of Ziklag, becomes the protagonist.

My comparative reading of the two novels, entitled "My Imaginary Offspring," appeared in print in the final issue of the Hebrew literary journal *Keshet Hahadasha*. After its publication, I received a telephone call from Aharon Barnea, father of the late Noam Barnea, who served in the IDF's elite bomb squad, YAEL, and to whose memory, along with Tzahi Itah, the Hebrew edition of Leshem's novel is dedicated. The dedication reads: "In memory of Tzahi Itah and Noam Barnea—who cannot become more beautiful than what they were back then"—a nod in the direction of "What He Can't Do Anymore." Tzahi Itah inspired the novel's Yonatan Spitzer, and Noam Barnea was the inspiration for Ziv Faran. Noam and Ziv—names connoting a soft glow and tenderness in Hebrew—led me to think, at least at first, that Leshem sought to retain the gentle spirit of the real-life person and therefore swapped the names in kind. Only later did I learn that the inscription on Noam's tombstone reads, "He left us with the glory of his resplendent youth," (*ziv alumav* in Hebrew), which is why the author changed his name to Ziv. The inscription was brought to my attention by Barnea's father, Aharon, who read my article and responded. As for the family name, both Barnea and Faran are synonymous with the Sinai Peninsula. Noam/Ziv Barnea/Faran did not serve under the command of Liraz (Erez) Liberti, the novel's flinty yet sensitive narrator. Rather, he arrived at Beaufort in order to carry out a bomb-clearing mission. He was killed five days before his scheduled discharge from the IDF.

His father, Aharon, chanced upon the final issue of *Keshet Hahadasha* in a doctor's waiting room and read my article. Before citing his response, I would like to excerpt parts of the article, which earned me the honor of a response from both the father of one of *Beaufort*'s protagonists and from its author as well. Interestingly, both Aharon Barnea and Ron Leshem, in separate and independent letters, refer to the same example in my essay regarding the link between a realistic detail that is dressed in literary garb in the novel, shedding more light on it. After all, my comparative reading of *Beaufort* and *Days of Ziklag* was written in 2008, without the extra-literary knowledge of the underlying story. Here is part of what I wrote in *Keshet Hahadasha*:

> *Days of Ziklag*, set during the War of Independence, follows a group of soldiers over the course of seven days of combat on an isolated hilltop in the Negev. Unlike Sami Michael's *Refuge* or Amos Oz's *My Michael*, it does not concern itself with the people who remained back home, nor does the experience of war figure on the margins of the story or in the epilogue, as in Haim Be'er's *Feathers*. And yet, *Days of Ziklag* is not merely a war novel replete with detailed and precise battle descriptions, but also a psychologically deep novel of ideas that is written in the narrative mode of a stream of consciousness. The vast tracts of text dedicated to the inner lives of the protagonists overshadow the war and the soldiers' performance under fire. Moreover, the novel deals with the yearnings, dilemmas, and thoughts of the young men, each conducting his own private reckoning, more than with the relationships between them. Their endless meditations sometimes soar to the lofty heights of universal questions regarding the moral justification, or lack thereof, for the act of war and the taking of human life. The continuum of the young men's meditative flow offers ample space for expression of their erotic desire, tinged with adolescent romanticism. Shards of memory from the pre-war days bring to mind girls with whom the young men had been in contact, while in the present there is no contact with women. Generally, all of the protagonists in *Days of Ziklag* are fleshed out with long internal monologues, weaving naive idealistic views with virginal erotic yearnings.[75]

We may think of the resemblance between the settings of *Days of Ziklag* and *Beaufort* as follows: Both novels follow an isolated group of young men caged in by war; in *Days of Ziklag*, it is a wooden outpost in the Negev (*Tel Najila*), which is merely four kilometers from the hill—Ziklag—they are ordered to take; in *Beaufort*, the setting is a mountain crowned with the Beaufort Crusader fortress, alongside which the military outpost is situated. In both novels, the groups of soldiers bear the brunt of the protracted defense of their outposts. Although *Days of Ziklag* spans seven days and *Beaufort* spans an entire year, the novels' dimensions of time and space (which Mikhail Baxtin calls "chronotope")[76] constitute a hermetic universe, a spatiotemporal bubble that sequesters the protagonists.

In both novels, the warriors face repeated enemy attacks. The authors of both novels, in their respective works, muse on the interplay between the troops' collective mentality and their individuality. Both novels attain an almost perfect imitation of reality, to the point that it is unclear whether they are documentary records or works of fiction.

Avi Ma'apil's 1988 PhD dissertation revolutionized the scholarly perception of S. Yizhar's monumental *Days of Ziklag*.[77] A comparison between this novel and contemporaneous historical documents chronicling the war indicates there is full and absolute compatibility, to the point of obsession, between the novel's literary universe and the historic reality of the battle on Hirbet Mahaz, which took place between Thursday, September 30, 1948, and Thursday, October 7, 1948. That is, the novel relies on a real-life event, reflecting in the literary narrative the true course of events starting with the framework of the plot and down to the minutest of details. Ma'apil also illustrated the ramified correlations between real-life persons and fictional characters. That is to say, *Days of Ziklag* is a novel that is completely subjected to the historical reality it depicts. Its tenacious recreation of the unfolding of events in the course of a mere seven days spans 1,156 pages of dense prose.[78]

It must be underscored: Generations of literary critics have read *Days of Ziklag* without knowledge of the historical reality in which the battle it portrays is grounded, and approached it as a work of fiction that is loosely based on wartime reality. Yizhar obscured the name of Hirbet Mahaz by replacing it with a charged, biblical name that suggests a comparison of the battle in the War of Independence with the ancient historical battle between King David and the Amalekites. In ancient Ziklag, the Amalekites surprise King David, burn the city down, and take his two wives captive. At the sight of the smoldering, empty city, David and his men "raised their voices and wept until there was no strength left in them to weep" (I Samuel 30:4). Yet after this bitter lament and after issuing the threat to have David stoned to death for allowing the defeat, the king musters up his strength and chases after the captors, raids them, takes back his women and loot, and shares his victory with the men who had just suggested stoning him. Thus, critics saw in the scorched Ziklag of the Bible an analogous conceptual framework for Yizhar's *Ziklag*.

Yizhar's obscurement of the concrete name of the site of events on the one hand, and his selection of a name that carries ancient memories on the other hand, have led scholars to believe that the novel adheres to Aristotle's call not to relay what has happened but rather what may happen.[79] They did not imagine that the events depicted in *Ziklag* are hard facts, which took place precisely as related in the novel. This, therefore, begs the following question: In the wake of the discovery of the profound, genetic-factual bond between the work and reality, does the novel lose its aesthetic value? It seems not. Perhaps, to a degree, it breaches a hidden contract between author and reader; but once one overcomes the surprise, it becomes clear that Yizhar embellished and elaborated the backbone of a gray and uninspiring battle narrative that took place in late September–early October 1948, with corresponding, but not necessarily factual, materials such as daily routines, rituals, actions, dialogues, and streams of consciousness, which do not, and truly cannot, be expressed in the historical chronicles of the war. The prodigious filling of the soldiers' inner lives, alongside the precise reconstruction of the historic events of the battle, is delivered in Yizhar's inimitable language.[80]

Ron Leshem's *Beaufort* also appears to protest against Aristotle's discrete and refined demand to keep literature and history separate. Leshem also challenges the hierarchy that places literature above history—that is, above reality. Hence, the second distinctive war novel of Hebrew literature also refuses to abide by the separation of literature and history and the elevation of the former over the latter. Though we have found Yizhar's elimination of Hirbet Mahaz and its replacement with Ziklag to be a ploy that allowed him to place his novel in the realm of the fictitious, *Beaufort* does not follow suit. The old, imposing Crusader fortress, overlooking breathtaking verdant landscapes, has the potential to be an invented site created by an author's wild imagination. Yet Leshem's novel had no need for eliminating the name of the real-life site and replacing it with a charged name to serve a fictional, literary aim because the ancient citadel, pregnant with historic memories, in and of itself so very "literary," is in fact solid reality.

The Golani Brigade's reconnaissance platoon, in a bloody, face-to-face battle, conquered the citadel in 1982, during the first week of the First Lebanon War; soldiers and commanders paid with their lives. The more well-known names of the fallen include Goni Harnick, Yossie Eliel, and Raz Guterman. Until 2000, the year of Israel's withdrawal, it served as a fortress in which soldiers were entrenched, and those are the characters that populate Leshem's novel. Realism and symbolism long intermingled atop Beaufort, though the soldiers manning the old fortress were not made of tin; they were soldiers of flesh and blood.

One individual who never served in a combat unit and never served in Lebanon was Leshem himself. As noted, he spent his compulsory military service in the Intelligence Corps in Tel Aviv, dressed in civilian clothes. He never experienced the difficult and surreal slice of reality that his protagonists are exposed to daily on Beaufort. And yet he managed to penetrate the mental, verbal, and spiritual world of a young platoon commander and relate a first-person account of what he and his soldiers endured. The account sounds accurate, reliable, and true, to the extent that no reader can doubt that the reality portrayed in the novel is stronger than mere fantasy. The Aristotelian assumption that literature deals with the possible but not necessarily with the actual is dwarfed by the novel's reality, which Leshem crafted with rare literary talent.

The men at arms and their impulsive, hotheaded commander, Liraz (Erez) Liberti, a twenty-year-old lieutenant, are no longer the fair young men we know from Moshe Shamir's *He Walked Through the Fields* and S. Yizhar's *Days of Ziklag*. Leshem's troops hail from the second and third tiers of Israeli society, those who today man the front: national-religious Jews, new immigrants, and residents of the periphery. Israel's demographics have changed, the language has changed, and the young soldiers' dilemmas have become more concrete and less universal. Therefore, when they argue over whether their presence at Beaufort is justified in the wake of the traumatic death of their comrade Ziv Faran, they sound so very different from S. Yizhar's 1948 war heroes:

On the third night, when I thought he'd calmed down, River caught me during one of my tours of the guard posts. . . . He said, "Erez, I just wanted you to know that when I asked what the fuck we're doing here, I really meant it." . . . "You have your doubts about our mission here, River? . . . Don't the towns and villages along our northern border interest you anymore?" But River didn't even take a breath or miss a beat before answering. "It has nothing to do with the northern border. We're just looking out for our own asses, that's all. We sit at Beaufort, disconnected from everything, drawing rockets and mortar shells and explosive devices, endangering our lives, just so we can continue sitting at Beaufort. That's the entire mission. What a shitty feeling. What on earth were we doing in that fucked-up operation anyway? All we wanted to do was open up some goddamned road, the goddamned road that leads back and forth to Israel, nothing more than that. You tell me, Erez, as an officer. What are we doing here?"

"What do you prefer?" I recited. "For Hezbollah to move freely right up to the fence and settle in there? You're talking bullshit, River. Chill out. If we weren't here, if we didn't have a string of outposts deep in Lebanese territory, the enemy would be pushed up against the border fence with their weapons drawn and ready to shoot at Metula and Nirit and Manara." (*Beaufort*, 148)

The argument between River the paramedic, who experiences his inability to save Ziv's life as a bitter failure, and Liraz-Erez, who adamantly justifies the IDF's presence in the Security Zone in South Lebanon, sounds completely authentic on the personal, political, social, prophetic, and linguistic levels. Leshem concocted the language of his characters after watching dozens of videos that soldiers serving in Lebanon shot as they went through their daily routines. In a random and seemingly negligible conversation like the one above, he presents the dilemmas and fears of an entire generation. He conjures up a hilarious-yet-terrifying reality consisting of wartime camaraderie and young people's dreams. After all, literature is about people, not about strategy and war tactics, which is why Lebanon and the war that raged on its soil until Israel's retreat is a mere backdrop for the story of eighteen-year-olds in Israel during the first year of the twenty-first century. Situated on the seam between childhood and adulthood, with their futures still looming ahead of them, their dreams and yearnings resemble those of people their age in other places around the world, but the conditions and chances of their fulfillment within Israel's singular reality are not similar. This is the dilemma to which Leshem gives voice.

Allow me to offer an example of how the novel manipulates reality, attempting to create literary conflict amid the documentary-like realism of a novel like *Beaufort* by staging a "probable" coincidence. The example I will use, which is one of many, points out the novel's compliance with the Aristotelian demand that literature convey that which may happen rather than that which did happen: *Beaufort*, which is based on real-life characters, is dedicated to the memory of Tzahi Itah and Noam Barnea, two combat soldiers killed in the line of duty during the course of Israel's final year of control over the "accursed mountain."[81] Tzahi Itah was the last IDF casualty in South Lebanon. Noam Barnea served in the elite YAEL bomb squad unit. In the novel, Ziv Faran, the literary persona of Barnea, is killed in a near-suicide mission to remove an explosive device a mere five days before his scheduled discharge from the IDF. Ziv's dramatic death also inspired the climax of the feature film *Beaufort*, which is based on the novel. When he arrives at the fortress, both in the film and the novel, Ziv is greeted by Erez with a mixture of suspicion and hostility, a response to his strangeness, to the fact of his being a scion of Israel's founding generation, a "fine young man-at-arms," whose Ashkenazi roots rendered him an outcast. This is how, in his typical style, Erez Liberti, Leshem's flinty narrator, a Generation X patriot, casts doubt about Faran and the "pretty boy's" professional skills: "If that little white boy really knows something about bomb removal, I'll cut my dick off" (112). But Ziv, with his different socioeconomic background, emerges, atop Beaufort, as one of the guys. He wins Erez over with his broad smile, his warmth and optimism, his courage and lack of condescension. All of these attributes counter the expectations of the deeply motivated and yet prejudiced commander.

Nonetheless, Ziv's otherness-foreignness comes to light unexpectedly when Erez and Ziv are in the common shower and Erez, to his dismay, notices that above Ziv's fancy toiletry kit hangs a white T-shirt imprinted with the slogan—"Leave Lebanon in Peace"—the slogan of the Four Mothers movement.

We might ask: Is this T-shirt story truth or fiction? Did Noam Barnea, the prototype for Ziv Faran, indeed own a Four Mothers T-shirt? Very possibly, but it is a possibility that adheres to the Aristotelian demand that fiction describe what may happen, while history deal squarely with what actually did happen. Either way, with the T-shirt story Leshem clearly seeks to expose the profundity of the Lebanon War quandary, and maybe the tragedy of Israel, in the year 2000 and at large: A young man with left-wing political views who opposes Israel's protracted military presence in Lebanon but nonetheless does not dream of refusing to follow his orders, arrives in Beaufort to carry out a dangerous mission and gets killed on the eve of his discharge from military service. Erez, the die-hard officer from the peripheral town of Afula, who suspected Ziv and was appalled by his leftist views, will never stop mourning the glow of the lost young life of Ziv Faran, the hero who was blown up next to him on their joint mission.

Leshem's novel concludes with an afterword entitled "Between Truth and Imagination." Few novels in Western literature, to which Hebrew literature belongs, either open or end with a chapter that reveals to readers the borderline between reality and fictional materials. And yet, the all-too-concrete reality on which *Beaufort* is based impelled its author to do so nonetheless. In his afterword, Leshem confesses that he, the author, was not "there," and also reveals his sources. Rotem Yair is the squad commander who told him about his experiences at Beaufort and whose story Leshem adapted into a novel. Yet after his full disclosure, the author tells his readers:

> Liraz (Erez) Liberti is not Rotem Yair. He's an invention. The soldiers he commands are also not based on real people. They are all of them, from the lowliest soldier to the highest brigade and battalion commanders, the live ones as well as the dead ones, though inspired by real people, are the children of my invention. (357)

The children of Ron Leshem's imagination are the true Israeli soldiers who are living the reality of their country, experiencing its intricacies, atrocities, torturous conflicts, and sense of unbearable loss. Surprisingly, however, they do not regret this experience, and are even prepared—in the event that peace does not prevail—to share with the coming generations an experience that only locals can understand: "I'm sane, don't worry. I'm not shell-shocked," says Erez-Liraz Liberti the narrator, close to the conclusion of his fictional-realistic confession:

> In our country I'm certainly not the only twenty-one-year-old who's held the body of a friend missing a head. You could almost say it's normal around here. And with a lot of pain and my hand on my heart, I've got to share my thought with you—and it's not exactly the most popular one at the moment: If peace doesn't come in the meantime, I want my own kid to go through what I did. The challenges, the pain, the fear. They made me look at the world in a different way, find myself and what's important to me. My love for my family and the love for my life, and how fragile they are. (310)

We would be hard-pressed to decide who is making this statement: the real-life combat soldier or the fictional character that Ron Leshem created with the inspiration of the real-life combat soldier, and in whose mouth he placed the aforementioned words. With considerable pain and with my hand on my heart, I must share my own thoughts: I believe his every word.

Below is an excerpt from the letter Aharon Barnea sent me in response to the above article, following an emotional telephone conversation between us, in which he told me that Noam Barena did not take a Four Mothers T-shirt up to Beaufort, but rather a campaign button. Also, thanks to his letter, I was able to understand why Leshem transformed Noam's name in the novel to Ziv.

> I was moved by our conversation today. I am amazed each time anew. More than nine years have passed since that accursed day, and all of a sudden, in the time and place I could least expect, the boy's wondrous memory keeps coming up in old-new contexts. The story of the Four Mothers button stirred quite a riot at the time. [Longtime journalist] Sylvie Keshet had published it in her column, which I enclose herein. By the way, when the Ministry of Defense offered us to add our own

words to his tombstone inscription (at that time the strict rules enforcing a uniform and somewhat Spartan language on the tombstones of IDF soldiers was finally breached), we asked Sylvie Keshet's permission to use a sentence of hers, stating how, "He left us with the glory of his resplendent youth [Hebrew: *ziv alumav*]." Then, as now, we believe that this phrase succinctly captures the full extent of Noam's joie de vivre.

As mentioned, I also received a letter from Ron Leshem (in January 2010), which I excerpt below. Such extra-literary accounts in the long and winding relationship between truth and fiction might help explain the secret of *Beaufort*'s success. (The novel was awarded the prestigious Sapir Prize, not without a heated argument between the members of the adjudicating panel.) Ron Leshem's letter also touches on the fascinating nexus between documentary and literary works, as well as the aspiration and talent necessary to transform journalistic research into an artistic novel:

> I write in order to experience worlds to which I have no access. I write instead of living. I write in order to get under the skin of the man I would like to be and I'm not. Or to cross a borderline I passionately want to cross, but cannot. And most of all, I write things that I have missed, things I will not get to fulfill. So I fulfill them in my imagination, and through writing. I was not on the Beaufort, but if you sat me down to take a polygraph test, I could very possibly emerge truth-telling when I say that I was there. I write my alter ego, which I think was the most powerful driving force for writing *Beaufort*. This is why I wrote [it]. I wanted to be that Liraz, I wanted to be in the company of that Zeitlawi. I was not Liraz in my real life, and I did not have a friend like Zeitlawi. Zeitlawi would not have even beaten me up in the schoolyard, because there weren't any boys like that at the school I went to. But I had always wanted to have around me such a boy who would be my buddy. That is why I wrote, and as I did so, I felt as if I was living among them.
>
> I have no desire to come back home at night from the life of a Tel Aviv media person, sit at the keyboard and write about the life of a Tel Aviv media person. That is why the research . . . was such a tremendous experience for me. I felt as if I was emptying myself completely, and filling myself with a new world, a new person, and then I shut my eyes, and woke up as someone else. What an enormous, spine-chilling

privilege. Pure joy. When I visit screenwriting classes and hear how they tell their young students, "look for the story at home, in the family, in your building, in the neighborhood, someplace close," it saddens me to see the way they are educated to indolence and advised to steer clear of research, and in that way the students are denied the right to be an actor who can really and truly change characters. For this reason, by the way, I like writing in the first person.

When *Beaufort* came out, the reviews in Israel were very cold, of course. Although I was not humiliated, cold, condescending winds blew in my face. No one considered it to be a piece of actual literature. They saw it as "journalism" . . . whereas I wanted them to think of it as a novel.

The choice of "If There Is a Heaven" for a title derived from my wish to endow the book with a poetic air. Not to be perceived as too close to current events. The publisher preferred the title *Coming Down from the Mountain*, which sounded to me as insufficiently sensitive. When the movie version was ready I was prepared to change to the new title *Beaufort*. I was also glad that the film's title is different from the book, because the film is different and consciously offered an entirely different commentary on the story; it did not compete with the book regarding the issues that the book sought to address. I was concerned that the book's cover would end up being overly militaristic and would smack of news-like reportage, but the publisher insisted on having an iconic, memorable image. That is why the army boots are turned upside down.

By the way, each of the characters in *Beaufort* was based more or less on a real-life person, who is either alive or dead. This somewhat tamed me and kept me from writing completely freely, as I thought to myself: Will Uri Glickman, who is the real-life Orthodox soldier from Beaufort, be offended by my portrayal of the Orthodox soldier in the novel? Only Zeitlawi is completely fictional. He is not based on anyone I know; rather, he is based on the greaser with the heart of gold friend I never had. That is why I felt free with him and ran wild.

To me, this book was to a large degree a social commentary. That is, my attraction to the story was the attempt to portray the face of the new Israel through the face of the new IDF. In my eyes, Ziv Faran, bomb squad fighter, polished Ashkenazi, arrives in the outpost as an ambassador of Goni Harnick—that is, of Israel's social elite. He arrives and then gets killed. And along with him, Israel's social elite dies, too. Forgive my pathos. Today's IDF regiments are the periphery's army: new immigrant and religious soldiers. Ongoing security, the battlefront, is largely maintained by an army of low-income cannon fodder, whose officers are either national-religious or from well-established farming communities who are yet to realize what is going on in Tel Aviv, for example. This is why I wanted to ask: Who are we sending over to die for our sake, and are we challenging ourselves enough when we do that? Are we asking questions? Naturally, I also wanted to create a microcosm of my own through the use of language. I love inventing languages. A large part of the words in Zeitlawi's military vocabulary are not genuine, but are rather derived from genuine meters of linguistic inventions that are characteristic of young people like him. Some of the [book's] publishers worldwide, its editors and translators, decided to use local military slang (in the American version, for example), and others decided to turn to the language of unruly slum youths (in the French version for example), and yet others held fast to the Israeli ambience. Unfortunately, some versions simply trimmed down heavily the slang and the language, to avoid having to confront this problem. Some editions published today are translated directly from the English, rather than the Hebrew, in China and Korea for example.

Another note: the late Noam Barnea, the combat soldier on which Ziv Faran's character is based, did not actually show up at the Beaufort with a Four Mothers T-shirt, which is why a national flag made of a T-shirt and ink was not flown [at the outpost]. He did land at the Beaufort with a "Leave Lebanon in Peace" campaign button on his T-shirt, underneath his uniform. The troops at Beaufort were flabbergasted. And they hated him. But he managed to melt their hearts during his short stay. And his death melted their hearts even more, and gradually he was idealized. The flag indeed disappeared on the night of the evacuation, as it was probably taken back to Israel in one of the first convoys [to leave Lebanon]; and they did fear before dawn that Lebanon would wake up and think that Beaufort had been evacuated and climb up to the fortress. That is why when it was decided to extend the stay by one more day, they flew a small makeshift flag. This is an example of how I permitted myself, just a tad, to improvise and mesh the stories together. I think that the spirit of the real-life events was untainted.

The ninth chapter of *War Lives* broadens the discussion on the relationship between fiction and reality by offering another comparison between two war and army novels: *Beaufort* and *Infiltration*.

Before the Second Intifada—A. B. Yehoshua's Friendly Fire

The novel with which *War Lives* concludes, A. B. Yehoshua's *Friendly Fire*, is linked both thematically and structurally to earlier chapters. *War Lives* opens with the theme of bereavement in Agnon's *To This Day*, which is also a central theme in my reading of *Friendly Fire*. Chapter 3 focuses on Amichai's *Not of This Time, Not of This Place*, where the protagonist is simultaneously present in two different locations: the novel's chapters alternate between Jerusalem and Weinburg (that is, Würzburg) in southern Germany. *Friendly Fire* employs a similar technique: It takes place simultaneously in two distant places, as its chapters alternate between Israel and Tanzania, in Africa. I have described Amichai's novel as "schizophrenic" because its divided protagonist undergoes parallel experiences in two different places, reflecting his bifurcated life. The author of *Friendly Fire* has called the novel "a duet," because its two main protagonists, husband and wife Amotz and Daniela Ya'ari—who maintain a symbiotic relationship typical of Yehoshua's novels—separate for seven days and undergo parallel experiences in two different places. Since Amotz Ya'ari, the main male protagonist, wanders across Israel during his wife's absence and, among other places, passes through an army base where Moran, his son, is kept in detention, this novel is also linked with *Infiltration*'s descriptions of army life. Moreover, A. B. Yehoshua even appears to make implicit references to the military novel of his friend, Yehoshua Kenaz. During Amotz's visit to his son, which the army camp descriptions hint is the basic training grounds Camp 80, Amotz smells Moran's work uniform that reeks of gun oil, "a fundamental Israeli aroma, an ever-present whiff of dread, the smell of one's first contact with the army, of basic training, which forty years cannot erase from one's consciousness" (*Friendly Fire*, 293). The passage is imbued with an impression of both Kenaz's own basic training experience and his novel.

On the face of it, the only-son motif that the first chapter of *War Lives* discusses in the context of the First World War bears no resemblance to the book's final chapter, which follows the attempt of the extended family of a casualty of IDF cross-fire in the summer of 2000 to come to terms with its grief. "Remember that our story took place before the Second Intifada, when the whole thing was a mess, when chaos reigned on both sides" (259)—this is the Israeli "war time" of the son's death in *Friendly Fire*, the way his bereaved father, Yirmi, describes it. The opening and closing chapters of *War Lives* share the focus on a son's unnecessary death. In *To This Day*, this topic is amplified through emphasis on the patriotism of Jews who are prepared to sacrifice their sons on the altar of the German nation shortly before its Nazification, whereas in *Friendly Fire* the topic is manifested by emphasis on the human error that led to the son's death. In Yehoshua's novel, the son is not even killed in battle or in one of the intifadas; he is shot dead by his close friends. The fathers in the two novels, Dr. Mittel in *To This Day* and Yirmi in *Friendly Fire*, deal with their bereavement in diametrically opposed ways: In Agnon's novel, the father clings to his life routine like an automaton, whereas in Yehoshua's novel the bereaved father runs away and obsessively turns his back on his previous life. The fathers' expressions of grief over their sons' pointless deaths are different, yet the motivations of both authors, Agnon and Yehoshua, are similar: to give literary expression to the pain of bereavement and the futility of war.

The chapter on *Friendly Fire* focuses on each extended family member's chosen way to deal with his or her grief, starting with the victim's parents (his father especially), and ending with his young female cousin. The novel is set in 2007, seven years after the son's death, by which time his mother is no longer alive. She appears to have died in order to disconnect herself from the pain over his loss. His father finds a different way to disconnect. Yehoshua's treatment of the subject matter is also exceptional when it comes to his representation of the mourning gestures of the soldier's aunt and uncle—his mother's sister Daniela and her husband Amotz—and their children, the soldier's cousins Nofar and Moran. Even Moran's wife Efrat, a "stranger" to the family, and her two children,

Daniela's and Amotz's grandchildren, find a way of sharing the family grief. Bereavement and mourning for the death of a nephew or cousin rarely receive literary treatment, which Yehoshua stages in *Friendly Fire* in order to acknowledge the powerful presence of bereavement in extended families.

The chapter also addresses both the concrete and metaphorical meanings of words and word combinations in the context of mourning and bereavement. The novel's oxymoronic, deceptive title "Friendly Fire" gives a small taste of Yehoshua's tireless play on words that is based on ambiguous expressions: fire, wind, roof, the color red, and the adjective real. In addition to the multivalence of the words that appear in different contexts in the plot as they acquire surprising meanings, and in addition to both concrete and figurative semantic manipulations obtained by their coupling, Yehoshua also juggles with time in his novel. The novel is set during Hanukkah and several chapters are devoted to each "candle," describing each hour of the day in both Israel and Tanzania and ending with the dating of animal bones to millions of years, the purpose of the anthropological expedition to Africa that the bereaved father joins. The Bible is placed between these two distant temporal markers, as events from 2,500 years ago have a significant presence in the novel. Yirmi, named after Jeremiah the Prophet, whom the protagonist resents, is visited by his sister-in-law for a few days, while Daniela's husband is in the company of his employees, clients, and especially his children, daughter-in-law, grandchildren, and aged father. They are all linked to Eyali, the soldier killed by friendly fire, whose name attests to his sacrificial role (*eyal* is Hebrew for ram). It emerges that in this novel Yehoshua continues processing the biblical Binding of Isaac story he first tackled in his early novella, "Three Days and a Child"; this time the boy sacrificed is a soldier killed in active service in the Occupied Territories, in the pastoral town of Tulkarem.

The dead soldier's name, an unmangled incarnation of Yali from "Three Days and a Child," proves that in the current novel Yehoshua continues to hold fast to the Binding myth. To be more precise, the fact that Eyali-Yali-*eyal* (ram) is killed by IDF fire indicates that Yehoshua continues with the same ideological move he initiated as far back as *Mr. Mani*, which he called "canceling the Binding by actualizing it."[82] In the author's view, the Binding story is a destructive myth because it has led Jews to believe that God's angel will always descend from heaven at the very last minute and call out "Do not touch the boy," thus saving the child from slaughter. This is why he employs the story as a way to battle against the myth. In *Mr. Mani*, he has a father kill his own son, while in *Friendly Fire* he has soldiers kill their brother-in-arms. In both cases, the death is caused by familicide; in both cases, the boy is the ram caught with its horns in the bush, rather than Isaac whose life is saved.

Women in the Novels of War Lives

The first ten chapters of *War Lives* focus on the military and war-related aspects of ten novels ordered chronologically by their story time, starting with the First World War in Agnon's *To This Day*, and ending with the eve of the Second Intifada in A. B. Yehoshua's *Friendly Fire*. The Yom Kippur War is represented in a range of works written in the first few years after that war, and most of all in David Grossman's *To the End of the Land*, written thirty-five years after the fact. Indeed, Grossman's novel also represents the dread that preceded the Six-Day War and the chaos of the Second Intifada in the early 2000s. Yet my analysis of the author's representation centers on the Yom Kippur War. Chapter 11 is an addendum, so to speak, that examines the status, presence, and role of women in the works discussed in *War Lives*, against the backdrop of the status, presence, and role of women in war and army literature at large. Since war has always been, and still is, considered a purely masculine sphere, war literature is a conspicuously masculine genre. Yet feminist undercurrents continue to subvert the salience of its masculinity, seeping into the IDF and other armies around the world.

The final chapter of my book explores women's representation in the corpus selected. The time has come, it seems, to update Virginia Woolf's pacifist manifesto *Three Guineas* (1938), which opens with the words: "For though many instincts are held more or less in common by both sexes, to fight has always been the man's habit, not the woman's. Law and practice have developed that difference, whether innate or accidental."[83] The time has come to update this observation: Women also share men's fighting habit and passion for victory. In any event, the works discussed in *War Lives* reflect the traditional conception of women's status in the army and war, as well as the perception that women and men are equally tough and rough and capable of collaborating with men-at-arms, rather than merely standing on the sidelines to cheer for them.

To conclude, *War Lives* does not purport to offer an exhaustive representation of all of Israel's wars in Israeli prose. It lacks, for example, adequate representation of the Second World War, or of Israel's War of Independence; these two wars are either mentioned in the context of other wars, or live in the hearts of protagonists whose story time either precedes or follows these wars (*The Brigade*; *Not of This Time, Not of This Place*). Furthermore, the works analyzed do not necessarily constitute war literature per se. War, the fear thereof, the military experience, vengeance against enemies, and the pain of loss are represented in Israeli prose in a manner that is restrained, implicit, and self-limited in comparison with life in the shadow of war—and in its midst—which is the cornerstone of the Israeli experience. For the most part, the novels selected to represent these issues in *War Lives* do not deviate from the escapism characteristic of the treatment of those issues in Israeli novels. The majority of works mix war with life stories of camaraderie, love, and family, together reflecting the intricacies of life, with which war and army are inseparably intertwined.

1

Only Sons and Bereavement in S. Y. Agnon's *To This Day*

A Novel of the First World War

> "But one war leads to another. After a second war and a third war, the Germans have been beaten to their knees."

The Narrator-Protagonist and Germany of World War I

Shmuel Yosef Agnon lived in Germany from 1912 to 1924, having left Jaffa, where he had landed in the second wave of immigration (the Second Aliyah) in 1908 from his native city of Buczacz, in Polish Galicia. World War I, which erupted about two years after his arrival in Germany, was one of the core experiences of his long sojourn in that country. His thoughts on the war and the deprivations he suffered as a temporary resident in Germany resound in some of his works, such as the monumental novel *Shira* (1970) and the short novel *To This Day* [Hebrew: *Ad Hena*] (1950). Both were written and published after the Holocaust, but while the Second World War (and not only World War I) is present in *Shira*, it is absent, at least ostensibly, from *To This Day*.

Shira is set in Jerusalem in the late 1930s—a time known in Jewish historiography as "the time of the troubles" and in Arab historiography as "the Arab Revolt." The World War I memories of the protagonist, Manfred Herbst, echo through the narrative. After emigrating from Germany, settling in Jerusalem with his wife Henrietta, and becoming involved in the city's life (Manfred Herbst is a doctor of history at Hebrew University, founded in 1925), he hears the wheels of the Second World War machine beginning to turn in Europe. That is, the war in *Shira* spans all dimensions of time: The present in the novel is the period of the Arab Revolt, the past is World War I, and the future is World War II, which is expressed in the novel in Henrietta's tireless efforts to obtain immigration certificates for her relatives in order to save them from the impending conflagration.

In contrast, *To This Day* describes only the acts, encounters, anxieties, distress, thoughts, and nightmares of the narrator-protagonist, namely Agnon, who went to Germany from Palestine as a "guest" for a short time, where World War I "caught" him, to his dismay. The short novel about the life of the narrator-protagonist, set in Berlin, Leipzig, and Grimma in 1916, portrays German Jews fighting for the German Fatherland without the slightest notion of what lies in store for them in Germany's next war against the world—unlike Henrietta in *Shira*, who senses what is about to happen in Berlin from far-off Jerusalem in the 1930s. In *To This Day*, World War I is called the "Great War," before the world knew that a war ten times "greater" and more terrible would follow. This highlights the fact that the novel was *not* supposedly written from the perspective of World War II. For only in hindsight is the Great War called the "First" World War, and in *To This Day* the narrator-protagonist, like all of the other characters, lives out the "Great War" as if it were the most terrible of all.

There is a fundamental difference between the hero of *To This Day* and most of the characters he encounters as the story develops, Jews and Christians alike: They see themselves as German patriots, while the narrator considers himself an émigré, trapped by chance in a war that is not his own, who must keep a low profile and wait out the war. "When the war broke out, I stopped working . . . All I wanted was to crumple the days into as small a ball as possible until it was over" (*To This Day*, 18).[1] His emotional and physical noninvolvement in the success or failure of the war allows him to observe it from the outside and to criticize those engaged in it. The novel is replete with paradoxical and ironic situations whose purpose is to emphasize the pointlessness of war. In particular, Agnon shines a tragicomic light on the Jews who regard Germany as their homeland and are ready to sacrifice their children on its altar.

The novel begins with the narrator lodging at a boardinghouse in western Berlin owned by Frau Trotzmüller, a German mother with three daughters and one son; the son went to war and is missing in action. The narrator hears his landlady weeping for her son at night. The boardinghouse is a microcosm of war life on the German home front. The landlady is a widow whose husband was killed in Germany's previous war—people are always living between two wars, as Yehuda Amichai notes in his epic novel *Not of This Time, Not of This Place*. And now her youngest child, her only son, has gone off to war and has not returned; no one knows if he was killed or taken prisoner. The narrator explains that any attempt to trace the lost son in the chaotic state of war would be futile: "Multitudes of soldiers were dead, captured or missing in action; who could locate a single mother's son, a speck of dust swept away by the winds of war?" (17). He expresses neither pity nor identification with the suffering mother, and attributes his indifference to the state of war that seals people off from each other: "Frau Trotzmüller and her daughters didn't impose their grief on their boarders, and their boarders didn't inquire about young Trotzmüller. Everyone had his own troubles; no one had time for anyone else's" (17–18). Even when the landlady recounts her sensational dream, in which he, her Jewish boarder, brings back her lost son, the protagonist remains apathetic toward the mother and her wishful dream. How could he, the uninvolved Jew, find a speck of dust while wandering the cities of Germany?

When this implausible dream becomes reality and the skeptical protagonist returns from his travels with the lost son, it is now the mother and her daughters who show indifference toward the very hero (the narrator) who made their dream come true. The protagonist's room in the boardinghouse had been the son's room before he went off to war and returned brain-damaged. Despite the son's head injury, the joy at his return is enormous, and in the great excitement the boarder who brought him home is forgotten. No one in the landlady's family cares that the narrator is left without a corner to lay down his head. The night of the return, when one of the chambermaids at the boardinghouse finally offers him the bathtub as a place to sleep, is one of the most surrealist nights portrayed in the novel. The fears of the mother, whose son is half-dead, materialize when he returns home without a brain; these fears are also expressed in the attitude toward the lone boarder, whose room was taken from him and is now considered as good as dead: "The chambermaid sized me up like an undertaker measuring a corpse for its grave. What she said next, dear reader, was this: 'I suppose the bathroom won't be needed until the morning. I'll make a bed for you there'" (85).

Only Sons of "Germans of the Mosaic Faith"

The case of the lost German son, who returns home a "zombie," foreshadows other only sons who went off to war and did not return, among them lost sons of Jewish families. The following example bears riveting witness to the psychological state of German Jews and to the existential predicament of those who were not authentic German Jews, but whose lives were bound up with Germany and its Jewry.

Dr. Isaac Mittel is an elderly man, witty and wise, a scholarly bibliographer who lives in Leipzig. He is not a German Jew; Mittel is a Polish Jew who had once been a Hassid, then later became a socialist and was therefore hunted by the secret police, which prompted him to flee to Germany. After settling in Germany, he earned his living compiling inventories of antique books for commercial houses and teaching Hebrew to Christian theologians. His proximity to those circles boosted his prestige among Jewish traders.[2] The following passage presents German Jews in a starkly ironic light:

> Hearing that he socialized with Christian professors—that is, with real Germans such as they, German citizens of the Mosaic faith, never rubbed shoulders with—they befriended him and invited him for coffee and dinner to their homes, where he became a frequent guest. In this fashion, he met the daughter of a wealthy family and married her. Her large dowry made him financially independent. (29)

Dr. Mittel, a native of one of the Polish townships, and his wife, the daughter of wealthy merchants who saw themselves as "Germans of the Mosaic faith," had an only son who went off to war. The Eastern European father feels bitter irony and heartache over this, while the mother, "an authentic German Jew," feels her heart swell with pride as she sends her son off to defend the Fatherland. When the narrator-protagonist visits his friend at his home in Leipzig and the mother is out—she, the German patriot, is taking part in the war effort on the home front—Dr. Mittel reveals to his guest the profound difference between his attitude and that of his wife vis-à-vis Germany's war and their son's eager enlistment in it. Mittel says bitterly:

> What's new in the world? Anything besides killing and being killed? First men go mad and start a **war** and then the **war** goes on by itself. My **only son** has taken up arms and is waging **war**, too. In case you've never seen him, here's a photograph. Doesn't he look the **war** hero in his uniform? A world conqueror! His dear mother has good reason to be proud of him. I never thought I would have a son who makes **war** (30, emphasis added).³

The word "war" appears repeatedly in Dr. Mittel's ironic remarks, underlining his comment that "war goes on by itself"—that is, it becomes an entity that is no longer controlled by those who launched it and takes on a life of its own. The elderly bibliographer, who works with letters and words, describes war's impact on the world and how the current war is transforming the world by diminishing its originality and humanity. In describing the new reality, he starts by citing minor changes and moves on to major upheavals, culminating in a surprise designed to shock his interlocutor: "One man makes ersatz letters, another ersatz food, another ersatz arms and legs, and the Reich makes ersatz men and calls them soldiers" (31).

As cited above, when Mittel emphasizes the difference between his and his wife's attitudes toward the war, he says, "in case you've never seen him [his son in uniform], here's a photograph." In fact, the narrator had indeed seen the son, and not only his picture. On an earlier visit to Mittel's home, the narrator had witnessed the son packing his bag to go off to war and observed the mother's look of approval: "I remembered the boy's mother scrutinizing every item that he packed in his kitbag, her eyes bright with joy at the sight of her boy going off to defend the Fatherland" (30). Did Mittel really forget that the narrator had visited his home on the day his son went off to war? Does he only remember his son and his son's enlistment by his picture?

The only son of Dr. Mittel, the "Ostjude," and of his wife, the "real" German Jew, fell in battle. The narrator hears this news after bringing the landlady's lost son, the mindless German soldier, back to his home in Berlin, leaving himself homeless. His homelessness continues after he is forced to leave another room, this time rented from German Jews. The narrator's tribulations with his lodgings are a central plot thread in *To This Day*. Agnon uses his protagonist's wanderings to describe life on the German home front during the Great War and the characteristics of Germans and German Jews. Agnon is unsparing in his criticism of both groups,[4] and he even treats his wandering hero, a literary embodiment of himself, with irony. The narrator notes that German Jews had begun to take in boarders and he shares his misgivings about renting a room from them:

> Like most of **my friends** from Eastern Europe. I had made a point of not living with German Jews. They were more German than the Germans and didn't like us **displaying our Jewishness**, which led to arguments. Now, however, after a homeless night, I was less choosy. When I found a room in a Jewish home the next day, I took it. (101, emphasis added)

When the narrator says "our" Jewishness and "my friends," he is referring to Eastern European Jews who recently arrived in Germany (like himself and Dr. Mittel) and who, unlike German Jews, do not hide their Jewishness. Still, the room and the kindness of Herr and Frau Lichtenstein, Berliner Jews, toward their boarder, the Galician Jew, made it worthwhile. However, the relatively good days for the narrator-protagonist in that room are few, as soon afterward the house is sold to a commercial firm. When the protagonist is about to leave, just as in the case of the room at Frau Trotzmüller's boardinghouse, the motif of an only son who is killed or badly wounded in the war emerges, except that here the son is substituted by a daughter and son-in-law: "Their [the Lichtensteins'] **only daughter**, whose husband was killed in the war, had been begging them to come live with her" (103, emphasis added). We see that the strong patriotic sentiment of German Jews for Germany—their "Fatherland"—demands a heavy price in blood.

Let us return to the only son of Dr. Mittel and the way in which the grim tidings of his death reach the narrator's ears. Simon Gabel, a functional architect portrayed in the story as pioneering a new stream in architecture (an apparent reference to the Bauhaus movement), comes to design the offices of the company that purchased the house where the narrator had found some respite. Throughout *To This Day* the narrator treats this Jewish architect with irony and distrust. The modernist seems to be involved in everything, erecting structures devoid of soul and ornament, both alien and cold. It is this man who informs the narrator, in an entirely offhand and indifferent manner, that the son of Mittel, the narrator's close friend, has been killed.

Unlike his indifference to the landlady who sobs for her son each night, the narrator responds in two ways to the dreadful news delivered incidentally by the architect. The first sounds like a lamentation that includes an ironic depiction of German Jews (and Dr. Mittel is not one of them): "A man has **an only son** who volunteers to fight Germany's war, and Germany's war sends a bullet to kill him. Isaac Mittel had paid his debt to Germany and his son had paid for his patriotism" (105, emphasis added).

The second response again recalls the day of the son's enlistment, when the narrator-protagonist was visiting the Mittels' home. While recalling this scene, the narrator relates for the first time a story Dr. Mittel told him that same day. For some reason, this story has not yet appeared in the text—not on the day of the son's enlistment (when it was actually told to the narrator-protagonist) and not on the later visit when Dr. Mittel tells him that he never imagined he would have a warrior son and prods the narrator to look at the photograph of the son going off to war. Only the title of the story is noted in this later visit, while the story itself remains untold.

Since Agnon's storytelling in *To This Day*—as in many of his writings—is eclectic and replete with digressions, he revisits essential events at various junctures in the text in order to sustain the central plot line. Furthermore, the hero-narrator, in service to Agnon the artist, sometimes postpones a side story in order to apply it later to another, analogous event.

Perhaps this is why it was "forgotten" (or suppressed) that the narrator was present when Mittel's son was packing his things and setting off to war, and that the father of the enlisting son then told a story, which the narrator has yet to deem appropriate to share with his readers.

So, let us return to the plot. When news of the death of his friend Mittel's son reaches him, the narrator is homeless once again. We recall that he had to leave his room at the home of the German Jews, the Lichtensteins, because they had sold it to a commercial firm (which employed the architect Simon Gabel) and had moved to live with their newly widowed only daughter. While wandering homeless through the streets of Berlin, the narrator decides to go to the post office to write a letter to Malka, his female relative, whose husband and only son have gone to war, leaving her all by herself in the village of Lunenfeld, near Leipzig.

The introduction of the Jewish woman whose two dearest ones have gone to war, and who knows nothing of their fate, further reinforces the motif of Jews sending their dear ones—an only son, a husband, a son-in-law of an only daughter—to fight Germany's war. In the case of Malka, her dear ones are perhaps still alive; in any event, no word has come of their demise—unlike the husband of the only daughter of the German-Jewish landlords who sold their house to the commercial firm, and unlike Mittel's son. Therefore, the narrator, now at the post office, apologizes for not devoting his thoughts to Malka, though she was the reason he went there:

> While I was picturing that dear woman living all alone, far from her husband and son at the front, I thought of Mittel's **only son** and the day he left for the war. Mittel was sad that he had raised a son to be a soldier, and his wife was glad that her boy was going off to defend the Fatherland. That same day Mittel told me the following story . . . (107–8, emphasis added)

As noted, the narrator already had several opportunities to share the story that Mittel told him on the day the latter's son was preparing himself for war. Indeed, the narrator comes to visit Dr. Mittel a second time during the middle of the war, when the son is already at war and his mother is not home. (She is busy with war-related activity on the home front.)

No one knows at this point that the son will be killed. This is when the narrator decides to inform his readers that during the previous visit (when he witnessed Mittel's son preparing to enlist), Mittel had told him "one of his stories about Heshl Shor, the author and publisher" (30). During this second visit to Dr. Mittel, the narrator mentions the story but still refrains from sharing the story's content with his readers, explaining that he will "skip" the story "to avoid getting sidetracked" (30). Those familiar with Agnon's storytelling techniques will recognize this as a delay tactic, intended to save the story for a place where it can take central stage. Once news arrives of the death of Mittel's son, the father's story evidently becomes relevant. It is therefore presented in the text for the first time. And here is the story Mittel told on the day his son enlisted in the war, the story the narrator recounts only after learning that Mittel's son was killed in the war.

"A Story Set in the Future"

Heshl Shor, the publisher of the Hebrew periodical *Hehalutz*, had an only son who was up for an appointment to a lectureship at the Sorbonne. One day, as Heshl Shor and his wife were having lunch, he looked out the window and saw the postman. "He must be bringing good news," Heshl Shor said. "Our son's appointment has come through." He rose from the table and went to greet the postman, who handed him a telegram with the news that his son had died. "What a pity!" Heshl Shor said, wiping the food from his mouth. "He was a good lad, a good lad!" And though he returned at once to his lunch, he never changed his menu or his clothes again for the rest of his life. Every day he ate the same meal and wore the same shirt and pants (108).

Why did the narrator recount this story only at this late stage and not earlier in the narrative? Why is Dr. Mittel's memory of the narrator's visit on the day the son went to war repressed? It is because Mittel told him a story during that visit that foreshadows the son's death. Horrifically, the father tells his guest the analogous story not after the son was killed, but when the son is still at home, when the young man is only preparing himself for war and the mother is relishing the sight and proud of her son. Thus, it appears that the father knows in advance that his only son is going to fall in the war, and the story he tells on the day of enlistment presages his future mourning. He did not wait for hearsay that would stop the hands of time for him. From his point of view, time stood still the moment his son volunteered for the war. The narrator, who feels he heard the story from the father too early, postpones telling it to his readers until the father's bleak foreboding has sadly materialized. Apparently, he could not tell this tale when he (and the soldier's mother) still hoped that the son would return safe and sound from the war. When the narrator is at the post office, about an hour after receiving the dreadful news, and is about to send a letter to his relative Malka (who still does not know the fate of her only son and her husband), he recalls this story about a father who sees a postman approaching his home, certain that the postman is bearing good news, only to hear the worst of all tidings. The post office provides an associative connection between the narrator's physical setting and Dr. Mittel's story about a letter that conveys bereavement.

If Dr. Mittel is a prophet—at an early and optimistic stage, he foresaw the death of his son on the altar of Germany—here are his remarks about the Germans and their wars:

> This war won't end so quickly. The Germans are a stubborn people. Once they start something, they see it through. They began this war and they won't stop it until either they or their enemies are beaten. As far as I'm concerned, it doesn't matter who beats whom. Both sides are war-crazed and victory-mad . . . If I wrote fiction, I'd write a story set in the future . . . But one war leads to another. After a second war and a third war, the Germans have been beaten to their knees. (35–36)

We began by saying that World War II is not mentioned in *To This Day*, but we do find an allusion to it in the "story set in the fortune" of the elderly bibliographer, Dr. Mittel, an Eastern European Jew who tied his fate to that of Germany.[5] Unlike the "original" German Jews, he is not blind to his place and standing in German society. His eyesight has dimmed from all of his reading and study of ancient books, but in his mind's eyes he sees that the Germans will continue to wage war again and again, and will desist from warfare only after they are utterly defeated. The fact that Dr. Mittel's son and other Jewish sons sacrificed their lives for the German Fatherland in the First World War will not win them any credit in the next war the Germans launch. Thus, Dr. Mittel—like Heshl Shor, whose tale he relates as a "story set in the future"—returns to his books after his son's death, clinging to his old habits as an expression of deep grief and grim reconciliation with the present and future.

2

Vengeance or Salvation? The Tragic Dilemma in Hanoch Bartov's *The Brigade*

A Novel of the Jewish Brigade

> "One wild Jewish vengeance. Just once to be like the Tatars. Like the Ukrainians. Like the Germans."

"Isn't There Going to Be War?"

The Brigade, relating the story of its narrator-protagonist as a soldier in the Jewish Brigade at the end of World War II, is one of four autobiographical novels by Hanoch Bartov. Though it was the first of the four novels to be published (in 1965, republished in 2011),[1] two of the later novels depict an earlier period in Bartov's life, prior to his enlistment in the Jewish Brigade.

The two later works, set in an earlier time frame—*Whose Little Boy Are You?*, published in 1970, and *Halfway Out*, published in 1994—are dedicated to the formative years of childhood and youth of Nachman Spiegler, the protagonist, in the farming community of Petah Tikva, until the day he joins the British Army. The fourth autobiographical novel, *End to End*, published in 2003, was the last of the four to be written and its setting is also the latest chronologically. It opens precisely at the point where *The Brigade* ends and follows the discharged Brigade soldier and his wife, his childhood sweetheart, over the course of fifty years, against the backdrop of Israeli life. Each of the works comprising this tetralogy is "a work in its own right, sealed within its own internal logic," as Avner Holtzman writes. Moreover, it is a work "with a tight dramatic structure that leads the hero from one exciting experience to the next, to the most exciting climax of all."[2] Hence, *The Brigade* is concurrently an autobiographical novel and a novel about war, the military, and vengeance.[3]

In this chapter, I wish to examine *The Brigade* as a novel in which Jewish soldiers from the Land of Israel (Eretz Yisrael / Mandatory Palestine) find themselves in Europe in the final stages of World War II as their military mission becomes a farce.

> We had faced an enemy we had never seen, not even once. We had fired into empty fields and were fired at from empty fields. The war had gone forever, the hour of vengeance would never be ours again. We would come home with unsoiled clothes and hands unstained with blood—we, the avengers (*The Brigade*, 55).

And yet, the experience is traumatic, unforgettable, hard to digest, and hard for the author-protagonist to record in writing. He needed twenty years to complete the task.[4]

Moreover, I wish to elaborate on the desire to wreak vengeance on the Germans versus the ability to actually carry out that desire, and assert that this tension between desire and ability is the main theme of the novel. Most of the critics who have written about *The Brigade* discuss the encounter of the soldiers from the Land of Israel with Holocaust survivors—a tormenting, jarring experience involving mixed feelings on the soldiers' part; less has been written on the topic of impossible revenge.[5]

I examine the same issues, while pointing out the merits of Bartov's text, which aspires to describe things as they were, on the one hand, without embellishment or demonization, while acknowledging the impossibility of full reconstruction with documentary precision, on the other hand. Thus, it is clear that the impressive, realistic-naturalistic materials of *The Brigade* were fused in the literary melting pot: It is the personal testimony of a person with a poetic soul. He projects his ambivalent feelings on landscapes and people; his protagonists say things that correspond with their persona, but are rephrased by the author.

The craving to take vengeance on the Germans may be found in another contemporary work, discussed in chapter 3: *Not of This Time,*

Not of This Place, Yehuda Amichai's only novel, published in 1963, two years before *The Brigade*. Both novels share the fact that they are not about acts of vengeance, but rather its futility. When Avner Holtzman says that in *The Brigade* the protagonist moves "from one exciting experience to the next, to the most exciting climax of all"—he is referring to sexual experiences, encounters with survivors, and failed attempts to carry out acts of revenge. By "the most exciting climax of all," he means a heroic-ironic act that embodies what Bartov will think of as a genetic, deep-seated handicap: the inability to wreak "one wild Jewish vengeance. Just once to be like the Tatars. Like the Ukrainians. Like the Germans" (*The Brigade*, 47).

In any event, the opening chapter of *The Brigade*, Bartov's war novel, is ironically entitled "Peace," and its first words read: "We first heard of the Germans' surrender as we lay out of sight on the far side of the slope" (1). That is, the novel is not about World War II, but about what happens after it.

The closing chapter of Bartov's childhood novel *Whose Little Boy Are You?* (1970) describes the bar mitzvah celebration of Bartov's autobiographical protagonist, Nachman Spiegler, in great detail and with extraordinary sensuousness. But the title—"There Will Not Be War"—given to this account of the feverish preparations for the bar mitzvah banquet, held in the summer of 1939 ("For five whole days Mom and *Mamme* shopped, peeled, crushed, ground, chopped, pickled, kneaded, stuffed, baked, and cooked"),[6] followed by a description of the gluttonous gorging at the feast itself, is essentially ironic, reflecting the "eat and drink today because tomorrow we will die" atmosphere in Palestine on the eve of the Second World War. While the naïve and ever-optimistic father unequivocally assures his guests, in oration and anecdote, that there will not be war, his feasting guests know that his promise of peace is implausible. Indeed, they do not pass up on eating and drinking, "chewing the meatballs and the stuffed neck, seasoning with horseradish, blowing on the steaming carrot." But when they finally rise from table and bring over the weekend newspaper, it is "to prove that there is no longer hope: There will be war. The heat is up in Danzig. And if there are eight and a half million men at arms in Europe, how could there not be war?"[7]

And indeed, Bartov's youth novel *Halfway Out* (1994)—which is a direct continuation of the childhood novel *Whose Little Boy are You?*—relates Nachman Spiegler's difficult and turbulent coming of age in the shadow of the war raging in Europe and threatening Palestine as well. Bartov captures well the collective mood at the time, vacillating between involvement and aloofness. On the one hand, there is a large map on the bedroom wall of Yigal, Nachman's best friend: "And after each conquest, [Yigal] changed the location of the pins with flags representing the fighting parties and drew colored strings between what Hitler had already devoured and what still survived of Free Europe."[8] On the other hand, the letters exchanged between Nachman Spiegler and Yonina Schein, the protagonist and his childhood sweetheart, though dated at critical junctures in the history of the war (June 21, 1942, for example), make no reference to the war situation. The father's optimistic vision that "there will not be war" (which ends *Whose Little Boy are You?*) is not outlandish when seen in the context of the farming community, Tel Aviv, and Palestine. The narrator in *Halfway Out* describes the summer of 1942 as follows: "Germans did not parachute from the skies, and even the brief days of anxiety were absorbed by life's routine, and vanished. The course of Nachman's life was changed in that summer only by the strike in the diamond industry, which continued on and on" (*Halfway Out*, 366). The closing chapters of *Halfway Out* describe a psychological, economic, moral, and erotic imbroglio in which Nachman finds himself. This is what compels him to lie about his age—he is only seventeen—and join the British Army in the spring of 1943, rather than any ideological or patriotic motives. Whatever drove him to enlist, once in the army, Nachman changes from a boy to a "man," as he was addressed by the British officer who swore him in.

A "Man" Indeed?

In *The Brigade*, Nachman Spiegler's name changes to Elisha Kruk. The novel opens on the morning when the narrator-protagonist and his friends—who, as usual, are "killing" the "dangerous hours" before noon with organized idleness in a "dead zone" in northern Italy, "recruiting" hands for a poker game—learn that World War II is over. The combat terminology is ironic, as it does not concern the war or the military regime to which the soldiers are subjected, but rather the opposite—to the evasion of both, as the danger lurking for them is not that of the battlefield or of ambush, but of roll calls and make-work jobs. It appears that the turning point in world history, May 8, 1945, does not affect the daily routine of these soldiers—HQ staff, stretcher bearers, radio operators, on-duty staff, those out on sick call—who hardly do anything anyway. Poker (both literally and figuratively), which helps them every morning to flee from these "war duties" and immerse themselves in collective idleness, is also the game played on this fateful morning. The opening scene foreshadows the novel's purview. This will be a post-war novel, in which military life, mannerisms, and mentality will be retained, but the protagonists will not be exposed to the dangers of the battlefield.

The astonishment that grips the narrator-protagonist, a combat medic modeled after Hanoch Bartov, over the soldiers' lack of exhilaration and excitement when receiving the sensational news of the war's end—indicative of their detachment from it—is conveyed well in the following passage:

> Just so—I still recall the moment vividly—the Second World War came to an end. Strange: a war should end on a field of slaughter, amid shattered bodies, smoking tanks, snorting horses and a mammoth groan cleaving the world apart. But we lay in a tranquil field of early May on the northeast slopes of the Apennines, with no one to make us rejoice, or tell us that this was no simple moment in time's flow, one of many waiting for ages to appear, preceded and followed by a stream of other moments. No, this was the one, the only moment that we and our youth could never reclaim. We were all silent. (6–7)

Therefore, it is no wonder that, ironically-tragically, the first casualty the soldiers encounter on their return from their hours of idleness that morning is one of their comrades who killed himself on the last night of the war with a single shot that no one heard. This suicide is at once similar and very different from an act of suicide described in Yehoshua Kenaz's *Infiltration* (which I discuss in chapter 4). While in Kenaz's novel the single shot is fired by a main character, tearing through the silence of night at a climactic moment at the novel's denouement, the casualty in *The Brigade* and the single shot he fires to kill himself open the novel but are never mentioned again. And yet, they assume a symbolic meaning at its ending: The single shot motif will frame Bartov's carefully structured realistic novel.

After the declaration of the war's end, the novel concerns itself with the platoon's logistics and peregrinations, life in the field and military equipment, forays of individual soldiers into the big city, relationships between people who would never have come across one another in ordinary life (another similarity between Bartov's *The Brigade* and Kenaz's *Infiltration*), all sorts of discoveries about human nature, military hierarchy, uniforms and emblems, the search for the reason and purpose of the presence of Jewish soldiers from Palestine on European soil, various and sundry frustrations and psychological challenges, euphoric moments, "wartime love affairs" (5) based on letters from home, and the soldiers' complex attitude toward women. Avner Holtzman has already written in the previously mentioned "Afterword" (2011 edition of *the Brigade*): "It is hard not to recall in this context episodes from Joseph Heller's *Catch-22* (1961), which grew from the same time and the same place."[9] Indeed, Elisha Kruk, protagonist of *The Brigade*, like *Catch-22*'s Yossarian, contemplates an early discharge from the army, but he is trapped in a different catch: Elisha Kruk will not necessarily be considered insane like Yossarian if he is discharged early, but rather, he will resemble his obsequious, whiny, self-righteous, broken-legged, little Jew of a father, who declared on the eve of the Second World War with pathetic confidence that "there will not be war." After all, Kruk Jr.'s volunteering for military service is in many ways another episode in his long escape from destiny's writ: resembling his father. However, the travails of Elisha Kruk in *The Brigade*—in contrast to those described in an impressive chronological continuum in the episodic novel *Catch-22*—come to gradually affirm the growing resemblance to his father.

Throughout the novel, the narrator hints at his true motives for enlisting in the Jewish Brigade: escaping his home and the suffocating community. Yet only at the end—a day before his discharge, after having done the deed that embodies his resemblance to his father, the figure whose shadow he seeks to escape with all his might, to no avail—does he engage in candid soul-searching on his decision to join the British Army three years earlier. The motives are complex: The rumors that had begun reaching Palestine from Europe on the fate of its Jews stirred Elisha's desire to act, ironically blending with youthful dreams of far-off places, the other side of the wish to escape the provinciality of his home community, the moshava:

> At that time, we heard of the fall of the Warsaw Ghetto. From Russia, stories began drifting in about what had been done in reconquered territories. And I—I was barely seventeen . . . So, at the very moment when dreams were becoming reality, I was whipped away from my destiny and my visions of being born a new man. I who had dreamed of rivers, oceans, who had yearned for glory, found myself in a camp at Sarafand?
>
> "Now?" everyone asked, eyebrows lifted. "You crazy, enlisting now? You got a screw loose or something?"
>
> There in the Black Forest, the day before the end, I could painfully face the truth; I had fled the stagnant waters of the *moshava*, raced off to save my warrior's soul; and on the morrow, I would head back where I had started from, a softie who could never make it. (238)

Childhood Illness and Adolescent Ailments

The war eludes Kruk even before the news of its conclusion. Due to a pathetic disease named rubella, German measles, or simply the measles, he ends up in a hospital and suffers a series of humiliations because of soiled pajamas in which he was dressed, feeling "like a baby who had made in his pants" (11). And then, just a week after his return from the hospital and the convalescence camp, the war is over.

Immediately after hearing of the war's end, Kruk joins his friend Brodsky, who is five or six years his senior. Brodsky had lived among the partisan fighters and had acquired considerable and cruel life experience in the woods of World War II Europe. The nineteen-year-old Elisha's feelings toward him are characterized by both attraction and revulsion. They are both headed for Bologna, and Brodsky's stated purpose of travel to the big city is to visit a brothel. At first, Kruk stands in the embarrassing queue, as this carnal lust always teems inside him: "When I would wander by myself, a stranger in foreign streets," he says, "[this lust] would suddenly seize me, whisper in my ear, tell me to take the plunge, burst out once again from the humdrum—no, hateful—world of Father" (23–24). But after standing in line with Brodsky for a few minutes, he realizes that he is incapable of going through with it. The anonymity of the woman and the blurring of her identity—she functions only as a sexual object—always stand in contrast to the singularity of his youthful love, Noga (Yonina Schein's name in *The Brigade*), whom he leaves back in Jerusalem and whose letters to him become less and less frequent. When Brodsky mocks Elisha and the women whose dignity he wants to protect, saying "it's the same with all women, Uzbekis, Poles, and Italians. Exactly the same" (24), the narrator-protagonist sees before his eyes Noga's singular personality, which deters him from being drawn into the realms of depersonalized and cold sex.

Eli Eshed has noted that *The Brigade* is the ultimate literary version of the despised and maligned genre of "Stalag" fiction. The genre was popular in Israel in the 1960s, and it emerged concurrently with Israeli society's first attempts to conduct a public discourse on the Holocaust and its repercussions. Rape, lustful Nazi women, and illustrations of broad-hipped, large-breasted, and thick-lipped women are the most frequent erotic representations in Stalag periodicals of the 1960s, and cultural critics consider them, alongside the Eichmann trial (despite the stark differences), as catalysts that brought the subject of the Holocaust "out of the closet" in Israel. Indeed, *The Brigade*, published in the mid-1960s, makes explicit references to Stalag literature.[10]

The novel's second half contains a murky "Stalag experience" that Elisha Kruk is dragged into, having successfully avoided a similar one earlier in the novel when accompanying his friend Brodsky to Bologna. Finnek, Elisha's relative—who was his childhood hero in the Palestinian farming community where he was born, Petah Tikva, and whom Elisha perceives as antithetical to his weak father—meets him in Venice and forces him to participate in a protracted sexual experience. When they randomly meet in summer 1945, Elisha discovers that his childhood hero has become debauched and ugly, a shameless gigolo. The distant memory of insult rises like a partition between the two relatives. Three years earlier, as the war was raging and its repercussions began to reach Palestine, sixteen-year-old Elisha got drunk at Finnek's wedding, held on a rooftop on Dizengoff Street in Tel Aviv, and leveled harsh words at the guests and at Finnek. Whether driven by a wish to avenge an old insult or by a desire to lead his young relative through a rite of maturation and show him a good time, Finnek drags him along to an elaborate erotic experience at the Lido near Venice. This is how Kruk describes the morning when, to his great surprise, he was left with a strange Italian woman by his side at the Lido, now emptied of the debauchees from the previous night (including Finnek, who had gone off to his day's work):

> We lay in a broad bed . . . Felicia leaned on her elbows, turned to me, her full thigh rising and her breasts surging toward the opening in her gown. She watched me with curious eyes, without all of those "veiled gazes" we used to read about in forbidden magazines. (*The Brigade* [Hebrew], 198; the English translation omits this)

By "forbidden magazines," Elisha Kruk is apparently referring to the Stalag magazines of the early 1960s. The description of the woman he awakes to find the morning after the surreal night corresponds with the image of women in those publications. The narrator describes the magazines from his perspective and speaks from the mouth of the soldier in 1945, some fifteen years before these magazines appeared. However, anachronism in literature, when the narrative time seeps into the story time, is a well-established practice. Moreover, pulp magazines, including detective stories and erotica, already appeared in Palestine in the 1920s and 1930s, and the narrator-author is apparently also referring to them.[11]

The Brigade, a belated record of Hanoch Bartov's experiences as a soldier in the Jewish Brigade, infused with the atmosphere of 1960s Israel, is in fact anti-Stalag: Ultimately, Elisha Kruk does not descend into Finnek's catacombs of lust because he remains an unwilling prisoner in the jail of his father's Jewish upbringing, which he had tried so hard to rebel against.

Something That "Would Wake up Children in the Night Five Hundred Years from Now"

The "base" sexual experiences in Bologna and Venice are the diametrical opposite of the protagonist's "sacred" love for Noga: "Even before my fingertips traced [Felicia's] smooth flesh, she drew close, hungry for me. 'Simple, simple, simple,' chanted a voice inside, but in the background 'Holy, Holy, Holy'" (200). These experiences, of course, deviate from the two missions of the Jewish corps on European soil: saving Jews and wreaking revenge on the Nazis. In the three-month setting of *The Brigade*—May, June, July of 1945—the soldiers seem to accomplish little in pursuit of these objectives. They are mentioned in discussions, plans, sporadic and random actions, some of them ludicrous, but they never materialize in any planned or systematic manner. Of the two objectives, vengeance remains particularly amorphous. At a certain stage, which is a turning point in the novel's plot, it is perceived as contradicting the Brigade's first mission: rescuing Jews.

The Brigade is "an army on wheels," alternating between rest and movement. The announcement of the war's end is a signal for the unit, camped in northern Italy, to move further north toward the Italian Alps, and from there into Austria and Germany. On the eve of their departure, the soldiers are given conflicting messages about vengeance: "You will be forced to prove the applicability of morality to men who butchered morality" (56) versus "cursed be he who fails to remember what they have done to us!" (57). The latter statement, uttered by Corporal Macover with a thunderous voice that shakes the entire formation, recalls the Bible's primordial commandment of remembrance: "Remember what Amalek did unto you," devoid of any modicum of forgiveness, morality, or compromise. In addition, the timing of the statement, at the war's end, also echoes the days of yore: "Therefore when the Lord your God shall give you rest from all of your enemies . . . you shall blot out the memory of Amalek from under heaven, you shall forget not" (Deuteronomy 25:19). That is, the arrival of peace marks the beginning of revenge.

In the twelve commandments for the Jewish soldiers on German soil, "vengeance" appears twice:

Four. Remember: The very fact that we [Hebrew soldiers] come as a military unit with flag and emblem in sight of the German people in its land—is vengeance!

Five. Remember. Blood vengeance is a communal task. Any irresponsible act weakens the group. (57)

It appears that these two commandments cannot satisfy the vengeance-hungry troops and create a conflict between their commitment to good order and the internal obligation they feel to take real action and imitate their enemies, at least verbally, if only once—"only one Kishinev, in round numbers: one thousand houses burned down, five hundred killed, one hundred raped" (46). The novel shows how the inherent contradiction in the perception of revenge, simultaneously calling for action and restraint, engenders tragedy.

In Yehoshua Kenaz's *Infiltration*, the ugliness of the boot camp (Sarafand) corresponds with army life, since it is a novel grounded in a specific place.[12] *The Brigade*, in which the soldiers pass through breathtaking landscapes, creates tension between nature's dreamlike beauty, which reiterates a nonpersonal memory passed on to the narrator-protagonist by his mother,[13] and what is perceived as a concrete nightmare:

> . . . the crystal clear air, the fragrance, the thick forest—it all seemed as though the stories that Mother had told of her distant childhood were coming true, as if we were in some dream world or a moving picture. Who would have believed that such lands really existed and that I would see them with my own eyes? Slowly the convoy crawled up the towering mountains, each one taller than the next, and suddenly we were in the midst of a nightmare. Coming in the opposite direction, southward, military trucks rumbled toward us—one, three, five, an entire convoy. At first we did not realize what it was we saw, but then someone shouted, in fright or amazement: "Germans. They're German troops." (67)

At the sight of the organized army, which actually seems to be in pretty good shape, not at all defeated—"What kind of war was it, if this is what the defeated look like?" (67)—the improvised vengeance initiatives by the stunned soldiers of the platoon begin to take shape. With savage lust, they pelt the trucks transporting German POWs with any "cold weapon" at hand: a hooked peg, a bayonet, cans of food, a wooden mallet, an iron try square. They even hurl a heavy statuette, a tin replica of Moses, which Hershler had purchased as a souvenir during his travels through Italy and kept in his backpack wrapped in socks. The paltriness and futility of these acts of vengeance stand in sharp contrast to the German-looking Corporal Bubi Meinz's pretentious call for revenge. The narrator is spellbound by Bubi and harbors homoerotic feelings toward him. Handsome Bubi wants to do "something that would frighten their children [on] winter nights. 'Ah, what the Jews did to us!' Something that would take the place of Grimm's fairy tales. That would wake up children in the night five hundred years from now" (48).

Two soldiers are mentioned here in reference to these initial acts of vengeance: Hershler and Bubi. Hershler is the owner of the statuette who was ready to part with it because a longing to take vengeance against the Germans burned in his bones. He came to Israel with Aliyat Hano'ar, leaving his parents behind in Budapest. He enlisted in the British Army on the same day as the narrator, and their military ID numbers are only one digit apart.[14] Despite spending years in the army, he plans for his civilian future: He dedicates every free hour to studying for his matriculation exams. The other soldier is the handsome Bubi Meinz, hence his nickname probably should have been "Baby."[15] Baby-Bubi has Aryan looks, charisma, and a determined manner of speech. Bubi and Hershler will play a central role in another exciting act of vengeance that will cast a heavy shadow over the Brigade's journey to Germany.

The Lineup of Shame

As the Jewish soldiers prod the sturdy Bubi to open the battle rations case containing shining cans of jam and margarine so they can use them to smash a few German skulls, someone voices objections to these "immoral" acts of revenge: "'You can't do this.' Tamari could no longer contain himself. 'Men, how can you wound defenseless war prisoners? We're not—'" (63). Tamari is introduced in the novel as the person writing "the damn 'War Journal of the Hebrew Soldier'" (7) and thanks to his age (a forty-year-old surrounded by a group of nineteen-year-old "kids"), serves as either the official or unofficial mediator between the members of the platoon and British headquarters.[16] He is described as short, with gray hair and dark eyes; his manner of speech is somewhat childish and his self-righteousness is infuriating. "Leave us alone," cry the annoyed soldiers who consider vengeance to be part of their mission. "You don't have to shit in your pants because we opened a few heads. We'll open some more . . . Write it in your diary. Write that we murderers pounced on the poor Germans. How horrible, what will they think of us in Germany! What kind of youth do they raise in Palestine, wild men" (66).

The unexpected encounter with the convoys of German POWs heading south, which stirs the platoon's soldiers to throw heavy objects aimed to hurt them, as well as the conflict between the platoon and Tamari, who rejects these acts and is presented as ridiculously self-righteous, are only the prologue to a volatile ideological conflict that forms one of the novel's significant climaxes. The sixth commandment of the Brigade, which prohibits personal revenge, is violated, triggering a harsh and scathing ideological debate.

"The human being in the novel," says Bakhtin, "is first, foremost, and always a speaking human being; the novel requires speaking persons bringing with them their own unique ideological discourse, their own language. The fundamental condition, that which makes a novel a novel, that which is responsible for its stylistic uniqueness, is the *speaking person and his discourse*."[17] The Bakhtinian polyphony of voices comes to life in *The Brigade* when the central dilemma regarding personal revenge initiatives erupts in all its complexity.

Still in northern Italy, an area embodying the anarchy, disorder, and confusion of post-war Europe, Tamari suddenly gathers the entire platoon, seventy men, to a "council" at the barn, an unusual convocation under a military regime in which an open-air roll call is the typical form of assembly. After much hemming and hawing, hinting, and insinuating, utterances that testify more than anything to his inability to speak to the point ("You're driving us crazy, Tamari. Can the philosophy and tell us what this crap is all about," 105), he tells his comrades that two women, a mother and her daughter, have complained to the British military police that two soldiers in British uniforms with a golden Star of David on a blue-white background on their sleeve (the insignia of the Jewish Brigade), broke into their home and attempted to rape and even murder them. The women screamed and managed to drive away the assailants, who stole money, watches, and other valuables. One of the soldiers spoke fluent German.

The gathering at the barn includes several trajectories of suspense and dramatic turns, as the people arguing there not only represent themselves, each with his own unique ideological speech communicated with his own language, as Bakhtin defines it; they also represent the rival voices within the group. Tamari, in the throes of a resolute struggle against a confused and enraged polyphonic collective, is the only representative of a unitary voice free from internal contradictions. A soldier named Giladi seems to represent Tamari's opposite voice, which also derives from deep internal conviction and a clear ideology, but Giladi's actions ultimately contradict his voice.

The first trajectory of suspense revolves around the identity of the assailants and complainants. Among the interjections and speculations flung into the air at the barn, after Tamari finally manages to explain the matter at hand, one clear and unequivocal voice is suddenly heard: "The two women aren't Italians" (106). The speaker is Giladi, who, as noted, is the salient opponent of the self-assured Tamari. Giladi thinks that the fact that the "rapists" did not hide their affiliation but, on the contrary, flaunted it—coming with their Palestinian Jewish badges and the German-speaking soldier presenting himself as a Hebrew soldier—indicates that the complainants are Nazis: The soldiers wanted them to recognize their identity because they sought revenge and wanted their actions to become public knowledge. Tamari claims that the victims' identity is irrelevant—"We're not a bunch of riff-raff thrown together under a British flag . . . We're not a gang of thugs, like those thugs of . . . Sienkiewicz . . . where everyone settles his own score, fights a private war . . . over some point of honor . . ." (107). But in Giladi's eyes, "this is the crucial question":

> You come here preaching about robbery, rape, murder. You lecture us on riff-raff, tell us we're not dealing with affairs of honor here. But you haven't answered the real questions: Doesn't it make any difference if

these soldiers—even if we assume they're really our boys—tried to rape and murder two peaceful citizens or tried to take revenge on the *Nazis*? Is there or isn't there a difference? (111, italics in the original)

The tense gathering at the barn focuses the argument on the issue of vengeance, and to this end Bartov stages a conflict between two opposites: Giladi is portrayed as Tamari's negative image. While Tamari, who opposes revenge, conjures up a plan that would cover up the assault, making the incident disappear without a trace, Giladi wants to make it widely known to serve as an example and model for others. The reader shares the turbulence and the emotional and ideological swings the platoon members experience, from feeling antagonism and repudiation toward Tamari and his self-righteous position, to siding with him and admiring the cunning and creativity of his plan, designed to extract them from a serious imbroglio. And when it seems that Tamari's plan is accepted by everyone, Giladi comes back to stoke resistance and revulsion. After all this comes one final twist: complete surrender to Tamari's sophisticated yet humiliating plan.

The drama that unfolds at the barn merits staging, and here is a short summary: Tamari declares that a lineup will be held, in which the two complainants will walk through the lines to point out the two "rapists-murderers." Commotion and a chaotic chorus of voices prevent him from continuing to describe his plan, as the horrifying notion of two Nazi women coming to a lineup to identify two Jewish soldiers who "went astray" is enough to stir an uproar. All hell breaks loose. Giladi, who cannot believe his ears, tells them firmly that he will not participate in such a lineup of shame. He even appears to be close to punching Tamari. But when Tamari is able to continue describing his plan, it emerges that he does not intend to hand over the two guys to the British authorities. The two "rapists" will not attend the lineup; they will be replaced by two soldiers from a different platoon. When the full plan becomes clear, the quarrel reaches an important turning point, with Tamari gaining the upper hand:

A murmur of amazement and admiration filled the granary. Well then, what had all the shouting been about? What was the big problem? If they want us to, we'll line up for them for two minutes. Let them send the German women through the ranks, they won't find anyone—and "peace upon Israel." (114)

But the spell of the simple solution is broken again by Giladi, who seeks the opposite of what Tamari is trying to achieve. Giladi wants to turn the ostensibly disgraceful act into a model for imitation. He wants the rumor to spread, for it to infuse the thousands of Jewish Brigade soldiers with a different spirit and encourage more acts of vengeance. In his view, the full exposure of the affair "would redeem the honor of the Hebrew flag we dropped right here as soon as we arrived at this cursed border" (115). And Giladi adds, appearing to merge the two missions of the Jewish Brigade: "All of us, not only Tamari and his friends, all of us want to reach the [survivors] Jews. But he thinks this goal allows us to forget about Jewish vengeance and to stain our military honor" (115). That is, while Tamari believes that the two assailants cast a shadow of disgrace over the platoon, Giladi sees them as heroes, and proposes that they identify themselves and serve as spokespersons, models for imitation and admiration for all those who are holding themselves back, whose blood boils within them:

> Fine, let them get up so we can see who they are. Let them get up and tell us what led them to that Nazi home, let them show us the acid eating away at every man's guts here: thousands of brave young men, all volunteers sworn to avenge the blood of our slaughtered brothers, to wreak vengeance in war or in peace on the butchers and their henchmen, on the people who applauded them and grew fat on the spoil—all of them, every man, woman, and child. We don't believe in turning the other cheek, Tamari. (116)

The piercing and articulate speech that Bartov places in Giladi's mouth in praise of vengeance and its psychological, national, and historical necessity, goes on and on (116–18), transfixing and persuading the platoon soldiers who only a moment earlier had agreed with Tamari's clever plan. The situation, in which two passionate disputants engage in a tug-of-war for their audience's support, masterfully conveys the predicament of a public that unexpectedly faces a conflict between instinct and reason, impulse and morality. Tamari represents the pragmatic and "moral" solution, while Giladi represents the instinct and impulse to avenge; the audience sways from one side to another, because the public is usually fickle.

Tamari's reply that follows Giladi's long and heated speech tips the scales in his favor once again. He makes it clear that Giladi's fiery call for wild acts of vengeance would hinder the task of saving Jews:

> And what will you tell our children if after a few murders, rapes, robberies, and burnings they take our weapons away, ship us out of here, disband us? What will you say when they ask you how was it possible we were here, thousands of young men, hundreds of trucks and didn't find a way to take the one chance history gave us, but . . . instead spent our time in theatrics? (119)

Zunenshein, a moderating voice, enters the discussion. "Unlike the two others, his face was not contorted with emotion, [so] his words were somewhat more convincing" (119). On the one hand, Zunenshein tells a parable whose moral is clear: A man and his family are passing through a forest. Bandits attack him and his dear ones, and murder his father and mother. Facing the dilemma of whether to avenge their blood or save the others, he opts for rescue. At first, the parable appears to support Tamari, but Zunenshein does not stop there and directs a rhetorical question at his audience, which listens to him intently. His question—how would that man feel, having saved his own life and the life of the others, without avenging his parents' blood?—was designed to bring Giladi back to the forefront of the debate and restore the rhetorical balance between the two passionate rivals. That is, Zunenshein, in his own way, further sharpens the dilemma and another commotion ensues, attesting to the collective emotional turmoil. No one is more upset than Tamari, who appears to be gradually losing his sanity:

> Tamari's muffled sobbing had become an unashamed wail. Like a madman he dashed for the door . . . We could not look at him, but at the same time could not take our eyes away from him. He was beating his chest with his fists, lacerating his face and shrieking. (120–21)

It seems, however, that it is not the absurd appearance of Tamari—"madly absorbed with the one truth in his heart" (*The Brigade* [Hebrew], 126; the English translation omits this)—that ultimately turns the scales, but rather Zunenshein's levelheaded argumentation. The night that the two "rapists" broke into the house of the two women, Zunenshein, the narrator, and three other soldiers were on a brief cross-border mission, in Klagenfurt. They met Jews and knew that those Jews were waiting to be saved by the Jewish soldiers from Palestine. That is, Zunenshein could not have been one of the assailants and also knew something about the need to stick to the task of saving Jews. And yet, he does not express an unequivocal position and does not preach. He is sufficiently wise and sensitive to lead a calculated psychological move. First, he clarifies the dilemma without siding with either of the diametrically opposed disputants; and then, while steering the audience toward the only possible solution, he describes the necessity of the decision as "a tragedy." By doing so, he removes the sting from the entrenched position of both disputants:

> There's no way out of this tragedy—none at all. Tamari, in discussing the practical problem confronting us—our responsibility to the surviving Jews—brought in his ethical position on the general question of vengeance; but these two issues shouldn't be confused. From the practical standpoint I share his feeling—because we're the dream of a nation, the last hope of all who have been saved from the furnaces . . . The fact that Tamari is right in no way detracts from the terrible truth of your remarks, Giladi . . . we'll never be able to forget how we couldn't take vengeance . . . never have peace of mind.
>
> Here you're right, Giladi; but you're wrong, as I see it, in thinking we have a choice. We have no choice. That's the tragedy . . . That's the tragedy, because God help us if we forego vengeance, but God help us seventy times more if we don't reach the Jews, for we are the last dream they have. (124–26)

The gathering, four hours long, finally ends with the lineup of shame. Giladi participates in the lineup with complete surrender. The two soldiers who do not participate are Bubi, whose beauty is German, whose language is German, and who mercilessly bombarded the passing convoys of German POWs; and Hershler, who sacrificed his statuette, a replica of Moses, in an attempt to pummel the Germans, and who studiously prepares for the matriculation exams he will take upon returning home and starting a new life. These two are sent to Milan that same evening, and Hershler takes advantage of this opportunity to search for his parents, lost in the Holocaust. But he is brutally murdered by Nazis on a train, as if the Holocaust was not yet over. Hershler will never experience the tragedy Zunenshein describes in his peroration at the barn, an eternal tragedy from which the platoon soldiers in particular and the Brigade in general will not be spared, "not now nor in the years ahead. Our children will ask us and we'll lower our eyes. Just so, just so we will live" (126). An invisible accusatory finger points at Tamari from now on, as if he is to blame for Hershler's wretched and tragic death on the soil of post-war Europe; Hershler, of all people, who had prepared himself more than anyone else for a normal life in the Land of the Forefathers. And we should not forget; a single digit separates the ID number of the protagonist-narrator from the ID number of the soldier who is murdered on the soil of Europe after the Holocaust. A hair's breadth separates their fates.

Story Time and Narrative Time

The time when the novel was written, twenty years after the events it depicts, is very present in *The Brigade*. This presence of narrative time is designed, in part, to examine, evaluate, and judge in retrospect the experiences whose impression on the narrator-protagonist is so powerful that he continues to struggle with them long after they occurred. The gathering at the barn ultimately concludes with the lineup, which had previously been considered an unimaginable disgrace. The lineup is described as a post-traumatic event, an illness that broods in the depths of the soul, and sometimes erupts to the surface:

> Many years have passed since then, but that day has stuck to me. For long stretches of time it fades from my mind as if it had never been. Then suddenly, without any warning, it swamps me as if it had not yet ended, as though I were still standing there in the barracks square on

the slope of the mountain . . . And when that day bursts to the surface I feel the shame burning beneath my skin.

How was it that in spite of everything we went out on lineup . . . How did we make the leap, in one fell swoop, from soul-searching to blind, soldiers' obedience? So often I try to reconstruct that leap, but never can figure it out. At times it seems to me we knew full well what the decision meant and that the itching under my skin began at that very moment; and at times I'm convinced we didn't understand what was said—by Zunenshein, for example—and that only over the years did that identification [lineup] become what is now a searing shame within me. (128)

The novel's final dramatic event, in which Kruk personally blocks vengeance from occurring, will apparently also be seared in his heart as chronic illness, a living shame.

After a six-week deployment of the "army on wheels" on the Italian border, it begins moving in late July 1945 toward Austria, en route to Germany. Elisha Kruk, the narrator-protagonist from the moshava, struggles to come to terms with the tension arising in his soul upon encountering those sites. On the one hand, these are the lands of his childhood dreams and stories—dense forests, blue lakes, tales of Hansel and Gretel, night elves, and yodeling songs; on the other hand, this is the land of nightmares, deep-rooted anti-Semitism, and ruthless murderousness. As they pass through a pastoral town, Zunenshein comments that for three centuries the villagers there have been performing the "Passionsspiele," in which the masses identify with "the suffering Jesus, whom the Jews put on the cross" (216). At the heart of this irreconcilable contradiction, as the soldiers advance slowly in military vehicles and loaded trucks, they come across a concentration camp. In light of the immensity of the surprise and excitement, the narrator acknowledges once again that the time of narration detracts from the fullness and accuracy of the documentary description. But that which was preserved in memory, or processed in the literary work—as we will see—is just as important:

The same cry swept over them and over us. They sang, they yelled, but out of the welter of shouts and songs, two words rang loud and clear—*shalom* and *eretz* [*yisrael*]—in a long continuous cry from the moment we saw the first of them standing by the road until their voices and faces faded in the distance.

Maybe it was different. Who can remember exactly how it happened? Our emotions gushed out like cataracts at the gate of that camp. (217)

Write Down That We Remained Jews

Burdened with difficult experiences—the gathering at the barn that led to a humiliating lineup; Hershler's arbitrary death in occupied Vienna that teemed with soldiers of the occupying powers, a murder that came in the wake of the lineup that will be remembered in eternal disgrace; the movement through enemy lands, the painfully beautiful Austria and Germany; the heavy bursts of water and mud of the summer storm that hit them overnight, reminding the protagonist of the filthy pajamas he wore when he had the measles; the concentration camp they came across, its victims yearning for redemption—the soldiers arrive at a field for yet another night of sleep out in the open. Elisha Kruk, the narrator-protagonist, and his friend Brodsky, the partisan boy from the snowy forests with hair-raising stories about his World War II experiences, are determined not to sleep in the open field. Moreover, without a word being said about it, an idea hovers in the air: Perhaps here is an opportunity to finally carry out the revenge they have dreamed of, and thus prevent the memory of the vengeance they had failed to take from spreading in their bodies like disease, like gangrene, as Giladi described it in the barn (117).

Demonstrating remarkable literary sensitivity, Bartov puts the two—who are walking toward the houses facing the field to find a lodging place and possibly to do something else—on a collision course with the smug Tamari, whom they hold responsible for the humiliation they were subjected to on the Italian border, as well as for Hershler's pointless death. This encounter is meant to further refine the tragic tension between vengeance and rescue, with the despised Tamari clearly representing one side only. The encounter, set in this particular situation, fans their drive and inclination toward vengeance:

We took our rifles and kit bags, closed the tent flap, and turned toward the houses. Suddenly, out of the darkness, emerged Tamari.

"*Nu?*" He embraced us both warmly, his eyes darting back and forth between us. I wasn't sure whether he had chanced upon us in the dark, thinking we were someone else, or whether he was suspicious because of the weapons in our hands and where we were headed. "Did you see the Jews?"

"Where?"

"In Landsberg. What a pleasure!"

"Sure we saw 'em, why not?" said Brodsky. "We see the Germans, too." (218–19)

This language of allusions, in which "the Jews" in Tamari's question represent the commitment to rescue and "the Germans" in Brodsky's response represent the commitment to vengeance, is the only reference here to this controversial issue. The two friends silently walk "tensed for what lay ahead" (219) when an additional encounter further stirs their commitment to revenge, but this time explicitly. A German citizen, leaning on his bicycle, is standing on the road, pointing at a particular house, and says: "There, that's an SS house . . . Yes, yes, there in the third house, that's where they live, the damn whores. The husband's vanished. He was a high officer in the SS, the swine!" (220).

The two friends presumably enter the strange, clean, and well-kept house as callous enemy soldiers, settling in some upper chamber, "a girls' room" (222), which the terrified women offer them. Here, at this hour and in that house, they can take revenge not only for the Jewish people at large, but their personal revenge too: for their mortifying encounter with the two Nazi women in that lineup, the memory of which gives them a rash, and for Hershler's embarrassing death. But neither the vision of vengeance nor Giladi's passionate speech change the fact that they cannot go through with it: "What was stopping us, Brodsky and me? Only the fact that we were what we were—impotent, impotent . . ." (227).

If they hesitate to sprawl onto the pristine beds because of the grime and mud that clung to their clothes, how will they dare "to do what Bubi and Hershler failed to do as soon as they crossed the threshold" (225)?

Their entire revenge will consist of treating the women rudely. When the young woman offers them on her mother's behalf a shower and a hot drink, the narrator drives her back with shouts. Brodsky says mockingly: "Ah, Jewish vengeance! . . . You won't rape her even if she cries for it. And you won't drink tea either." Elisha responds in kind: "So what about you, Brodsky? Why are you sitting there on the bed scared to move? Afraid of getting the room dirty?" (224–25).

But some of them are not afraid. Elisha Kruk wakes up from a nightmare to the sound of punches and screaming women and realizes that others have come over to carry out the deed that he and his friend Brodsky only contemplated as a possibility.

This, in a nutshell, is what follows: Since the narrator and Brodsky do not dare to lie in their clean beds, they get up and leave the house, head back to camp to pick up their belongings, and return to the locked house that reopens for them only after they kick the door with the tips of their boots. Upon reentering the house, they muster the courage to stretch out on the beds. Elisha's dream in the house of the SS women—where he and his friend have the opportunity to fulfill their retributive fantasy but are incapable of going through with it—mixes childhood fears from his family's cabin in the moshava in Palestine with Holocaust events that Elisha did not witness directly. Perhaps only Brodsky, lying awake in the bed next to him, had experienced them. When Elisha awakes from his dream, he marvels: "You will not believe that in your dream you can live a place, voices and a destiny that are not yours" (*The Brigade* [Hebrew], 227; the English translation omits this). By that he appears to affirm the "philosophy" of Jung, father of the theory of archetypes: "A dream, like every element in the psychic structure, is a product of the total psyche. Hence we may expect to find in dreams everything that has ever been of significance in the life of humanity."[18]

But is it true that this dream—which includes traces of the previous day (for example, the tricycle of the German snitch who led them to this house) and Holocaust symbols (a train, forest, horses and their riders, long rifles, Cossacks galloping on cobblestones), simultaneously placed in a nondescript location and in his childhood village—expresses a life he did not live and could only live in a dream? One thing is clear: Elisha's dream, like all dreams, is meant to protect sleep as much as possible, as Jung believed following Freud, but it ends when the dreamer and the dream can no longer bear its difficult, intensive content.[19] The sound of women screaming on the ground floor, transformed in the dream into the squawking of geese and the shrieking of Hollander's daughter from the moshava, ultimately overpower the dream and Elisha Kruk wakes up.

One nightmare is replaced with another, a dreamlike nightmare with an actual nightmare: Elisha rushes to help the women. Brodsky's call, "They're our boys," and his warning, peppered with a Russian profanity—"*Yebyuhamat*, Kruk! Your first bullet in the war you want to put into your buddies!" (229)—materializes in a different way: Kruk fires a warning shot in the air to prove his serious intention to prevent the rapists from carrying out what they see as revenge.

Two lone shots are fired in the dead of the night in *The Brigade*. The first occurs at the beginning of the novel, when a soldier named Freedberg shoots himself several hours before the war's end is declared, and the second comes at the end of the novel, when Elisha fires in the air to prevent Jews from brutally raping SS women. Freedberg's suicidal shot is heard by no one, and the pit in which the desperate soldier killed himself "was left deserted like a gouged eye" (*The Brigade* [Hebrew], 65; the English translation omits this). The platoon members are devastated by the news of the suicide, but not necessarily because of Freedberg the man, who was seen in retrospect as "destined for such an end" (13) or because of the tragic timing of his self-planned death—just as the war ended. His friends react with shock because there are no witnesses who heard the shot: "And how was it that no one heard that lone shot? That's what bothered us" (14). Elisha Kruk's warning shot, however, sounds like an explosion of a hand grenade in the dead of the night (229) and becomes multiple "gunshots" the next day in the accounts of witnesses. And though the single shot actually aborts the acts of revenge, the soldiers interpret the events otherwise:

> "After the shots last night and the fire, they won't forget us," said little Ostreicher. . . . "There was a regular massacre last night," the story went . . . Our men believed the rumor and their eyes lit up with joy. Even I began to have doubts, so anxious was I to forget what had happened.

Maybe there were other shots besides my one. After all, everyone else seemed to be sure of it. (234)

Two shots, which are not fired on the battlefield, frame the novel as a motif and underline the sense of missed opportunity that accompanies the Brigade soldiers along the entire way. And here is a partial list of missed opportunities: They miss the war, having arrived in Europe too late; Freedberg misses the "momentous hour" when he "chose" to commit suicide the night before the news of liberation; Hershler is murdered when he set off to search for his parents who perhaps survived the Holocaust, and his studies for the matriculation exams in Palestine are all for naught; Elisha Kruk misses the opportunity to commit "one Tataric" act of vengeance when he rushes to the aid of the SS women. This is how he despises himself:

In an instant all the hymns of hatred had dissolved, leaving me my father's son. Crawling with impurity. A **man**. A misfit.
   Now I knew: such were we, condemned to walk the earth with the image of God stamped on our forehead like the mark of Cain. (232, emphasis in the original)

The narrator's ambivalence toward himself (whose name "Bartov" becomes "Kruk" in the novel, suggesting a blend of crookedness and goodness [*tov* in Hebrew]) is reflected not only in what he says about himself (for example, calling himself a "misfit" after thwarting the fulfillment of the vengeance fantasy), but also in his future attitude to the three would-be rapists, whose "revenge" he prevented, and in his ongoing interaction with Tamari, whose "imperative" he followed. The names of the three are erased. They will not be remembered when the narrator puts those memories in writing: "I knew the three of them, and I clearly remember how they looked and their names, but I skip over that today as well" (*The Brigade* [Hebrew], 229; the English translation omits this). The narration time noted here aims to emphasize that the three will always be seen in a negative light, even decades later. Moreover, the narrator is assaulted and beaten by one of them one night. Tamari, who is sitting and writing by the light of his flashlight, notices the narrator's injuries and demands an explanation. The narrator-protagonist does not reveal the secret of why he was beaten and by whom; instead, he accosts Tamari for the identification lineup, the lineup of shame, which had become fixed in his heart as a disease, as the ultimate defilement:

> "You did a terrible thing to us over there, Tamari."
> "A terrible thing? What are you talking about?"
> "About the identification [lineup], that's what. About Bubi and Hershler. About all of us."
> "Kruk, you're—"
> "I'm perfectly all right. Didn't you have any nightmares after that [lineup], Tamari?"
> "No, definitely not. Kruk, come here, sit down a minute . . ."
> "I want to go to sleep." . . .
> "You don't want to hear me out?" asked Tamari.
> "I have already. Myself, too. Write in that notebook of yours that weaklings have no choice. Write that we remained Jews. Write that the memory of all this will keep coming back at us like a boomerang. We know all the rest." (245)

"Write down that we remained Jews," says the narrator to the establishment figure writing down in his diary the story of the war. That is, we tried to resemble our enemy, to shake off the heritage of our ancestors, of weak, whiny, and exilic forefathers, and we ended up like them. It seems that the only revenge taken in *The Brigade* is that of Finnek, an impressive family relative who became corrupt and drags his tender young relative, now fully grown, into a vile, Stalag-like situation in Lido, near Venice.

In contrast to Yehuda Amichai's *Not From Now and Not From Here*—a novel of fantastic realism in which the Israeli protagonist is simultaneously present in two locations (Jerusalem and his German hometown of Weinburg) and undergoes two contradicting experiences, all in order to illustrate the rift in the narrator's psyche—Hanoch Bartov's *The Brigade* is a realistic novel par excellence, and the narrator's torn soul is revealed against the backdrop of the newly concluded Second World War. The soldiers in *The Brigade* experience deep frustration at this turning point in world history.

With rare psychological insight, Bartov depicts complex relationships between people in pursuit of an objective that is not entirely clear. At the center of the novel is a protagonist with a torn soul: He seeks revenge and acts to prevent it, and is attracted and repulsed by his friends, his girlfriend, his family members, his biography, and himself. There is no other novel in Hebrew literature that tells the story of the Jewish Brigade, yet it is also a universal novel about the Second World War and its horrors, about soldiers who search for vengeance and find themselves.

3

The Vengeance of the Skull in Yehuda Amichai's *Not of This Time, Not of This Place*

A Novel of Two Wars

> "Because you drowned others, you drowned, and the fate of those who drowned you is to be drowned."

Bifurcated Novel, Bifurcated Soul

Two wars live within the hero of Yehuda Amichai's novel, *Not of This Time, Not of This Place* (Schocken, 1963): World War II (the Holocaust) and Israel's War of Independence. Contrary to expectations, the events of the novel, based on the memories of the two wars, occur not on the axis of time but on the axis of space: In the single summer of 1959, Joel, the protagonist of Amichai's novel, is present simultaneously in two different places. In Weinburg (a fictitious name for Würzburg, Amichai's native town in northern Bavaria), he searches for traces of the Holocaust and comes to realize that the "economic miracle" is happening there.[1] In Jerusalem, the city in which Amichai resided most of his life, Joel meets a foreign woman and plunges into a passionate love affair with her. Fragmentary memories of what he underwent in the War of Independence and of the Holocaust, which in fact he did not experience, permeate his mind and mark his emotional world and his actions. Vestiges of the two wars, some of them actual and some imagined, emerge in Weinburg and in Jerusalem. The two wars are not mentioned by name, but merge in the hero's consciousness.

This lengthy novel (619 pages in Hebrew), the only one the poet Amichai published, bifurcates from beginning to end into two parallel plots. The first deals with a consuming love affair that takes place in Jerusalem in 1959 between Joel, a lecturer in archaeology at Hebrew University who had gone through fierce battles in the Negev in the War of Independence that will not leave him in peace, and a gentile woman, a doctor, named Patricia. The second deals with Joel's obsessive project of vengeance, which is grotesque and quite unfeasible, in which he tries to uncover within the German city of Weinburg skeletons and skulls that he imagines were buried in dark cellars and at the bottom of rivers. The two plots unfold side by side in an amazing schematic design: A chapter belonging to the Jerusalem plot is almost always followed by a chapter belonging to the Weinburg story. The dramatic tension within this schematic structure—with its reiteration of events, wild associations, and multivalent imagery—is one of the novel's most distinctive features, along with the startling bond between the two plots.

Joel is a bifurcated hero living in two different spheres and simultaneously undergoing experiences that appear contradictory, but are in fact complementary. In hot and dusty Jerusalem, he is totally immersed in the carnal love relationship with a foreign woman; in cool, rainy, hedonistic Weinburg, he is caught up pathetically and hopelessly in the search for body parts and incriminating details of the death of his beloved childhood friend Ruth, a search that will justify his coming there for revenge. In the Jerusalem chapters, he is spoken of in the third person; in the Weinburg chapters, he speaks about himself in the first person.

In each of the plots, the divided hero carries within him two wars that have already ended, which crystallize in his consciousness as a single amorphous bloc of war. At all times and in all places, he experiences an inner post-traumatic condition with different and sometimes contradictory manifestations. In each of the cities, he encounters various people who mirror his past and present condition. The worlds of memories—images and attitudes—depicted in each of the plots are both different and similar. In fact, this novel, built on a synchronization of events, moves between fidelity to time and place and a freewheeling hallucinatory association of ideas. It is an experimental work, rich in repetitions and contradictions, at once riveting and repelling, with the metaphor of self-revelation that bears within it unresolved tensions. Motifs, images, wordplay, objects, perceptions, and characters link the two parallel plots.

One example of the linguistic play, the false semantic field, the illogical logic and the fabricated continuity that links the two simultaneous plots, is found in the Jerusalem chapter (chapter 82). Here the reader experiences Joel's great distress inspired by his total immersion in the love of the foreign woman with whom he betrays his wife, his teacher, his milieu, and all his everyday obligations. "And once Joel awoke and words screamed within him as though not from his mouth: 'My God, my God, why hast Thou forsaken me?'" (571, from Psalm 22:2 and Matthew 27:46). In the Weinburg chapter that follows (chapter 83), which manifests the plot of revenge that will never be realized, the narrator awakens and the Psalmist-evangelist cry of the Jerusalem Joel is screaming within him, but with a twist: "And once I awoke: My God, my God, why hast Thou forsaken me? And immediately, My God, my God, why did You not forsake me, not leave me alone and in peace, with no vengeance and no love?" (572).[2] The vengeance belongs to the Weinburg plot, and the love belongs to the Jerusalem plot. In both, Joel is put to the test, and the cry from Psalm 22 and Matthew expresses his disappointment and despair in the crucifixion, which encapsulates this dilemma.

The heavy sense of survivor guilt and the guilt for his marital betrayal that Joel carries within him like a cross are the motivations underlying his movements both in Jerusalem and in Weinburg. This guilt is directed toward two women named Ruth, the shared name connecting the two plots. Big Ruth is the wife of the adult Joel in Jerusalem; Little Ruth was his closest childhood friend in Weinburg, who perished in the Holocaust. Each Ruth is associated with a different milieu, with a different period in his life, and with a different war living within him. The connection between them is his abandonment and betrayal of each, albeit in different ways. In the Jerusalem plot, he betrays Big Ruth by falling deeply in love with another woman; in the Weinburg plot, he betrays Little Ruth, who shaped his world and his personality, when he immigrated to Palestine a few years before the Holocaust. He left her behind and, with the passage of time, did not even answer her letters that reached him in Palestine. Big

Ruth represents the soldier's longing for a woman, for when Joel came back from the burning desert, he found her waiting: "Once you waited for me after the battle at night when Avraham was killed. You stood at the approach to the wadi when we came back at dawn. Then we decided we would become man and wife, if we remained alive. We remained and we became" (606). Little Ruth represents those in his town who were burned, shot, and drowned, and who turned into smoke, skeletons, and skulls, whom the narrator seeks to avenge in an ostensibly different Germany. The two different women are fused into a single Ruth toward whom Joel feels a sense of obligation: "'Why do you act badly toward Ruth?' my mother suddenly asked. I did not know what to say. Did she mean Ruth my wife or Little Ruth, who was burnt in the camps?" (36). For Joel: "Many thoughts and many memories arose within him in a whirl, the face of Little Ruth and the face of Ruth his wife and her father the commander, and his own dead father" (142).

Joel finds that the Germany to which he returns in the summer of 1959 is a place where people appear to have ignored their past; they repress and hide the horrors that they perpetrated. In his view, they are concerned only with rebuilding their world as quickly as possible just a decade and a half after the Holocaust:

> I went to my favorite street, all of it gentle and European after the World War. In the shops, there was merchandise in delicate colors, everything neatly arranged and splendidly presented, a delight to the eye . . . And the white snow of all my life came upon me as I stood on a summer night in the elegant renovated street of Weinburg. (406–7)

In her study *Yehuda Amichai: The Making of Israel's National Poet*, Nili Scharf Gold provides a detailed and reliable biographical basis for Amichai's poetry and fiction. She demonstrates that substantial portions of it are clearly autobiographical. In his poetry, Gold argues, Amichai refrained from explicitly revealing his European origin and sought to appear as a native Israeli. In the novel, however, the "childhood world" from which he had fled continued to pursue him. The fact that the narrator did not himself experience the Holocaust, while the flourishing Jewish community of Würzburg—and Little Ruth within it—was cut down, is the source of the sense of guilt accompanying his life and expressed in the novel in all its gravity.

Gold writes that in 1959, when he was thirty-five, Amichai traveled for the first time to Würzburg, which he had left in 1935. She claims that despite the actual late visit, the depiction of the city in the novel juxtaposes childhood memories with current realities. Two scholars, Christian Leo and Hans Steidele, were able to draw a map of Würzburg in the 1930s based on the novel and identified its streets, buildings, architectural monuments, fountains, and statues. Gold reports that when *Not of This Time, Not of This Place* appeared, Amichai said in an interview that he discovered there places he had thought were taken from his dreams.[3]

In the Weinburg of 1959, Amichai portrays disguised Nazis, wanderers seeking vengeance, sundry people demanding justice, and among them the remaining Jews—all of them, as it were, living witnesses to what had happened. But the lively, colorful summer does not allow for vengeance, which turns into an illusory idea that cannot be carried out:

> First, life struck Little Ruth in winter, on a snowy day. Now it's summer. A wonderful summer in which it rains on and off. A summer of joy, a summer of flowing streams and decorated rowboats. And to a summer like this, I have come from parched Jerusalem to avenge. Since Ruth is alive [at a certain point in the novel, he fantasizes that she is still alive and living in a convent], I will at least avenge the kick they gave her. I will search for the one who kicked, the one who bit, the one who burned, the one who hit, the one who whipped, the one who crushed, and the one who tore to pieces, and again there will be no end to my searching. (490)

The "snow" of all Amichai's life is the past that lives within him, and the "summer" is the hedonistic present that does not allow the implementation of acts of vengeance.

The understanding of the Holocaust by the first-person narrator is seemingly unconnected with the experience of the War of Independence that is reflected in the Jerusalem chapters, where Joel is immersed in a love relationship that makes him forget everything else. But remembering and forgetting are two sides of the same coin. The childhood memories of the first-person narrator, who is seeking to fill in gaps of knowledge about what happened in the Holocaust, repeat themselves obsessively and mingle with fragmentary memories of the War of Independence, referred to only as "war" or "battle." These fragments resurface in Weinburg when an appropriate stimulus presents itself, often when the narrator is in a half-waking state before falling asleep: "Woe to the man in whom the inner partitions have collapsed," says the first-person narrator, in whom the drive for vengeance is confused with the carnal desire of Jerusalem, over which dreams rule: "Love mingles with revenge and dreaming floods reality." (190)

> I got up to pee . . . Before the battles, in which I took part, I too would pee, so that I would be quick in movement and wouldn't soil myself with urine if I were torn by a bullet or a piece of shrapnel. Why did Platoon B arrive late and why was Platoon C lost? Actually, it was the fault of the other platoon that took part in the action. Little Ruth would certainly have been very proud if she had seen me then fighting in the Land of Israel for our people and for our land. The thought of the battles soothed me and I finally fell asleep. (190)

The idea of the mingling of memories from childhood with memories of the war recurs again and again. All the memories of the war in Israel are suffused with irony, a catalogue of failures, errors in strategy, and uncompelling historical analogies (he calls his army uniform "khaki shrouds," mocks the cake his mother gave him "to sustain him" and, like the prophet Elijah, walks with the power of that walking until the evil horizon of the south appears and swallows him up in the battles, 37), gratuitous disaster, and death:

> Only when I sat in the bus did all the walls break within me. I was like Jericho, and a fearful army of conquerors arose and went wild over my ruins—songs of nuns [nonsense], songs of Ma'oz Tzur, fragments of the play Judah [a Hanukah play in which he took part to the dismay of Little Ruth, a childhood event in which he, the hero Judah, was exposed in all his weakness, and which haunts him], "behold thou art betrothed"

from my wedding, everything was mixed up in me with orders from the time of war: "Open fire only when you see them approaching. Silence! Don't be nervous, don't expose yourself unnecessarily." Then my brain shut down, one part after another, like cabins on a sinking ship. (433)

A flash of memories from the War of Independence opens the shell of repression that Joel cultivates when he falls in love with a foreign woman and neglects the practical world. This is also because Jerusalem—the eternal city—is always plunged into a kind of war that preserves within itself the memory of all the wars and does not allow a total retreat into love: "Whoever comes to Jerusalem enters a city under siege. Always, even in times of peace, Nebuchadnezzar and Titus and the Crusaders are all around. A person who lives in this city—is always under siege" (105). Love, with no limit and no borders, was intended to make Joel forget the first Israeli war, but he cannot suppress the fragmentary memories that constantly float up and mix one war with another, the city where he was born with the city in which he lives, beautiful Weinburg and eternal Jerusalem.

A Guest for the Night

Amichai evidently drew the topos of return to the native town from Agnon's *A Guest for the Night*. The two narrator-protagonists, both literary avatars of the two authors, return belatedly to their native city to see what a world war has inflicted on it. Agnon's narrator goes back to his city after World War I and Amichai's after World War II. Each finds a city that is changed: The narrator of *A Guest for the Night* finds a city in ruins, ruins that obliterate the glory of its past. The narrator of *Not of This Time, Not of This Place* finds a reveling city of wine, its past buried beneath it. Agnon's novel abounds in symbols and characters, and deploys a dense and rich intertextual network. Amichai's novel surpasses it in the flood of details, metaphors, realistic and symbolic representations in its rich figurative language, the interweaving of calculated analogies, the cataloguing (lists and enumerations of all sorts of inventories), the fragments of memory reiterated in different variations—all these bearing witness to troubling thoughts from which the hometown visit and writing about it purport to free the protagonist.

Here is what the Weinburg narrator says about his return to his hometown, supposedly for the sake of revenge:

> Whoever returns after many years to the site of his childhood cuts off his childhood from his life. For a person always carries within him the site of his childhood. When he returns to it, he wipes away the imagination of it with the eraser of reality. And now I have discovered that this is why I came here. This is my true revenge; not to carry anymore the beauty of Weinburg in my heart, but to erase its memory and entirely break with it. (549)

Many motifs connect Agnon's novel of belated return with Amichai's. The motif of severed limbs is one of these. It seems that almost fifteen years have passed from the end of World War I until the visit of Agnon's narrator to Szybucz (another spelling of Agnon's distorted name of his hometown of Buczacz, in Galicia, is Szibucz) and the town is still immersed in destruction. The ruins have not been rebuilt, and the town is falling apart. This devastation is also visible in the appearance of the people with severed limbs whom the visitor encounters immediately upon his arrival: "Along came the dispatcher called 'Rubberovitch'; his left arm had been lost in the war; the new one they gave him was made of rubber. He stood erect, waving the flag in his hand, and called: 'Szibucz!'" (*A Guest for the Night*, 1).[4] Daniel Bach, whose right leg is made of wood, shows him to his hotel (3–4). It should be noted that this prosthetic leg is not the result of the war, just like Little Ruth's prosthetic leg in Amichai's novel, which also is not from the war but from an accident before the war. The wooden leg in each of the novels is represented with black humor, as though the prosthetic provided some advantage. Daniel Bach tells the narrator: "In fact, this man-made leg is better than the other, which is the work of God. It doesn't have to worry about rheumatism, and beats the other for walking" (3). The irony regarding Ruth's leg is still more shocking. Surely, the Nazis, before they burned Ruth, removed her leg for reasons of thrift—perhaps they would need it for the wood or other materials (metal bands and screws) from which it was made:

> I thought of Ruth's body that was burned after it was killed. How the fire in the crematorium must have been disappointed, for it was knowledgeable about human bodies, when it reached the place of the leg that wasn't there, and how the flames must have pulled back and flickered out. (*Not of This Time, Not of This Place*, 331)

The motif of the one leg has dozens of reflections in the waking and nightmare world of Amichai's narrator. For Agnon's narrator, after he has made the acquaintance of the one-armed Rubberovitch and the one-legged Daniel Bach, he meets Ignatz the beggar, "whose nose has been destroyed in the war, and who has a hole in place of the nose" (*A Guest for the Night*, 25). The world of severed limbs sums up his first day in Szybucz: "I said to myself: This night I shall know no sleep, Rubberovitch's hand or Bach's foot will come to terrify me" (8).

For Amichai, the significance of maiming, severed limbs, a leg without a body, a body missing a leg, and especially a skull floating on the water or borne up over the smoke of the crematoria or of cigarette smokers, depending on where the divided self of Joel finds himself in the summer of 1959, in hedonistic Weinburg or decadent Jerusalem—this is the motif on which this section about the vengeance of the skull in *Not of This Time, Not of This Place* will now concentrate. This motif amounts to a detail that indicates the configuration of the whole. The skull and the disembodied limbs are a metaphor for the novel's central theme, which is the Israeli, a divided Jew, who after the Holocaust and after Israel's first war, has not achieved an integration of the self.

To Drown and to Be Drowned, to Forget and to Remember, to Love and to Hate

Although the Jerusalem love plot is no less powerful than the vengeance plot set in Germany, Amichai gives his novel a motto that appears to be directed only to the vengeance plot. The motto is taken from the Mishnaic text, *Ethics of the Fathers* (2:6):

> He [Hillel the Elder] saw a skull floating on the surface of the water, [and] he said to it: Because thou hast drowned others, they have drowned thee, and, in the end, they who have drowned thee shall themselves be drowned.

This motto, which amounts to "the entire doctrine of retribution in one sentence," is ironically appropriate in a frightening way to the plot, in which the narrator leaves Jerusalem for his hometown to avenge the blood of his dear ones who perished in the Holocaust: He will pay them back. He will drown them as they drowned his dear ones; he will turn them into skulls floating on the water as they did to Little Ruth, Dr. Manheim's daughter, the innocent and blameless girl whom the Germans burned in the crematoria.

The human desire to follow two parallel courses of life simultaneously and to compare them—as Joel himself puts it, "I'd like to be at the same time in all places" (220)—is expressed in the novel's fantastic structure. Joel's split personality, the lack of comprehensible integration within the person, his contradictory longings and his unreconciled concerns are reflected in the structure of the twin plots. But, beyond the psychological expression of a divided self, the protagonist's character is complex, and the vengeance motto of the book also applies to the love plot.

Love and vengeance are two powerful emotions that threaten the balance between reason and emotion, wherein emotion overwhelms reason. The emotions of love and vengeance, when manifested in all their power, can lead a person to mental or physical collapse. However, these antithetical emotions also consume or contradict each other. Whereas love immerses one in forgetfulness and alienation from one's past and from one's quotidian obligations, vengeance plunges one into the past and requires the rigorous planning of acts in the present. Joel, who stays in Jerusalem, wants to fall in love, body and soul, and to forget the whole world, and especially the experiences of the war in which he met his wife, Ruth: "and the face of Ruth, his good wife, disappeared, the wife with whom he had enjoyed a life of tranquility ever since their first encounter in a yellow blazing Negev dawn in the sun and in the war" (314–15). However, Joel, returning to the landscape of his childhood, wants to remember a whole world, a remembering that will enflame his hatred for those who destroyed his world and rouse him to acts of vengeance. But Amichai turns memory and forgetting into perfect complements. "What is in the river, forgetting or remembering? I could not tell, but once I saw a skull floating in the water" (422). Invoking the motto from *Ethics of the Fathers*, Joel suggests that the river on its own would have drowned the horror of Europe in forgetfulness, but the ancient skull floating in its water does not allow the enemy to be forgotten. The skull is the very embodiment of the memory. The skull in the water is the symbol of hatred whose opposite side is love. "You came to remember and to hate, but you know that to hate and to love amount to the same thing psychologically" (137).

Amichai tells us repeatedly that hatred is the natural and absurd continuation of love, and love is the natural and absurd continuation of hatred. Although both remain opposite emotions, both are in the heart of the person seeking to remember and to forget, to forget and to remember. These contradictory feelings threaten to tear Joel apart; yet in the absence of either, his identity and his life are incomplete.

The words that Hillel the Elder addressed to the skull could be a curse or a dirge over a sad reality or the assertion of a solid fact of life experience and broad historical perspective. The victim becomes the avenger, the avenger the victim; the drowned becomes the drowner, and so it goes to the end of time. The eternal cyclical process of victimhood and vengeance to which Hillel bears witness is changed by Amichai into a fluid and arbitrary cycle of love and hate. Hillel's historical perspective shows how these reversals of roles and emotions constitute a continuing process occurring on the linear axis of time. Amichai sees the interchange between the two roles of victim and victimizer, love and hate, from a spatial perspective in which they occur at the same time and in two different places.

"My good friend told me," the narrator says to himself, grateful that he has not stayed in Jerusalem but followed the advice of his friends and has gone to Weinburg:

> Either you finally go there and get rid of the tension, or you betray your good wife and become involved in an affair, an adventure of flesh and adventures of blood, which will end in disaster, tears and terrible deaths. To such an extent I was tense and calculating and plotting before I went. (176)

While in Weinburg, Joel realizes, to his disappointment, that there is neither hatred nor vengeance in him but rather reconciliation and tranquility. Thus, he sees himself as being unfit for the battle that was his motive for coming. At the same time, he imagines the story of his hypothetical love in Jerusalem from the perspective of distance as the story of a bloody war, and that it was good that he had come to Weinburg and prevented it from happening.

A Living Skull—A Dead Skull

The skull from *Ethics of the Fathers* would seem to fit the Weinburg plot. In the European city, in which the river is an integral part, Joel stands on the bridge and sees below, or so he imagines, that skull from the ambiguous utterance of Hillel the Elder. At that moment, Joel becomes the Hillel who curses or asserts an empirical fact of life. On the one hand, he seeks vengeance for the victims of the Holocaust for whom the skull is their representation. On the other hand, he experiences schadenfreude that the floating skull represents the collective head of the perpetrators of the Holocaust, a material testimony of the retribution that has overtaken them. Paradoxically, to his horror and relief, Joel realizes that Hillel's "dead skull" has, in the city of his childhood, become the heads of people hungry for life.

The context of the skull's first appearance in the novel is evidence of the fiasco of the proclaimed vengeance and of the incapacity to implement it. The romantic atmosphere of cafés and of fishing boats on the banks of the river, the nocturnal swimming of women and men in the river, and the relaxed mood of Joel, make Hillel's accursed skull seem false:

> I feared that this was not the right moment for plotting revenge, and I was apprehensive that I would be too conciliatory and tranquil. Meanwhile, I

strode through the gravel on the riverbank. I saw a skull on the surface of the water. I said *al de'ataft atafukh vesof metifayikh yetufun*. Because you drowned others you drowned and the fate of those who drowned you is to be drowned. Then I repeated those Aramaic words in Hebrew and in German. The skull turned to me with its black mouth and said: I know the Holy Tongue. I asked: Why, are you Ruth? But the skull went on floating with the current. I accompanied it for a time. I saw that it was the skull of a boy and that I had been mistaken. When I reached the Lion's Bridge, I saw that it was the skull of a girl. I asked it: How did it happen? You are very quick. How did you manage to go down from the bridge so soon, to undress and to get into the river? The skull disappeared and there was total darkness and I did not know whose skull it was. The river began to glisten with the reflection of lights from the opposite bank. My feet stumbled over a pile of woman's clothes. I sat and thought that I'd wait till she came out of the water, but I heard nothing. (156)

The skull that Joel, the modern Hillel, sees is the skull of a living person. In the darkness, it is hard for him to tell whether the skull is a man's or a woman's, a girl's or a boy's, or both alternately. This is an elusive skull, changing shape and appearance. And rather than representing victims and avengers, it represents lovers. But if it is the skull of a living person, it is not actually a skull but a head, the head of someone with a body immersed in the water and a head held up above water. "A dead person's skull" is a tautology, like "a dead person's corpse." But in fact, in what follows, Joel clarifies for himself the concept of "skull" and whether the living skull (an erroneous concept, essentially oxymoronic) can relate to the ancient Aramaic curse:

> The skull was no longer in the water. A skull means the bones of the head. Can one call a living person's head a skull? To what end, then, would one add the qualifier "dead" to "skull"? This is what I thought: During the war, they didn't bring people to the river to their death, for the river goes to the west, and the river is not guilty like the railroad tracks that go to the east. (175)

The river and railroad had always been distinctive features of Weinburg, but after the war these two dynamic elements of the landscape, which were a kind of soundtrack of the city, became freighted with suspicion, blame, and a need for vengeance, like every person and object in Weinburg. The skull in the water and the black smoke in the sky embody the narrator's subjective perception that imbues whatever he sees with his unbearably heavy inner world.

Because of the return to life of the skull that turns out to be the head of a boy or girl swimming for pleasure in the water, the Weinburg revenge plot changes its character and direction. With his incapacity to hate, the revenge plot becomes a plot of sober reconciliation. From this tolerant viewpoint, the plot of the love affair in Jerusalem is transformed into a war story. But what war can be taking place in the Jerusalem of the late 1950s, and how can there be a skull floating on the water in a city with neither river nor sea?

The skull from *Ethics of the Fathers* floats in Jerusalem, not in a river that divides it, but rather in a mined no-man's land of walls and towers—symbols of a continuing war, of perpetually opposed views, of geographical and political divisions, of an arbitrary border, and of the danger of death.

Opposite the ancient wall and the Tower of David, on the same seam that divides the city, in the place where high defensive walls have been set up against snipers, and in the walls in which narrow slits have been made to peek into the territory of the enemy, a sign has been affixed warning "Border ahead!" On the sign, written in four languages so there will be no room for mistakes and as an indication of the cosmopolitan character of the place and its "international status," there is the iconic image of a "death-skull with two crossed bones beneath it" (157). It appears that this frightening skull bears within it both an accusation and a sense of guilt, but it immediately becomes clear that this iconic skull is not frightening. Moreover, the ancient skull is given a new interpretation here: "Over time," says the narrator of the Jerusalem plot, "the skull was no longer terrifying and people in the street became accustomed to it as to the skull from *Ethics of the Fathers* that floats gently on the water" (157). That which is familiar, routine, and common loses its power, loses its terror through overuse. Just as birds are not afraid of the scarecrow, people are no longer afraid of the skull. The story of the love affair, which had been seen from a distant viewpoint as an adventure of flesh and blood that ends in "disaster and tears and terrible deaths," turns out to be not in the least like that. Everything is relative and everything depends on the distance from which one views an event, a person, or an object.

The mutable symbolic identifications of the skull become dominant thematic features of the novel. The skull from Weinburg has had its menace neutralized, and the skull from Jerusalem has its announced threat also neutralized, indicating that the two plots reflect each other despite their difference. The skull can turn into the head of a swimmer in the river in one plot and into a two-dimensional iconic sign in the parallel plot. But both the resuscitated skull and the silenced skull have the same source: The skull floating on the water and the words addressed to it are an inexhaustible source of imaginative transformations and creativity and atemporality. An eternal atavistic skull achieves concretization and revivification in a modern world that is fissured, comical, and illusory; and within Joel's divided self, it can be understood in different ways that finally are very similar.

In the Weinburg plot, the skull is the symbol of unrealizable vengeance, and in the Jerusalem plot it is a sign of "Border ahead," announcing danger that has lost its terror through routine. It marks a divided life and the fusion of opposites; it illustrates the failure of integration within the so-called "new Jew," who has a geographic limit in front of him, but who sets no limits to his desires, to his impulses, and to the contradictory feelings that surge within him as the results of war that are manifest in the conflicted condition of his life's routine and in the impairment of his creative abilities.

A real border divides both the protagonist and his cities in two, but in his mind, he and his cities—one in the Diaspora and the other in Israel—are transformed into a single entity. When the new Jew, the Israeli and archaeologist-warrior, sheds his mask, a naked skull is exposed. The fearless Israeli warrior is suddenly exposed as a survivor of the Holocaust, a skull searching for its body and its identity. The skull, besides being stripped of flesh, is without disguise, devoid of makeup, of pretense; it is unconnected to anybody and can be in all places, simultaneously floating on the water in German Weinburg and emerging as a sign in Israeli Jerusalem. In Weinburg, it floats on the surface of the river that divides the town; in Israel's capital city, it is a marker, a testimony, and a warning about the division of the city that bears the word *shalem*, "whole," as part of its name and its spiritual nature. In both cases, the skull appears on the seam, and the two divided cities mirror the double sensibility of the protagonist, who lives and acts in both beneath a mask and armor. Although he is exposed and cut off like that hapless skull torn from its body, he bears its ancestral freight for eternity. The inner split, this lack of wholeness of the protagonist, who represents his generation, is concretized by Amichai in dozens of images in which the human body is divided into disjunct members scattered in every direction. The split is also seen in the schizophrenia that afflicts one of the protagonist's close women friends, a lucid psychotic who gives Joel "ambiguous advice" to be in both Germany and Israel in the same summer, to return to himself, there in spirit and here in body.

Not of This Time, Not of This Place begins with a detailed description of a summer farewell party held in a large stone house in Jerusalem belonging to Mina and Yitzhaq, friends of Joel. Gradually, the house is transformed into a metaphor of Jerusalem and the entire state. The party is called a "Roman revel," in part because it is mainly characterized by a decadent atmosphere and lack of purpose. Yitzhaq intends to sell his home with everything in it. Amichai's skull symbolism is extended into the "Israeli Romans" who stay late into the night in their revels, and into the description of the museum-like accoutrements of the house that is about to be liquidated. When Joel enters the "Roman chamber" into which his friends from the Palmach and the War of Independence have crowded, it seems to him that he sees only the skulls of living-dead Romans floating on the surface of the room. The face of Mr. Cohen, the melancholy musicologist, is the face of Emperor Nero. The face of Yitzhaq the doctor is the face of a Roman tyrant, thin and lined with vertical furrows. The head of Meinzer the painter is "too big." The face of Yoska the archaeologist somehow resembles the bodiless heads laid bare in archaeological digs: "His nose is straight and his forehead high and broad and his hair curly." The lawyer, Dr. Gulglus, whose name is a Hebrew pun on *gulgolet* ("skull"), has a "jaw that juts out forcefully" and his "blue eyes are deep-sunken and penetrate into whoever looks at them." Into this room full of seemingly decapitated heads, a question is tossed: "Who wants Beethoven's head?"—a broken sculpture, one of the art objects in this crumbling house. Afterward, "Yitzhaq's head arose from among the discussants, and he saw Joel and nodded to him through the smoke" (21–22). Just as Joel's head is revealed as though separated from his body, the head of Professor Oren, an eminent archaeologist, with whom he has a love-hate relationship, is revealed before Joel's eyes: "His face, the face of a Roman imperator crowned with years, was still tanned and drawn from the last expedition of discoveries in the desert and in its caves" (22).

The skulls of Jerusalem are different from the skulls that are revealed to Joel in Weinburg. In Jerusalem, they are the skulls of his friends and acquaintances from the army and the university, and they thrust up from the smoky room and from the archeological digs of heat, dirt, and sand. They are the heads of "Romans," all of them sunburned men covered with dust, crowding into a room for the sake of "the group," the Israeli collective that seems to be falling apart. In Weinburg, the gender of the skull floating in the water is ambiguous; it is not clear whether it is a young man or a young woman who has come to swim in the river without guilt feelings and without knowing that there is somebody looking for revenge. The sexual and collective identities of the Jerusalem skull are clear: They are males who have experienced war, sand, and the Israeli blazing sun. In both cases, these are living skulls, harboring within them the oxymoron of the "living dead" or the "dead that live."

The "amputation of limbs" is also a central motif in the novel that is given original expression in the book's rich imagery. Its thematic justification refers to Little Ruth, whose leg had been amputated, and whose death Joel wants to avenge. A childhood episode linked to the leg continues to trouble Joel: "Hitler's Jugend hold him and prevent him from coming to her aid, while one of them kicks her." Ruth's prosthetic leg makes "a sound of hard materials, of clasps and buckles, and leather" (182). Joel imagines that her prosthetic leg symbolizes her toughness, endurance, and maturity; thus the prosthetic leg must have survived when the Nazis burned her in the crematorium, and he, returning to the scene of his childhood, looks for this unusual leg. It is of course an absurd, hopeless quest, reflecting the surrealist-symbolic shaping of the revenge plot.

Joel is haunted by this unresolved childhood trauma, which is reflected in the images he sees when he comes as an adult to settle accounts with the torturers and the killers of his dead friend. He sees in a store window "a flesh-and-blood person alongside human parts and heads," and he tries to arrange them "in a new order" (182). The narrator, captive of his imaginings, is of course hinting at "the new world order" that the Nazis aspired to establish, in which they turned their victims into disassembled and lifeless mannequins. But in the context of a "new Germany" rising from its ruins, the arrangement in the shop window is an innocent, routine act in an urban world teeming with life, although the belated avenger tries to establish its connection with the Nazis.

Images of detached limbs in shop windows are frequently repeated. On the one hand, these windows recall Kristallnacht, an important motif in the novel, in which the odor of perfume mingles with the odor of the blood of the innocent (517). On the other hand, the memory of shattered windows of Jewish stores and broken bodies of Jews in the Holocaust is juxtaposed to the new shop windows that embody the hedonistic economic world that proceeds as though there had been no Holocaust: "The latest fashion lines in shop windows do not display the whole mannequin, but only parts, such as a hand carrying an elegant purse or a leg wearing a silk stocking, or a hand in a glove" (234). For Joel, these synecdochical objects represent dismemberment and horror, but at the same time hedonism and the disavowal of any burden of emotion or conscience. He sees the heads and feet of the young women in a lovely café as if their whole bodies were not there: "From the railing of the balcony one could see the heads of young women . . . Besides the heads, I could see only the feet" (183). The railing of the café, hiding the bodies and allowing only the heads and the feet to be visible as if they were not connected, is devised to serve the guided, selective vision of the narrator, for whom disjunct members recall the body that was destroyed. The dead Ruth and her missing leg constantly live in his memory of her life and his consciousness of her death.

These instances of disjunct heads and legs illuminate the vengeance motto of the book—"Because you drowned others, you were drowned"— and the search for the leg of the dead Ruth is an element of Joel's grotesque constellation. From his point of view, a world that goes on as it always has after tearing hands and legs from living bodies, turning them into disembodied wanderers, is a monstrous world.

How will Joel, who was driven from childhood's Garden of Eden into the forest of predatory life, cope with his frustration, his outcry, his impulse for vengeance? After all, he too is wandering through the world like a dangling limb, cut off from body and spirit. His spirit is perhaps in Jerusalem and his body in Weinburg, or perhaps the other way around. The answer lies in the recognition that "When they burnt Ruth, they burnt her avenging, and the earth was left empty of mercy and of vengeance and of any human being" (182). The unresolved doubling, represented by the living-dead skull with an oscillating gender identity floating in the river of Weinburg, amounts to the end of all flesh, alongside ordinary life as though nothing had happened. In Jerusalem, the sign of the skull with two crossed bones beneath it serves as a warning against crossing the border that runs through the heart of the city. The divided structure of the novel embodies the tension between crossing all borders in time and space, and strict recognition of disassembly and wholeness, chaos, and order.

In one of the novel's most evocative scenes, during Joel's futile search for Ruth's leg, he comes to a workshop for prosthetics, "in the forest of prosthetic limbs" (232). Before the owner has a chance to help him, Joel recalls how "one day in the garden of the palace by the pond, in which there was a stone nymph pouring its water into a marble basin," the twelve-year-old Ruth proposed that they share their future, and he was shocked (232). This shock marked the beginning of the estrangement between them, an estrangement in which the sheltered childhood Garden of Eden was displaced by the forest of prosthetic limbs, the forest of adulthood, which happened four years before they burned Ruth in the crematoria. Now, after almost two decades, Joel asks for a "used prosthetic leg" for a sixteen-year-old girl. In his fantasy, this artificial leg might have survived the burning.

The German owner conducts a thorough search. "After a few minutes he appeared, his head hidden by several legs he was carrying. One leg was bent around his neck like a lamb around the neck of a shepherd" (233). This provocative visual image is another symbolic version of the living skull floating in a paradoxical amoral world in which the borders have been blurred between reward and punishment, between mercy and cruelty, between forgetting and remembering, between love and vengeance, between past and future, between terror and suffering, and "quixotic hedonism." A living head adorned with dead legs marks all these blurrings, especially the blurring between life and death. The used artificial legs may have been taken from victims of the Holocaust (they were manufactured in 1935) whose flesh-and-blood bodies were turned into smoke. The leg bent around the owner's neck, like a lamb around the neck of a shepherd, also indicates these blurrings. It is a cruel parodic image of the shepherd's compassion for his flock. However, what the owner carries around his neck is not a lost lamb but the cruel essence of Nazism, which had no compassion for millions of human beings but did have "compassion" for their property. The artificial body parts gathered by the frugal Nazis are, ironically, the only embers saved from the burning and from annihilation.

Joel, too, was saved from the burning, and his divided self and double life in Jerusalem and Weinburg reflect an artificial schematic existence, a well-wrought artifice. Thus "Hillel's skull" becomes alternately his own skull and that of his double—or both, one alongside the other.

In Weinburg, the narrator becomes friends with an East Indian who is undertaking a comprehensive research project on the sources of human despair and its manifestations. The Indian is the Jew's "secret sharer," not only because they both are people from the East who have ended up in the hedonistic Bavarian city searching for the opposite of appearances, but also because the Indian is one of the persons to whom Joel reveals his innermost secrets.

In one of the most grotesque scenes, in the Weinburg Yoga Institute, Joel crawls on all fours toward the Indian, who is sunk in meditation (277). Half-naked people, some of them lying on their backs, pay no attention to the stranger crawling among them. How different this room filled with still heads on the floor of the Yoga Institute is from the heads of the "Romans" jutting out in the "Roman chamber" in Mina and Yitzhaq's Jerusalem home. There, the heads borne up through the smoke in the room are a kind of "first person plural," a solid collective about to fall apart; in Weinburg, they are incidental private persons who happen to come together in one place to be alone, together. "I identified the Indian's head by his bitten fingernails. I lay down beside him and we spoke, head alongside head, like heads upon the water" (277). These two heads are conducting research, each in its absurd way, into the sources of human despair and how it floats on the surface.

But the Indian, who floats in the endless cyclical stream of victims and vengeance, reward and punishment, meaning and emptiness, love and hate, memory and forgetting, is not the only person who becomes Joel's friend in Weinburg. Joel, the narrator, also makes the acquaintance of Melvin, an American film director who has come to make a film on the Holocaust. Melvin had accomplished in Weinburg what Joel is unable to do. He was the commander of the military unit that destroyed the city toward the end of the war; he carried out vengeance in a brutal military manner, and now he has come to confront the Holocaust through art. Ironically, Melvin is the husband of Patricia, who has painfully separated from him, and who has become Joel's lover in Jerusalem. Joel fulfills in Jerusalem what Melvin no longer can: a great, fatal, mythological love for a woman they share. Melvin says to Joel: "If you only knew her, you would understand me" (363), but he is unaware that the Joel who stayed in Jerusalem knows her very well. Joel in Weinburg asserts: "This friend of mine is not a typical American. He is unusual. The Indian, too, is not a typical Indian, just as I am not a typical Jew. That's why we've gotten together" (363). He summarizes this remarkable encounter in Weinburg with his two secret sharers: All three are individualists, investigators of the time, of human nature, of the place, of the era, and of peoples. In Amichai's imagination, they are skulls floating on the stream of an ephemeral and eternal life, symbols of the impossible possibilities of life within death and death within life, living the life of war and life after war.

Joel becomes Melvin's adviser on what should be filmed of all the things in Weinburg of the late 1950s: "He should film the flowing river in which a skull is floating or the image of his wife carried along in the gentle current toward the Bridge of Saints" (364). The floating skull is thus part of the landscape of Weinburg, just as is the image of Melvin's wife swept up in the current of the river when she herself is in Jerusalem. Space and time and intimates are joined in a unitary vision that negates conventional boundaries and limits.

For Amichai, Hillel's image of the skull embodied in Joel's imagination takes on multiple symbolic significations in the endless flow of mythological time and space. It symbolizes the metaphysical connection among people beyond religion, color, nationality, and blood. It becomes the symbol of every human being, of radical individualism, which is at the same time the unmediated, natural connection with the other, who is the self:

> How does time rise in people; not the time that can be measured and not the time of night and day and seasons. Like the level of water this time rises in people, like the level of water rising and falling in wells, according to the law that controls it, which is also a law from the depths of the earth. This is the sense of history, not the history of schools, of dates and eras and acts of kings, migrations of peoples, and not the history of orators and leaders and not that of scholars sorting truth from falsehood; but an all-encompassing sense of history . . . a sense of a single generation sharing this or that war, those feelings of fear, sharing hope, and sharing an incipient despair, and sharing qualms and a retreat into the self. (345)

This sensual and sensuous description of time rising in people through an inner, primal, immeasurable force matches the skull that floats and rises intermittently within Joel. The pulsations of another time cause the ancient skull to rise in him like the primal water that rises and falls in wells, and they have no connection with the pulsations of the human clock or with the external cycle of natural seasons. This is a different cycle of wars of the collective after which the individual retreats into himself. Like Joel and his peers, who fought together and then each went his own way, they will again unite should a new-old war occur. The cycle of drowning and the floating of the skull from time immemorial embody this idea in the novel.

Amichai states this idea explicitly: "The only historical principle is Hillel's, who saw a skull on the surface of the water and said to it that it was drowned because it had drowned others and that the fate of those who drowned it was to be drowned by still others, and on it goes" (592). This is an idiosyncratic historical principle, just like the floating skull that appears to Joel in his own private vision: "The children, Sybil and Heinrele, saw rowboats and saw ducks and saw branches and saw swimmers and saw pieces of paper. Everything floated in the river, and the children called out: 'Look at this, look at that!' But I saw a skull and remained silent" (541). Joel is aware of his selective, subjective vision and therefore does not join in the game of calling out and pointing to objects floating in the water. What the children see he also sees, but he—who has experienced two wars and depression and introspection after the war—sees what the children cannot see. What Joel cries out to the skull, then, is interior, another version of Hillel's epigrammatic declaration: "Because you skidded, skull, you shall skid onward. There is neither reward nor punishment. There is no act of love and no act of vengeance and no return, but only the skidding of the skull in the flowing river" (541).

That is how things are in Weinburg. In the river-city, there is no principle except the principle of rolling. In this city, Joel does not manage to love or to hate, to avenge or to punish, or bring back his lost childhood. He only stumbles from one grotesque adventure to another quixotic experience. His eyes filled with visions of skulls manifest to him the law of the stream in which there is an exchange of drowner and drowned, but without any moral virtue or natural principle.

The children whom Joel befriends, recalling Ruth whom he befriended as a child, throw breadcrumbs to the ducks in the river or skip flat stones across its surface. And Joel, even in their animated presence, sees skulls. Joel plays with Sybil as he had with Ruth, but Sybil's father "was Ruth's murderer and the murderer of all the dead, and made many skulls skid onward" (541). Nevertheless, Joel does not hate her and does not seek vengeance through her. He merely wonders: "How did I become an avenger and how altogether did I arrive in Weinburg? Many rivers flow. Not only this river flowing before me, but unseen rivers. One of them has brought me here and another river will carry me away" (541). In Weinburg, he is essentially a skull carried on the surface of the water or on the surface of time; ancient waters or ancient time, in their endless flow, have swept both the skull and him to this place.

Because You Loved, They Loved You, and the Fate of Your Lovers is to Drown

Back in Jerusalem, there is love and the possibility of halting the flow: "Jerusalem has a new role. It is not Torah that will come forth from Zion, but love" (533). Within it occurs "the miracle of a second chance . . . the moment when the record goes back to the previous groove so that one can hear again and again a beloved piece of music with eyes closed" (533).

Joel first meets Patricia in Jerusalem after the "Roman party," when she is coming out of the bathtub, her lovely head dripping water and her long black hair wet. Her head immediately replaces the heads of the "Romans," his confused friends, and it becomes everything for him. In Weinburg, when Melvin wants to show his wife to his new friend Joel, he takes out a small bag and pulls out a photo. At that moment, "a breeze arose and the photo dropped into the river before I could see it. The photo of his wife's head dropped into the river; it was barely visible in the murky water; and then disappeared into the darkness of the depths" (327). Patricia's head, which in Weinburg is a photo, mingles with the rest of the skulls carried along in the river's gentle current (364). For Melvin, Patricia's photo, like Patricia herself, is lost. But in Jerusalem, she emerges from a bath as the living, enchanting head of a beautiful woman who becomes involved with Joel in a love relationship. For Joel, her head appears in all its splendor.

Toward the end of the novel, this first defining image is repeated, and this is "the miracle of the second chance": Patricia is sitting in the bathtub, making little waves around her neck. Regarding this vision of Patricia's head, Amichai reveals a great transformation of Joel as the Weinburg narrator to Joel in Jerusalem. The former sees skulls and repeats the substance of Hillel's words. The latter, the Jerusalemite in love, when beholding his beloved's head floating in the water, her eyes closed, whispers to himself: "Because you loved, they will love you, and the fate of those who love you is to drown" (552). What does it mean to "drown" in love?

This new and radical version of Hillel's words interrupts the eternal flowing of the skull in the river. There is no river in Jerusalem, and the head that floats in the water of a domestic bathtub is without doubt a woman's head. The elusive gender of the swimmer's head in Weinburg is refocused in Jerusalem in the head of a particular woman, who is altogether captivating, bursting through fortified walls. Joel remembers her first entrance into the room as "a proud entrance, head held high, like a **conquering army**" (60, emphasis added). And near the end of the novel, "Patricia entered, as when he first saw her: with an emphatic sweep, her head inclined forward a little, slightly lowered, like a battering-ram for the breaching of a besieged wall" (552). The martial language used for Patricia makes her a conqueror, and the conquest is one of love. Joel, who in Weinburg waited a long time for a woman to come out of the water, experiences in Jerusalem with his own eyes and with all the pleasure of his senses the big woman coming out of the water: "Patricia rose from the bathtub, water dripping from her. Her body was large and sturdy, like the bodies of women in ancient Greece. Her legs were strong and shapely and her hair was gathered on her head" (552). The strong legs of the beloved woman in Jerusalem are juxtaposed to the prosthetic leg of Little Ruth, the girl he loved in his Weinburg childhood, she whose leg was the target of the kicks by Hitler's Jugend. Whereas most of the motifs and images in this novel in which doublings and proliferating versions are emphasized, here there is no real opposition. The legs of both his loves are strong, and each represents a different version of the strength of body and spirit: "I remembered Little Ruth's precision and her confidence in walking, even after her leg was amputated" (492).

However, a great love of this kind for Patricia, the big woman coming out of the pool of dreams, cannot survive forever. Only skulls can float upon the water forever. The end of great loves is death, and in fact, the Jerusalem Joel steps on a landmine left after a prior war and is killed. He envisioned his own death when he whispered to Patricia's head the version that broke the framework, broke the rules, broke the law of history concerning the drowning of others and being drowned: "Because you loved, they loved you, and the fate of your lovers is to be drowned" (552). Only a great and powerful love like Joel's and Patricia's can deflect river and time from their fixed course, but just for a moment, for the fate of the heroic lovers is to die, and the river again will flow as it has from time immemorial, now and then bringing up its repressed skulls to the surface.

The Jerusalem Joel figuratively drowns at the end of the summer with his great love for Patricia intact. He was "drowned" (killed) not by love, but by the buried remnant of hostility that haunts his Jerusalem world. However, the Weinburg Joel comes home armed with a deep "redemptive insight" about justice and vengeance:

> Justice, too, is a great river always flowing. And everyone pours into it his great or small vengeance. But the river is quiet and all the motives for revenge do not trouble the surface of its water. There is no sign in it of the spate of actions or the foam of wrath and violence. It flows quietly and carries along on its surface the skulls, which are endless in number. (612)

The ambiguous and multifaceted metaphor of the floating skull, together with the words addressed to it by Hillel, require Amichai's readers to wait patiently for the full revelation of their meanings. This revelation has a hidden and manifold character that takes us back to the beginning of our journey on the trail of Hillel's message and its semantic proliferation in Amichai's unique novel of vengeance and love.

The first-person narrator, who embarked on an alternative quest for vengeance in Weinburg, finds support in Hillel's words to the skull; Joel, who embarked on a quest for a great fateful love in Jerusalem, puts Hillel's ancient words to creative use. The "historical principle" of the Weinburg narrator confronts the "fateful principle" of the Jerusalem Joel. "They drowned it because it had drowned others, and the fate of those who drowned it is to drown" is confronted by "they loved her because she had loved others, and the fate of her lovers is to drown." Is death the common thread connecting the avenger who drowns others and the life-saving lover? Perhaps. In any case, the lover who realized a great love steps on a mine that awaited him as a fate "from another war," a landmine that is, as it were, "not of this time, not of this place" (611). By contrast, the avenger whose vengeance was unrealized comes home with his eyes still filled with skulls "endless in number" (612), while he himself is alive.

Joel, who has stayed in Jerusalem and has not gone to his native city to close a door that was left open, steps on an old mine on the Mount

Scopus of the late 1950s and is killed. The Mount Scopus of that period, cut off from the city, is still another symbol of the lack of wholeness and of a limb separated from its body. It recurs as well in Eli Amir's *Yasmine* (see chapter 6). In *Yasmine*, too, one of the characters dies in a place thought to be the Hill of Good Counsel, but death lurks among its walls and its rocks.

4

Abjection, Camaraderie, and Passion in Yehoshua Kenaz's *Infiltration*

A Novel of IDF Basic Training in the Early 1950s

> "What do you know about comradeship between fighters like them? It's a form of longing, like love."

Individuals, Virgins to Horror

The story in Yehoshua Kenaz's long novel *Infiltration* (1986) takes place in 1955, between the War of Independence and the Sinai War.[1] Thus, the State of Israel's first war, in 1948–49, is the only war that echoes in the novel. But it is overshadowed by the massive presence of the reprisal operations, clouded in mystery and stirring the imagination, conducted by Paratrooper Unit 101 against the *fedayoun*—gangs of infiltrators from Egypt and Jordan that plagued the young state in the first half of the 1950s. Kenaz conveys the centrality of these operations in the novel through the consciousness of Alon, one of the heroes of the novel. Alon is from a kibbutz in the Beit Shean Valley and is the only kibbutznik in the squad of new recruits at Training Camp 4 "and perhaps in the whole platoon" (*Infiltration*, 21). The tales of heroism and sacrifice of the paratroopers and the elite Unit 101 live inside Alon and spark his imagination, his actions and the things he tells his friends, his behavior, his worldview, and his perception of love, life, and death.

The historical background of *Infiltration*, therefore, is crucially important for understanding the meaning of the novel: an Israeli initiation story in the state's formative years, when, like today, the army is accorded a central place in the lives of young people fresh out of high school.[2]

This novel is the fifth "chapter" in a series of works that compose the history of the Kenazi "self," from childhood through adolescence. The four previous chapters are stories published in the collection entitled *Musical Moment* (1980),[3] while the fifth chapter grew into the voluminous *Infiltration*. The novel's broad canvas and the mythical-fateful character of the young recruits' experiences during their basic training reflect the profound impact of these initial army experiences on their lives; these experiences outweigh everything they encountered during their childhood and pre-army adolescence, and everything that comes later. In 1955, Kenaz was eighteen. The time and place (Training Camp 4) of his army induction, and his artistic inclinations, match the novel's description of the narrator Melabbes, a member of the platoon of new recruits. His nickname is based on the name of the abandoned Arab village (Mulabes or Umlabes) where Petah Tikva was built—and where Kenaz was born and grew up. However, despite the clear autobiographical elements, it is not an autobiographical novel: Melabbes is not the main character, and his life story and family history are not center stage in the novel.[4] The narrator is one individual in the heterogeneous collective that comprises the platoon of basic trainees, who together constitute the real protagonist of the novel.

The novel traces the relationships that develop during basic training among the recent high school graduates and the newcomers who arrived in Israel during the waves of mass immigration in the 1950s—all placed by the army in the same "melting pot." They are strangers, but this foreignness is variable: It waxes and wanes; sometimes it completely disappears, and sometimes it reemerges even between old friends.

The heroes of the novel are young recruits who arrive at Training Base 4 from the IDF induction center and form one of the platoons stationed at the base. They come from different socioeconomic classes: from well-to-do families in the Rehavia neighborhood in Jerusalem and from the transit camps, from agricultural settlements and from cities, and from various ethnic groups, Ashkenazi Jews and Sephardi (Mizrahi) Jews. Most of them are secular, but the platoon also includes Avner—a central figure in the novel, colorful, enigmatic, and complex—who comes from a traditional, Sephardi home and grew up among Ashkenazi Jews; Nahum—who is religiously observant and is portrayed in an exaggerated stereotypical way; and a recruit they call Hedgehog (a nickname inspired by his bristly hair)—who used to be religious (or might be considered "ex-Orthodox" or "religious lite" in the sociological codes of today).

In light of the tense and painful encounter between the native sons and the new immigrants (primarily those from Arab lands, but also with Miller, the strange and detached recruit from Germany who writes notes in a foreign language, and with Zero-Zero, the recruit from Romania), *Infiltration* can be considered not only a novel of Israeli initiation, but also an immigration novel. The broad human diversity that converges into one narrow place—a basic training camp, where the rigid hierarchy rules over everyone with pointless cruelty—intensifies the experience of this convergence, which is already highly charged and serves as a mirror of Israeli society in the 1950s.[5]

Infiltration seeks to examine "the melting pot" concept in the State of Israel's first decade. It is the story of individuals who arrive at a place that is surprising in the horror and humiliation it metes out to those entering its gates. These individuals share a lack of physical fitness and all line up in the novel (that is, during their basic training) in pairs or in groups, and even sometimes coalesce into a single cohesive unit, yet they essentially remain individuals. Each must contend in his own way—hour by hour, from the day they arrive at the base until completing their stay there—with the wickedness that is heaped upon them.

In *Powers of Horror: An Essay on Abjection*, Julia Kristeva cites a motto taken from Louis-Ferdinand Céline's *Journey to the End of the Night*: "One can be a virgin with respect to horror as one is virgin toward voluptuousness."[6] All of the recruits who arrive at Training Base 4, the scene of the novel, are virgins in experiencing horror. The horror hits them with cruel suddenness and accompanies them throughout their months of basic training at the base. Some survive the horror and others break. Their sexual ("voluptuous") virginity—whether they have had some sexual experience or none at all—is not necessarily related to how they deal with horror, humiliation, and abuse, and their commanders' relentless efforts to break their spirit. Creative tactics must be employed against the commanders, who are viewed as the enemy, in order to avoid their malicious treatment. Ultimately, however, the commanders have no direct impact on the connection forged between the individuals, who would never have met and gotten to know each other so intimately if they had not been "sentenced" to this "penal colony." *Infiltration* is a twisted mirror reflecting, on the one hand, a person's basic human need for others, and on the other hand, the fear, humiliation and ridiculousness of this dependence.

The relations between two pairs of friends deserve close analysis: Melabbes, the narrator (as noted, the Kenaz-like figure), who somewhat grudgingly becomes friends with Avner, a fascinating character who does not fit any specific ethnic or social mold; and Micky, the famous soccer player from Hapoel Hadera, who becomes friends with Alon the kibbutznik from Beit Shean. The ethos and education that Alon received, as well as his physical fitness and his readiness to faithfully and enthusiastically carry out any mission assigned to him, are contrary to his placement among those who are physically unfit. The relationship of these two "elite" characters, the soccer player and the kibbutznik, who find themselves in a place which is incompatible with their own self-image and with the way others see them, is examined later in this chapter, which is devoted to the story of the basic training of unfit soldiers in the mid-1950s.

"Invalids, Unfit!"

The first pages of the novel are infused with the atmosphere of a bad dream, quivering between life and death, and confusion, apparently following a loss of consciousness and a difficult reawakening. It is hard for the reader at the beginning of *Infiltration* to understand what the narrator is saying when he tells about seeing "images in black and white," with "a strong sense of urgency in the speed with which they changed places" (3). Where does he see these images and how and why did he fall into this state of disorientation? Only in the second chapter, about ten pages after the nightmarish and idiosyncratic description, the context becomes clear: a military exercise of silencing a sentry. In this exercise, recruits pair off and take turns pressing down on the other's artery to stop the flow of blood to the brain and induce an ugly loss of consciousness. Through a graphic description of this exercise, Kenaz tries to give the reader a taste of the emotional and physical shock the new recruit experiences. The reader and the basic trainees share this sense of disorientation, trepidation, and helplessness. The dangerous training exercise Kenaz chooses to open the novel exemplifies the trainees' traumatic encounter with the army.

And to be sure, these trainees are not destined for combat duty. On the contrary: "All the people you see here are sick," declares Micky Spector, the narrator's partner in the silencing-a-sentry drill. "All of them, for your information, are cripples. Defective combat-worthiness" (7). Micky, a well-known soccer player, belongs—to his great dismay—to the category that he condescendingly criticizes with such scorn and revulsion. Indeed, scorn and revulsion are words that appear frequently in the novel (in addition to humiliation, insult, fear, disgust, nausea, and so on), thus making *Infiltration* a work of twentieth century "abjection" literature, which, according to Kristeva, continues from where the apocalyptic and carnival genres ended.[7] Micky was diagnosed with a heart murmur and he studies this "hated heart murmur" (12) in an effort to overcome the humiliating fate imposed upon him. When the narrator Melabbes is about to grab him, block his artery, and incapacitate him, Micky urges him on: "Don't go easy on me, you hear? Put all your strength into it, because I'm sure to resist. My life instinct is awfully strong; it can break out and rampage like a wild animal" (16).

Kenaz is a shrewd author. If he speaks about the life instinct—libido, eros—at the beginning of the novel, it is reasonable to assume that Thanatos, the death drive, will later join it. The two play a game of opposites in the novel and leave their mark on its ending. Moreover, the silencing-of-a-sentry training exercise that knocks people to the ground at the beginning of the novel will become a reality in the end. This is foreshadowed in the description of what the narrator sees when slowly awakening from "death": "Without moving my face, I let my eyes wander round and saw my friends lying on the ground like me in a circle, their faces pale as death, coming slowly back to life as the ones standing at their heads watched them wake" (4).

By alluding to Haim Gouri's poem "Here Lie Our Bodies," which was written after the Lamed Heh disaster on January 16, 1948, and acquired canonical status in the Israeli culture of mourning, Kenaz parodies the situation: In our case, the soldiers did not embark on a secret mission to save the homeland and their death is not certain and final. Instead, they are a physically unfit bunch whose training, like a game, has rendered them "temporarily dead." But perhaps this exercise contains a hint of what will happen to one "sentry" whose life instinct, unlike Micky's, is not "awfully strong."

But we are getting ahead of ourselves. Kenaz's typical extended family, which is heterogeneous in essence, has yet to be introduced and take shape.[8] It is true that the individuals who arrived at the Sarafand (Tzrifin) camp have something in common—"all the people you see here are sick," as Micky declared—but this is not an element that unites them. On the contrary, each individual bears his own sickness, along with the humiliation and suffering it confers upon him and his surroundings: "Over here, anyone who's weak or falls down on the job gets everyone into trouble, not only himself. Over here, being weak is like being a thief or a traitor" (10), says Micky, for whom the world is divided into sick and healthy, weak and strong. This dichotomous worldview is congruent with the tough military framework, which places extreme demands on both body and spirit, and where sickness is viewed as an enemy. Since *Infiltration* is a story about basic training, there is no fear stemming from the horrors of war or an external enemy. The war is waged between the basic trainee and his commanders, who belittle him, disparage him, and pound him to the dust—and most of all, terrorize him. Moreover, many of the wars described in the novel are internal, fighting the enemy that resides within us.

For example, Zero-Zero, a new immigrant from Romania, whose insulting nickname has an ostensibly rational explanation—his military ID number ends with two zeroes—already asks to see a doctor on his first day at the base, claiming that his heart is racing. Zero-Zero is the only married soldier in the platoon. In the silencing-a-sentry drill, he thought he was going to die and the fetal position—from which he was slow to emerge—expresses his desire to return to the womb, to the prenatal period, and perhaps also foreshadows the son he will have.

Zero-Zero is a hypochondriac, but his ailments extend beyond this. His sadistic commander threatens to charge him with attempted suicide because of Zero-Zero's constantly inflamed eyes and the shaving scratches on his face. This type of threat against a person like Zero-Zero is an example of "creative hazing typical of previous generations," as Amos Harel explains in his book on the new IDF. These are old phenomena of abuse for the sake of abuse.[9] But just as the simulated death of silencing-a-sentry later occurs in reality, the imagined suicide of Zero-Zero, which was intended only to mock and humiliate him, will later play out in a frightening incident. In one of the live fire exercises, Zero-Zero pulls out the grenade pin, but instead of tossing the grenade toward the ditch at the bottom of the hill, it slips from his hand and falls behind his back. The kibbutznik Alon, an exemplary figure—it is not clear why he is here, in this platoon of inferior and sickly trainees—rushes to the grenade before it explodes, picks it up and hurls it downhill, thus preventing a tragedy. Zero-Zero is ordered to stand in front of his comrades, and the platoon commander, Raffy Nagar, tells them about Zero-Zero's "dreadful designs and the massacre that had been averted thanks to the alertness of our instructors and the resourcefulness of Alon. 'You can thank your lucky stars that there are a few men in this platoon.'" Alon was crowned a hero, while Zero-Zero, humiliated and terrified, "put all the blame on his old enemy, his long-suffering body" (366). It is interesting to learn at the end of the novel that a robust life instinct flows in the sick body of this "zero," who is accused of attempting to kill himself and of plotting to kill his comrades, while Alon—handsome, resourceful, physically nimble, and valiant—is the one who succumbs to emotional infirmity.

Another stark contrast between the two is evident during the course of basic training. Zero-Zero never stops complaining about strange palpitations in his heart, "clinging to them as to his last salvation" (14). Alon, on the other hand, who saved the platoon from a "massacre," hopes the army will quickly realize it erred in assigning him to a group of frail losers. In Alon's mind, his natural place is with the paratroopers.

Alon's depiction in the novel is complex and deceptive. He fits the stereotype of a kibbutznik—an idealist, he excels in obeying and executing orders, and speaks the language of collective uplift. The consideration and assistance he always gives to his comrades in the platoon stand in contrast to the manifestations of egocentrism, narcissism, isolation, distrust, disloyalty, sectarianism, and antisocial sentiments he sees only in others. He alone is free of such negative characteristics, he believes. On the other hand, his perfection calls for a closer look and his hidden illness gradually comes to light. Still, it is unclear whether Alon is the one who is ill, or whether it is the kibbutz society, whose values he has internalized.

"During the first four decades following the establishment of the state, the combat force was primarily led by members of the labor settlements (moshavim and kibbutzim, who, in those years, sometimes accounted for over 30% of IDF commanders, fighters, and casualties, more than four times their proportion of the population)," Harel writes in his book.[10] Alon, therefore, belongs to this society, which raised its children on the mythos of mobilization and sacrifice, and is convinced that only in the Paratroopers Brigade can he fulfill the values on which he was educated. At the end of this chapter, we again compare the feeble-bodied Zero-Zero to Alon, who is always ready for any order or mission.

On Friendship, Life, and Death

As noted, the story in *Infiltration* takes place in 1955. The platoon's basic training begins in late summer of that year; it includes the High Holidays in early fall and concludes as heavy rainfall threatens to disrupt the graduation ceremony. During this period, the trainees return to their homes on leave for Rosh Hashanah vacation, but spend Yom Kippur and Simchat Torah on the base. A seminal event in the state's history is noted among other historical incidents that seep into the novel: the discovery of oil in the Negev.

A few days after returning to the base from Rosh Hashanah vacation, Hedgehog bursts into the platoon's hut and announces: "They've found oil in the Negev! There's oil in the State of Israel!" (360). He saw a newspaper with a sensational picture of the mighty black stream, gushing from the depths of the earth at a site called Hulikaat (today: Heletz). On Friday morning, September 23, two days before Yom Kippur in 1995, oil surged from the rig, and the event precisely places the novel on the axis of time. Hedgehog, the Jerusalemite, a hyperactive character, screams out the exciting news as if warning of a disaster. Alon, the kibbutznik, responds in the more restrained, noble manner that typifies him: "If they've already hit on the place, from now on they'll find more and more. It changes everything. This is a great day!" (360).

I noted earlier that the reprisal actions against the fedayoun in the early 1950s have a presence in the novel. Like the oil find at Heletz, these raids help to set the plot on the axis of time and connect it to historical events. In the novel, Alon describes the secret operations of bold fighters. The tales about the reprisal actions captivate him and he adds his own touch to them when telling the stories to his only friend in basic training, Micky Spector. The friendship between the two begins with heated ideological arguments early in basic training: Micky, the cynic and individualist, constantly challenges Alon's innocent collectivist worldview. In time, they stop their wrangling after Micky realizes that Alon is exceptional in remaining true to himself and his core beliefs. At a certain stage in the development of their relationship, Micky examines how Michel de Montaigne's essay *On Friendship* (which his aging father reads to him during the Rosh Hashanah vacation from the army) pertains to the deepening friendship between him and Alon. The realization that Alon is capable of total, utopian friendship in the spirit of Montaigne and that he, Micky, is incapable of this, gradually takes root in his consciousness.

Infiltration deals with muck, latrines, bodily excretions, stench, and illness. Moreover, this story of basic training, which includes intense scenes that go far beyond a realistic-documentary depiction of the experiences, is based on dread and self-pity. The narrator himself explains at the beginning of the novel that his description is not objective because of "the fear that had numbed me for the past few days, preventing me from taking anything at face value" (9). He continues, "perhaps because the fear and the meaninglessness had made me feel sorrier for myself than I had ever felt before in my life, and tempted me to take off for the borderland between reality and fantasy" (9–10). Against the backdrop of the novel's many manifestations of abjection, and due to the inclination of the narrator (a frightened and humiliated trainee himself) to mix reality and fantasy, and to assign a mythological quality to events, the novel rises here and there to peaks of beauty, unity, and purity.

One of these peaks occurs during an extraordinarily beautiful night, one of the wonderful religious moments in the novel, when Alon and

Micky are on guard duty together, and the first autumn rain catches them by surprise. The drama of the weather plays an important role in the emotional process the trainees undergo: They enter the army in the heat of summer and feel the blaze of foreignness and fear for weeks, which the novel portrays as a period of shock and suffering. Then autumn arrives, slightly cooling the fears and relieving the pain to some degree. By now, the commanders' caprices, harassment, and hollering have become a tolerable and less threatening routine. The first rain of the season is a sign of hope, of time moving toward the end of the ordeal: The bad air is becoming purified.

Micky and Alon are on guard duty by the armory. The other soldiers in the platoon, including the narrator Melabbes, are asleep in the hut, filling it with the sounds and smells of slumber. But the sound of rain also reaches the hut. A cry of joy rises in the narrator's heart: The first rain penetrates his sleep in the hut, stirs his dream, and wakes him. What a contrast between this beautiful awakening by the first rain and the rough awakening at the beginning of the book after the ugly loss of consciousness in the silencing-a-sentry drill. They are lying there on the hard ground scorched by the summer heat and now the ground is softening from the first rain. The hut, the platoon's home—which fills at night with the sickly sounds of sleep, snores, mumbles, coughs, bad breath, and body odor—is instantly purified. The sound of the rain reaches Melabbes's ears:

> I raised my head to hear more clearly, to banish the remnants of the dream. Was it really the common, monotonous, domestic sound that was always capable of touching my heart with delight, like an unexpected meeting with faraway places? I listened to this sound, wanting to be certain that I wasn't mistaken and that I wasn't sleeping . . . Everyone was sleeping. I got out of bed, went over to the door, and stood looking at the first rain. (398)

Melabbes experiences the first rain in the hut while the platoon sleeps, and is swept up in a wave of nostalgia for his childhood in Petah Tikva. At the same time, Micky and Alon are guarding at the armory, each one experiencing the first rain in a way commensurate with his respective personality. Alon, the secular kibbutznik, with his typical religiosity, is enchanted by the loud rumbling of the first rain and Micky begins to see him as a religious person. This is when Micky takes an introspective look at their friendship. "The more I know him, the less I know him," Micky says to himself.

> The obsessed, lonely expression on Alon's face reminded him of the hostility the kibbutznik had aroused in him during the first weeks of their friendship, when he had taken advantage of every opportunity to provoke ridiculous quarrels and arguments over matters that he had never, in fact, felt very strongly about. Did he already understand that it was a kind of battle to establish the conditions of their friendship, its limits, its depth? (399)

The first rain that falls on the earth and saturates it sometime after the oil discovery at Heletz can be seen as a thesis and antithesis, complementing and contradicting the surge of oil from the earth, reflecting its power. The oil springs from its depths; the rain seeps into it. The paean to the earth that Alon recites to Micky as they stand on night guard duty, surprised by the first rain, makes it clear to Micky how different he is from his friend, who can identify with the soil, who can personify and extol it, and whose love for it is greater than a man's love for a woman. It later becomes apparent that Alon, the Zionist patriot, knows that the soil covers secrets pertaining to identity, nationhood, and affiliation that are not necessarily Zionist. In the end, we see that he is prepared to live for this land, but also ready to die for it and be buried in its soil. Micky is not cut out for such romantics. Here is the paean to the land that Alon recites at the end of that fateful summer of basic training:

> After the death of summer, it comes to life, it breathes. Can't you feel the warmth of its breath, its marvelous smell? See how sweet it is, like the breath of the girl you love. The smell of the dust and the dry soil beginning to wake up. Sometimes it seems to me that if only it was quiet, perfectly quiet, you'd be able to hear that breathing. You'd be able to hear the earth breathing. Can you just imagine it? (399)

After Alon's effusive display of emotion toward the soil—soaking up the first rain, rising like a phoenix from its summertime death—Micky notes laconically: "It's always like that after the first rain." This dialogue illustrates the extremely different personalities of Alon and Micky. Nonetheless, on this night of the first rain, the two friends become closer and bare their souls to each other. Micky, a proud and reticent person, tells Alon that he is a virgin. "Maybe you won't believe this, but I've never gone to bed with a girl . . . When it comes to sex, they don't want me" (406), he discloses in response to Alon's candid stories about his parents, his special relationship with his girlfriend Dafna, and especially his love of country, which goes beyond ordinary patriotic sentiment and borders on sickness: "I love this country. I really love it. A thousand times over I'm prepared to give everything for it—my blood, my life" (404). Alon is aware that his love of country, for this land, is seen even by his kibbutz friends as sick. One time, on Mount Arbel, he says: "I had to turn away to hide the tear of emotion, of love, that came into my eyes when I looked down at that landscape" (404). This confession is no different—in its intensity, depth, and intimacy—from Micky's disclosure about his erotic frustration, and he says to Alon: "I told you because I wanted to share something personal, something that hurts me, with you. Like you told me all kinds of things" (407).

The things that Alon tells Micky are all connected in one way or another to love and death for this land: his emotional description of the soil's rebirth ("after the death of summer") and his readiness "to give everything for it—my blood, my life." The respective secrets of Alon and Micky seem to be very different: One speaks of his longing to love and engage in intimate relations with a woman; the other speaks of his love for the soil and his erotic relationship with it. However, the land in Zionist romantics is always compared to a virgin woman, as an object of sexual conquest, and the woman and Great Mother are always associated with the land. An example of an explicit sexual connection between the land and the first rain can be found in Yehuda Amichai's novel *Not of This Time, Not of This Place*, which takes place one summer in the late 1950s. The two parallel story lines in Amichai's novel come to a close at the end of the summer. Here is one of the signs of the end of the Jerusalemite love: "because the summer reached its long-drawn-out conclusion, with man and land in a state of exhaustion. Exhausted, the land is laid on its back, breathing heavily after its summer-long struggle. And now it's waiting for the great rapist, the first rain" (*Not of This Time, Not of This Place* [Hebrew], 600).

Montaigne's essay on accepting the other—"because it was he, because it was myself" (*Infiltration*, 224)—which Micky's aging father, a teacher by profession, reads to him, legitimizes and explains the deep friendship that develops between Micky and Alon, despite their differentness—or maybe because of it. "How different we are," Micky says to himself. "Everything about us is the opposite, even our fathers" (406). We later learn that their biological mothers are also completely different and play an opposite role in the lives and perspectives of the two friends. And of course, each has a different connection to Mother Earth, and this difference is significant and fateful.

Togetherness, the Individual, the Unit, and Love of Country

The great disparity in their attitude toward the homeland is evident in the following comparison: In the silencing-a-sentry exercise at the beginning of the novel, when Melabbes is about to "silence" him, Micky declares jokingly: "It's good to die for our country!" (17). It seems that what Micky spouts as a parody of Joseph Trumpeldor's words, which became the slogan of the Israeli culture of self-sacrifice, is regarded by Alon as profoundly serious. Alon was raised on the value of self-sacrifice, and he has internalized this in a literal and dangerous way.

Kenaz establishes a convincing family biography to explain the different views of the two friends vis-à-vis what is called "love of homeland." Alon's father was killed in one of the pre-state battles. Alon was ten years old at the time; his father was thirty. Alon always carries with him the last photograph of his father—"a young man, tall and thin, in short khaki pants, a submachine gun dangling from his shoulder" (400–401). While the image of Alon's father remains young and frozen forever, Micky's father is growing old before his eyes, and his hatred of the state, kibbutzim, and Ben-Gurion increases with his age. Alon believes that if his father were alive, he would act like Uri Illan (an IDF soldier who killed himself in a

Syrian prison on January 13, 1955, in order to avoid divulging state secrets, and left a note saying "I didn't betray"). Micky's father, in contrast, says that the State of Israel will not survive and Micky, in analyzing his father's frustration, believes that his father even wishes for the state's demise (400). The mothers of the two friends are also fundamentally different. The reader meets Micky's mother when the platoon goes on holiday leave. The mother is portrayed as a vibrant woman who looks after her son and husband, and keeps her family on an even keel. Alon's mother, on the other hand, suffers from bouts of depression and in Alon's opinion, "It's worse than death" (405).

Alon is captivated by the cult of death—molded by the loss of his father, his mother's depression, the sanctification of kibbutz members who fell in battle, and his own special personality. He obsessively reads *Scrolls of Fire*, which includes letters his father wrote to his mother. The fact that he prefers to read them in the book and not "the actual letters themselves" shows the extent to which the public-propaganda perspective has taken over him. His private father has disappeared, replaced by a condensed figure encompassing the world of all of the fallen who have been memorialized in written tributes as heroic figures worthy of glorification and imitation. After they take the book from him—the kibbutz sees that he is becoming a victim of the literature of heroism and death—Alon continues to read other memorial books, such as *Friends Tell About Jimmy*. Eventually, all of the fallen take on a single face: the face of his father. Micky, on the other hand, argues that love of country is only one type of love. He explains, "A person can't only experience his country . . . But there's the world outside your country too, and there's the world inside yourself, your most private world, that accompanies you wherever you go, whatever you experience. The world that distinguishes you from other people" (405).

Alon's response is that everything is mixed together. Social life and national life are part of one's private life. "There's no difference" (405). Just as all of the memorial books for the fallen merge within Alon, and just as his private father becomes a symbol for all of the fallen (or perhaps the opposite, all of the fallen blend into the portrait of his father, erasing the distinction between his private and national father)—Alon's private world is swallowed up by his patriotic fervor.

In his book *Commando Unit 101*, Dan Margalit writes:

> The name 101, cloaked in mystery, spreads in the kibbutzim and moshavim. Few know about it at first, and then their number grows ... The rumor of the unit's existence spreads like wildfire in the kibbutzim. In the dining halls, they speak of it aloud and admiringly. They say that its members cross the border on patrols and participate in reprisal raids. Young members want to join the unit, and look for inside connections to get into the camp. "It reminds me of Ali Baba and the Forty Thieves," someone jokes. "Everyone wants to know the magic formula for opening the gates of the cave."[11]

Alon, like the other teenagers on the kibbutzim (and even more so), is enthralled by the tales spun around the unit. "The unit's existence is not a secret, but there is little talk about it," Dan Margalit writes. "Those who are not among its fighters hear more rumors and legends than facts, and there are still many in the army who don't know and refuse to believe."[12] Alon knows and is drawn into believing, and on that magical night of the first rain, on guard duty, he shares some of the secrets about the unit with Micky. "I trust you not to talk about it to anyone" (408), he says, and reveals:

> They're real people, I know them. I've seen them. I've heard them talking about their missions. I've seen them relaxing and having fun. Most of the things are secret and I can't talk about them. But even from the little I have told you, you can see what kind of fighters they are. (403)

After declaring that "they're real people," and that he saw them with his own eyes, he reiterates that they are indeed extraordinary:

> Once Meir Har-Zion himself came to spend the weekend with us. And other guys from the unit came too, and they all sat and talked and joked and laughed. And me, I was just a little kid, I sat in the corner and tried to make myself invisible. Listening to every word that came out of their mouths. Looking at them as if they were gods come down to earth. You can't imagine the kind of men they are. I'd already heard of

their operations and their hikes and trips to all kinds of places across the border. (408)

Unit 101 was created in August 1953 and operated for only five months before being absorbed into the Paratroopers' Brigade in January 1954. Its short existence and small number of fighters undoubtedly contributed to the legends it spawned, but this does not diminish the derring-do of its fighters. Even today, Meir Har-Zion, who settled in Kochav Hayarden, a hilltop overlooking the Jordan Valley, is considered a son of gods, residing on Mount Olympus. Alon, Kenaz's protagonist, regrets the fact that Unit 101 was absorbed into the Paratroopers' Brigade: "When they broke them up and attached them to the paratroopers, in my opinion it was a mistake" (403)—and he continues to listen with unparalleled attention to every story about them. During the night guard duty with Micky, Alon tells him, with fervent reverence, about the reprisal raid known as "Baruch 1," which took place on June 29, 1954. Alon heard about it "about a month before my conscription, from someone on the kibbutz, an officer in the paratroopers who knows all the fighters from the commando unit and is really friends with them" (408).

Alon tells the well-known story of heroism in a palpable way, as if he had witnessed the scenes and heard the sounds. His short account of the story shows his emotional involvement in the action. He tells how Meir Har-Zion carries the injured Yitzhak Jibli on his back, as heavy gunfire surrounds the fighters returning from their mission against the Arab Legion in Azzun, near Qalqilya. Jibli was injured twice, in the leg and in the neck, and Alon describes his blood spilling onto Har-Zion: "It covered all his clothes, and he went on carrying him, panting like a bull and hearing Jibli's groans and his cries of pain the whole time" (40). At two o'clock in the morning, the fighters reach an olive grove. They still have eight miles to walk, "over difficult mountain terrain, full of enemy ambushes. And Jibli began to plead with them to leave him behind and go back without him. Wounded as he was in the leg and with a hole in his neck, bleeding, he thought about them and he didn't want them to fall into enemy hands because of him" (409). The painful negotiation between the injured fighter and his comrades, the excruciating decision to accede to his pleas and leave him lying on the ground in the olive grove, his awful night there "suffering terrible pains, barely conscious," falling into captivity and the torture he undergoes—all are described by Alon as if he had actually observed the events. The description of Jibli's interrogation in captivity includes a comparative reference to Uri Illan, another Israeli interrogated in captivity, who acquired a mythic status in Israeli consciousness. Alon concludes his account with observations about the connection between the body and the mind during torture, as if he had personally experienced this:

> Whatever they asked him, he repeated his name, rank, and serial number. And if he added anything, it was only his blood type and shoe size. It drove them wild. They tortured him without stopping and he didn't say anything. He didn't betray us. Like Uri Illan behaved in the Syrian prison a little while later. None of us knows what it means to be tortured. We can't imagine it. What happens to a man when he's subjected to such pain, when his body's broken? What happens to his will then? To his mind? To his life force, which is so strong, so dominant in us? What kind of strength do you need to remember who and what you are, when they break your body, when the most terrible pains cloud your mind, so that you begin to forget who you are? (409–10)

This heroic description undoubtedly foreshadows the torture Alon will himself experience, but in a wretched and humiliating context that will dampen his life instinct. Jibli's comrades left him injured in the field because they had no other alternative, but remained with him in spirit and soul as brothers-in-arms who shared an uncompromising commitment. Alon's innocent rendition of the story emphasizes the deep identification of the fighters he reveres toward the comrade they left behind, bleeding. "Har-Zion and all his other friends suffered terribly. They identified with what was happening to Jibli all the time; they understood exactly what he was going through there. Every single one of them felt as if it was happening to him personally, that Jibli was suffering for them" (410). When Alon remains behind bleeding, albeit in completely different circumstances, there is no one who feels the same way and no one to support him. The mythological unit's brotherhood-in-arms is the antithesis to the somewhat forced and mundane friendship that develops between Alon and Micky. Alon, naive and pure, does indeed see his friendship with Micky as akin to the sublime camaraderie of Unit 101. However, Micky—skeptical, cynical, and rational—is unable to meet Alon's larger-than-life expectations. Tragically, the fate and achievements of Unit 101 fighters stand as an antithesis to Alon's fate and achievements as a fighter. Alon desperately wants to be like those "sons of gods," but is unsuccessful. He remains alone, without camaraderie and without a unit.

On that night of the first rain, Alon does not yet know that Micky will be absent when he needs him, and he shares his secrets with him. He decides to share with Micky secrets from the paratroopers—those who are "continuing the tradition of the Palmach, of the War of Independence . . . the chosen few, the elite, who voluntarily sacrifice themselves for all the rest" (403)—because Micky had referred to them in the past as "mercenaries." Now, on the night of the first rain, the night of their greatest intimacy, Alon demands of Micky his/their rightful due. Micky is not entirely convinced. His individualist-pragmatic worldview is also reflected in the psychological explanation he offers to explain the daring of the elite unit that was absorbed into the Paratroopers' Brigade. In his opinion, their daring and actions are not only spurred by a pure love of country, as Alon believes:

> You didn't understand what I meant when I spoke about mercenaries. There was no reason to get insulted. I didn't say they were hired murderers, that they did it for money or anything like that. I only said you couldn't be sure that they risked their lives purely out of Zionism and patriotism and all that. It's possible that they need that stuff for psychological reasons—that it's necessary to them for themselves. It's possible that if they didn't have the opportunity to live that kind of life in a respectable military framework, and to be considered heroes of Israel, they would find other ways of expressing their instincts. It's possible that they have to prove something to themselves: that they're not afraid of death, that they're superior to other people, that they're permitted what's forbidden to others. I don't know. But it's possible, just possible that some of them might have turned into murderers to find an outlet for their instincts. (403–4)

Alon dismisses Micky's thesis and emphasizes the value of devotion and fraternity among those fighters, something you cannot find among gangs of murderers. Then he goes on to tell his good friend the story of Jibli falling into captivity. He ends the story by describing how the injured Jibli sang to himself in the olive grove in order to stay awake. In his "hoarse, throttled, grating" (15) voice, "twisting in pain and intense emotion" (410), Alon sings "The Cannons' Roar" and it is no longer clear whether the lone soldier left at night in the field is Jibli or Alon. Kenaz blends the two, while leaving Micky outside to observe them from a safe distance. It is difficult to say which of the two is Kenaz's favorite, Micky or Alon. It seems that he has strong love for Alon and respects Micky's clear choice in life, despite his despised heart murmur. Kenaz's humanistic perspective sanctifies life rather than land.

And thus ends the night of first rain, one of the high points of lyricism and religiosity in *Infiltration*.

A Mirage of Heroism

Alon is assigned to be the leader of the group of basic trainees at the beginning of the novel. Thus, from the outset, his ambition to excel as a soldier and his readiness to serve as a role model are apparently evident. His fellow soldiers in the platoon and the reader meet him for the first time near the end of the opening chapter, entitled "Heart Murmur."[13] This title is intended, of course, to convey the chilling fear and trepidation the military camp casts upon the young trainees during their first days at the base. At the same time, the title refers to a specific protagonist, Micky Spector, Alon's close and only friend, whose heart murmur is the reason that he is here, in the platoon of unfit trainees at Training Camp 4.

Micky, the product of a completely different home and family than Alon, is depicted as the antithesis of Alon—in his essence, his worldview, his aspirations, his appearance, and his emotional makeup. Even Micky's bodily heart murmur is the opposite of Alon's latent emotional "heart murmur," which is revealed slowly and gradually. The two trainees also appear in the opening chapter at opposite times. Micky is the first trainee the narrator, Melabbes, encounters when awakening from the silencing-a-sentry exercise, and Alon is the last trainee introduced to the platoon and to the reader.

The trainees are mentioned, briefly or at length, in the context of that ugly exercise, when they are described as dreamers, sick, or dead; or in the context of the camaraderie that begins to develop among them— "Once again the barriers fell, conversation flowed freely and the sound of laughter rose loudly in the air. The last vestiges of shyness and strangeness, which only a short while before had still kept the individuals and groups apart, were dispelled" (10). But Alon is not part of the collective that is coalescing. He makes a dramatic entrance in the story, and the first chapter ends in surprise with his unique entry onto the scene. His arrival generates suspense and curiosity about his identity. Who is that person who appears suddenly out of nowhere, sort of hovering, like a god?

> At the end of the path, we saw someone running towards us at last. A tall, broad-shouldered fellow, his kitbag on his shoulder, running with light, very springy steps. But for the badgeless beret on his head and the new, still dark uniform, we would have taken him for one of the instructors. He came up and stood in front of us. His face was sunburnt and slightly freckled, his hair was fair, his expression somewhat tense and arrogant. He dropped his kitbag to the ground, put his hands on his hips and said in a hoarse, throttled, grating voice: "Hi fellows, my name's Alon." (15)

Alon, who was already chosen as leader of the trainees at the beginning of basic training, is appointed to serve as platoon leader during one of the nighttime training exercises. The roles assigned to Alon and his ardor to excel in them do not prevent Benny—the sadistic, cynical, cruel, and fanatical instructor—from heaping abuse and scorn upon him. (Melabbes recognizes Benny from elementary school as someone capable of disgusting actions.) Alon's natural excellence makes him a target for all of the commander's satanic urges. Perhaps Kenaz wanted to say something about the army's distorted hierarchies that place the pure-hearted Alon in the hands of a heartless commander.

In any case, after the wonderful night of the first rain—when Micky and Alon discover each other and their secrets, and when the reader, who admires Alon and loves him for his perfection, begins to realize that this angelic Alon is a bit psychologically unstable—there is a night exercise in a citrus orchard less than an hour from Sarafand. During this exercise, Alon's infirmity is exposed in its full severity. We already learn during the night of the first rain that Micky will leave for soccer practice and miss some of the platoon's activities, in effect abandoning Alon. This exercise, like other nighttime exercises, simulates military operations. Like Alon, who wants to be a fearless paratrooper setting out in the dead of night on perilous missions, the others are also caught up in a momentary illusion that these are real military operations:

> Everything was carried out with an air of tight-lipped gravity; it was all so real that this time too, as on the other night-training exercises, the strange suspicion stole into my heart that this time it was serious, like in the combat units, and I longed to enter into it whole-heartedly, with total identification. (415)

But while the basic trainees ultimately know to distinguish a simulation exercise from a real operation, Alon falls easy prey to nocturnal visions: He thinks he sees a suspicious figure carrying a weapon, one of the fedayoun, and fires a shot at him. It is not an accidental discharge; he opens fire deliberately.

"You're nuts! You shouldn't be allowed to carry a gun" (425), cries Raffy Nagar, a relatively moderate commander, and this time it is clear that the insult is not just for the sake of insult, but is actually a true statement that finally and saliently exposes Alon's hidden "heart murmur." He is not facing an external enemy he should shoot; rather, he is his own enemy. In a moment of clarity, he realizes that "something inside you is working against you, like a fifth column. Tripping you up, deceiving you, flattering you" (427). That is, he himself is aware that another force, perhaps another Alon, is operating in his psyche and threatening the coolheaded and well-respected Alon. Early in basic training, Raffy Nagar lauds Alon as a resourceful soldier for saving the platoon from a "massacre" when he pounced on the live grenade that slipped from Zero-Zero's hand and hurled it down the slope. Now Raffy defines Alon as a crazy person who is not responsible for his actions.

In the following pages, Kenaz juxtaposes psychological disturbances, mental illnesses, and sadism versus masochism. The sadist is Benny, the instructor, and the masochist is Alon, the basic trainee, who now, when the game turns into live reality, can become like Jibli and Uri Illan, who stood steadfastly against a brutal enemy, because "what's all this compared to the torture of Uri Illan in the Syrian jail, or the suffering of Jibli in the Jordanian jail? Here it's only a game of humiliation" (432). Anyone wishing to learn about the abuse and humiliation IDF commanders were capable of inflicting upon their subordinates in the 1950s can read the detailed and shocking description of the brutality toward Alon. God endowed Alon with a pure heart, but planted a sick spirit in it. One of the symptoms of his illness is his attraction to the soil, which we begin to see on the wonderful night of first rain. However, while we learn of his erotic connection to the soil on the night of first rain, here this connection is mixed with a powerful death wish, with the desire to become one with the beloved land and snuggle in its lap. The connection, seen on the night of first rain as romantic, turns morbid. Eros and Thanatos, pride and humiliation, vigor and infirmity, wage battle against each other in the character of Alon, foreshadowing the tragic denouement of the beautiful Israeli:

> Benny leads him to the platoon and the mess for lunch. Enemy to the left! Enemy to the right! Up! Down! Up! Down! . . . The mud in this place smells like rust. His face is stuck in it, his body suddenly refuses to rise. Benny kicks his thigh: "Up! You miserable nut! Get up!" No one's coming to rescue him. No one's waiting for him anywhere. There's no other place for him . . . Benny's boot pushes his face into the mud, his eyes are closed, and like a sigh of relief the temptation wells up in him not to open them, to go on burying his face in this soft, damp lap whose taste is the taste of rust, and to fall asleep. (433)

Hints of Alon's longing for death appear even earlier: Alon knows there is no suspicious figure in the citrus grove and that he is inventing this in order to experience the role of the fearless warrior, even if only for a fleeting moment. Deep inside, Alon understands that he is shooting at himself, because he is his own enemy. In the wake of this embarrassing act ("you can forget about your dream of a transfer to the paratroops"), death begins to seduce him. Kenaz provides a number of lyrical expressions of the longing for death that captivates Alon. One of them is taken from the speech by Eleazar Ben Yair to the people besieged at Masada:

> Why, pray, should we fear death if we love to repose in sleep? And is it not absurd to run after the freedom of this life and grudge ourselves the freedom of eternity? It might be expected that we, so carefully taught at home, would be an example to others of readiness to die (427).[14]

Alon wonders whether Eleazar really meant this "or was he just trying to rid them of the natural, physical, paralyzing fear of the deed? Of the hatred of death?" Because if the latter is true, then death is merely a "good deal, worth their while" (427). After all, if it is good and pleasant to die, as the politician Eleazar Ben Yair declares, then "life is the calamity for man, not death. Death gives freedom to our souls and lets them depart to their own pure home where they will know nothing of any calamity" (428).[15] This means that there is nothing heroic about the act of suicide. On the contrary, it is egotistical and entails no sacrifice. Alon, however, is seeking a different death, "performed in pain, in the love of life" (428). He longs for a sacrificial death that brings no reward:

> Without any consolation. Flying in the face of self-interest. Under an olive tree, with the summer sky above you clear and deep, full of stars like windows into infinity, on enemy territory full of the smells of an ancient, rural Canaan, you feel the blood of belief ceaselessly flowing out of you and soaking into the earth, returning to it after its wanderings, homeward bound. (428)

Again, the romantic-heroic picture of Jibli lying on the beloved land—the land of Canaan, the homeland, even if part of it is in enemy territory—serves as a model for Alon of sacrifice and readiness to die for a sacred purpose (nation, state, comrades). While Jibli did not die during that starry night in the olive grove, he was ready to die. And so is Alon.

Micky returns to the base from his soccer practice on the eve of Simchat Torah. As noted, basic training started in late summer and continues until November. When Alon tries to persuade Micky that he really did see a man in the dark, in the citrus grove ("his face covered with a keffiyeh, and only his eyes showing. You know I'm not crazy"), Micky answers dismissively: "Alonchik, before long you'll forget all about it . . . Basic training doesn't go on forever" (439). Micky, who sought to encourage Alon, has yet to realize that this basic training is eternal in Alon's mind: Alon will eternally be considered a victim of this horrible basic training, which brought humiliation that he cannot bear to live with. And he will always be remembered as a failure by Micky, his only friend during this period of his life.

Mud, Shifting Sands, Potsherds, and Orchards

Alon's ambivalent attraction to the soil is expressed in numerous ways in *Infiltration*. We see his excitement when the first rain rouses the land from its summertime slumber. We see how Alon responds when Benny, the brutal instructor, presses his head into the mud with his boot: Instead of feeling absolute humiliation, Alon seeks to snuggle in the soft and damp lap of the earth, close his eyes, and fall asleep. Alon perceives this urge to sleep, which Kenaz likens to a longing for death, as an awakening of libido, as a pulse of life. "Listen," he tells Micky when the two try to update each other upon Micky's return to the base,

> Something really weird happened. At the height of my tiredness, the climax of despair and humiliation and pain, with my face in the mud, I suddenly felt sexually aroused . . . Don't laugh. Seriously. I don't understand why, but suddenly, when my head was deep down in the mud, I could hardly breathe, it happened, without any connection to a particular girl or desire, just like that, of its own accord, for no reason . . . I did feel that it had some connection to what was happening to me, as if it was some kind of rebellion of the natural life force against the pressure,

against the repression. When he yelled at me to get up, I didn't want to. As if he was interrupting me in the middle of making love to the most beautiful girl in the world. (439)

Thus, the land simultaneously embodies eros and Thanatos for Alon. But the land is not only mud or solid ground. It also includes sand dunes, and Kenaz makes full use of the many metaphorical, national, and political meanings he can elicit from the sand dunes of Ashkelon, where the platoon goes to train.

The shifting sands are mythicized because of the fear they stir among the trainees, who are supposed to navigate this arid, borderless space, without any paths or landmarks. The land they tread upon is treacherous; it is as if they are walking in place, sinking up to their knees in the deceptive dunes and getting nowhere. And their destination, where they need to set up their tents, is nowhere in sight. "Was this the wilderness that had to be crossed in order to experience the transformation, to forget the journey, to lose our way in it, in order to reach the real destination?" (459) the narrator Melabbes wonders. In his mind, he compares the platoon trudging in the sand to the Israelites who wandered in the desert for forty years before reaching—very belatedly, and only after undergoing a process of recuperation—an inhabited land. While Melabbes is part of "a small group of stragglers, wandering amid the dunes, not looking at each other, like the survivors of a shipwreck each trying to save his own life" (460), Alon, who was worried at first that he would not be allowed to participate in the navigation exercise because of the shot he fired in the citrus grove, set out on the mission with his usual passion to excel. To prove to himself and to the others that he is strong and superior, Alon forcibly lifts Rahamim Ben-Hamo, the laughing-stock of the platoon, onto his back. Again, Alon is trying at every opportunity to emulate the Unit 101 fighters he so reveres. Meir Har-Zion carried the injured Yitzhak Jibli on his back in difficult terrain, and now Alon too is carrying on his back an "injured soldier" in sand dunes that are difficult to traverse.

As on the night of the first rain, which saturates the land awakening from its slumber, here too, among the dunes that cover the solid ground,

Micky and Alon express their views, each in his own way, on what will be revealed in the sands.

Twice in *Infiltration* the sand covers a reality buried underneath it: archeological artifacts from ancient times and the life that existed before the Israeli reality of 1948 repressed, buried, or expelled it. In both cases, remnants of an Arab reality are found.

Alon notices Zero-Zero tossing something into the sand. This time, it is not the platoon Alon rushes to save from a "massacre" (as in the incident of the live grenade that slipped from Zero-Zero's hand), but rather an archeological artifact that expresses the richness of this land. It turns out to be two pieces of ancient pottery that broke in Zero-Zero's pouch. He found the pottery intact on a mound but was no longer interested in the pieces of clay after it broke, so he cast them into the sand. Alon, poking in the sand, finds the two shards and pieces them together to restore the artifact, which he believes was used as a lamp. He explains to his fellow soldiers who gather around him that it is not of biblical vintage. Though they were in the dunes of Ashkelon, which was part of Philistine, the pottery is from the Arab period. In Alon's opinion, the lamp indicates that their navigation exercise is taking place in an area full of ancient mounds containing valuable archeological artifacts. But Hedgehog, who comes from a religious home, does not find the juxtaposition of antiquities and Arabs plausible: "If it's from the Arab period like you say . . . then it's not so old, is it?" (466). Alon responds: "Do you know when the period of Arab rule dates from? Do you know how many hundreds of years they've been here? You don't know the first thing about the history of Eretz Israel [the Land of Israel] . . . All you know about, if anything, is the persecution of the Jews" (466).

Alon distinguishes, perhaps like the Canaanite movement in the 1940s, between the history of the Jewish people and the history of the land. The history of the place includes all of the periods; and the peoples who lived during these periods left their fingerprints on the land. The ancient Arab period in the Land of Israel lasted for 458 years (641–1099), and Asqalan (Ashkelon) was an important port city.[16] This city was chosen in *Infiltration* to illustrate both the disregard for the Arabs' ties to the land, as reflected in Hedgehog's complete ignorance, and Alon's broad knowledge about these ties. But Kenaz does not only reference the ancient Arab period whose traces are found in the sand dunes. The ancient lamp is a lead-in to a surrealistic sight that unfolds before the soldiers' eyes, testifying to the fact that Ashkelon is situated alongside the ruins of an Arab town (Majdal) that began to sink into the sands and suffocate only seven years earlier (in 1948):

> We circled the sand hill, and when we were behind it, a very strange sight, which at first sight seemed like a mirage, was revealed: On the plain, a few dozen yards from where we stood, we saw a small group of trees rising out of the desert of sand. We approached the spot. We were standing on the edge of a wide, shallow pit, about a yard deep, with a few sabras and acacia bushes that had almost completely dried up around it, the remains of a hedge with only a few bits of green to testify to the remnants of life still surviving in it. And in the middle, crowded closely together as if for protection, five or six trees, figs and pomegranates and a single plum tree. Thin trees, whose few slender branches stretched up like arms crying out to heaven. And their fruits were still hanging on them, some shriveled up for want of anyone to pluck them, some still good to eat: The pomegranates looked dry and shriveled, but the figs looked juicy and sweet as honey, bursting out of their skins with over-ripeness. (468)

While most of the group feel frightened and confused when this dead life appears before them in the heart of the arid expanse, Alon again offers a historical-geomorphological explanation of the puzzling sight. Bluntly and unequivocally, he identifies this as a direct result of the War of Independence:

> Before the war, this whole area was full of Arab villages and orchards . . . and after they fled, the sands spread and covered everything. Seven years is a long time for shifting sand, when there's nothing to stop it. In another year or two, this place will be covered too and these trees will die. In the meantime, their roots draw nourishment and water from the soil that can still breathe. But in the end, it will be suffocated when the sand covers it like it covered everything around. (469)

At this point in time and in this emotionally charged setting (where the remnants of life from the Arab town of Majdal sprout in the dunes that are now part of the Jewish city of Ashkelon), Micky and Alon briefly resume their ideological arguments from the early days of basic training, when Micky still believed they were on equal footing. Micky says, "People lived here, for generations. At least in other places new immigrants came and moved into their houses, and life somehow goes on there. Here everything's been buried, not a trace will remain" (469).

In response to Micky's pessimistic, general, and somewhat simplistic assertion, Alon delivers a long and persuasive speech that shows extensive knowledge about the geopolitical situation that led to the flight or expulsion of the Arab population from the Negev, with the vestiges of its existence drowning in the sand. Alon is portrayed very favorably at this moment in the novel. He is granted the last word, enabling him to demonstrate his erudition about the battle heritage of the War of Independence and to express—clearly, logically, and at length—his firm worldview. Kenaz places the kibbutznik, whose knowledge of the land is enormous and whose political views are complex and well-thought-out (even if somewhat Darwinist), in front of a diverse audience that includes new immigrants (who remain exilic in the State of Israel), the "spoiled darlings" of the Rehavia neighborhood (as they are called throughout the novel by Avner, the Mizrahi Jew), and the cynic Micky, who is no less an urban ignoramus than the haughty Jerusalemites from Rehavia when it comes to knowing about the Land of Israel. Alon seems to be directing his words to Micky, his eternal antagonist, but everyone is gathered around him, listening in astonishment. If the readers are not already aware of his infirmity, they might mistakenly think that an ideal hero is emerging here, one that will serve as an antithesis to all the others.

This is how Alon responds to Micky:

> Look, this is the Majdal-Bet Guvrin line, where the Egyptian forces cut the Negev off from the rest of the country. They intended holding that line and expanding it more and more. And Bernadotte already had a plan for a state of Israel without the Negev. The Negev and Yiftah Brigades fought here in the Yoav campaign. A lot of fighters spilled their

blood so that the Negev would be ours . . . We wouldn't give up. Until the Egyptians broke and fled to the Gaza Strip. And the inhabitants fled with them. And anyone who didn't flee was expelled. Because there wasn't any choice. There was no room for them here. Today they're over there in refugee camps in Gaza. And you can feel sorry for them, Micky. There's certainly good reason to feel sorry for them. But you should know that most of them are still hoping, dreaming; they haven't given up hope of returning to their homes one day. And now that the Egyptians are getting all those weapons from the Russians, and preparing for the second round, those hopes aren't so fantastic. So you can save a few tears for us. Because we have to be awfully strong. Only the strong will last here. Only those who believe in what they're doing here, those who're prepared to sacrifice everything for it—only they have a chance of prevailing and surviving here. (469–70)

After this fiery speech, the narrator says that he feels, for the first time, a sense of general agreement and great admiration for Alon's erudition, profound humanism, and eloquence. "The silence which fell when he finished speaking was pregnant with the seriousness of the moment, the kind of moment at which a man might become a leader" (470).

Impersonation

This aura of an admired leader is short-lived and Alon falls to the depths of disgrace. The full extent of his shame is revealed to Micky when the latter comes on one of their weekend furloughs to visit Alon at his kibbutz— Micky's first-ever visit to a kibbutz. As noted, Micky's father hates the state, the kibbutzim, and Ben-Gurion. So Micky, unlike his friends, had never participated in a summer work camp at a kibbutz. Now he regrets this. Perhaps he wishes to relieve the pangs of this missed opportunity by visiting the kibbutz of his friend from basic training. But when he arrives, Alon is not there to greet him. Instead, Alon's girlfriend Dafna explains, in a gentle and understated way, that Alon went out for a "victory lap" in the big city, dressed up as a paratroop officer. Micky is shocked: Alon, the man of integrity, with great breadth of knowledge and absolute values, has succumbed to his illness and pretended to be someone he longs to be with all his might. Micky senses the beginning of a parting of the ways between the two friends, an emotional parting that precedes the physical parting:

> A line has been drawn between the past and the present moment. And in his longing for the figure who has departed never to return, he feels a kind of hatred for the usurper of this identity, the other Alon, shamelessly mad, setting out alone on a hopeless journey, a ridiculous adventure, to act out his sick fantasies, like some lousy Don Quixote, like a parody of Don Quixote, like a parody of a parody. (509)

Dafna sees Micky's discomfort and beseeches him, in a voice that seems to be on the verge of breaking: "Please, don't hurt him. You know him—he's got a pure heart, really pure. He doesn't know how to be mean, or petty. There's no limit to what he's capable of doing for others" (508). Undoubtedly, she sees right away how differently Alon and Micky perceive their friendship. Therefore, her request is not only for the here and now, but also for the future: "I feel something hard in you, something evasive. And he expects you to be at his side when he falls, to help him up" (508).

When Alon returns to the kibbutz and puts on his kibbutznik clothes, shrugging off his act of lunacy as a joke, everything ostensibly returns to normal. But Micky feels that something was destroyed beyond repair: "There isn't the same intimacy between them now as there was on that night guarding next to the armory, when the first rain fell, when he told him that he had not yet known love" (514). Alon, on the other hand, continues with his characteristic passion and warmth to tell Micky about his two great loves: Dafna and the land. In late afternoon, he leads Micky to his favorite spot. A lyrical spirit hovers over the description, in congruity with Alon's passion for the land:

> They walk past an orchard hedged in with a row of cypresses. At the foot of one of the cypresses they sit down, leaning against the trunk. In front of them is a plain surrounded by hills, steeped in a golden, dusky light, part of it sown, part plowed, part stubble, a patchwork of dark brown and light brown, yellowish squares. And opposite, on the mountain range on the border, the omnipresent Gilboa again. (514)

After Alon shares with Micky his love for the land, he goes on to tell him about his love for Dafna. He shows Micky nude sketches he made of Dafna, which no one other than he and Dafna have ever seen. Micky suddenly discovers that Alon is a talented artist. Moreover, Alon has firm opinions about art. When Micky is ill at ease with Dafna's nudity, Alon explains: "You didn't see her naked. Of course you didn't. You saw my drawings, the nudity that I invented for her. It's not her. It's not a photograph of her. It's how I see a nude woman. And I'm not ashamed in front of you. I have no secrets from you either. Does that embarrass you?" (526).

While Alon is always able to reveal to Micky his deepest secrets, Micky does this only once, when he confides in Alon about his sexual virginity. He knows that contrary to Alon he is also an emotional virgin, but he never tells this to Alon. Micky is also unable to disclose to Alon that he is both thrilled and put off by him at the same time. He is totally in awe of Alon's unique capabilities, but also recoils from him, from his only good friend in the platoon.

The Spectacle of Horror

After skillfully piecing together the shards he retrieved from the sand, Alon offers the restored lamp to Micky as a gift, wholeheartedly and with a feeling of exaltation. But Micky wants no part of it, flinching from it as if it were touched by "some mystery that carried a curse." He tells Alon that he knows nothing about history or archeology, so the lamp means nothing to him. Alon responds with his typical pathos: "The history of Eretz Israel is the history of us all, including you, even if you don't know anything about it. It belongs to you as much as it belongs to me" (523). For Micky, the Alon he knew and liked, whose contradictions and strangeness he had become accustomed to, was no longer the same Alon after the impersonation incident, and the two parts of the lamp are a metaphor for this. Two Alons are racing around inside the body of his good friend, who suffers from schizophrenia. However, the basic training experience they shared prior to the impersonation incident, the watershed event in their relationship, forged an alliance between the two and a decision began to emerge:

As one man, as in response to a command, they stop to get their breath back and relax their limbs. Then they go on bounding over the dunes, in an imitation of running. And Alon says, panting:

"Maybe I'll apply to go on a squad-commander's course. To come back here and keep coming back with a new intake of recruits . . ."

"You like this place."

"Yes. A lot."

"That makes sense."

"You come too. They're sure to let you, all you have to do is apply."

"Can you see me instructing recruits?"

"Why not?"

"Do I know?"

"We'll be together."

"Maybe I will. You know what, it's a possibility." (490)

This possibility did not become a reality. Instead, after completing basic training, Alon is assigned to a course for military policemen—the most contemptible assignment imaginable from his perceptive. Alon is devastated. When Micky tries to suggest that Alon might end up in the Criminal Investigations Division (CID) of the military police, and "that could be interesting," Alon snaps: "Are you crazy? Can you see me in an MP's uniform? Can you see me coming home to the kibbutz like that? It's all over for me. I won't be an MP. Never" (538). Micky realizes that Alon, who wore the uniform of a paratroop officer, would not put on a military policeman's uniform. For Alon, this would make him even more of an imposter than when he impersonated a paratrooper. Still, Micky does nothing to help Alon. Moreover, Micky is not at Alon's side at the critical moment, even though Alon is clearly in distress.

Micky knows that his friend is liable to hurt himself and pleads with Alon: "As a friend, I'm asking you. Control yourself, even if it's awfully strong, even if takes hold of your imagination. Promise me you won't do anything silly, that you won't break" (540). As in the night exercise when Alon fired that unfortunate shot, Micky is absent—on leave for soccer practice. The shot fired in the citrus grove against a figment of Alon's imagination foreshadows the shot he fires at himself; in both cases, Micky is missing. Dafna's request that Micky be at Alon's side to lend him a hand when he falls is not fulfilled.

The split in Alon's personality, when one of his two personalities is his most powerful nemesis (the one Micky calls the "usurper" of its counter-personality), and Alon's erotic-thanatotic lust for the soil (a strong temptation that Micky warns about)—two factors that lead to his death—are reflected in the following passage, where Alon is struggling with the forces that are pushing him to take action:

> The enemy is hiding inside you. The longings for the meeting are terrible; they are impossible to overcome. On the ground, in the shade of the olive tree, on a bed of earth which nothing can surpass, as dawn begins to break, and the cries of the hunters are not yet heard, life runs out; it runs out, the blood returns to its source, like the payment of a debt of love. Hard, hard, are the fathers to die, as the oak to be torn asunder. (555)

With psychological, detailed, and very credible realism, Kenaz sets the stage for the suicide of the best of the boys. Alon's split personality and his ability to defamiliarize himself are expressed in different ways in the novel—not only in the figure he imagined and shot at, and not only in his impersonation of a paratroop officer and his rapid return to himself, but also in a shrill scream that sprang from the depths of his tormented soul, "a short scream, full of terror and cruelty" (557). He is jolted awake by this scream after learning that he will not be assigned to the squad commanders' course and will not return to instruct trainees at Training Base 4, a compromise he is ready to reluctantly accept. Instead, he receives an assignment he can never accept.

"Who had screamed? Perhaps someone outside the hut. Perhaps someone had screamed in his sleep. And perhaps the scream had come from within him. Perhaps it had only been heard inside him . . . like a cry of horror and warning against an enemy unexpectedly discovered" (557). When Alon steps out of the hut on a cold and clear November night, "something has been purified inside him. He feels like a man who has made his reckoning and whose reconciliation with himself is approaching" (557). But when he comes back to the hut to sleep, the nightmare continues to haunt him, and perhaps the scream that woke him came from this nightmarish dream.

In his dream, he is lying motionless on the ground, and soldiers in a command car that burst into the camp look at him with "disapproval and disappointment," waiting for him to join them. Micky, "whose stories about soccer training were nothing but a cover-up for his treacherous secret" (558), is already one of them. In his dream, Alon knows that Micky had abandoned him. Micky, who had claimed that he was "not so keen on being an instructor or an officer. I want to finish as a private" (490), had crossed over to the other side. "As if rent by a knife, his body is split by a bitter cry: 'You were like a brother to me, a brother!'" (558). The dream of the betrayal adds another dimension to Alon's suicide. Micky was not at his side to pick him up when he fell. Micky will go to the squad commanders' course and Alon will lie on the ground and become one with it.

On the morning after the dream of betrayal and the scream, a mischievous grin spreads across Alon's face, and he volunteers for night guard duty. While guarding, he encounters Benny, the sadistic instructor, who unequivocally informs him that he is assigned to the Military Police. Each hunkers down in his position: Alon declares over and over, like a mantra, that he will not go to the Military Police. And Benny, as if failing to understand, remains resolute: "I tell you that I know you've been posted there. You're going from here to a course for MPs. So you're telling me that you're not going there?" (564). From a distance, Avner watches the two standing and conversing; Benny finally walks away and disappears behind a bend in the fence, and the sound of a gunshot echoes in Avner's ears. Avner could not make out what Benny and Alon were saying, but he clearly heard the gunshot that followed the conversation and knew for certain that he had already heard this gunfire once before (565). Alon thus fired two shots at himself—one in the citrus grove when his gun was pointed away from him, and the second on the night of the guard duty with Avner when the gun was pointed at his body.

Will These Bones Live?

Micky returns to the base and tries to understand from Avner what he saw and heard that night. Avner recounts that when Alon was lying shot on the ground, he tried to sing. Micky knows immediately that the song was "The Cannons' Roar," which Alon had sung with religious fervor on the night of the first rain. The line about the lone soldier was relevant to his situation then, and now the line about the vulture descending upon the corpses took on relevance. Alon was conscious after the shooting and his comrades in the platoon did not yet know whether he would survive his suicide attempt. The mix of emotions Micky feels again illustrates how different he is from Alon, his antithesis:

> What does it matter if Alon lives or dies? Everything's over in any case. The remnants of the anger and the hatred, which filled his heart when he stood opposite the kibbutz that Friday waiting for him to return, well up in him again: Lousy Don Quixote. I won't be your Sancho. A huge desire to be rid of it all, to get back to himself, not to feel guilty. What could I do? I wasn't here. He was waiting for it. He had it all planned. There are limits to friendship, the borderlines between the self and the other. So what's the meaning of the pain? (567–68)

Even before they officially announce Alon's death, a soldier named Ze'evik from the neighboring Platoon 3, who was known for his ability to communicate with the afterworld, informs them that Alon is "gone" (575). Alon and Micky had already encountered this necromancer during training exercises and then too had seen things very differently. Micky, the rationalist, plainly expresses his opinion about the conjurer from Platoon 3: "Disgusting . . . How morbid can you get? How can they take freaks like that in the army?" (458). Alon, on the other hand, connects the spiritualism to the value of comradeship, which he considers the loftiest of values. He believes totally and innocently in this value—as he believes in everything related to combat soldiers:

> When one of them falls, they can't forget him. It's as if he was taken prisoner and they have to keep in touch with him, not to forget him.

They leave no stone unturned in the attempt to make contact with him. As if a limb has been cut off their body. They won't let him leave them. He has to come back. Don't you understand? What do you know about comradeship between fighters like them? They used to go to a woman in Tel Aviv to teach them how to get in touch with that other world. What do we know about it? Nothing. The important thing is, not to give up. To keep up the struggle to go on being together. It's a form of longing, like love. (458–59)

On one of the last days of basic training, when torrents of rain disrupt the arms drill prior to the graduation ceremony, Micky goes to meet with the necromancer from Platoon 3. (The drama of the weather parallels the experiences of the trainees from the moment they arrive at the base through the end of their stay, and here the downpour symbolizes release and the turning of a new page.) Undoubtedly, Alon's distant words about fidelity to memory—about not forgetting a comrade, not giving up on him and trying to communicate with him even after his death—bring Micky to shed his cold armor of rationalism and seek to conjure up Alon. "It's too early," the spiritualist replies. "Some time has to pass first. A few months at least. Then I can try to do it" (590). In the same breath, the conjurer predicts that Micky will forget and will not return to communicate with his dead friend. (Kenaz cleverly assigns the necromancer to the Signals Corps.) Ze'evik and Micky are slated to remain at Training Base 4, the site of both the course for signalers and the course for squad commanders. (Tragically and ironically, Micky is the one going to the squad commanders' course and not Alon.) However, Ze'evik the spiritualist knows from his experience that most people "get over it and they forget" (591). Micky vows not to forget and to come looking for him. Their conversation ends with a wager.

Hedgehog, who witnesses this strange conversation, reminds Micky about how he had previously spoken contemptuously about this spiritualist. Now, as Micky is about to fulfill, alone, the decision he made with Alon to go together to the squad commanders' course, he replies to Hedgehog in the spirit of Alon: "You know that the toughest paratroopers went to séances? After their mates were killed" (591).

Alon's spirit not only finds its way into Micky's soul and fate, but also into the newborn son of the hypochondriac Zero-Zero, the fainthearted trainee who always had inflamed eyes and a bloody face from careless shaving, whom Alon had saved from death by hurling the grenade Zero-Zero had dropped. Zero-Zero mourns Alon and is bewildered by what Alon did:

> How can anyone do such a thing to his own body? Why? Why? Look at me, a sick man, with a useless body—I want to live so much . . . And him—a sabra, strong, healthy, handsome, with such a good heart, who loves our state so much, why should he do something like that to his body? What happened to him? . . . He's better than all the rest of us. He saved my life on the firing range. Except for him, I would've died on the spot. (567)

In the end, Alon is the one who died on the spot. Zero-Zero's comparison of his body to the body of Alon—the strong, healthy, and handsome sabra—does not include the personality makeup of each and their respective impulses vis-à-vis life and death. Zero-Zero, the weak, sickly, and exilic one, who feels inferior, is willing to live "like a dog, like shit, but to live" (567), while Alon prefers to die rather than give up his dream of being a combat soldier in the IDF. Zero-Zero's will to live begets a new sabra, the child of immigrants, in place of the perfect kibbutznik sabra who gave up on life. When they deliver the news of the birth to Zero-Zero, the only married soldier in the platoon, he says in astonishment and boundless joy: "I've got a sabra son . . . He'll be like the kids who grow up here from the beginning. He'll talk Hebrew like them. He won't know no foreign language, only Hebrew, and he'll sing their songs" (592). And when he mentions the songs his son, the new sabra, will sing, he is surely not thinking of "The Cannons' Roar," which Alon sang on the wonderful night of the first rain and at the time of his sad death. Instead, what he had in mind was the song bursting from Platoon 3, which was practicing for the graduation ceremony, as the torrent of rain poured down on the earth and cleansed the air.

In harsh harmony, discordant to an untrained ear, Platoon 3 sang the immortal line from the prophet Ezekiel's vision of dry bones: "Son of Man, will these bones live" (593). And with this human longing for the resurrection of the dead, the curtain closes on the story of the sad demise of Alon, the good and troubled soul, one of the fascinating heroes in the novel *Infiltration*.

5

Dream and Illness in Amos Oz's *My Michael*

A Novel of the Sinai War in 1956

"Yesterday the Israeli army climbed up Mount Sinai with tanks. Almost apocalyptic, I would say."

Hannah Gonen—"Sweetheart," a Detached Dreamer

My Michael,[1] the only Israeli novel that the Bertelsmann Publishing House placed on its illustrious list of the "Twentieth Century's One Hundred Greatest Novels," is the story of Hannah Gonen, a young frustrated housewife, set in Jerusalem in the 1950s. In a distinctly Israeli literary and social milieu, it shares a common theme of the stifling routine and disintegrating marriage of Hannah and her husband Michael with the nineteenth-century realistic novels *Anna Karenina* by Leo Tolstoy, *Emma Bovary* by Gustav Flaubert, and *Effi Briest* by Theodor Fontane, which all end in depression, despair, and death. In these earlier novels, omniscient narrators tell the protagonists' stories, and are therefore able to narrate the accounts of their death at length. In *My Michael*, Amos Oz chose to tell the story from Hannah's perspective in her own voice. She hints that her suicide may be a possibility in the future; but it is equally possible that her "confessional narrative" is therapeutic, and that suicidal intentions might be exchanged for a life of writing. Those familiar with Amos Oz's biography know that in his novels he and his mother merge: She committed suicide, while he is forever writing the story of her life and death in multiple variations.

Hannah Gonen's narrative follows a precise timeline of events. A date is cited at the beginning of the novel, as well as the place: "Jerusalem, January 1960." It soon becomes clear that the narrative will encompass the prior ten years of Hannah's marriage to her husband Michael. In her first-person narration, Hannah does not name her story after herself. It is named after her husband, whom she considers the central figure in her sad life. In the title "My Michael," one hears her possessive voice; Michael belongs to her and he is also that part of Hannah's self that inspires her distress, a motif that is sustained throughout the text. Hannah writes the story of her accidental meeting with the geology student Michael Gonen and her marriage to him in 1950, a decision she regards in retrospect as hasty and which she will ponder again and again while writing her memoirs.

> I am thirty years of age and a married woman. My husband is Dr. Michael Gonen, a geologist, a good-natured man. I loved him. We met in Terra Sancta College ten years ago. I was a first-year student at the Hebrew University, in the days when lectures were still given in Terra Sancta College. (1)

A substantial part of the novel is devoted to that fateful year of 1950, when Hannah made the most consequential transformation in her life: marriage and pregnancy. She then goes on to reveal each subsequent event in her life with careful attention to details, using specific dates to endow the passing time with mimetic authenticity. Most of the dates are connected with her private or family experiences: "Our son Yair was born . . . in March 1951" (56); "There was a day, for instance, late in July 1953, a bright blue day full of sounds and sights" (87); "I bought Michael the first volume of the *Encyclopedia Hebraica* as a present on our fourth wedding anniversary" (97); "One evening in the autumn of 1954, Michael came home carrying a grayish-white kitten in his arms" (105); "In the summer of 1955, we took our son for a week's holiday in Holon, to relax and swim in the sea" (122).

Periodically, some outside news items filter into the closed family chronicle. Hannah recounts them accurately, though channeling them through her narrow domestic consciousness. For example, in July 1953,

Michael bought an evening newspaper "which mentioned South Korea and gangs of infiltrators in the Negev" (87).[2] These events occurred three years before the 1956 Sinai War, which is the "climax of the novel's thematic structure,"[3] but the reader is given a hint that Hannah has no real interest in geopolitical events. Similarly, in the autumn of 1956, when the signs of war are multiplying, the reader becomes aware of the imminent war through various characters who express their opinions of the unfolding events. One of them is Mr. Kadishman, a frequent visitor to Hannah and Michael's home, who says:

> There is going to be a war. This time we shall conquer Jerusalem, Hebron, Bethlehem, and Nablus. The Almighty has wrought justly, in that, while He has denied our so-called leaders common sense, He has confounded the wits of our enemies. What he takes away with one hand, as it were, He restores with the other. The folly of the Arabs will bring about what the wisdom of the Jews has failed to achieve. There is going to be a great war, and the Holy Places will once again be ours. (163)

To this premature "prophecy,"[4] Michael retorts[5]:

> Since the day the Temple was destroyed, the power of prophecy has been granted to men like you and me. If you want to know my opinion, the war we are about to fight will not be over Hebron or Nablus but over Gaza and Rafah. (163–64)

Both men's opinions about the Sinai War illuminate their personalities. Analytical, straight-thinking Michael forecasts the events rationally and correctly; he serves as an antithesis to those who dream grandiose nationalistic dreams, like Kadishman, and to those who dream grandiose private dreams, like his wife Hannah. The cause of Hannah's dissatisfaction with her married life is her husband's mild and balanced character: He does his utmost to protect their tranquil life routine from her overexcitement, her fantasies, and her illness. His name, Gonen, means "protector" in Hebrew, and his correct prediction about the Sinai War can perhaps protect Hannah from feeling anxious, but he cannot protect her from her dreams, which will induce a grave illness that coincides with the war.

Hannah's distance from the political situation and from her husband's correct "prophecies" do not gain him any favor with her:

> At lunchtime Michael commented on the radio news: There is a well-known rule, established—if his memory did not deceive him—by the German Iron Chancellor, Bismarck, according to which when one is faced by an alliance of enemy forces, one would turn and crush the strongest. So it would be this time, my husband declared with conviction. First of all, we would scare Jordan and Iraq to death, then we would suddenly turn around and smash Egypt.
>
> I stared at my husband as if he had suddenly started talking Sanskrit. (165)

Unlike war plans and strategies which are nothing but "Sanskrit" to Hannah, the romantic woman does not recoil from the sight of soldiers clad in masculine-enhancing uniform: "In Café Allenby on King George Street, I saw four handsome French officers. They were wearing peaked caps, and purple stripes gleamed on their epaulets. Only in films had I seen such a sight before" (166). Not only the French officers appeal to her; she also finds Israeli soldiers attractive: "On David Yellin Street . . . I passed three paratroopers in mottled battle dress. Submachine guns hung from their shoulders . . . One of them, dark and lean, called after me—'Sweetheart.' His comrades joined in his laughter. I reveled in their laughter" (166–67).

Hannah would like "to live in films;" she detests what for her is a dull real life, and she does not join the home front's preparations for war. She merely buys matzah (normally bought in springtime for Passover, not in autumn), while others are grabbing canned foods, candles, and paraffin lamps from the grocery store's shelves (166).[6] Moreover, while the frantic food hoarding and the tense atmosphere make most people alert and overactive, she becomes ill and ceases to function. The fact that the soldiers had called her "sweetheart" left her half-satisfied. In her fantasies, "The soldiers thronged and closed around me in their mottled battle dress. A furious masculine smell exuded from them in waves. I was all theirs. I was Yvonne Azulai. Yvonne Azulai, the opposite of Hannah Gonen" (170). She fantasized that the masculine soldiers proceeded to gang-rape her. They are the extreme opposite of her husband, who receives his call-up papers with the utmost restraint while Hannah inwardly shouts: "When will this man lose his self-control? Oh, to see him just once in panic. Shouting for joy. Running wild" (177–78).

Michael Gonen—Neither a Pilot nor a Paratrooper

The noble way in which Michael receives his call-up papers is accompanied by his typical voice of reason, which drives Hannah, literally, out of her mind. Describing that scene, she narrates Michael's words rather than quoting them directly. The indirect telling, or "free indirect speech," is meant to ridicule his assessments and his character, although what he says is very sensible:

> Michael explains tersely that no war was likely to last longer than three weeks. The talk is of a limited, local war, of course. Times have changed. There wouldn't be another 1948. The balance between the Great Powers is very unsteady. Now that America is in the throes of elections and the Russians are busy in Hungary, there's a fleeting opportunity. No, this war won't drag on, for certain. Incidentally, he is in Signals. He is neither a pilot nor a paratrooper. (178)[7]

Hannah's repeated emphasis of the fact that Michael serves in the IDF Signal Corps adds a sarcastic dimension to his pronouncement, which he repeats with a chivalrous apology, that he is not a "real" fighter: He is neither a pilot nor a paratrooper.

Hannah's piercing irony is directed at Michael not only through requisitioning his words and reporting them in indirect speech, but also by ways of analogy and projection. Of all the radio broadcasts on the eve of the war, Hannah reports that "an excited newscaster spoke of an ultimatum issued by the President of the United States. The President called on all parties to exercise restraint" (175). That ultimatum is clearly an impossible demand at a moment when the conflict between the parties had already reached the boiling point. It is an analogy to Michael's absurd ability to accept his call-up papers with restraint and to speak, even at that moment, with cold logic. Even the "excited" newscaster cannot maintain composure when reading the president's demand. It seems that Michael is the only one able to do so. Michael repeats for the third time his measured and reassuring estimate concerning the war, and once again his words and actions are recounted from Hannah's point of view, who adds her own ironic touch:

> He is leaving me a hundred pounds. And here on a piece of paper under the vase are written his army number and unit number . . . The war won't last long at all. He means to say, that is what political reason dictates. After all the Americans . . . never mind now. (178)[8]

Michael is only marginally aware that his estimates of the length of the war or the deployment of forces are not a major concern for Hannah. Her lack of interest in the war on the national and political levels can be seen through the way she reports the frequent radio bulletins, once again through indirect speech. She begins by quoting authentic news, but changes them into clipped reports, picking from the news trite combinations, "white-washed expressions," and unrelated clichés, which portray the war's aims and triumphs ironically:

> At nine o'clock the radio announced:
> Last night the Israel Defense Forces penetrated the Sinai Desert, captured Kuntilla and Ras en-Naqeb, and have occupied positions near Nahel, sixty kilometers east of the Suez Canal. A military commentator explains: While from the political point of view. Repeated provocations. Flagrant violation of freedom of navigation. The moral justification. Terrorism and sabotage. Defenseless women and children. Mounting tension. Innocent civilians. Enlightened public opinion at home and abroad. Essentially a defensive operation. Keep calm. Must not wander outside. Must enforce blackout. Must not hoard. Must obey instructions. Must not panic. Must be on the alert. The whole country is the front. The whole nation is an army. On hearing the warning signal. So far events have proceeded according to plan. (180–81)

Except for the first sentence, Hanna's report of the radio's nine o'clock bulletin is devoid of real information. Hannah creates a parody of the news, especially in the parts of alternative "musts and must nots," giving the public instructions in a sterile fashion.

Hannah carries on with her subjective and ironic reporting of what is heard on the radio every fifteen or thirty minutes:

> At a quarter past nine:
> The armistice agreement is dead and buried and will never be revived. Our forces are overrunning. Enemy opposition is giving ground . . . Till half past ten the radio played marching songs from my youth: "From Dan to Beersheba we'll never forget," "Believe me, the day will come." (181)

If we thought that Hannah would not refer to these familiar patriotic songs with any sense of irony, we were wrong. From her responses to the lyrics, it is clear that she is taking no part in the national celebration. All the messages, all the slogans, are worthless to her: "Why should I believe you? And if you don't forget, what of it?" (181).

A dramatic report at half past ten describes the Sinai Desert as the "historic cradle of the Israelite nation." Hannah sarcastically remarks "as opposed to Jerusalem," neither affirming nor rejecting the purported national importance of the Sinai Desert. Then she says either earnestly or ironically: "I try my hardest to be proud and interested" (181), hinting that her ostensible effort is fruitless. As far as she is concerned, the war is a golden opportunity to fall ill, to abandon all her obligations, to indulge in fantasies, to get even with her "square" husband. Hannah, like the war itself, represents the rearrangement of orders, the breaking of routines, and thus she does not have the ability to see things outside of herself.

Hannah is ill during the Sinai War. During a visit by the German-born physician, Dr. Urbach speaks alternatively of her state of health and the state of the nation as an analogy between two states of sickness that are simultaneously states of exhilaration. Dr. Urbach declares:

> These are important days, fateful days. At times such as these it is difficult to refrain from scriptural thoughts. Is our throat still inflamed?

Let us look inside and find out. It was bad, very bad, dear lady, what you did when you poured on yourself cold water in the middle of winter, as if it was possible to bring peace to the mind by bringing afflictions to the body . . . Well, today the news from the war is optimistic. The English and the French also will fight together with us against the Moslems. The radio this morning spoke even of "the allies." Almost like in Europe. (186)

Both Hannah's mental illness and the ecstatic state in which the Israeli nation finds itself in the autumn of 1956 are brought together in the physician's words: "There is a serious defect of the intellect in some Jews; we are unable to hate those who hate us. Some mental disorder. Well, yesterday the Israeli army climbed up Mount Sinai with tanks. Almost apocalyptic, I would say, but only almost" (186–87). In his medical diagnosis of both Hanna and the Jews—"defect of the intellect," "inflamed throat," "to bring peace to the mind by bringing afflictions to the body," "mental disorder," "almost apocalyptic"—Dr. Urbach uses expressions that work on both levels. Hannah's psychosomatic and psychotic state serves as a metaphor for the state of the Jews, while the State of the Jews serves as a metaphor for Hannah's fantastical despair. In one of her most startling fantasies, she dreams about her relationship with two Arab boys, with whom she played as a child and "bossed around," but now have become fantasy figures who attack and rape her. This rape-fantasy is similar to the one she has about the soldiers who called her "sweetheart," but this time the fantasy involves Arabs raping her and "raping" the State of Israel, and it follows the argument about Hannah's "mental condition" as an analogy to the "war."

It is worth noting that Amos Oz was not pulled into the "scriptural thoughts" and the feeling of elation shared by Israelis during the short and relatively easy first war following the War of Independence. He also remained detached from the messianic wave that flooded the country during the Six-Day War. Through Hannah, who remains unmoved by the decisive victory and turns through her dreams and illness into a mirror for the distorted, abnormal state of a nation during war, Oz reveals his reservations concerning the dreams of grandeur that cause illness and war. Perhaps there is a literary-ideological message here: If you tell your own story and are aware of your misleading dreams and self-imposed illness, you will not commit suicide and may exchange illness for a life of creative work.

The fact that Oz entitles Hannah's story with the name of her husband may suggest another ideological message contrary to the reader's expectations. The husband disappoints Hannah, who is a prisoner of false romanticism, but he does not necessarily disappoint the reader. First, he accurately foresaw the events of the war. And once he is safely back home, he is unable to tell his son Yair, who is waiting impatiently to hear heroic war stories, anything about the front itself: "Unfortunately, Daddy didn't capture the Egyptian destroyer in Haifa Bay or visit Gaza. He wasn't parachuted near the Suez Canal, either. Daddy isn't a pilot or a paratrooper" (209). Precisely because Michael Gonen did not actually fight, did not come face to face with the enemy, and can only tell about patrols, ambushes, and alarms rather than Michael Strogoff-like heroic deeds that would excite and impress his son and wife,[9] Amos Oz hints that his readers should ignore Hannah's judgment of her husband as "Goofy Ganz" and see him as a sane and sound Israeli patriot.

6

Language Barriers, Roadblocks, and Frustrated Love in Eli Amir's *Yasmine*

A Novel of the Six-Day War

> "I want to love you in Arabic and in Hebrew and in all the languages of the world."

To Speak a Language Is to Adopt a Culture

Eli Amir's fourth novel, *Yasmine*[1] (2005), is the provocative love story of Nuri Imari and Yasmine Hilmi that takes place against the background of the tense encounters between Israelis and Palestinians in the aftermath of the Six-Day War. Nuri is Jewish and was appointed after the war to be an aide to the "minister in charge" of forging Israeli policies regarding the Arabs in the newly conquered territories.[2] Yasmine is a Christian Arab with a high degree of political consciousness, whose family had fled West Jerusalem for the eastern sector during the 1948 War when she was a young girl.[3] She had been living in Paris, and has returned to her parents' home after the Six-Day War.

Prior to the story of their romance, Amir begins the novel with a two-chapter prologue. In the first chapter, Amir depicts the exaggerated Arab confidence in their armies and aspiration for victory inspired by prewar Egyptian propaganda and radio broadcasts of false news, which change to disbelief and depression when shocked by the reality of the Israeli victory that exposed their expectations as bitter illusions. In the second chapter, Amir depicts the Israeli point of view: the three-week period before the war when Israelis were in a fearful state of anxiety about what was about to happen, inspired by listening to those same Arab broadcasts; and then the sudden change to euphoria when the Israeli army was victorious, a victory tainted with an increasing arrogance of power, problematic messianic sentiments, and an insensitivity toward the defeated Arabs.

Nuri, a moderate Mizrahi Jew with a deep understanding of the language, culture, and sociopolitical situation of the Arabs, served in the Israeli army during the war, but emerged with a remarkably nuanced psychological and geopolitical understanding of what the significance of this amazingly short war had brought about for Israelis and Palestinians. He sees the multifaceted conflict between Palestinians and Israelis that began long before the Six-Day War and will continue due to the seemingly implacable mindsets of both sides. He has this realization before he meets Yasmine, the woman he will fall in love with, whose name Amir has chosen for the title of his novel.[4]

The remarkable attraction between Nuri and Yasmine derives in part from a sense of linguistic and intellectual similarity. Nuri is a "son of Arabia," a native of the East, fluent in both Hebrew and Arabic, and Yasmine too has command of both languages. However, they will speak neither in Hebrew nor Arabic, but in English, a neutral language in this land, which is dear to both. Yasmine believes that "speaking a particular language means, above all, adopting its culture" (330).[5] This quotation explains why this proud Palestinian is unprepared to speak Hebrew, a language she spoke freely and without accent before her family's flight from Talbiyeh to Sheikh Jarrah in 1948. "Why," Nuri asks himself, "couldn't we communicate in Arabic, which was our mother tongue, hers and mine? Why did she set up this language barrier between us, like a throwback to the days of the British Mandate?" (302).

Language, which has the potential to connect the lovers, turns into a barrier, a roadblock, which Nuri regrets repeatedly. Apparently, he does not want to acknowledge that Yasmine's superior command of English is intended to prove her superiority over someone she considers an enemy and an occupier. Against the backdrop of the Six-Day War, this "language war" becomes a measuring stick of relations between occupier and occupied, and of the dynamic proximity and remoteness between two lovers and their respective conceptions of themselves and others in this new geopolitical reality. Yasmine represents her people and Nuri represents his, but he wants to speak of love in her language, which he claims as his own.

Ihna Yahud min hon: We Are Jews from Here

Yasmine opens at dawn, symbolizing the opening of a new era. East Jerusalem, Al Quds according to the Arabs, has just been conquered by the soldiers of the Israel Defense Forces (IDF). This is a very specific time marker, for indeed, the narrative of the Six-Day War is characterized by precise demarcations of time: three weeks of waiting before the beginning of battle, three hours during which the Egyptian air force was wiped out, six days of combat that changed the face of the Middle East, and the delusion on the part of the Arabs that within two or three weeks the Israelis would retreat from the conquered territories. Amir does not overlook the central motif of this "war of time markers":

> At daybreak on Wednesday, the seventh of June 1967, As-Sayed Antoine Salameh, senator of the Hashemite Kingdom of Jordan, peered out of the window and saw a group of soldiers approaching slowly, wearily, as if scarcely able to walk. With torn and dusty clothes, they paced down the street. (1)

Before daybreak, "4:34 AM exactly," the slow, heavy walk of unidentified soldiers, in torn, dust-covered clothes, the recognizable "traces of the toilsome day and of fire-filled night," evoke images of Natan Alterman's famous poem, "The Silver Platter."[6] Amir begins with an omniscient narrator who knows Hebrew literature and who can make such references to canonical works. Nuri, whose mother tongue is not Hebrew, laments his weak knowledge of Hebrew literature, and considers himself a lesser speaker of Hebrew than the "minister in charge" in terms of knowing the language, its nuances and sources:

> I'm always rattled when I have to prepare the report. Afraid of the minister's criticism, I struggle with the wording, write and rewrite, feeling him

> breathing down my neck. His Hebrew is superb, drawn from the geological strata of Bible and Talmud, the Revival writers and poets, innovations made by Bialik, Mendele, Agnon, Shlonsky, Alterman . . . As for me, I'm an immigrant with a limited command of the language. (293)

The fictional apparatus here thus differentiates between an omniscient narrator who knows how to employ literary allusion and a protagonist who knows many languages but none of them completely. Later, when Nuri, an immigrant from Iraq, quotes Bialik's "Let My Lot Be With You,"[7] he explains his expertise by saying that he learned the text at an evening school for working boys (367). His purpose is to make clear that his native tongue is Arabic, whereas Hebrew is a second language. Still, he has acquired a command of Hebrew. In contrast, his brother Kabi, an Israeli spy who easily learns Persian for his missions and whose girlfriend has translated Agnon's "*Harofe Ugerushato*" [The Doctor's Divorce] into English, "has an awkward relationship with Hebrew" (110).[8] It appears that the knowledge of a language is a psychological matter, a function of a decision and an emotional state of mind.

In "The Silver Platter," a boy and a girl "march slowly" and are "full of endless fatigue" at the end of the battle for independence.[9] In the opening scene of Amir's novel, after another cessation of combat, a group of soldiers walk down the street "slowly, wearily, as if scarcely able to walk," now that they have reached the end of the bloody battle on Ammunition Hill (Giv'at HaTahmoshet in Hebrew, al-Mudawara in Arabic) and the conquest of the Sheikh Jarrah neighborhood in Jerusalem (1). However, there is a great difference between these two groups of walkers, and from this difference a great, cutting irony emerges about the defeated side that remains mired in its delusions. Amir's soldiers, unlike Alterman's girl and boy, are not marching "toward the nation" and are not dead. They are Israeli soldiers walking down a street in East Jerusalem, in the cultivated, garden neighborhood of the now occupied northern part of the city, moving by happenstance toward the home of a senator of the Kingdom of Jordan, whose name is As-Sayed Antoine Salameh, and they lean against the fence that surrounds his house. They are tired, but are beginning to recover from their great fatigue.

The cosmic-mythic event of Alterman's "Silver Platter" is replaced here with an earthly, realistic one. In "The Silver Platter," the "nation"—a collective, disembodied, symbolic entity—poses a rhetorical question: "Who are you?" However, the Jordanian senator, who has not been able to sleep and has been restlessly pacing through the rooms of his house amid the sounds of gunfire and exploding windowpanes, does not ask this question. For some reason, he is confident about the identities of the soldiers, who are resting their heavy combat backpacks and weapons on the ground and kneeling for a moment's rest. From the balcony of his elegant house next to the Ambassador Hotel, he is quick to bless and express to the tired soldiers the appreciation of the Hashemite Kingdom for their bold combat. He believes that they are the first of the vanguard Iraqi soldiers who enlisted to help the Jordanian Legion in the holy battle for Palestine.[10] Now that they have driven off "the despicable Zionist enemy, the cruel contemptible, miserable and cowardly infidel" (3) with a sword's thrust, they deserve to receive cold water from his Sudanese maid to refresh their souls from their victorious night of battle. The mistake that Amir attributes to Senator Antoine Salameh is intended to illustrate the depth of the denial that the senator has enacted on his own psyche, which compels him to believe that in front of his house stand Iraqi soldiers actualizing in his mind's eye a sense of imagined Arab solidarity.

This initial "linguistic drama" is accompanied by an "optical error," a kind of trompe l'oeil, since the soldiers standing by his house are not Iraqi Legionnaires who have joined the Jordanian army to wipe away the shame of 1948 (2–3); rather, they are Israelis who have just captured his neighborhood. Indeed, upon hearing the senator's warm blessing, the eyes of the soldiers open wide in amazement. The omniscient narrator penetrates the senator's thoughts and explains the soldiers' surprise. The explanation is concealed within a linguistic impediment: "Perhaps they didn't fully understand his speech since he addressed them in the Palestinian dialect, and Iraqis had a dialect of their own that he himself scarcely understood. He should address them in literary Arabic, which all Arabs understood, but let them first refresh themselves with cold water" (3). The senator does not have a chance to repeat his Arabic blessing, for at that very moment a soldier with a ripped shirt and a bandaged arm approaches the porch of his house, and taking off his steel helmet, announces in an Arabic comprehensible to all Palestinians, Arabs and Israelis alike, "*Ihna yehud min hon*—we're Jews, from here, from Israel" (3).

Notably, Amir deals with multilingualism and multiple dialects in Hebrew and Arabic—words, idiomatic expressions, and esoteric sayings that create confusion in both their messages and ideas. Unlike A. B. Yehoshua in *The Liberated Bride*,[11] Amir does not relegate confusing translations to footnote; he makes them an integral part of the story. The Hebrew appears immediately as a natural continuation of the Arabic. This form illustrates for the reader that Hebrew and Arabic are correlative if not synonymous. This ostensibly technical matter shows that whereas the characters can inhabit both languages, they also could share both cultures and the same territory. Herein lies Amir's principal political and autobiographical message. Against the definition of "the nation" as "one people, one land, one language," which was suggested by the literature of 1948 (including Alterman's "The Silver Platter"), Amir's Six-Day War novel offers an alternative perspective of bilingualism and biculturalism. The pathos of the 1948 War literature is thus replaced with cultural and religious relativism, with flexibility and irony.[12] However, the linguistic roadblock serves to introduce even more serious impediments to follow.

The two dead soldiers of "The Silver Platter" who come to face the nation provide, in clear Hebrew and with great pathos and metaphor, a heartbreaking answer to the question of identity: "Who are you?" They declare, "We are the 'Silver Platter' on which the Jewish State is given." In "The Silver Platter" from the 1948 War, a glorious dialogue unfolds between the Hebrew nation and its soldiers, who sacrifice their lives for its freedom and affirm the nation's assumptions and expectations of them. How different those dead soldiers are from the lightly wounded soldier in *Yasmine*, in whom the spirit of life, humility, and respect for the other still pulsate within him, and who approaches the porch of the conquered house to correct in simple words, devoid of pathos, the mistaken assumption of the Jordanian senator. Unwittingly, the tired soldier not only shines an ironic light upon the senator's error, but also upon the entire Arab nation, which has been bragging loudly about imagined victories. Amir shows that a dialogue of the deaf is taking place between the victorious

Israelis and the defeated Arabs, replete with contradictory diagnoses and painful optical errors.

"Baba, They Stuck Their Flag There! They Beat Us!"

"The Silver Platter" is not the only work that resonates as an ironic background in the first chapter. Hans Christian Anderson's "The Emperor's New Clothes," a social allegory in which a small child dares to tell the truth that the "king has no clothes" while the adults are too fearful or embarrassed to admit the fact, is used by Amir to illustrate the false consensus that proliferated among the Arabs during the Six-Day War and that intensified their insult and anger when they learned the bitter truth of their defeat.

From the rooftop of the Church of the Redeemer on the third day of the Six-Day War, three Arabs—Abu George, Abu Shawkat, and his young son—look out over the Temple Mount and observe the capture of the city that culminates with the famous blowing of the shofar by Chief Rabbi Shlomo Goren. Abu George is Yasmine's father; he is an affluent Christian Arab, a journalist with a political consciousness, the head of the tourism association, and the owner of a restaurant. Abu Shawkat is a famous newspaper photographer. The two adults and the small boy watch the scene unfold before their eyes and perceive the conquest of the Old City (which the Arabs call El-Balad [The City]), with its biblical signification. and the arrival of Israelis at the Western Wall from two different points of view. The adults cannot believe what they are seeing; from their point of view, they must be the victors. The small child is the only one who sees the truth.

Abu George sees the fortified positions of the Jordanian Legion snipers, which allay his concerns, but it is not clear whether these positions are still occupied or vacant. His concerns had begun to trouble him at sunrise when his neighbor, Senator As-Sayed Antoine Salameh, phoned to tell him that Israeli soldiers were wandering around his street. Abu George had dismissed the senator's eye-witness account, reasoning that the caller was old, that a senseless fear had overtaken him, that he must have been seeing things, or was simply losing his mind. Even so, the idea that Israeli soldiers had been seen leaning against his neighbor's fence makes him uneasy. He climbs to the roof of his house to see what is happening with his own eyes, aided by his binoculars; but as if fulfilling the desires of one who wants at once to see and not to see, a eucalyptus tree, dubbed the "Jews' tree," blocks his view. With no alternative, at the climax of the battle and to the great chagrin of his wife, he leaves his house to ascertain for himself what is happening on the streets of Jerusalem. Contradictory visions and testimonies confuse him and fail to offer him a straightforward answer. He is just about to return home, with no real knowledge of the direction of the war, when he decides to take a look from the rooftop of the Church of the Redeemer. There he gazes upon the city's gates and walls, and for a moment he calms down.

This momentary calm is disturbed at ten in the morning, when the little boy, son of Abu Shawkat, standing next to him at the lookout point, screams out: "Daddy, look, look, they're shooting at Bab al-Asbat!" (18). Bab al-Asbat is the "Gate of the Tribes," next to the "Lion's Gate," through which the IDF's 56th Paratrooper Brigade entered the Old City and progressed to the Western Wall. The little Arab boy discerns their presence first and calls the attention of the two adults to what is happening. Only then does the photographer see a thin metal rod, apparently the antenna of a vehicle, upon which a small flag waves. The two adults cannot believe their eyes: How on earth could an Israeli armored vehicle make its way through the narrow gate of Bab al-Asbat, and how is it that the road is clear as if it were the King's Highway? They easily dismiss what they see and conclude that the image of the military vehicle is merely a mirage. But the boy, who is trained to tell the truth, does not allow them to shove aside what they have seen, and shouts out again: "There! There it is!" And with that, the armored vehicle suddenly becomes a reality. The little Arab boy who forces the two adults to see stands in contrast to the "Jews' tree" that hid what the men refused to see. The boy's responses to his father's evasive answers recall the plot of "The Emperor's New Clothes," where a young boy reveals to a group of adults what their eyes have seen, but which they refuse to acknowledge in their heart of hearts:

> "Baba, are those the Jews?" the child asked. "Baba, why don't you answer?"
> "It seems so," said the father in a low voice.

"Where are our soldiers?"
"They are firing from all sides," the father said.
"Then why don't the Jews stop?" (18–19)

In his innocence, the child sees and asks questions; but his father, who denies what he sees, does not answer. Instead, he whispers, continuing to deny the truth, until he has no choice and begins to lament like his son: "Abu George, what is going on here? Where is Allah, where is the Legion, where are Hussein and Nasser and the Arab states and Russia? Where? . . . *Ya-ra el-alamin*, Lord of the Universe, what will happen to us? Wasn't one *Nakba* enough? The land is gone and so is our honor!" (20). When the soldiers reach the "Jews' Wall" from which they had been denied access since 1948, Abu George is on the verge of fainting at his observation point, but the child continues to describe the bitter truth in loud tones: "Baba, they stuck their flag there! They beat us!" (20).

With the sound of the shofar declaring victory, a historic, fatal moment, the observers atop the Church of the Redeemer can no longer deny what their eyes have seen and their ears have heard. The celebratory sounds of the shofar ring out sharply and clearly. And yet Amir, wanting to bring in the Palestinian perspective, attributes to the shofar a sorrowful tone transformed into the inner wailing of the Arabs who are witnessing the Israeli victory. This is no victory blast, as it is perceived by the victors; rather it is the moaning voice of weakness and lament, as perceived by those who have been defeated. For this reason, the first chapter of *Yasmine* concludes with a depiction of Abu George, the father of Yasmine: "His tears flowed freely, and he felt no shame" in his lament (22). The role of the small boy, who speaks difficult truths, has concluded. Now the adults too must admit that the emperor is naked.

Between Sound and Meaning

Amir's narrative method is an excellent example of a conflict between *fabula* and *syuzhet*. The fabula is the chronological order of events; the syuzhet is the order in which these events reach the consciousness of the reader, an order that is not necessarily chronological. Amir's syuzhet first presents the reader with the Arabs' twisted grasp of reality, which does not change even by the third day of the war, and only later describes the Israelis' existential trepidation on the eve of the Six-Day War. However, Amir's primary ironical focus on the Arab side, which seems to outweigh his criticism of the ecstasy of victory that later swept Israel, does not mean that Israel's intoxication with power, insensitivity for the Arab population, and delusion that "the wars are finished"[13] (236) after the Six-Day War are not subjected to sharp criticism in the novel. Nevertheless, in *Yasmine*, Amir presents the Arabs as being much blinder than the Israelis, and entrenched far more deeply in their illusory ideologies.

Against the backdrop of the arrogance of the Arabs, whose optimistic forecasts are refuted before their eyes, and against the backdrop of the terror of the Israelis that melts away, Amir begins the second chapter with the phrase: "Some time before the Flood, or before the earthquake, ages and ages ago" (23), which conveys a sense of subjective time. Objectively speaking, only three weeks have passed since Nuri was called for reserve duty, but the lightning-fast war that overturned their world order endows the short time that has passed with a metaphysical quality. In the second chapter, Nuri emerges as a person who knows Hebrew and Arabic and is familiar with Israeli and Palestinian cultures. The linguistic drama of the novel that begins with *"Ihna yahud min hon"* continues in the second chapter.

In the middle of May 1967, Nuri finds an emergency call-up order on the door of his one-room flat in Jerusalem. The next day he takes two buses, filled with army reservists, to the Bilu camp, where his tank brigade does practice exercises, before they eventually move out and camp in a garden on the outskirts of Gaza City. During this time, Nuri listens carefully to the radio broadcasts in Hebrew and Arabic. Already at six in the morning, he hears the radio broadcaster announce in a deep, dramatic voice that "Nasser has closed the Straits of Tiran and barred our shipping to the Indian Ocean." Then, "without stopping to draw breath," the broadcaster goes on to state that "Israel regards this move as a *casus belli*" (24).

The subject of Egyptian propaganda-news is ever-present. On the morning of his ninth day at the Bilu camp, presumably May 24, Nuri asks the soldier in charge of the canteen to turn the radio dial to the Israeli

Arabic-language station. The soldier, who does not pay attention to the fact that Nuri was asking specifically for Kol Yisrael [The Voice of Israel] in Arabic, responds expressing his attitude toward this enemy language: "Again? . . . What the hell do you want the Arabic station for? Screw them!" (30). On this Israeli radio station, from which Jews broadcast in Arabic, Nuri hears the Israeli reaction to the Egyptian president, Gamal Abdel Nasser's speech at Bir Gafgafa: "President Gamal Abdel Nasser, yesterday at Bir Gafgafa, you said you would not retreat a single inch. Well. Listen to these words from Israel: the Straits of Tiran are an international waterway; open them up or they will be opened up some other way, and an Israeli ship will pass through, flying the Israeli flag" (30).[14]

In his book *Through Arab Eyes: The Six-Day War and its Aftermath*, Shimshon Yitzhaki notes that on May 19, 1967, the UN peacekeepers began their evacuation from Sharm el-Sheikh and the first Egyptian soldiers established positions there and on the islands of Tiran and Sanafir. The Egyptians took complete control of the straits on May 21, and the last of the peacekeeping forces left Sharm el-Sheikh on May 22. That same day, Egypt announced its decision to close off the Straits of Tiran to Israeli vessels. Nasser made a formal tour of Sinai in the company of the Egyptian military top brass and gave a speech at the Bir Gafgafa air force base, in which he explained the decision to close the straits. This speech by Nasser, Shimshon Yitzhaki writes, was broadcast on Egyptian radio in the afternoon of May 23. The Egyptian president said:

> Since yesterday and the day before, the world has been speaking about Sharm el-Sheikh, about the fleet in the Gulf of Aqaba, and about the Port of Eilat. This morning I heard on Radio London . . . that Abdel Nasser obligated himself in 1956 to open the Gulf of Aqaba. There is no truth to these words. These words never were, and Abdel Nasser cannot relinquish any of Egypt's privileges, and I have said, we will not renounce a single grain of sand of our land . . . Yesterday the armed forces [of Egypt] occupied Sharm-el Sheikh. What does this mean? It is an affirmation of our rights, our sovereignty over the Gulf of Aqaba, which are Egyptian territorial waters. Under no circumstances can we permit the Israeli flag to pass through the Gulf of Aqaba. The Jews threaten war; we are ready for war, our armed forces, our people, all of

us are ready for war, but under no circumstances shall we abandon our rights. These are our waters.[15]

Nuri, who should have been serving in military intelligence rather than in the tank corps (56), continues to listen to Arabic radio at every possible opportunity. By the time they deploy near Gaza City, it is clear that war is about to break out. Nuri approaches the intelligence officer and volunteers to translate an important speech that Nasser is scheduled to give in the afternoon—this he knows from the newspaper. The officer places him in a side office with a radio, pencil, and paper so that he can translate the speech. Nuri confesses that like all other Arab boys, he had always been captivated by the stirring charisma of Gamal Abdel Nasser and his warm, pleasing voice, and had always dreamed of being a leader like him. But here was the hero of his youth, "giving the signal for his armed forces to pour into the Sinai Desert and entrench themselves in its gullies and ravines to kill me. And for what? The Straits of Tiran were zipped open and then zipped shut. Was that a reason to kill and be killed?" (33). Nuri goes on to say: "I am listening to Nasser's speech on the intelligence officer's radio, and I hear him declaring that his goal is to restore the situation as it was before 1948" (33). Nuri realizes that Nasser intends to nullify the major accomplishment of the Sinai War (1956): the opening of the Straits of Tiran and the free access of sailing vessels in the Gulf of Eilat-Aqaba. But before he can even absorb the military import of all of this, he is drawn back into the magic of Nasser's voice that had always captivated him:

> I try to concentrate on his words, not on his voice, but I can only retain the words when I listen to the tone and the music. It is thanks to the music that I remember his old speeches verbatim, like something learned in childhood—the emphatic repetitions, the rise and fall of the voice, the rage he let loose and the insults he flung, the stormy outbursts, the dramatic silences, the measured imprecations. (33–34)

Nuri finds it difficult to separate the content of Nasser's words, which threaten him as a Jew and as an Israeli, from his attraction to the pleasantness of Nasser's voice and his rhetorical power; he oscillates between intellectual understanding and romantic adventure in his dual relationship with the two warring nations. Amir concludes the second chapter with this same motif of conflict between voice and meaning. Nuri is captivated by the voice of Umm Kulthoum rising from the radio, which reminds him of his distant, childhood lullabies: "Umm Kulthoum used to sing to me in my sleep in my mother's arms . . . For a moment I forgot the war. The queen was singing!" (37). But this "queen" is the friend and ally of Nasser. Both have wonderful voices that awaken longings for his Edenic childhood. And if Nasser and Umm Kulthoum are not enough, there is also Sheikh Abu al-Ayneen Shaisha reading verses from the Quran, whose voice is melodious, moving, and intoxicating, but the content of the verses is horrifying: "The bitterest enemies of the believers of Islam are the Jews and the idol worshippers. Jihad is the duty of the very devout Muslim, the only way to treat the enemy. It is a religious duty to kill them, and whoever does so has his place in heaven" (38).

To be in a Movie

Two related questions arise in Amir's *Yasmine*. Can the voice of a speaker be absorbed apart from the semantic meaning of his words? Can the eyes of a beholder see something apart from what reality presents? The answer to both questions is yes. Nuri illustrates the separation between voice and meaning when he confesses how he revels in the voices of Nasser, Umm Kulthoum, and the sheikh at that very moment when they are threatening his life. Senator Antoine Salameh, the journalist Abu George, and the photographer Abu Shawkat demonstrate how people can deny the meaning of what they see. In wartime, senses and sensibilities are distorted. To contrast these two differing approaches to the war, Amir employs the metaphor of film, which is the equivalent of a dream—a nightmare or a wish fulfilled. An Israeli soldier, Trabulisi, who has just celebrated the *brit milah* [circumcision] of his son and then joined his fellow reservists, tells of what seems to be happening in Tel Aviv at the end of May 1967:

> You can't imagine what's going on in Tel Aviv . . . It's a ghost town, the streets are empty and apparently thousands of casualties are expected.

The rabbinate has prepared land for a mass grave in Independence Park, and secondary-school kids are being enlisted to dig trenches. It's terrifying! People are running away, making macabre jokes. "The last one out of the airport turn off the light!" that sort of thing. (25)

Amir describes how Tel Aviv appears before the war through the eyes of an Israeli only after having presented in the first chapter a description of Jerusalem from the opposing perspective of the Arabs. Jerusalem's conquest, which occurs before their very eyes, does not induce them to correctly understand their city's situation. According to the report of the governor, whom the journalist Abu George and his partner, Abu Nabil, had interviewed on the morning of the third day of the war, the stores in Jerusalem "are open as usual. There's plenty of everything, and the main roads to Amman are open" (12). This is juxtaposed to Trabulisi's vision of Tel Aviv, where people purportedly are digging mass graves. The Israelis sitting on the outskirts of Gaza City envision the destruction of Tel Aviv, while the Arabs inside Jerusalem, in the line of fire, continue to the very end to view their city as bustling with life.

After the two journalists leave the governor's home, relieved by his unfounded testimony, they see a colorful billboard outside a movie theater, showing a scene from the old romantic film *Al Wardah al Baidha* [The White Rose]. Abu Nabil tells Abu George that he will reserve seats for the two of them and their wives to see the film on Sunday. "That would be nice," Abu George replies. This conversation again reveals how totally oblivious they are to the significance of the Israeli conquest of Jerusalem that is unfolding before them (15). Watching a movie serves as a metaphor for their distorted vision of reality. The "film" that Nuri sees in his own mind is fundamentally different: "Fear haunted me. In the darkness, I saw a man with his hands tied, being shot in the head. He fell and that was the end of him. One moment he existed, the next he didn't. **A scene from a film**. Was that going to be my fate?" (32, emphasis added). The exaggeratedly dark view of the Israelis juxtaposed to the blindness of the Arabs makes the Israelis' fears irrelevant and ironically points out the arrogance of the Arabs.

The "Jews' Tree" and the Arab "*Tarab*"—Hybrid Identity

Amir uses landscape and trees invested with symbolic meanings to emphasize the dichotomy between the Arabs who deliberately evade the reality and the Israelis who amplify the danger awaiting them. In the first chapter, when Abu George receives a phone call from Senator As-Sayed Antoine Salameh about the Israeli soldiers wandering around their neighborhood, he goes up to his roof with binoculars to see with his own eyes what is happening. A "spreading *shajarat al-yahud*, a Jews' tree—the eucalyptus tree—blocked his view of the hill" (5). Eucalyptus trees were originally brought from Australia to drain the swamps in the Hula Valley, and thus became symbolic of the Zionist ethos of reclaiming the land. Eucalyptus trees were also planted along a road near the demarcation line between Israel and Syria to prevent Syrian snipers from seeing and shooting at Israeli farmers. Amir uses the tree as Abu George's excuse to cover over the truth of the Israeli presence in Jerusalem, which in any case, he has no desire to see.[16]

The eucalyptus tree plays a more complex role in the second chapter. Nuri and his fellow reservists are crammed together during the waiting period before the war trying to comprehend their tense, drawn-out expectations. He begins to suffer a severe headache and seeks refuge under an old eucalyptus tree that stands adjacent to where the tanks are parked. He sits under its shade and listens "to the wind riffling through the leaves as if they were pages in a book of poetry, now stopping for a quiet read, now skimming fast, glancing and flitting on" (28). The poetry arising from the meeting between the wind and the eucalyptus leaves stands in marked contrast to the sounds of Ahmad Shukeiry, the chairman of the Palestine Liberation Organization on the transistor radio, mocking Israelis: "Isra'il . . . your head is made of wax, so why are you walking in the sun?" (27).[17] The eucalyptus tree, a symbol of Jews taking root in the Land of Israel, provides the shade that alleviates Nuri's headache and indirectly offers a remedy to the Israelis' head of wax, melting as it were in the heat of the Middle East. "Heat. Emptiness. Unease. Once again, I drag myself to the silent shadow of the eucalyptus, lean against its trunk with my eyes shut, and try to calm myself by crushing leaves between my fingers" (36). Indeed, the "poetical rustle" of the eucalyptus leaves and the healing fragrance of its leaves satisfy his sense of sound, touch, and smell, alleviating his headache and providing support and rest from fear. Because he took refuge under the "Jews' tree," he can put on his headphones again and listen to the enchanting Arabic music [*Tarab*] on the radio with a kind of sensual intoxication of losing oneself in the music and nostalgia of Arabness—where Queen Umm Kulthoum lends her voice in song. The "Jews' tree," with its associations with Zionism, and the Arab "*Tarab*" both offer him temporary moments of pleasure during these difficult days of anxiety and doubt in the face of impending war. Amir creates a character who is a juggler of cultures, capable of combining the two cultures in whose midst he grew up, and melting them into a great love and a message of peace. Nuri's Jewish identity and Arabic sensibility contain binary oppositions that become even more pronounced over the course of his later relationship with Yasmine, a Palestinian Christian.

Eshkol and Nasser

Amir initially focuses on the difference between the Arabs' and Israelis' perceptions of themselves and of their enemies. The Arabs' perception is absolute: They constitute the absolute good and the Jewish enemy embodies absolute evil. In contrast, Nuri, the Mizrahi Jew, is enchanted to the point of intoxication by the singing of Umm Kulthoum, despite her hatred of Israel. He is delighted by the pleasing voice of a broadcaster reciting hateful verses from the Quran calling for Muslims to slaughter Jews, and he is impressed by Nasser's charismatic radio voice in contrast to the paternal and rhetorically limited voice of Levi Eshkol, the Israeli prime minister. Indeed, these first two chapters present sequentially the contrasting perspectives of the Jews and the Arabs with respect to their leaders in the leadup to the Six-Day War.

In the first chapter, during the interview that Abu George and Abu Nabil conduct with the governor on June 7, the governor praises Hussein for joining the war precisely because Eshkol has suggested that he not join. According to the Arabs, Eshkol's request, which they understand as a plea and betrays his weakness, must be exploited by doing the very opposite of what the Zionist enemy requested. It is important to note that the governor's praise of King Hussein and mockery of Eshkol proves the incorrectness of the Arab leaders' assumptions: "You remember how a few days ago, he [Eshkol] addressed his people on the radio and stammered with fright? *Miskeen*, poor thing! Ha ha . . . Our King, who is as wise as his grandfather Abdullah, immediately spotted this and decided that now is the time to attack them" (13). The governor caps his haughty statement with these words: "We have learned the lessons of *al-Nakba*, the catastrophe of 1948. Our new leaders, primarily Nasser and Hussein, God preserve them, are leading us to a splendid, speedy victory" (14). This is how the Arabs spoke about the leaders of both sides of the conflict during the Six-Day War.

Amir makes the point that Israelis also admired the Arab leaders. "Just look at Nasser," Afflalo went on. "Young, handsome, tall, sturdy, charismatic, a brilliant speaker. And his opposite number? Eshkol! Old, bearish, balding, with a black beret flat on his head like a pitta and belt under his armpits, and on top of all that, he's a lousy orator. Bugger it!" (26). According to historian Motti Golani:

> The story of Eshkol's stammering in the May 28th broadcast, a week before the war, already has a prominent place in every consideration of the waiting period before the war . . . This story illustrates, by way of the public's response to this speech, the extent of the Israelis' terror before the war. It is possible, however, that the response to the unsuccessful speech itself amplified the nervousness so that it became outright terror.[18]

Like Trabulisi, the reservist who describes the tense atmosphere in Tel Aviv, the public response to how Eshkol delivered his speech exaggerated its dark aspects and contributed to Israeli fears. Amir gives meticulous literary expression to this speech. Ironically, its role in stoking Israeli fears contributes to the Arabs' delusions about their impending victory. Afflalo's superficial description of the two leaders expresses his fear that an Israeli leader cannot prevail over such an impressive Arab foe. The ultimate outcome of the war places these superficial descriptions—of Eshkol as a pathetic weakling, of Hussein as a master strategist, and of Nasser as a great leader—in a distinctly ironic light.

Jephthah's Daughter

Nuri demonstrates his own fears on the eve of the war in various ways: He listens obsessively, perhaps even masochistically, to Radio Cairo, which bursts with arrogant invective; heretical thoughts arise in his head about his very presence in this stormy, insane country; he remembers the fate of his maternal uncle, Nuri Elias Nassah, who died before age thirty and after whom he is named, worrying that he like his namesake will not live to age thirty; he asks one of his friends to look at his palm to tell him what he sees in terms of life and death; he suffers from nightmares and makes a vow. "That night on the outskirts of Gaza, I made a vow: If I survive this in one piece, I'll change my life" (32). Amir alludes to the biblical Jephthah the Gileadite, who vows that if God will "deliver the children of Amnon into my hand, then it shall be, that whatsoever cometh forth of the doors of my house to meet me when I return in peace . . . I will offer it up as a burnt offering" (Judges 11:30–31). Jephthah's vow was monstrously fulfilled: Upon his return from the war, his only daughter came out to greet him with drums and dance, and her father must offer her as a sacrifice to God (Judges 11:37–40).[19]

This vow was adapted intertextually in S. Y. Agnon's *To This Day*. During the First World War, as he wanders around looking for a room, Agnon's narrator-protagonist, a literary incarnation of the author, spends a night sleeping in a bathtub in a Berlin pension:

> Somehow I managed to fall asleep. The reason I know I did is that I had a dream. What did I dream? I dreamed that a great war had broken out and that I was called to fight and took a solemn oath that if God brought me home safe and sound, I would sacrifice to Him whatever came forth from my house to greet me. I returned home safe and sound and behold, coming forth to greet me was myself.[20]

In contrast to both the biblical Jephthah and the protagonist of *To This Day*, Amir's Nuri makes no vow to sacrifice someone else upon his return from war; rather the very opposite—that he will change his own life. His vow is connected to life and not death. Surprisingly, the fulfillment of his vow is connected to Yasmine, the titular heroine of the novel and the only daughter of Abu George.

Abu George is not the sort of father to sacrifice his daughter; she is the joy of his life and his separation from her breaks his heart. When her husband Azmi died at a very young age and she miscarried their child, Yasmine left Al-Quds to pursue her education in Paris. For five years, Abu George and his wife have been longing for her to come home. Now, in the aftermath of the war, she is about to return, and each of her parents have a recurring dream of her. Abu George dreams of her departure for France:

> Again he recalled the parting scene that he was unable to get over—Yasmine walking towards the departure lounge in Amman airport, her back to him. He wanted to say something but his vocal cords would not obey him, until at last, a weak cry burst form his throat: "Look after yourself!" (122)

While Jephthah's daughter goes out to greet her father with drums and dance, Yasmine turns her back to her father; while Jephthah tells his daughter of her impending death, Abu George asks his daughter to take care of herself. These are two opposite pictures of fathers lamenting a forced separation from their daughters, and both invoke God in the process. Jephthah cries out: "Alas my daughter! Thou hast brought me very low, and thou art become my troubler; for I have opened my mouth to the Lord, and I cannot go back" (Judges 11:35). Abu George cries out: "You bring up an only daughter and she abandons you. How could that be, oh Lord Almighty?" (122). Yasmine's mother also has a dream for several nights, but it is a dream of homecoming: "Yasmine, wearing white slacks and a white shirt with a red kerchief around her neck, disembarks from a ship and runs into her arms" (121).

One night after the Israeli conquest of East Jerusalem, when Abu George was back to his routine of publishing his newspaper, "He returned home close to daybreak, and was met at the door by Umm George looking excited and pleased." As if going out to greet him with drums and dance, like Jephthah's daughter, Umm George tells him that Yasmine will be returning. Indeed, though we learn that "working on the newspaper in its new form was good for Abu George, making him feel young again," Abu George's wife explains to him that his good mood was not because of the first issue of the newspaper that he and Abu Nabil printed that night. "It's because of Yasmine—she is coming home soon!" (132).

Yasmine's actual return does not resemble her parents' dreams. When she disembarks from the plane, even before her parents embrace her, the white rays of Middle Eastern sun strike her and she hurries to protect her eyes with her sunglasses. The sun has a violent connotation in literature: Marceau, the protagonist of Camus' *The Stranger*, shoots an Arab to death "because of the sun" blinding his eyes; and in Joseph Conrad's *Heart of Darkness*, Marlow, traveling up the river, learns about the Swede who hanged himself—perhaps because "the sun was too much for him."[21] Amir employs the sun in a similar way: beginning with his quotation from Ahmad Shukeiry's words of contempt: "Isra'il, your head is made of wax, so why are you walking in the sun?" (27), and culminating with Heskel, Nuri's uncle, whose eyes squint in the sun (245), like Yasmine, when he arrives at the airport after years in an Iraqi prison. Sun, blood, and multilingualism are the motifs that accompany this "Palestinian Jephthah's daughter" on her return to occupied Al-Quds, while her father, in contrast to Jephthah, is not the victor but the vanquished, and for this reason, needs her alive and breathing next to him.

At the Allenby Bridge Barricade: Yasmine on Her Way to Al-Quds

The war slogans that catch Yasmine's eyes on her way from the Amman airport to the Allenby Bridge are ironic remnants of Arab arrogance before the war. They are written in Arabic, of course: *Al-nas'r karib!* [Victory is coming!] and *Ta'ish al-wahda al-Arabiya!* [Long live Arab unity!]. These slogans on the bare walls contrast with the graffiti that decorates the walls of Paris "like lipstick on a woman's lips" (134). Amir seems to be visualizing the slogan: "Make love, not war," since the rouge on a woman's face in the City of Lights appears much more stark and stable than the empty war slogans in Jordan, and especially those that decorate the walls of the West Bank where these Arabic slogans seem absurd in the reality of the occupation.

When Yasmine arrives at the Allenby Bridge, returning to her homeland, she comes to a roadblock. The image of the roadblock rather than the bridge will serve as a significant motif in her return to Jerusalem and her love story with Nuri Imari—himself a kind of bridge or roadblock standing in the way of her re-acclimation to life in this old-new place. At the Allenby Bridge roadblock, a reservist Israeli soldier asks for her documents in "a strangely accented Arabic, which reminded her of North African Arabs she had met in France" (135). When the soldier hears that Yasmine has come from Paris, he begins humming one of Yves Montand's songs and surprises those sitting in the car with his knowledge of French. A sergeant, looking to hurry up the inspection process at the border, directs his soldier: "Why are you messing around? Get on with it! Can't you see the queue?" Yasmine's ears prick up. After all, she knows Hebrew; she learned it as a young girl at the YMCA, and her best friend as a child in Talbiyeh (an upscale neighborhood in Jerusalem) before the expulsion of '48 was a Jewish girl. She just does not understand the word *mitmazmez* [messing around]. She does not recall this expression from childhood. Could it be a kind of code? Amir's readers know better than Yasmine that Hebrew has not incorporated code words over the years between 1948 and 1967 as much as civilian and military slang. When Yasmine is taken out of her parents' car for passport and bag inspection, the customs officer questions Yasmine in English (137). The soldier inspects her bag and finds a couple of cardboard boxes containing small white cylinders. "What's this?" he asks, and she answers: "Cotton tampons. Women use them for their periods. They're more hygienic and convenient than cotton pads" (139). The soldier is so embarrassed by her allusion to menstrual blood and feminine hygiene that he sends her on her way without inspecting the suitcase that includes three letters that Fayez, the Fatah head in Paris, had sent along with her to Jerusalem.

Arabic, French, Hebrew (formal and informal), and English are the languages that will roll off her tongue in her relationship with Nuri, the civil servant her father had befriended—at first to her dismay, before he became the object of her love. At this first roadblock on the way to her new life, these four languages play a central role. When the soldier who speaks Arabic, French, and Hebrew refers to her as "mademoiselle," she instantly corrects him: "It's madame not mademoiselle" (136). In her widowhood, she does not consider herself single and available. The motifs of the sun and blood also figure prominently as well, in a foreshadowing capacity. The sun's white rays that lash her eyes when she disembarks from the plane strike her mercilessly once again as she awaits inspection of her passport and her suitcases. As if she is punishing herself for some mysterious reason, she refuses her mother's offer of her scarf so that she might protect her head from the oppressive sun.

References to her menstrual blood bracket her stay in the land at its beginning, and will become the final symbolic impediment at its end, blocking her relationship with Nuri. With the help of the tampons, her path is paved to return to Jerusalem, and it is menstrual blood that will pave the path of her escape from Jerusalem back to Paris, where the slogans are written in red lipstick rather than blood.

When she returns to the car after the inspection of her suitcases, her father goes out to greet her: "Her parents had waited for her in the car, their nerves fraying. Seeing her come out, her father rushed to carry her cases and they drove off. Yasmin's gaze was frozen and her mouth tight-lipped as the car **crossed the bridge** and turned onto the road leading to Al-Quds" (139, emphasis added). But a long journey awaits her. Roadblocks of religion, nationhood, political and military power, and familial status all accumulate in the language Yasmine and Nuri will use to speak to one another and will painfully hamper their relationship, making their love short-lived. The war, and its physical and spiritual roadblocks, will prove stronger than love.

"It Is in the Nature of War That It Alters Reality and Creates a New Balance of Power"

Before analyzing the relationship between Nuri and Yasmine, it is important to consider their family background and particularly their fathers. Abu George, Yasmine's father, lives in Sheikh Jarrah after fleeing from Talbiyeh during the '48 war. Nuri's father lives in Katamon, after having been exiled from Baghdad following the establishment of the State of Israel. The wars and exiles of these two fathers radically transform their lives and adversely affect their health. Nuri's father has a heart attack resulting from the Six-Day War, when his four sons are called up to fight. Yasmine's father falls ill after the war with a mysterious illness, with a persistent cough and a sense of depression and disinterest in life. Both fathers depend on their children to justify their existence and help them maintain a hold on their lives. Nuri's father had nurtured the hope of establishing a rice farm in the Hula Valley, but that plan evaporated. He lives in a dismal apartment, but justifies his life in Israel based on the success of his sons: "I immigrated for the sake of your future. Here you and Kabi graduated from university, Moshi has his own farm in a cooperative village, and Ephraim is being educated on a kibbutz. Thank God you are all nicely established and have a good future before you" (311–12). Abu George consoles himself with a similar rationalization about the war and its aftermath: "There is even some good in your conquest—we got Yasmine back" (325). He does not know that continuing conflicts in the aftermath of the war will cause Yasmine to leave him again.

The analogy between the two fathers extends to the public sphere: Both have the capacity to offer poignant criticisms of their respective communities, further evidence of their deep frustration. In one of his arguments with his Muslim partner Abu Nabil, Abu George declares:

> Come on, Abu Nabil, we're always blaming others for our problems—the Ottomans, the British, the colonialists, the communists, and now the Jews. When are we going to accept responsibility for our own mistakes? . . . We're stuck in the past, brother, and we won't move forward until we stop blaming everybody else. Look at how the Israelis have succeeded in combining the old with the new, modernism and religion. Look at their enthusiasm when they reached that wall of theirs. (124)

The criticism of Nuri's Iraqi-born father is directed toward the members of his community and is ignited by his brother Heskel, who offers new insights about the Mizrahi community vis-à-vis the Ashkenazi founders of the state:

> Our culture is not a culture of revolutions. We are fatalists like the Arabs. We sat under the palm trees and waited for the Messiah. We lamented "by the rivers of Babylon" while the Jews of Europe got up and did something. They came from the incandescent world of the Bolsheviks. Such people are irreverent, they have no God, they have decided to become the Messiah themselves. If there is a mountain in their way, they move it. We see a mountain and we stop. That's the difference between the East and the West. (315–16)

When Kabi and Nuri oppose their uncle's trenchant critique of the ethnic conflict within Israeli society, Nuri's father agrees with his brother:

> Nuri, my son . . . your uncle may be right. Revolution is blood and these people had the hard heads of world-savers who believe only in their own truth and God can't budge them from it. Like in your kibbutz, where the children sleep separately from their parents. Can you imagine such a thing among us? Parents and children getting together for a couple hours a day, as if at a café? (317)

Amir's ability to adopt different points of view and to confront these divergent opinions turns *Yasmine* into a kind of *Rashomon*.[22] He not only manipulates the confusion engendered by multilingualism and multiculturalism, but also expresses conflicting insights about issues within Palestinian and Israeli society after the War of Independence and the Six-Day War. The analogy between the fathers of Yasmine and Nuri indicates Amir's attempt to portray the similarity between the tragedy of the Palestinians and of the Jews, and to bind the two narratives together in a bond of fate. Amir does not let one side in the struggle be dismissive of the other because there are many similarities between them. Amir implies that the Mizrahi mentality, which is close to that of the Arabs, might have been a mediating, clarifying, and calming force in the ongoing, bloody conflict.

This complex argument is expressed in a discussion between Senator Antoine and Nuri's father. In defiance of the Arab policy of not mixing with or discussing political issues with Israelis, the senator has accepted an invitation from Nuri and his father to come to Nuri's office in Sheikh Jarrah, which before the war had been the house of Ahmad Shukeiry. The senator comments:

> I see that except for the pictures you have left everything as it was. I used to come here often. The head of the Palestine Liberation Organization, Advocate Ahmad Shukeiry, was a friend of mine. He was at my house the night before he left Al-Quds. (302)

When the senator asks, "What do you [the Israelis] have to do with Al-Quds?" Nuri's father explains the Israeli position in an exemplary and diplomatic manner: "Jerusalem is mentioned in our Torah 667 times, and the Land of Israel, 4,584 times. On the other hand, Jerusalem is not mentioned even once in the Quran" (302–3). When the senator complains that the character of the city has been changed, Nuri's father answers with the principle of measure for measure:

> It is in the nature of war that it alters reality and creates a new balance of power. In 1948, you captured the Jewish Quarter and did whatever you wanted with it—you killed some of the inhabitants, exiled others, and destroyed all the houses. Did that policy not change the character of the ancient Jewish Quarter? (303)

Nuri's father mentions the seventy generations of Jewish inhabitance in Iraq, and how they were slaughtered on the Shavuot holiday in 1941[23] and later expelled. (He still has a key to his house in Baghdad.) By adapting the Palestinian complaints to explain the Israeli story, Amir gives voice through Nuri's father to a repressed and silenced fact: Jews too were expelled from the lands of their fathers. Nuri's father concludes his striking analogy between the fate of the Jews of Arabs lands and the Palestinians with a surprisingly daring message of peace, something his son will do again at the end of the novel:

> We are aliens? This is our home, your Excellency. Half the Israelis are children of Arabia, from Asia and the Maghreb, speakers of Arabic and

products of its culture. It is time to turn over a new leaf. We offer you good neighborliness, we court you the way a cousin courts a cousin. Why do you not respond? (306)

Perhaps this vision of perilous peace foregrounded on bad blood between "cousins" provokes Yasmine to flee from Nuri, her parents, and her homeland.

Sun, Blood, and Roadblock

The paradox of the *roadblock* and Yasmine's *crossing* of the Allenby Bridge relatively in peace is part of the motifs that foreshadow the opposition-ridden world she will find in Jerusalem in the aftermath of the Six-Day War. It is a binary system that does not necessarily fit the stereotypes that have been passed down to her and are enshrined in her consciousness. How will "cousin" Yasmine respond to "cousin" Nuri's courting? While previously she perceived Nuri as a cruel and sly conqueror who toppled her father from his seat of power, she comes to recognize that he is an open-hearted and considerate person: "[H]e's a different [sort of] Jew, unlike the image depicted by Fayez and his comrades in their struggle for public opinion; a new kind of Israeli, without machismo, not a battle hero or a hoe-wielding pioneer, as they like to project them" (333–34). In the wake of her falling in love with Nuri, she sets out to change her attitude toward life. Recall that it was Nuri who had vowed that if he survived the war he would change his life, a vow that alludes to Jephthah's. Here the vow pertains to the daughter of Abu George, the "Jephthah's daughter" of *Yasmine*:

> She longed to start living again, to leave behind the pointless mourning, the bitterness, the loneliness, and the patriotic struggle. Surely life was not all wars and vengeance and restoration of rights and that whole ideology. Perhaps real life was simply loving, finding a partner, raising a family, like her friend Nehad and people all over the world. Ever since meeting Nuri she had felt deep down inside that she was yearning to conceive, longing for life given and received, for a man's caress, his warmth, his friendship, for life with a twin soul. She dreamed of

waking in the morning with her man beside her in bed, of listening to his breathing, caring for him and giving him pleasure, putting her arm through his in the street, dreaming together. (334)

Yasmine's feminine love renders war superfluous. Nuri's love transforms the image of blood into a life force and the sun into an emblem of adoration.

She had entered my bloodstream. Was this the immediate, instinctive love, the kind you can't resist? They say that everyone has a halo around his head, a small sun, which dazzles, creates a sweet illusion, an action. When two such haloes touch, love happens. Was her halo responding to mine? And where would it lead? (324)

At the Allenby Bridge roadblock, the images of a blinding sun, blood, and death were linked to war. Here the images of sun and blood are linked to love and life. They will come together again at another roadblock at the end of the novel.

Nuri comes out of the war unscathed—only his brother Kabi was wounded—but the chapter dedicated to his return from battle in the south to his home in Jerusalem ends with him cutting himself while shaving. "Drops of blood dripped from the blade."[24] This blood foreshadows the blood of two Arab women—both refugees from '48 whose families settled in East Jerusalem, one on Mount Scopus and the other in Sheikh Jarrah—with whom Nuri is deeply connected and who will both wallow in blood at the end of the novel. The shepherdess Ghadir is killed by members of her family for "family honor"; Yasmine's menstrual blood is natural, but is associated with the end of her relationship with Nuri. Still the two women are connected to him through the common motifs of the sun, blood, and roadblocks, and through that connection, each in her own way, to the prototype of Jephthah's daughter.

Whereas Nuri's acquaintance with Yasmine comes at a later stage of life (he has experienced battles and has reached what he considers the fateful age of thirty years old[25]), he met Ghadir nine years earlier, when he was still a young soldier doing his regular military service for a short period on Mount Scopus. At his first meeting with her, a symbolic roadblock goes up between them:

> I had met her on the mountain my first morning there, when I woke up at dawn to see the sunlight polishing the mountains of Jerusalem. Suddenly, beyond the barbed wire fence that surrounded our enclave in East Jerusalem, a shepherd girl appeared with her flock. Her walk was supple and springy, like a wild colt's, and her long dress flapped in the morning breeze. She seemed mysterious and secretive and she charmed me from a distance. When I approached the fence, she stopped where she was. (182)

When Nuri is informed that the convoy[26] on which he had come up the mountain was planning to stay an additional two weeks on the mountain, he responds with joy: "I loved the place, the tranquility . . . and of course, Ghadir, the wild colt on the other side of the fence" (186). The allusion here to Bialik's "On the Other Side of the Fence" is significant: Nuri and Ghadir, fire and water in Arabic, like Noah and Marinka, the Jew and the gentile in Bialik's story, will not be able to mix. Even clothing constitutes a kind of impediment. Ghadir's clothing covers her completely and arouses the protagonist's interest: "I have always been enchanted by pretty women covered from head to toe. I sensed in them a mysteriousness that was much more intriguing than the provocative behavior of women in our society" (184). When Nuri later meets Yasmine, she generally appears in Western dress, "in an aubergine-colored shirt and black jeans" (223).

When Ghadir senses that the emotional relationship between them is beginning, she becomes frightened, foreshadowing her horrific murder, more than nine years before the fact: "Night is falling, what am I doing here? They'll kill me" (186). It is not mentioned that the scarf that Nuri tries to give Ghadir as a present is red, but only that it is colorful. However, this scarf is connected to the recurring dream of Yasmine's mother, correlative to the story of Jephthah's daughter, in which Yasmine "wearing white slacks and a white shirt with a red kerchief around her neck, disembarks from a white ship and runs into her [mother's] arms" (121). The red scarf around her neck, as if to strangle her, set against a background of white, suggests the death of the possibility of realizing the love between Nuri and Yasmine; at the same time, it is related to the death of Ghadir that followed the occupation of Jerusalem.

Nine years later, after the conquest of East Jerusalem, Nuri hopes to meet Ghadir. When he left the mountain at the end of his reserve duty, he remained "confused by what had and had not happened" between them: "I knew that Mount Scopus had been besieged during the most recent war and heavily shelled too, but in my dreamy way, I kept on hoping that I would still find Ghadir on the slopes, herding her flock as before" (187). His dream comes true, but within a few months it turns into a nightmare. A joyous fulfillment occurs next to Senator Antoine's villa, that same villa where the soldiers were seen wandering around on the third day of the war, turning the senator's dream of victory into a nightmare. A woman who is "covered from head to toe" stops next to Nuri and asks, "Nuri?" It was Ghadir. It becomes clear that since she last met him, she had been forced to marry a cousin from Amman, whom she does not love. Her Jordanian husband, who had gone to see his family before the war, is now stuck in the Jordanian capital with no way of returning to the East Jerusalem that is now in Israeli control. Nuri tries to help Ghadir, but all his efforts to return her husband to Jerusalem so that the "little shepherd girl" will not have to go live in Amman come to naught, and her situation becomes even more complicated. The Israelis dealing with the occupied Palestinian population create bureaucratic impediments, another kind of roadblock, to reuniting the husband and wife. In the end, it is the young shepherd girl (whose sheep serve as a metonymy for her innocence) who pays the horrific price, when the fanatic men in her family slaughter her in cold blood.

In a formal tone, Nuri reports on the end of Ghadir's life:

> Ghadir was murdered, her body shattered against the rock on which she used to sit with her sheep around her. A local Arab woman, probably a neighbor, was waiting for me at the office to give me the terrible news. I informed the police and then made my way to the foot of Mount Scopus. Ghadir's broken body was still lying on the boulder, helpless under the wide blue skies and hot sun, covered with her darkening, drying

blood. Who killed her? Her husband? Her cousin Karim? Her father? Or all three? (363)

The white rock that serves as a backdrop for Ghadir's crimson blood, which blackens in the oppressive sun, recalls Umm George's dream in which a red scarf is tied around the throat of her daughter Yasmine, who disembarks from a white ship dressed in white from head to toe. But Ghadir is the real Jephthah's daughter, the one whose father and kin murder her. In contrast, Yasmine's connection to Jephthah's daughter remains implied. Her connection to white and red is encapsulated by white tampons meant to obstruct the flow of menstrual blood, and by her repeated appearance in her mother's dreams in red and white. Even so, both women are sacrificed to a war that is not theirs; and their fathers play a central role in their fates, just like that nameless biblical daughter, known by her father's name.[27]

Toward evening, when Nuri returns to Mount Scopus (Jabel Scubus, in Arabic), he meets Fathiya, Ghadir's mother. For the mother, red and white represent her sacrifice, not in a dream, but in reality. The setting sun plays a symbolic role of lost hope: At that moment, Fathiya was "turning gold in the light of the setting sun . . . and she said: I had only her, one ray of light, and they went and extinguished her too" (365–66). The sun, the light and Nuri's Arabic name, together with the stream, the water, and Ghadir's Arabic name—continue to play a game of complementary opposites even after her disappearance:

> Ghadir's death elevated her in my mind, drew all the light to her, forced me to clarify to myself what I had taken for granted while she lived, to understand what I had unconsciously sensed in her. (366)

Amir concludes the chapter on Ghadir's murder with a reference to the clear water suggested by her image and name, and with a quotation from Bialik's poem of praise to the simple man. In contrast to the hidden allusion to the biblical Jephthah's daughter and to the female sacrifice that remains behind the fence in Bialik's story, this time the allusion to the national poet is straightforward. Nuri is separated from the woman who was and is no longer: "[Ghadir] this one little bird under the sky, a stream of pure water, brought back to my mind some lines from Bialik's poem, 'Let My Lot Be With You,' which I had learned at the evening school for working boys" (366–67).[28] In this way, he bids farewell to a modest, innocent woman, whose voice of clear water has been silenced forever. The immigrant from Baghdad, who ostensibly lacks a strong command of Hebrew and its literature, nevertheless pays tribute to Ghadir with exceptional Hebrew linguistic expression.

The Final Roadblock

After Ghadir's death, Nuri realizes that his memories of her serve as a foil for Yasmine, and he compares the two women:

> I had always seen Ghadir as a sweet appealing creature, an innocent girl-woman walking down a marginal path, far from the centers of power and influence, simply living and letting others live, like a little bird under the sky, a flower of the field. In a way, she was the opposite of Yasmine, the educated, analytical, political Yasmine, who lived at the head of things and rallied to the flag. (366)

Ghadir always spoke to Nuri in Arabic, "practiced in the art of silence and verbal restraint," in Bialik's terms. *Sabah el-khair* [good morning] is how Nuri greets her on the third morning of their acquaintance on Mount Scopus in 1958, when he was twenty-one years old. The two days beforehand the dialogue between them had been carried out almost without words. "We looked at each other in silence. 'For you all,' she said, laughing [with a thousand eyes], pointing to the heaped spring onions, mint, parsley and other vegetables in the basket" (182). In response to his good morning greeting, Ghadir answers "*sabah el-nur*," which means "morning of light." When Ghadir hears that the name of the Jewish soldier who speaks Arabic is Nuri, she exclaims, "An Arabic name! Nuri, it means light, fire." When Nuri hears her name, he says, "Ghadir—stream. A beautiful name, musical, like water running through gullies." Ghadir sums up the connection between these two names as follows: "Stream and fire, water and sun, *ya salaam*, it's beautiful!" (183). Nine years later, East Jerusalem has been conquered, Mount Scopus has ceased to be an enclave, and suddenly they meet again. The evening sun lights her tawny face and she says, "*Allah yinawer alaik*, may God shine his light upon you! Light and water, stream and fire" (188). The connection between their first meeting and this one is thus reestablished.

In contrast to Ghadir's Arabic name, Yasmine's name is international. She does not bring Nuri a basket of vegetables and fresh pita from her tent, for she can offer a much greater culinary experience: Her father is the proprietor of a large restaurant in which he can eat to his heart's content whenever he likes. Even more than through names, food, fathers, and fate, the contrast between Ghadir, the Muslim Arab from Mount Scopus, and Yasmine, the Christian Arab returning from Paris, is sharpened by the issue of language. While Ghadir and Nuri converse in Arabic, whose register is rendered beautifully by Amir when translated into Hebrew, Yasmine insists on speaking with Nuri in English. Nuri laments this artificial, diplomatic choice:

> I always admired the matter-of-fact clarity of her speech. At the same time, I wished that she wouldn't insist on speaking to me in English, which she spoke so much better than I did. Sometimes what she said sounded like a complex, mathematical equation and I often felt tongue-tied when speaking to her. I could understand why she did not want us to talk in Hebrew, though when working at the village she sounded like any Jewish Israeli woman. But why couldn't we communicate in Arabic, which was our mother tongue, hers and mine? (329)

It is interesting that Nuri refers to Arabic as his mother tongue. In their book *The Babel of the Unconscious*, Jacqueline Amati-Mehler, Simona Argentieri, and Jorge Canestri suggest that one's first linguistic experience connects the voice of the mother to the primal pleasure of nursing.[29] No wonder that Nuri delights in the voices of those who excel in speaking and singing in his mother tongue—Nasser, Umm Kulthoum, the sheikh reciting verses from the Quran—and distinguishes between voice and meaning. Only in his relations with his beloved Yasmine is he deprived of this primal pleasure. English, the language of the West, serves as an impediment to a warm and authentic connection between them.

But Yasmine softens with time. Love is good to her. She changes and becomes willing to get to know the Israeli cultural world of Nuri, who, in turn, is willing to tell her in "seventy different languages" how he loves her (393). About a year after the war, they leave Jerusalem to travel to Kiryat Oranim, the kibbutz where Nuri lived as a new immigrant. Now that he has become a public servant, he has been invited to deliver a lecture there.[30] On the way, Nuri and Yasmine pass by Ramallah, Jaffa, and Tel Aviv, and they also see the remains of an immigrant camp near Pardes Hanna, which had been the home of the Imari family, but now stands desolate. During this trip, their love reaches new heights. The places they pass undergo a depoliticization for them. Nuri invites Yasmine to occupy the land with him in a non-warlike way. Until this point, romance defeats politics, but roadblocks await them at the end of their journey. Meanwhile, on the beach at Jaffa:

> Yasmine held my hand and led me towards the sea. We took off our shoes and walked along the sandy beach. Two elderly men, bent over fishing nets they were mending, smiled at us. The air smelled of fish. A flock of gulls circled above us and then took off over the sea. (405)

In their intimate excursion, Amir employs the well-known literary convention of making the climax of one experience serve as an introduction to its collapse in another experience. The menstrual blood that floods the lovers during their first sexual encounter at the kibbutz, which will have ramifications for their entire relationship, is foreseen by Nuri in the crazy dreams he has in the kibbutz guest room while Yasmine is resting in the room next door: "Crazy, restless dreams filled my sleep, and one image shook me: The ruddy Tigris overflowed and flooded the loamy soil, bursting furiously on to the white dunes of Pardes Hanna" (411). Once again, the coded colors of the novel, red against a background of white, signal tragedy. When they leave the guestrooms toward the dining hall, where the lecture will take place, "red hibiscus and long-stemmed poppies glowed in the twilight" (412).

Nuri, a Mizrahi immigrant from Arab lands who as a pupil at the kibbutz had sat "on the back benches" of the dining hall (419), is now a person of authority presenting his political vision to the old-timers of the kibbutz; it is a sort of victory demonstration for a second Israel. Earlier in the novel, Kabi, the brother who was injured in the war, turns to Nuri and asks a challenging question: "Little brother, what do you think was the most important thing that happened in this war? It was our war . . . Look around you, most of the wounded are from the mass immigration, as they call us. Jews from Iraq, Romania, Morocco, Tunisia, Libya, Turkey, Iran . . . It's a revolution. From now on the State is as much our as theirs" (79). At the end of the novel, it becomes clear that not only the war belonged to the mass immigration, but the possibility of peace rests in their hands too, which is what Nuri tells the pioneering members of the kibbutz:

> Today we need a new beginning, a revolution that will take into account both the Arabs of Israel and us, the immigrants from the Muslim countries who fought in this war shoulder to shoulder with you.
>
> The question is, what will be our place in the leadership? Will our knowledge, our intuition, our cultural connection to the Arabs be put to good use, will we be a formative element in the culture and the new political reality, or will we continue to be second-class?
>
> And another question—Will the Arabs of Israel continue to be the third class? I believe that what we do today will determine whether the Arabs of Israel will be our neighbors or our enemies. Are we capable of sensitivity to the other and consideration for his difficulties? Will we have the wisdom to carry out the necessary revolution and usher in a new era of peace and co-existence? (419)

Nuri's words are those of Eli Amir, the publicist, directed to his readers. But within the fictional framework of the novel, they are directed to the members of Kibbutz Kiryat Oranim, and more than that, to his "cousin" Yasmine. He wants her to know that it is possible to remove roadblocks. This is what Nuri—the hybrid person, who floats freely between two languages and cultures—offers as an answer to the various questions that rain down on him at the end of the lecture: "In my opinion this country has two histories, two languages, two cultures, two visions, two dreams. Anyone who tries to claim the whole thing will end up with nothing." And about Jerusalem, his city and Yasmine's, he says: "In my opinion, Jerusalem should be open to all, and if you ask me, the Temple Mount should fly not just the flag of Israel, but the flags of the Vatican and all the Arab states" (421).

Nuri's statements are greeted with applause, something "which is not customary among us." He suggests a social and political solution to Yasmine from his point of view, and with that their love story reaches its climax: "Hand in hand, Yasmine and I walked up the dark cypress path, just the two of us, closer than we'd ever been before. Here in Kiryat Oranim, my first home in Israel, the barriers between us finally fell" (422). Can it really be so? When they return to the guestroom they are ready to give themselves over to love, to remove the emotional, physical, and psychological barriers and unfulfilled desires that had been deferred. Nuri's affinity with the culture and mentality of the Arabs expresses itself in his hesitation to come to her until their arrival at the kibbutz, a place that in its time exemplified an attitude of free love. But when the longed-for moment finally comes, "She was bleeding and I was smeared with her blood. 'Sorry, it's my period,' she said" (423). There is no doubt that the expression *"lehitboses bedam"* [to be smeared in blood] can be interpreted in varying ways.

The meaning of blood in *Yasmine* is referential to war: If the Arabs come to us in blood, we shall do the same to them. However, in this situation, blood and being smeared with it indicate an intimate connection between the couple. Yasmine's menstrual period, during which the love between her, the Palestinian, and Nuri, the Israeli, is finally consummated, suggests that only after the spilling of blood are peace talks possible. If not for the final roadblock that will make clear to the lovers that their love is doomed, we might see in this expression a sign of revival or a literalization of the common expression "Make love, not war."[31]

Yasmine and Nuri return to Jerusalem via Beit She'an and Jericho, and at a roadblock, a young soldier asks for their identity papers. Unlike the reservist at the Allenby Bridge, who addresses Yasmine in Arabic, who sings in French, and whose behavior was light-hearted and considerate, this young soldier speaks only Hebrew and his behavior is dogmatic and intransigent. It does not help Yasmine that Nuri is equipped with official papers attesting to his high government status. The soldier warns him: "Sir, to me you are a citizen like any other. If you continue like this, I'm going to have to take measures against you too" (427). Here too, Nuri, who had been unable to save Ghadir from death or prevent the expulsion of Senator Antoine Salameh, is unable to prevent the humiliation of his lover. Yasmine returns from the body search embarrassed and sober. When she first entered the land, she encountered a roadblock, and after a long period of acclimation, during which she thought she might be able to put down the flag that was her responsibility to carry as a Palestinian, daughter of an occupied people, she stumbles once again on a roadblock. The roadblock frames the sojourn of this Jephthah's daughter in the land. She decides to return to Paris, even though she leaves heartbreak in her wake. Her ill and suffering father, a stranger in his own land, will find no further consolation from her; and her lover, Nuri, who is bitterly disappointed to have lost his lover—who embodied his dream of peace—resigns from his job and leaves his office in Sheikh Jarrah. In the letter that Yasmine leaves for him, she writes: "It turns out that our dream journey was in fact a farewell trip. I didn't intend it to be like this. On the contrary, I tried to remove the obstacles to my heart . . . To you I'm Yasmine, but beyond that I'm an Arab woman in the Jews' country" (439).

It appears that the roadblocks that Israel places in the West Bank after the Six-Day War are nothing in comparison to the obstacles within the heart. Yasmine insists until the very end on speaking English and refuses to let a common language—Hebrew or Arabic—take root in their relationship. She also ignores the fact that Nuri, the refugee from Baghdad, has offered a solution to the refugee from West Jerusalem; as a person entrusted with responsibility for Arab Affairs, he suggested in his bold, authoritative words at the kibbutz the idea of two states for two peoples, and even received applause from the kibbutzniks who normally bask in their own self-righteousness. In the face of this message of peace from someone with authority who is meeting her halfway, she returns to her original stance that he is an occupier and she is a stranger in a land that is not hers, proving that the roadblocks in her heart are more formidable than she is. Yasmine sees the reality of the war and its aftermath, and she decides to leave it all behind her and escape to another foreign place that imposes no obligations on her.

7

The Human Voice in Inhumane Wars in David Grossman's *To the End of the Land*
The Yom Kippur War in Israeli Prose

> "The voice is the most important thing for me, always, even before a girl's appearance. She has a voice that no one I know has, an orange voice, I swear, don't laugh, with a little bit of lemon-yellow around the edges, and it has a spring, it has a pounce."

When the Turning Point Is Both Surprising and Expected

There are literary storylines that stick in our minds for years, and there are others that slip into oblivion soon after reading the last page, and we struggle to remember what we just read. One of the important elements in a powerful story is the turning point. When the turning point in the storyline is surprising, amazing, but also, in the back of our minds, expected, we feel that the story is good, credible, taken from real life. The Yom Kippur War, unfortunately, is a dramatic turning point in the chronicles of Israel, as if taken from a good story.

It ostensibly came as a complete surprise, like a bolt of lightning or a sudden sandstorm. But when the dust settled and the shock subsided, we knew it had been expected, that the writing on the wall had been flashing in front of our eyes, and we had preferred to ignore it. Because how long could the euphoria have continued after the Six-Day War, which had infused the army with an exaggerated sense of confidence, a feeling of omnipotence? How long can a person—or a nation—rest on their laurels and meanwhile become depraved and arrogant, scorn the enemy, treat the occupied territories as their own, maintain a hedonistic lifestyle, and think and declare: "No one matters but me." The Yom Kippur War was a glaring and brutal response to the sense of superiority Israelis felt in the wake of the Six-Day War and their derisive attitude toward the occupied population. The brilliant victory in 1967, which seemed to be straight out of a captivating bestseller, a bit surreal, blinded our eyes, inflated our chests, and made us slow to emerge from the euphoria that swept over us after the somewhat miraculous war, which in six days generated a dramatic change in the geographic and mental map of the State of Israel.

The Events Occurred in Reality, the Characters—Obscured

The siren that blared in the heart of Tel Aviv at 2 PM, in the middle of the Sabbath day, in the midst of Yom Kippur 1973 (and during the Ramadan fast for Muslims), announcing the sudden outbreak of war to the shocked, fasting residents of the State of Israel, epitomizes the aforementioned mix of the opposites "surprise" and "expected"—an oxymoron that helps etch the storyline in our memory. The sudden siren, in the afternoon of the most sacred day in the Jewish calendar, is shrill and deafening evidence of a complicated political and historical reality, capable of unleashing real and metaphoric thunder out of the blue; it is doubtful whether the greatest and boldest of writers could pull off such a feat without being accused of sensationalism. The siren on that sacred day, which also fell on the Sabbath that year, terrified the ultimate symbol of the Israeli home front: the city of Tel Aviv. The siren in the heart of Israeli existence is a jarring embodiment of the precise time and place in which it was sounded, which endowed them with further symbolic meaning.

All this seems to reinforce and affirm the rhetoric about Jewish fate and the Israeli reality, which is sometimes stranger than fiction and beyond imagination. How did Hebrew literature contend with the trauma and upheaval of the Yom Kippur War? How did literature address—if at all—the symbolic time in which the war erupted and the fact that it was a prosaic, harsh, and traumatic antithesis to the miraculous Six-Day War?

Hanoch Bartov is an author who knows how to weave complicated stories, including detective fiction. At the end of his detective novel *The Dissembler*, published in 1975, there is a brief glimpse of the Yom Kippur War when the multifaceted hero is killed on his way to the front. The author refrained from addressing the war itself through the genre of fiction,[1] preferring to contend with it by writing a diary. The second volume of *Dado: 48 Years and 20 Days* deals with the twenty days of the Yom Kippur War (October 10–25, 1973, A War Diary). Every minute is documented in the diary, every conversation, every gesture, and every testimony. The detailed-documentary, factual, and understated nature of Bartov's book speaks for itself: There is no need to invent a story like this; it was already invented. It exists and only needs to be told.

On the cover of *Fire*, a documentary novel by Yuval Neria, the author announces, "Many of the events described in the book occurred in reality. All of the characters are obscured." That is, Yuval Neria also had no need to make up a story; he just protected the identity of the people.

Fire is a chilling document about the smugness of the army's senior command; about the prophetic feeling of young officers in the armored corps who decided not to go home for Yom Kippur, despite the unequivocal statement by IDF military intelligence that war was not imminent; about their crazy personal war during the initial days of battle, alone, frantic, pitted against the entire Egyptian army; and about their unheroic return to the beaten and alienated home front, though their valor should be recorded in the annals of human history, because there is no greater heroism or sacrifice. Yair, the deputy company commander, the hero of the novel, agonizes when laid up in the hospital:

> I knew there'd be a war, I knew just like Amir knew, and I didn't have the courage to go to the top [brass], if necessary, punch them all in the face, if necessary, to say you're blind, deaf and blind. There's going to be a major war. I didn't go. I didn't shout. I didn't speak and I remained alive. Like Cain. And nothing, nothing in the world will help. (143)[2]

And he wants to die.

Time Broken into Days, Hours, and Minutes

Guilt is the strongest feeling that overwhelmed the fighters who survived that war, soldiers and officers alike. They remained alive while dozens of their comrades fell and they felt a mark of Cain on their foreheads, stamped by their own devastating emotions and by the society around them—especially the relatives of the dead and missing: bereaved parents, widows, and orphans. The heavy and unprocessed feeling of guilt is the subject of Yitzhak Ben-Ner's story "Nicole," published in a collection of stories entitled *Rustic Sunset*. Unlike the heroes of *Fire*—Yair, Amir, and Eran—who were deployed at the banks of the Suez Canal when the Egyptians opened fire and were caught in the inferno, Berko, the hero of "Nicole," a brigade commander, is at a hotel in Beersheba with his young girlfriend Nicole on October 6, 1973. The guilt that torments Yuval Neria's Yair is that he chose to keep quiet—that he didn't voice his gut feeling about the imminent outbreak of war—and that he survived; the guilt of Yitzhak Ben-Ner's Berko is tenfold, and his girlfriend Nicole uses his guilt feelings to take revenge against him, refusing to support his efforts to absolve himself. Berko's burden of guilt is focused on his soldiers and officers, who cried out for his help, in vain: "He [Little Jonathan] called out to him for thirty-nine straight hours, until his batteries died out and the Egyptians came."[3] The military two-way radio and the radio operator have a clear vocal presence in the literature on the Yom Kippur War, as evident below when analyzing that terrible war in David Grossman's *To the End of the Land*.

Berko's whereabouts at the time the war broke out—at a hotel for a weekend of lovemaking and rest—illustrates the suddenness of the war. Even more, it underlines the terrible irresponsibility of the senior army commanders, their smugness, their arrogant and pompous behavior, which stemmed from excessive self-confidence and a mentality of "don't worry, everything will be fine."

Wars, in which time is broken into days, hours, and minutes, also dictate the emphasis on the precise (fictional) time in the literature written about them. This also applies to place; each waypoint is measured. Concreteness is critical in war, as well as in the documentary literature written about it and in the literary fiction that reflects it in tendentious and sharp perspective. Thus, A. B. Yehoshua decided to emphasize, from the very first conversation of *Mr. Mani*, that Hagar's father Roni was killed on the sixth day of the Six-Day War. In *Fire*, Yuval Neria describes not only the chaos of the first days of battle, but also the four days that preceded Yom Kippur in 1973, including a letter a soldier named Eran writes to his family on the morning of the war: "Sinai, October 6th, 11 AM. Dear Dad, Mom and Nirit." Eran, who would die three hours later in the war that broke out on the banks of the Suez Canal, where he sat to write the letter, asks his parents in central Israel to buy a string for his guitar to replace one that broke. His imminent death was unimaginable.

Berko, tucked away with Nicole in a Beersheba hotel, left a message on Friday at 11 AM that he would be spending the Sabbath at Hotel D in Ashkelon. Midway, the couple had a change of mind and turned to Beersheba instead of Ashkelon. Berko notified his unit about the change in a careless way, conveying the information to a telephone operator whose name he could not recall. On that Friday, he also disdainfully dismissed his security officer's assessment—"They shouldn't get all hysterical every time an Egyptian farts."[4] Was this war indeed a total surprise? Or was it engendered by a total disregard and dismissal of anything that might ruin the hedonistic plans of satiated, adulterous, and self-satisfied officers? The literature's emphasis on time and place helps it to contend with the absurd, to pointedly express the operational negligence, to capture the moment and illustrate the abrupt transition from a false national sense of peace and security to a reality of all-out war, a war that sowed death and bereavement in thousands of Israeli homes one clear day, during the twenty-fifth year of the State of Israel.

In *To Know a Woman* by Amos Oz, the war is mentioned indirectly. Yoel Ravid, the protagonist of the novel, which takes place in the 1980s, is a retired spy, a Jerusalemite who rents a spacious home in Tel Aviv. In the library of that home, he occasionally peruses a biography of the late IDF chief of staff, David Elazar ("Dado"). This is apparently a reference to Hanoch Bartov's *Dado: 48 Years and 20 Days*. The protagonist reaches a section of the biography where the "patron" (his boss in the "organization") is praised for being one of the few who warned about the impending disaster of Yom Kippur 1973.[5] The title of Bartov's book on Lt. Gen. David Elazar, implicitly referenced in Oz's novel, again emphasizes critical days of war, twenty days weighed against forty-eight years. Here again, literary fiction implies that the war was expected—after all, the patron sounded a warning—but it was more convenient to divert attention, to suppress the knowledge.⁶

A Flash of Lightning, a Continuous Roll of Thunder

The novel *Feathers* by Haim Be'er describes the story of the wonderful friendship of a boy of religious background with an eccentric man named Mordechai Leder, who is driven by a single obsession. The friendship develops in Jerusalem of the early 1950s, despite strong objections by the boy's parents.

The boy is Leder's confidante regarding the latter's vision of establishing a Nutrition Army, a vision based on the ideology of a Viennese-Jewish thinker named Josef Popper-Lynkeus, who distinguished between the individual's essential needs and luxuries, and demanded that the state take responsibility for meeting its citizens' primary needs; the state could fulfill this obligation by enlisting the citizenry in compulsory civil service.

The intensive friendship between Leder and the boy is severed toward the end of the book, when the "visionary" loses his mind and is placed in a psychiatric hospital near Rehovot. Leder's disappearance from the landscape of the boy's life does not stop the inquisitive boy from puzzling over his enigmatic friend. He is particularly interested in the most recent chapter of Leder's life, because a stubborn rumor circulating in Jerusalem claims that Leder, despite his insanity, married a young Yemenite from Nes Ziona and that a son was born to them. At the end of the Yom Kippur War, twenty years later, this rumor is confirmed in tragic circumstances.

It should be noted that the narrator's captivating story of childhood is told by the now-grown boy to evoke what he saw and experienced at the end of the war, on the western banks of the Great Bitter Lake.⁷ As a reservist in the army—in the IDF Rabbinate and not in the Nutrition Army—he and his comrades in the unit are assigned to identify the remains of soldiers. In "Africa," as the reservists call the west bank of the canal, disengagement talks were then underway between Egypt and Israel on Kilometer 101. During the day, soldiers serving in the IDF Rabbinate persistently and devotedly continue to search for MIAs; at night, they are regularly haunted by nightmares. One day, a telephone call jolts the soldiers, then based at Fayid. An emotion-charged voice asks them to come immediately to the dock at Fanara. The soldiers and their commander hope this means that the remains of the last MIA have finally been found. After arriving at the site, however, they discover it is not the body of a soldier killed in the battles there a month earlier; another person has now joined the list of casualties. Three truck drivers went down to bathe in the lake, despite the warnings about mines planted under the water and in violation of orders. Two of them emerged from the water bleeding profusely, one of them without a leg. The third was killed.

The narrator and his comrades retrieve the dead truck driver from the water and they will never forget the sight: "His leg and stomach were ripped to pieces, but his head, crowned with curls, and his swarthy face looked alive."[8] When it turns out the dead man is the son of his childhood friend Mordechai Leder, the narrator knows, about twenty years after the fact, that the rumor mill in Jerusalem in the 1950s was correct: After Leder left Jerusalem due to his insanity, he became a father. It was no surprise that Leder named his son Yosef Popper Leder, but his wife changed the boy's name to Yosef Shelah. This genetic remnant of the father's vision of a Nutrition Army became a truck driver, delivering conserves and basic goods for the army. When the son dies, the father's vision and line of descent are buried with him. This death, after the war had already ended, was so superfluous. All he had to do was heed the warnings. The writing, in this case too, was on the wall. The father's insanity is passed down in inheritance to his son, and the insanity is actually a transition to the personal and familial level, because war is complete, systemic insanity. Therefore, "the end of this story is also pinned to death,"[9] as stated in the concluding words of the novel.

And the general insanity is not only exemplified by the insanity of an isolated individual. The superfluous death of Yosef Shelah, who failed to listen to warnings, symbolizes the superfluous death of the 2,223 soldiers killed in the superfluous war, whose hallmark is the disregard for warnings.[10] The postmortem discovery (that rumors about the dead driver's father were indeed true) fits in with this chapter's depiction of that sudden–expected war, whose catastrophic dimensions could have been reduced if more attention had been paid to those who saw it coming. The game of opposites Haim Be'er plays in this novel—with determinism and chance, with "all is foreseen, yet freedom of choice is granted,"[11] with the obligatory and the avoidable—is a game we play with the fate of our lives. The story of the narrator's friendship with Leder, ostensibly a chapter closed long ago, resurfaces "at the end of the Yom Kippur War, illuminated by the blinding lightning flash of Jewish destiny," Be'er writes toward the end of *Feathers*, and "the inevitable roll of thunder that comes in its wake accompanies this story from start to finish."[12] The blinding lightning that preceded the thunder appeared in a flash and was easy to ignore, but the roll of thunder that continues to echo is deafening—and can no longer be denied.

The Human Voice as Vision

"Hey, girl, quiet! . . . Be quiet! You woke everyone up!"[13]

David Grossman's *To the End of the Land* opens with this call, hushing a dreaming teenager who shouts and weeps in her sleep. The human voice is accorded a central role in driving the plot in this novel, in characterizing the five protagonists and in reconstructing their lives. In fact, the human voice in the novel is an image that at times stands alone, detached from the semantics it is supposed to bear, and overshadows the scene. The acoustic aspect of the novel competes with its visual aspect, and these two, hearing and seeing, collaborate to capture a complex and unique Israeli reality. The hidden struggle between the two senses begins already in the novel's opening chapter, which takes place in a hospital during the Six-Day War, when a total blackout is imposed throughout Israel. "Turn on the light," the dreaming young woman says to the youth who tells her she had shouted or sung in her sleep. He replies, "Are you crazy? . . . They'll kill us if we do that."[14] That is, the initial acquaintance between the two, which will develop into great love and an everlasting bond, begins in a hospital, in wartime, and under a blackout, when only the human voice can connect the patients.

As in childbirth, before the newborn sees the light of day, like creation before "Let there be light" was uttered, Grossman constructs the first meeting of Ora, Avram, and Ilan—three young people who will form an unusual romantic triangle for almost forty years—as the incubation of a catastrophe. The Yom Kippur War will leave a mark of disaster on the lives of the three. Thus, the Six-Day War, when they meet in the isolation rooms of a hospital, is the progenitor of disaster. And the conditions in the "incubator"—darkness, fear, uncertainty, nightmares, stifled weeping, and screams—presage the catastrophe that will fully unfold six years later, in a war that follows the one in which the three become acquainted in complete darkness. The name of the dreaming young woman who wants to illuminate the room with forbidden light is, ironically, Ora ("light" in Hebrew) and she is the one who must make do with sound and forgo light. The sounds of war, illness, and nightmare that open the novel during the Six-Day War will become louder and more powerful in the Yom Kippur War, and the sounds will echo in the horrific terror attacks and military operations of the 2000s.

To the End of the Land is a story of motherhood, of parenthood, of "family work" (a concept that appears again and again in the novel), of a woman's love for two men, and of the love of two men for her; it is a story of a boy who at the age of eighteen will become an Israeli soldier—a role that will continue even after his formal service is over. In this sense, *To the End of the Land* is also the story of Israel's wars from 1967 until who knows when. In all of these, the human voice is present as a symbol designed to express Israeli familial existence in the shadow of a war that has no end. This complex and multidimensional existence is expressed not in a "still, small voice,"[15] but through stories and confessions spoken in intimate circles at critical junctures in life; through dramatic sentences stated again and again to articulate the absurdity and dreadfulness of the complicated situation; through unforgettable phone conversations; and through the voices of despair transmitted over military two-way radios in wartime. Without a doubt, the other side of the never-ending words streaming through the novel is silence: The words that remain unspoken, the stories that are too heavy to recount, are bottled up and only emerge years later. These silenced words that slowly come to light, primarily due to Ora's humanistic and enlightened nature, possess no less vocal power than the words spoken when the events occurred. For the novel begins, as noted, with a call to Ora to stop shouting from the depths of her nightmare: "Hey, girl, quiet! . . . Be quiet! You woke everyone up! . . . Singing, shouting, everything. Now be quiet."[16]

But at sixteen, Ora does not keep quiet, just as she will not keep quiet thirty-four or thirty-five years later. In the Six-Day War, as during the military operations of the early 2000s, she finds a single address for the voices of her soul and for her stories: Avram, a child prodigy at the time of the Six-Day War, whose verbal future lay before him—his turns of phrase, his sharp wit, the elaborate radio play he wanted to write in which only the human voice would be present, because the human voice had always fascinated him—and Avram, who became broken and only a shadow of his former self after falling captive in the Yom Kippur War. Then and now he is the attentive ear for Ora's life stories.

The novel begins like a Dadaist text, with meaningless syllables, words that do not combine to make any coherent statement, calls that contain an expression of confusion, disorientation, and horror. It tries to introduce three adolescents joined by illness, a dream, and war—three words with a similar ring in Hebrew: *mahala*, *halom*, and *milhamah*. The short lines, the hasty questions and unsatisfying answers, convey a feeling that this text speaks in the voice of young people and that the high fever of illness and the quickened heartbeat from fear of war dictate the pace of their speech, and their measured and incomplete dialogue:

> "Tell me something."
> "What? Who is it?"
> "It's me."
> "You . . ."
> "Tell me, am I alone in this room?"
> "How should I know?"
> "*I can't see anything. Hello, is anyone here?*"
> "*It's me here.*"
> "No. Is there anyone else?"
> "*Here we go, I'm standing up.*"
> "What was that?"
> "*I fell down.*"
> "Are you, like, shivering?"
> "Yeah, shivering."

"How high is yours?"
"It was forty this evening."
"Mine was forty point three."
"Gotta get back to my room."
"Tell me."
"What?"
"When do you die?"
"At forty-two."
"That's close."
"No, no, you still have time."
"It's very close."
"You'll feel better in the morning."
"Don't go, I'm scared."
"Do you hear?"
"What?"
"How quiet it is suddenly."
"Were there booms before?"
"Cannons."
"I keep sleeping, and all of a sudden it's nighttime again."
"Even when I'm lying down, I feel like I'm falling."
"Every time you open your eyes—night."
"Cause there's a blackout."
"I think they're winning."
"Who?"
"The Arabs."
"No way."
"They've occupied Tel Aviv."
"What are you . . . who told you that?"
"I don't know. Maybe I heard it."
"You dreamed it."
"No, they said it here, someone, before, I heard voices."
"It's from the fever. Nightmares. I have them, too."
"My dream."
"Gotta get back now." (*To the End of the Land*, 5)[17]

In this passage, the national reality outside the hospital walls, war, blends with the personal fear of death from illness within the hospital walls. The sounds of war reach the patients' ears—booms, cannon fire—together with baseless rumors that spark existential panic and anxiety: "They've occupied Tel Aviv," "They said it here, someone, before, I heard voices"—and this while their body is battling illness: "When do you die? At forty-two." These fears of war and illness are constantly accompanied by a soundtrack of sobs, the reedy weeping of the Arab nurse in charge of them; and no one knows why she is weeping.

Writing about the voice and its effectiveness is somewhat absurd, because written words do not make any sound; and when we read about a voice, it remains mute. That is, writing may describe the voice, but it cannot make it audible. Accordingly, in this novel, Grossman tried to endow the voice with form, color, and expression in order to make the voice visible and audible in writing. The following example illustrates how he presents the fragmented, crushed, and crumbled utterances that emerge from the mouths of the young people, who are burning with fever and a secret fear of the unknown. By scattering letters and using numerous hyphens, he seeks to imbue the self-represented human voice with graphic mimesis, adding an interpretive, living and breathing aspect to the written words:

> The trembling wouldn't stop, and sometimes it turned into long shivers, and when they talked their speech was choppy, and they often had to wait for a pause in the trembling, a brief calming of the face and mouth muscles, and then they would quickly spit out the words in high, tense voices, and the stammering crushed the sentences in their mouths. How-old-are-you? Sixteen-and-you? And-a-quar-ter. I-have-jaun-dice, how-a-bout-you? Me? He said. I-think-it's-an-in-fec-tion-of-the-o-va-ries. Silence. He shuddered and breathed heavily. By-the-way-that-was-a-joke. Not funny, she said. (7–8)

In another passage, Avram—the young man with the soul of an artist, who will be mutilated in spirit and body in Egyptian captivity—is Grossman's vehicle for expressing fascination with the human voice. Through a concomitance of senses, synesthesia, Avram tries to describe to Ora the spell her voice casts upon him. He speaks to her, about her voice, in the third person:

And I want to tell her about her voice, Avram said *afterwards, sitting at her feet again, curled up on his chair and hunched over her bed*. Because the voice is the most important thing for me, always, even before a girl's appearance. She has a voice that no one I know has, an orange voice, I swear, don't laugh, with a little bit of lemon-yellow around the edges, and it has a spring, it has a pounce. (32; the italicized lines do not appear in the English translation.)

Without having seen Ora, Avram describes her voice as the sun, as light, as her name suggests.[18] What could more fully express the power of the human voice than two young people in a pitch-black hospital during the Six-Day War, trying through their voices to absorb, sense, and draw close to each other? The intonation of their voices corresponds to the content they convey when they talk about themselves, and the things they say about themselves revolve around the voice. Their situation is unwittingly the fulfillment of the ideas Avram pours into Ora's ears.

Here is an illustration of this: Ora asks Avram with a shout, almost wailing, to explain what he is actually writing: "*I'd like to know about these masterpieces of yours!*" The answer Grossman puts in Avram's mouth is accompanied by a description of the intonation that Avram tries to impart to his voice: "'*At the moment I'm only writing for voices . . . Sketches like they play on the radio*,' he replied, trying to make sure she heard the exertion in his voice." The exertion in his voice is a reaction to the fact that Ora, whom Avram earlier described as possessing a sun-like voice (orange, "with a little bit of lemon-yellow around the edges"), does not relent and asks in a sort of repetitive mantra, "*What does that mean?*" Avram suspects that she is deliberately "*using that voice of hers, purposely sounding like a broken record, asking what does it mean, what does it mean*," and he answers her: "*I want to make radio theater, that's what I'm most interested in. Just human voices, with music in the background, but the main thing is the voices, without seeing anything. So just the imagination works.*" Avram ignores an expressive sound—a sniff—a derisive note she tries to sound in response to his words, and he continues: "*And with me it's not just like the regular radio shorts. Those guys make their lives easy. With me, I'm always mixing up reality with fantasy. Sometimes I even record real people, all kinds, on* the street, at the grocery, and I work the things they say into my pieces." And though Ora, for some reason, goes on making that noise, meaning that she does not understand her interlocutor's artistic credo, which is actually winning her over, she cannot cool the ardor of his impassioned words about the human voice: "'What is there to understand?' he yelled. 'I think there's nothing more moving than the human voice, and I think radio art is the most powerful thing that could exist in art in general.'"[19]

The Human Voice as Delirious Reality

Only when readers reach one of the breathtaking emotional peaks of *To the End of the Land*, in the last quarter of this massive novel, will they grasp the significance of the conversations that opened the novel, the long conversations between Ora and Avram about the human voice. These conversations, which took place during the Six-Day War, are a sort of preview, a prologue to a monstrous fulfillment of Avram's ideas on the human voice during the next war, the Yom Kippur War.[20]

In the final part of Ora and Avram's trek together in northern Israel—which among other things can be interpreted as an additional leg in Ora's years-long quest to restore Avram to life after the captivity that killed his soul—she will tell him what she knows about his vocal connection with Ilan, his good friend and her husband, a few hours before Avram fell into captivity.

This story about the vocal connection between Avram and Ilan traverses three temporal levels before it reaches Avram's ears.

The first level is when the story occurs: at the outbreak of the Yom Kippur War in 1973, several hours before Avram is taken captive. The story's timeframe is the basis for the two narratives that emerge from it—that is, the second and third levels are the telling time.

On the second level, Ilan tells the story to Ora some ten years later, a few hours before Ofer (Avram and Ora's biological son) is born. The story, sealed up in Ilan's consciousness for years and shared with his wife Ora for the first time in the context of near parenthood—when the couple still has time to make love once more before the birth, an unconventional time and situation that cannot be forgotten or denied—essentially designates

Ilan to serve as acting father of his closest friend's child, soon to be borne by his own wife.

On the third level, Ora tells the story to Avram twenty-one years later, when Ofer, the son of the trio—Ora, Avram, and Ilan—is in the midst of a military operation, and Ora and Avram set off on their hike in northern Israel. Inspired by Ora, the hike is an attempt to flee from the news that might reach their ears.

The situation in which Avram hears the story recalls the situation in which Ora heard it, and Avram is thereby placed in the role of the father, a role he has rejected since the birth of Ofer, his biological son. In the previous narrative time, Ilan was assigned the role of the father; in this narrative time, Avram is assigned the mantle of fatherhood.

We will focus here on the third temporal level, because that is how the story is told in the novel, by Ora to Avram; and that is how she claims she heard it from Ilan, and that is how he says he experienced it in the Yom Kippur War. More than thirty years separate the time the story occurred from the narrative situation in which it is recounted.

The narrative situation is this: After the hike together through the landscape of northern Israel, when Avram becomes increasingly attentive to Ora's stories of the stormy dynamics among the four members of her family (Ora, her husband Ilan, and their two boys Adam and Ofer), and after the two of them, Ora and Avram, have slept night after night side-by-side in the open air at the end of full and exhausting days of hiking and storytelling, they are swept away by their passion one night. Two acts of love between Ora and Avram are described in the novel. In the first, Ora tries to restore Avram's virility, which he lost in captivity. From that single lovemaking encounter in his dingy apartment in Tel Aviv, she becomes pregnant and nine months later gives birth to Ofer. They make love for the second time during their hike together, when mortal danger looms over their son Ofer. At the end of this sexual encounter in the midst of nature, Ora finds herself telling Avram the story that Ilan had told her at the end of her rare and dangerous lovemaking with him, just hours before Ofer came into the world. The narrative situation in 2002 or 2003 not only reconstructs the narrative situation that prevailed twenty-one years earlier; it also has characteristics that call to mind the fragmented conversations of Ora and Avram during the Six-Day War, thirty-five or thirty-six years earlier.

And here is the beginning of the conversation that will later reveal the vocal connection between Avram and Ilan in the Yom Kippur War, before Avram was taken into Egyptian captivity, a horrible experience that changed the lives of all three of them:

> "Do you know that Ilan went to look for you?" she murmurs into his shoulder.
> "When?"
> "Then."
> "When the war was over?"
> "No, at the beginning."
> "I don't understand. What . . . ?"
> "He got all the way to the Canal—"
> "No way."
> "From Bavel. He just walked off the base."
> "That can't be, Ora, what are you talking about?"
> "I'm telling you."
> His back hardens under her hand, and Ora is amazed at her stupidity: All she had in her mouth were the pleasurable murmurs and purrs of afterward, and then this came out. (*To the End of the Land*, 470)

Even before the pleasurable sounds of the act of love have faded, Ora tells Avram "what she heard from Ilan one morning twenty-one years ago . . . in detail—she remembers quite a bit, in fact—finally bringing the story full circle" (471). Her tale is no longer fragmented now. It is continuous and complete, oddly imitating Ilan's determined trek then—toward the strongholds on the waterline, which fell one after another into Egyptian hands; and oddly imitating Ora's resolute trek now—toward an unclear destination. Ilan set out then because his friend Avram was at the end of the trail, and Ora sets out now because her son Ofer is at the end of the trail. The parallels drawn between Ilan then and Ora now, and between Avram then and Ofer now, underscore war's ability to reenact the same fate and the same patterns of behavior. Regardless of gender and generation, Ilan then and Ora now set out on a Sisyphean mission to save their loved ones.

"'Hello hello hello hello,' came a ghostly voice, exhausted and despondent"—Avram's human voice over the two-way radio reaches the ears of Ilan, who had entered a stronghold that had not yet fallen into the hands of the Egyptians; it was about a kilometer and a half away from Avram's stronghold, where he alone was still alive and waiting to die (483). The short geographic distance between Avram and Ilan was in inverse proportion to the enormous distance, which would always remain unbridgeable, between the destinies of the two close friends. Ilan listened intently to Avram's words and their meaning, while also noting the changes in his voice. Years later, Ilan would tell Ora about this, and she in turn would later recount this to Avram, thus enclosing the three friends in a vocal circle that began in the first days of the Yom Kippur War and ended in a military operation of the early 2000s. If we add to this the human voice that emerged from Avram in the Six-Day War, we see that in this novel he is the representative of the *human voice* that erupts in *inhuman wars* from the depths of a person's soul. His voice is the voice of clinging to life when there is no longer any chance of survival, as if asserting: If I make a sound, it means I'm alive, the sound is me, it's my essence, my soul. His voice is the voice of hope, a voice that draws its strength from art. "'Though I walk through the valley of the shadow of death,' Avram whispered, 'I will fear no evil, for my story is with me'" (508, based on Psalms 23:4). This is what Ilan transcribes from the mouth of Avram, who spoke over the two-way radio without knowing whether anyone would pick up his voice.

In great chronotopical, technological, and psychological detail, aimed to create a credible combination of events, Grossman describes the amazing vocal connection forged between Avram and Ilan amidst the sounds of the Israeli war, the direst of all:

> "Hello hello hello," a distant voice whispered weakly again. "Hello hello . . ." The voice faded, disturbed by the breezes of radio noise, someone from Ismailia shouting in Arabic at a squad commander of Sagger missiles. Ilan tried to calm down and convince himself he'd

been wrong—there was no way to identify a single voice in this hellish commotion. (483)

But Avram's voice, more specifically his language, is identifiable: Avram's inimitable turns of phrase, his special ability to "say out loud what everyone isn't thinking" (484), his relentless plastic descriptions of his wound, his tenacious insistence on continuing to declare, over the entire range of human voices at his disposal, that he is still alive and wants to live, and above all his ability to create a story when his life is about to end. Perhaps precisely when Avram faces certain death, the story suddenly emerges from within him and is heard in his voice, because this is his destiny. This is Avram's strength. Ilan is acutely aware of his friend's human singularity, and yet even he is taken by surprise.

In a private lament for his friend, listing the things Avram would never be able to do in life because he is about to be killed, Ilan says, "There would be no more quotes from the sacred poetry of David Avidan and Yona Wallach or from *Catch-22* or *Under Milk Wood*—a song of praise for the human voice, from which Avram could recite entire pages by heart" (540).

To create an unexpected alliteration, Grossman juxtaposes the translated Hebrew title Milkud-22 of Joseph Heller's *Catch-22* with the English title of Dylan Thomas's well-known radio drama *Under Milk Wood*. These two works are relevant to Avram's world; however, before his death and contrary to Ilan's expectation, Avram creates a radio play that is the opposite of *Under Milk Wood*. While Dylan Thomas's Welsh village comes alive in the morning and the day the drama describes serves as a metaphor for life, Avram composes a play about the end of the world. He lays out his ideas orally, and Ilan, listening to him over the two-way radio, writes them down word for word: Humanity is aware of its death, and people behave accordingly. In this passage, where Avram lets his story unfold, a story that reflects his present situation as the representative of humankind facing annihilation, his addressee is Ora. During the Six-Day War, burning with fever in the hospital, Avram told her that his greatest ambition was to write a masterpiece for the human voice. And now, in this "Judgment Day War," in unimaginable conditions, his human voice is able to vocalize his longed-for masterpiece. Dylan Thomas, who wrote the marvelous vocal play, also had a hypnotic voice when he read aloud the works he wrote, but Avram's voice is several times more hypnotic, and not because of its vocal quality. Avram does not read or memorize his work in order to recite it. He creates his work on the spot with his voice, and someone writes it down as he speaks. Ilan, the person closest to him after Ora, realizes two things in this bizarre situation: that true artists often reveal more of themselves to their attentive audience, through the voice of their art, than they reveal to their partner in an intimate relationship, and that Avram is the ultimate artist:

> He muttered, intermittently excited and fading, and Ilan struggled to keep up, and knew that no one had ever opened up to him like this before, not even Ora, not even when he slept with her. As he scribbled, something was being written inside him: a new, cool, lucid knowledge that he himself was not a true artist. Not like Avram. Not like him. (507)

This situation, in which Avram dictates to Ilan his masterpiece about the end of the world from within a stronghold where he is the last person alive—that is, a situation that marks for him the end of the world—concludes as follows:

> Ilan's ears filled at once with shouts in throaty Arabic. An Egyptian soldier, who sounded no less startled than Avram, was screaming. Avram pleaded for his life. One shot was fired. It may have hit Avram. He screamed. **His voice was no longer human.** (509–10, emphasis added)

Avram did not know that he was dictating to Ilan, and Ilan, who writes it all down, never let Avram know that he was recording his words. Avram's nonhuman voice, which is wounded in the shooting and later in captivity, symbolizes his spiritual death, the song of his life that is aborted in the middle. What transpires between Ora and Avram on their hike together in the Galilee thirty years later moves in the opposite direction. Here, Ora dictates the family story to Avram with her own voice (orange? with a little bit of lemon-yellow around the edges?) so that one day he, the true artist, will be able to tell it in his own voice. The hike that was meant to save Ofer from the present war is, in fact, another effort by Ora to rescue Avram from the previous war. On this trip, she restores Avram's voice.

The following is an extract from the dialogue that ends the novel. We have long since grown accustomed to this fragmented dialogue, crushed and crumbled, in which Ora and Avram mutter single words and half sentences, understanding each other in supreme intimacy:

"I want you to promise me."

"Yes, whatever you want."

"That you'll remember everything."

"Yes, you know I will."

"From the beginning, from when we met, when we were kids, and that war, and how we met in isolation, and the second war, and what happened to you, and Ilan, and me, and everything that happened, yes?"

"Yes, yes."

"And Adam and Ofer. Promise me, look me in the eye." She holds his face in both hands. "You'll remember, right?"

"Everything." (576)

In particular, Ora wants him to remember all the twenty-one years of Ofer's life. And Avram will remember. In a human voice and with boundless love, he will relate in his unique artistic voice the life story of his son and the life stories of those who feared for Ofer's safety.

8

Brothers in Blood in Sami Michael's *Pigeons at Trafalgar Square*

A Novel of the First Intifada

> "The next time you meet your brother, it'll be on the battlefield . . . it looks like he'll defeat you."

Sami Michael's *Pigeons at Trafalgar Square* and Ghassan Kanafani's "Returning to Haifa"—a Dialogue

Theoretical Introduction: Hypertext and Hypotext

In creative writing courses, a common exercise is to read a story to the budding writers, stop at a certain point, and then ask them to continue it and concoct their own denouement. There is also another version of this creative exercise: The entire story is presented to the students and they are asked to compose a standalone story that begins at the point where the previous story ended. The result—a story that is essentially independent of the original story. A reader familiar with the underlying story will naturally compare the two stories intertextually. On the other hand, a reader unfamiliar with the story that inspired the sequel will analyze the new story with literary tools that do not necessarily include intertextuality. That is, analysis of the intertextual aspect requires familiarity with the underlying text.

At the beginning of Sami Michael's novel *Pigeons at Trafalgar Square* (2005), the Israeli author notes: "A dialogue with the writer Ghassan Kanafani," and thus declares a deliberate connection between his novel and the work of the Palestinian author. Michael does not cite a specific work by Kanafani, perhaps because the latter's novella "Returning to Haifa" (1969)[1] has already become a canonical text among Palestinian Arabs, who comprise part of the readership the Jewish-Arab writer Sami Michael is addressing. Michael assumes that his Arab audience, and his Jewish readers too, are familiar with the novella, or will become acquainted with it through his novel, which offers a continuation—an additional developmental layer, historical and ideological—to the storyline of the novella. *Pigeons at Trafalgar Square* was published thirty-six years after the publication of "Returning to Haifa," which deals with the relations between Israelis and Palestinians in the wake of the 1967 war. Michael apparently seeks to conduct a dialogue with the ideas of the Palestinian author—that is, to offer a different and more complex formula as an alternative to the Palestinian writer's unequivocal war formula. In *Pigeons at Trafalgar Square*, the two literary works blend into a novel with a single plot sequence that accommodates two different worldviews vis-à-vis the Israeli-Palestinian conflict: Kanafani's and Michael's. Michael responds to Kanafani with an ambivalent message; some would say this message is more optimistic than Kanafani's, and others would deem it more pessimistic.

From a theoretical perspective, we can define this blended text, using Gérard Genette's term, as "hypertextuality." This is defined as any type of connection linking any Text B to an earlier Text A upon which it is constructed; Text B is creative in nature and does not necessarily focus on interpreting Text A. Genette calls Text B "hypertext" and Text A "hypotext." Actually, hypotext is what other literary critics refer to as intertext: the text that can be clearly identified as a primary source for attributing meaning to the new text. Genette calls the new text (Text B, hypertext) "a text in the second degree" or "text derived from another pre-existent text."[2]

The meaning of hypertextual works depends on the reader's familiarity with the hypotext (a primary work), which the hypertext may rework in a satirical way or mimic to create a pastiche. In the case of *Pigeons at Trafalgar Square*, the hypertext is designed to chronologically continue "Returning to Haifa," the hypotext, and thus perhaps reexamine it.

In an interview published in the Israeli daily *Haaretz* in April 2005—an interview that ignited a media firestorm—Michael told the journalist

Dalia Karpel that prior to the outbreak of the Second Intifada in late 2000, representatives of an Italian production company approached him, saying that Kanafani's widow had suggested that an Israeli author and a Palestinian author jointly write a screenplay, a sequel to "Returning to Haifa." Michael apparently accepted this offer in part. Rather than partner with a Palestinian author to write a collective cinematic work that would continue the story of "Returning to Haifa," he wrote a novel on his own, his own sequel to "Returning to Haifa," and chose the First Intifada as the time setting.

Haaretz interviewer Dalia Karpel sparked the media controversy by noting the ostensibly problematic connection between the hypertext and hypotext: She accused Michael of concealing the fact that the plot of his new novel was based on the sensational and surprising plot of the novella "Returning to Haifa," the fruit of the Palestinian writer's imagination. The interview was published in the newspaper's weekend magazine under the headline "Writer under influence," an allusion to the legal term "under investigation,"[3] hinting that the influence or appropriation was not sufficiently highlighted. Michael was offended by this headline, which carries the scent of plagiarism.

Five months later, on September 15, 2005, *Haaretz* published an apology that opened with the following paragraph:

> *Haaretz* apologizes to the writer Sami Michael for the article by Dalia Karpel, published in the *Haaretz Magazine* on April 15 of this year, following the publication of his book *Pigeons at Trafalgar Square*. The article and the headlines attached to it were misleading and tarnished Sami Michael's good name and professional integrity.

The accusation and apology indicate that intertextuality in the case of *Pigeons at Trafalgar Square* extends beyond the narrow literary context and has political implications—apparently, because both Kanafani's novella and Michael's novel are not only works of literature; each carries an explicit or implicit political message. The soft and "cultural" term Michael uses to describe the connection between the two works—"dialogue"—is actually very explosive. The Israeli writer's appropriation of a core segment of the storyline from the Palestinian writer, along with the Israeli's description of this appropriation as "dialogue," is an apt metaphor for the problematic dialogue between Israelis and Palestinians in general, and for the rapprochement efforts between the two peoples as presented in *Pigeons at Trafalgar Square* in particular.

"Returning to Haifa"—Hypotext;
Pigeons at Trafalgar Square—Hypertext

If someone informs you one morning that you are not actually a Jew like you thought, but an Arab; or, if you regard yourself as a proud Arab, connected to an Arab tradition that includes inherent opposition to Jews and Judaism, and one fine morning your mother tells you that you are not an Arab, but actually a Jew—this kind of revelation would undoubtedly shake the foundations of your world and generate enormous emotional turmoil. Few people would be able to emerge from such tumult unscathed. In this situation, when you suddenly discover that you are not "you" but actually "him," and not just "him" but a despised "him"—a "him" who is an enemy—all of your certitudes and convictions collapse like a house of cards.

Ghassan Kanafani's novella and Sami Michael's novel are both based on this sort of discovery. We will start by focusing on Michael's work (hypertext), ignoring the foundation (hypotext) upon which it is built: Kanafani's work.

For many of Michael's readers, *Pigeons at Trafalgar Square* brought to mind *A Trumpet in the Wadi* (1987), which also deals with split, dual, paradoxical, and tragic identities. A large part of these two stories (as well as Michael's novel *Refuge*) takes place in Haifa, a mixed city. All three novels present war lives from the perspective of Palestinian Arabs, those living in Israel since 1948 and those living in the territories conquered by Israel in 1967. The ability to connect with the other side in the Israeli-Palestinian conflict, which appears in Sami Michael's books, can also be found in *Yasmine* by Eli Amir—two writers of Iraqi descent.

In *Pigeons at Trafalgar Square*, Riva, the widowed mother of Ze'ev Epstein, is a Holocaust survivor whose husband Ephraim fell in the Sinai

War in 1956. About a year before Ze'ev's conscription into the IDF, Riva tells him that he is not her biological son; in fact, he was an Arab boy abandoned in his crib during the Arabs' panicked flight from Haifa in 1948. Riva found him in the apartment she received upon her arrival in Israel. A "gift child"—that's how Riva would refer to her beloved son throughout his childhood, and Ze'ev would relish this term of endearment used by his devoted mother, who derived such great joy from her only child. Experiments conducted on her body during the Holocaust had left her infertile, and thus the child she found in her home was indeed a "gift child." From his perspective, on the other hand, the revelation that he was randomly adopted suddenly adds demonic significance to the term of endearment: To be a "gift child" means not to be born to the mother who raised you, but to be arbitrarily found by her in an abandoned apartment.

Ze'ev, who until that moment regarded himself as an entirely Jewish boy, the second generation of proud Israelis, whose family embodied the nation's two foundational narratives—Holocaust and rebirth—realizes at age seventeen that he is not who he thought he was. He is not the son of Holocaust survivors and is not an Israeli war orphan. He is an Arab. The same Arab who, in the fearful eyes of Israelis, is conniving schemes and plotting war against them, against the person he thought he was just a minute ago. Thus, one fine day, Ze'ev discovers that he is someone else, a sort of antithesis, a negative, an opposite of himself. This discovery leads Ze'ev to break up with his girlfriend Anat in order to avoid deceiving her about his identity: "I'm not at all an Epstein, he said to himself, and I'm not the son of Holocaust survivors, I didn't come from Europe. I'm an *Arabush*, just a dirty little Arab" (42).[4]

To identify with "the other" is very difficult, and is a key part of education. There are a number of sayings in Judaism that encourage a person to "step into the shoes" of the other in order to feel him, to experience his life and fate; to be him. "Love your neighbor as yourself" and "Don't judge your friend until you've stood in his place" are just two of many sayings intended to make the other's life experience more accessible and turn it into the subject's own life experience. Indeed, empathy is one of the values that guided Michael in writing a sequel to "Returning to Haifa," in which he gives expression to the Palestinian side of the political map.

After the initial shock, Ze'ev Epstein tries to come to terms with the devastating discovery:

> In a frenzy, he pored over books on psychology. When he discovered the behaviorist school, he breathed a sigh of relief. Skinner became his prophet. Everyone is born as a clean slate. The environment and learning are what shape the individual. Ethnic origin, race, and genes make no difference. He's Israel. He's Jewish. He's more an Epstein than Riva herself, because he became an Epstein during his infancy, while Riva received this name when she married Ephraim. (43–44)

Michael portrays a young man of remarkable psychological resilience, who contends rationally and heroically with the upsetting discovery. There is no doubt that B.F. Skinner, the psychologist who believed that people are capable of controlling their behavior, is not only the prophet of Ze'ev Epstein; first and foremost, he's the prophet of Michael, Epstein's creator.[5] Ze'ev's devoted and loving mother instilled confidence in him, and he is endowed with the fortitude to embrace, after the shock of discovery, another family—his Palestinian family, of which he knew nothing until the age of seventeen. Ze'ev is the second generation of both the Holocaust of the Jews and the Nakba of the Palestinians, and he does his utmost to lovingly and courageously bear this twofold and impossible burden. He has two mothers: his adoptive mother Riva and his biological mother Nabila, who enters his life at a late stage. Nabila and the son who resurfaces in her world develop a wonderful relationship of warmth and tenderness, clearly Oedipal in nature. The two mothers, who respect each other and share their love for Ze'ev, are a declaration of Sami Michael's faith in mothers as such, regardless of their origin, religion, or race. Indeed, he dedicates his book to "all mothers, who are the promised land of the human race."

As noted, Sami Michael took the idea and the platform (Text A) from the Palestinian playwright and journalist Ghassan Kanafani: An Arab child is abandoned in the turmoil of 1948 when his parents are pushed out of Haifa; his parents return to Haifa after the 1967 war and find their son in a Jewish family of Holocaust survivors, who have adopted him in his/their home. Kanafani served as the spokesperson for the Popular Front for the Liberation of Palestine and wrote extensively on the Palestinian tragedy. His novella "Returning to Haifa," published in 1969, describes a tense encounter between the biological parents and their abandoned son, nineteen or twenty years later. To their dismay and horror, he appears before them wearing an IDF uniform and is absolutely certain of his Jewish-Israeli identity. Kanafani names the young man Dov, and Michael conducts a dialogue with Kanafani over this name too: Kanafani's Dov [bear] becomes Michael's Ze'ev [wolf]. Both heroes have the name of a wild animal that is also used as a person's name. The parents who adopted Dov, Kanafani's abandoned child, are Miriam and Iphrat Koshen. Iphrat in Kanafani's novella becomes Ephraim in Michael's novel. (Perhaps Kanafani was unaware that Israeli boys are not named Iphrat [more commonly spelled Efrat] and Michael intended to "correct" the name.) In both literary works, the adoptive fathers are killed in Operation Kadesh (the Sinai War) in 1956 and the widowed mother—Riva in Michael's novel and Nabila in Kanafani's novella—is the dominant parent in the life of the adopted boy. However, in Michael's novel, which continues the events of the novella, the Palestinian mother plays an increasingly significant role in the son's later life, while the first mother (or the second, depending on how you look at it) begins to fade before the very eyes of her son due to her age.

Michael's novel (Text B) centers on the development of the relationship between Ze'ev and his Palestinian mother, which started more than a decade after his formative encounter with his biological parents in Haifa. Ze'ev is now married to Anat (the same Israeli girlfriend he had abruptly left at age nineteen upon learning he was an *"Arabush"*) and they have a son named Adiv. Nabila, Ze'ev's Palestinian mother, is now flourishing in her personal and public life, and Ze'ev is enchanted by her, but does not abandon Riva, his Jewish mother. Two partners help him care for Riva: his wife Anat and Shmil, his business partner. Shmil's love for Riva is eternal. It began in Europe before her marriage to Ephraim, and continued after Ephraim's death.

For over a decade, Nabila and Ze'ev, the Palestinian mother and the Jewish-Israeli son, have conducted a secret relationship. At a late stage in the novel, Ze'ev also gets to know the rest of his Palestinian family—his brother, sister, niece, and nephew—and a complex connection develops between them. All this comprises the additional layer Michael builds upon Kanafani's basic text.

Let us return, therefore, to the climax of Kanafani's novella: the meeting between the adopted son and his biological parents, where the son hurls harsh accusations against them. This scene appears again in Michael's novel, but the tables have turned: The father chastises the son, and the son keeps his cool and is portrayed in a nobler way.

In Kanafani's novella, Dov returns home from the army late at night, calls "Mama?" and wonders why she is sitting in the living room so late at night. His mother Miriam says, in English: "Come here, Dov. There are some guests who wish to see you." The perspective changes: Those seated in the living room see a tall man stepping into the room. "He was wearing a military uniform and carrying his military cap in his hand." His mother introduces her son to his "real" parents. The great flurry of emotion and surprise does not temper the scathing and unequivocal words the Israeli soldier fires at his lost parents, Safiyya and Said, who abandoned him and returned twenty years later to Haifa to meet him. Dov's tirade sounds like it had been planned long before the fateful meeting, and that the time had come to recite it. The text of the abandoned son, Khaldun who turned into Dov, is not at all pleasing to the ears of his Palestinian parents.

"I didn't know that Miriam and Iphrat weren't my parents until about three or four years ago," Dov launches the speech he had prepared, as if knowing that this sort of encounter would occur one day.

> From the time I was small, I was a Jew . . . I went to Jewish school, I studied Hebrew, I go to synagogue, I eat kosher food . . . When they told me I wasn't their own child, it didn't change anything. Even when they told me—later on—that my original parents were Arabs, it didn't change anything. No, nothing changed, that's certain. ("Returning to Haifa," 181)

The son's words stung the biological parents, especially Safiyya, the Palestinian mother, who had earlier stated: "I'm certain Khaldun will choose his real parents. It's impossible to deny the call of flesh and blood" (172). Michael toned down the dramatic question of the mother in the novella regarding the mystical connection of flesh and blood; in his novel, the mother asks her son whether he does not sense that she is his mother. In both literary works, the son answers in the negative. It seems that Kanafani, like Michael, and without stating this explicitly, subscribed to Skinner's psychological premise that a person's behavior is shaped by the education he receives and not by a genetic-intuitive "call of flesh and blood." The child who was born Arab, but was raised and educated as a Jew, is a Jew and not an Arab. His Jewish context is what dictates his personality, and not an ancient genetic code of which he is unaware. As the mother Safiyya weeps, the father Said confronts his biological son Khaldun (Dov) and promises him that he will meet his Palestinian brother on the battlefield one day. He concludes his visit to the home in Haifa by saying: "You two may remain in our house temporarily. It will take a war to settle that" (187). Kanafani's belligerent conclusion, expressed through the father Said, is repeated a number of times in the novella. Even before his son appears before him, wearing an Israeli army uniform, he tells Miriam, his son's adoptive mother: "We didn't come to tell you to get out of here. That would take a war . . ." (164).

Kanafani's novella contains a parallel story that occurs in Jaffa. In that side story too, the Palestinian from Ramallah, who comes to visit his former home in Jaffa and finds another Arab family living there, tells the current resident: "I came to have a look at my house. This place where you are living is my house. Your presence here is a sorry comedy that will end one day by the power of the sword" (174). It seems that these simplistic, vitriolic, and bellicose conclusions spurred Sami Michael to write a novel that would continue Kanafani's novella, adding another diachronic layer to the storyline and reflecting a future reality that is far more nuanced than the one envisioned by the Palestinian writer and his protagonist in the late 1960s. The Israeli writer was challenged, in particular, by the prediction of the Palestinian father in Kanafani's novella—that someday the Jewish son would meet his Arab brother on the battlefield. In his novel, Michael repeats the militant prophecy of the father, whose name the Israeli author changed from Said to Rashid: "The next time you meet your brother, it'll be on the battlefield . . . it looks like he'll defeat you" (*Pigeons at Trafalgar Square*, 50).

Armed Struggle and Brothers in Blood

The independent storyline of *Pigeons at Trafalgar Square* stretches over twenty-three years, from 1967 to 1990, without citing specific years. The points in time are measured by the evolving relations between Ze'ev Epstein and his mother Nabila, who appears in his life for the first time in 1967. And, of course, there are allusions to historical events that can be tied to specific times and places.

"When the first letter from her arrived, Ze'ev was already thirty years old" (*Pigeons at Trafalgar Square*, 83), we are told regarding Nabila's first communication with her son, immediately after her husband was killed by the Israelis. Since the late-night verbal confrontation, when Ze'ev was a nineteen-year-old soldier, they have been out of contact. Now, eleven years later, Nabila dares to make contact again. The year, therefore, is 1978. The letter, the first one Ze'ev Epstein has ever received from his Palestinian mother, opens with the salutation "My dear son." It is written on both sides in Arabic. Shmil, Ze'ev's partner and benefactor, who is lovingly devoted to Ze'ev's mother Riva and is like a father to him, the only father who acts like a father to the orphaned Ze'ev, brings the letter to a translation institute in order to maintain confidentiality and avoid endangering the woman who had sent a letter into enemy territory. The letter reads: "I'm sad to inform you that two days ago several armed men, presumably agents of the Israeli Mossad, killed your father in Athens, where he was staying as part of his political activity. The funeral was held yesterday and your father was buried in Ramallah" (84). The death of the biological father, a Palestinian obsessed with the idea of obliterating the State of Israel, enables his wife, the Palestinian mother, to make contact with her Israeli son.

Another eleven years pass before Nabila finds the courage to inform her other two children—Karim, head of the municipal engineering department, and Sana, a gynecologist—that they have a Jewish sibling: "And how old is he, our brother?" Karim asks mockingly. "He's forty-one, two years older than you and six years older than Sana. He was born at the beginning of 1948, when . . ." (121). That is, Nabila makes initial contact with her son in 1978 and surreptitiously conducts intensive relations with him for eleven years: "For a long time, about a decade, he responds to her letters, reciprocates affection, secretly meets with her several times a year" (86). She reveals her secret to her children in 1989, when the First Intifada is raging. Sami Michael ties the bitter events of the intifada to the disclosure about the secret sibling in order to emphasize the absurd situation in which both the Israeli and Palestinian protagonists are living.

About six months before Nabila decides to share with her children and grandchildren the shocking revelation that they have a Jewish brother and uncle, she orchestrates a tense situation in which her Arab offspring see her Jewish son and grandson—they see them, but do not know who they are. Only she and her son Ze'ev are aware of the blood ties. As the Palestinian family is picnicking in the Ma'ayan Harod National Park, her two children and two grandchildren feel the presence of a dark-skinned Israeli man in front of them, right next to them, playing ball with his fair-skinned and green-eyed son. The Palestinian siblings have no inkling about any connection with him. Sana, who also is widowed as a consequence of the Israeli system of targeted killings, seethes with hatred toward her enemies. Yet she is attracted to the foreign Israeli man. All of this Oedipal web—that includes elements of incest, conflicting blood relations, a mix of enmity and attraction, hidden and open knowledge, and the crossing of boundaries—is intended to serve as a metaphor for the complex relations between Israelis and Palestinians. The novel opens with the scene at Ma'ayan Harod, and the reader, like the Palestinian branch of Nabila's family, is left uninformed and puzzled about the nature and significance of the encounter. The mother Nabila and the son Ze'ev, who have forged a pact of secrecy, stand alone at a higher vantage point than all the others.

Many chapters separate the novel's opening scene, where the two parts of the family meet, ostensibly by chance, and a description of Nabila's efforts to reveal the secret to her children.

In chapter 13, Nabila finally plans to tell Karim and Sana her secret, but her plan is foiled:

> Over half a year passed since the picnic at Ma'ayan Harod. The scent of spring floated in the air and Nabila prepared the house festively, but another wave of the struggle between the two peoples again threatened

to shatter the illusionary quiet. Those were the first months of the uprising, of the surging violence between the two sides. (86)

Nabila's festive preparations, as spring was knocking at her door, stand in contrast to the violence that ultimately bashes down her door, shoving aside the festivity and the spring. Instead of her home serving as an intimate setting for discreetly revealing the secret about the Israeli sibling, as she had planned, Israeli soldiers storm into her home. "An officer about the same age as Ze'ev approached Karim and sized him up with a searing and threatening look before saying in English: 'We're looking for a terrorist, and maybe you're sheltering him'" (90). Michael devotes the entire chapter to the terrifying moments the family experiences. During these moments, Suhail, Sana's son, faints. Suhail is already emotionally scarred from ghastly scenes he has witnessed in clashes between Israeli soldiers and the Palestinian population, and is sensitive to any real or imagined threat. His mother, a physician, attends to him and revives him. When the soldiers leave the home, Sana curses them, while Nabila finds consolation in the fact that "the members of her household are all alive, and the electricity was not cut off and the telephone works" (94). She is also secretly grateful that the soldiers did not discover the big box containing the letters from Ze'ev, her other son.

Another attempt to reveal the secret is also made in the shadow of harsh events. Faithful to his approach of giving voice to the Palestinian side, Michael describes Nabila's family under curfew: There is no electricity, the refrigerator is empty, and the television and radio are silent. This gloomy atmosphere is described before the reader learns the reason for the curfew: "Many Jews were killed . . . another one of our fighters. He forced a bus to tumble down into a ravine. The bus flipped over and burst into flames. Lots of dead and injured" (111), Karim says, pressing a tiny transistor radio to his ear. This a reference to the horrible terror attack on Bus 405 on July 6, 1989; a terrorist grabbed control of the wheel near Kiryat Ya'arim, on the way to Jerusalem, and steered the bus off a cliff, killing sixteen passengers and injuring twenty-seven. Karim calls the terrorist "another one of our fighters" and Suhail receives this news with a joyful cry of "bravo." And then, in this atmosphere of schadenfreude and in the darkness of the curfew, when the whole family is stuck together, and as the Israel-Palestinian conflict reaches a new peak and is again present in the home, Nabila opens her mouth and says: "You've already seen him, him and his son in that park" (114). And after a few moments of bewilderment and confusion, she explains: "your brother, who remained with the Jews in Israel" (115). Nabila realizes that she cannot wait again for a period of calm, which will never come, and decides to share her secret with her family:

> For many days, Nabila waited for the right opportunity to tell her children about their older brother, but the confrontations and conflicts between the two peoples did not let up and even intensified, until finally she said to herself that if she continued to postpone telling them, she would never find a comfortable time. (87)

During the stormy conversation that ensues between Nabila and her two children, she unfurls the story of her life. The reader is offered another version of the flight from Haifa, in which the mother, only seventeen at the time, stepped out of her house "and was suddenly swept up into a crowd spooked by the sounds of shooting and explosions, and she got caught in a thick trap of terrified and screaming people, fleeing for their lives, and when she remembered that she had left a baby in his cradle at home, there was no longer any way back." Versions of the flight in 1948, and of the dreadful late-night encounter in 1967—"between the father, the leader who advocated armed struggle until the final eradication of Israel, and the Jewish soldier whose father was killed in war and who suddenly learns that his real parents are actually Arabs" (116)—are repeated like a mantra throughout the novel. As noted, these are details of the story written by the Palestinian author Ghassan Kanafani, and Michael retells them in various versions in order to establish them as seminal events from which his independent storyline emerges.

The fact that Nabila decides to begin studying, so that she will be able to communicate with her son, also reappears again and again throughout the novel. However, this already belongs to Michael's independent story, which seeks to raise the woman's status and make her into a dominant character, a mediating character, overshadowing her extremist husband, who was assassinated by the Israelis. While her husband, the extremist father, says about his offspring, "they took a Palestinian infant from us and returned a despicable Zionist soldier" (54), the mother tries, with determination and sensitivity, to bring the "despicable Zionist" into her home. And to help pave his way into the family, she tells her two children, in the presence of her two grandchildren, all of the versions of her life story in one continuous sequence. This is the personal and national narrative of the Palestinian mother who seeks understanding and forgiveness from her family.

The mother's story is interrupted by the ironic, caustic, and cynical comments of Sana, who inherited her father's uncompromising temperament. Her widowhood and the emotional condition of her son Suhail further embitter Sana and quicken her tongue-lashing. For example, Sana has this to say about Nabila's secret meetings with her son, the tall and handsome Jew: "Come on, mother . . . let's hear how the romantic story between the two of you developed" (148). Nabila's agitated response indicates that her relations with Ze'ev indeed extend beyond son-mother relations and contain a clear Oedipal element. Ze'ev's wife Anat also complains about the growing intimacy between her husband and that mother, who surfaces late in his life, captivates him, and is captivated by him.

Three days after the mother's momentous announcement, which changes the self-perception of Sana and Karim—"not only would this change their future, it also compelled them to reconsider their past" (134), Nabila enters the living room with a large cardboard box in her hands. The box contains many fistfuls of letters, photographs, photocopies of documents, newspaper clippings—all of the "incriminating" documentation of the relationship Nabila has secretly conducted with her Israeli son. This time, it is as if Sana's sarcastic wit has dried up. She and her brother look at the box, which is full to the brim. "After a moment or two, Sana blurted, in a frozen voice, an off-topic remark: 'Where did you get such a huge box?'" (145). This "off-topic" remark suggests that Nabila has presented her family with a Pandora's Box that will sow tragedy or hope.

"The Normal Situation"

The mood and everyday life in the territories under Israeli occupation in the West Bank are therefore depicted in *Pigeons at Trafalgar Square* via the Palestinian family in Ramallah. The double widowhood of a mother and her daughter, a scarred child, curfew, closure, and fear breed fierce animosity toward Israelis. When the Israeli brother "pops up" in the family, the attitude toward the enemy naturally becomes more complex.

The mood in Israel vis-à-vis Palestinians is also portrayed in the novel. Ze'ev Epstein, who lives with his wife Anat and their son Adiv in Haifa's upscale Denia neighborhood, and is already well aware of his dual identity, has a neighbor named Joshua Reshet, a bereaved father and widower, whose main function in the novel is to serve as a sort of Greek chorus, expressing the prevailing views of the Israeli public. The wealthy, quiet Denia neighborhood, built on the slopes of the Carmel Mountain range, overlooking the sea—"the tranquil neighborhood was not threatened by rifles, planes, or tanks" (155)—serves in the novel as an antithesis to the city of Ramallah, whose homes the Israeli army invades and whose streets it treats as if they were its own. Nonetheless, the horror also reaches the spotless, isolated neighborhood, immersed in greenery and illusionary quiet. The son of Joshua Reshet, the neighbor whose porch is adjacent to that of Ze'ev and Anat, was murdered by Arab terrorists, who also mutilated his corpse. And here, in dark irony, Joshua Reshet speaks about his "Israeli" situation:

> Here they don't suffice with murder . . . they stole his severed head. Gladys said we won't put up a tombstone; we'll wait for the head. In the end, she didn't wait very long. They say that women are stronger than men, that they withstand sorrow better than us. But Gladys, like the young man, did not obey rules. Her heart broke into pieces . . . I'd throw everything away and flee from the blood–drenched Middle East, but now, I already have a complete grave and a headless corpse. Who could abandon such property? (35)

It turns out that Joshua Reshet, a lone wolf who cannot sleep at night, found an original way to contribute his part to the war life in Israel—he will prevent disasters:

So I decided to take advantage of this plague of insomnia. The moment I feel my mind alert, I get up, get dressed, and go down to the car. It's because the Palestinians have again started to carry out abductions; their organizations are competing with each other over who can be the most violent. Our problem is that we have young people who take this lightly. They take no pity on themselves or on their parents . . . Soldiers forget themselves with their girlfriends and remember at the last moment to return to their base. So I drive around on the roads and pick them up. (160)

Sami Michael wrote *Pigeons at Trafalgar Square* during the Second Intifada and attaches some of the horrible events of the early 2000s, and the fear they sowed in Israeli cities, to the First Intifada, which took place in the late 1980s. Planting bombs in restaurants and attacks by suicide bombers wearing explosive belts are characteristics of the Second Intifada. But the writer, for whom historical documentation is secondary to documenting the state of mind, does not intend to separate them. In the words of Joshua Reshet, Ze'ev's neighbor, who is tied to this place by "property" consisting of a grave and a headless corpse: "Here, war is the normal situation. Pulling out a knife, shooting and murdering, lighting fires. Someone wrote that only here, in Israel, a Jew can be normal. But I think that he doesn't really believe it's a normal situation with the atrocities occurring here" (36–37). Indeed, the "normal situation" is spread across all of Zionist existence. Even Shmil, the most balanced and cool-headed character in the novel, expresses a pessimistic assessment, similar in essence to that of Joshua Reshet, the strange neighbor: "One hundred years of enmity and bloodbath have poisoned the souls" (194).

Thus, the citing of specific years would not change the feeling that war lives are a continuum, with some lulls. Nonetheless, as shown, the novel is set in identifiable times. The precise time of the events can be deduced by following the evolution of Nabila's relationship with her son, and via notorious terror attacks. The Bus 405 attack is an example of an event that ties the story to a specific time and place. As described above, the bus was en route to Jerusalem from Tel Aviv when it was forced over a cliff by a "fighter" or "terrorist." (The term you choose reflects where you side in the conflict. As noted, Karim, a Palestinian, refers to the bus hijacker as "another one of our fighters.") Here is another example: Joshua Reshet, who is always eager to speak about the Palestinians "who reproduce like maggots and poison the air" (181), tells Ze'ev in one of the last nighttime conversations they conduct between their adjacent porches in the novel:

> Those bastards, they murdered our soldier who entered the Al-Bureij refugee camp in Gaza by mistake. That's what you call a lynching in broad daylight, to torch a car like that with a person inside, and the couple with the infant in the car! You didn't hear the news? A three-month-old baby. Bullets made for killing lions shattered the infant's bones. A detestable race. Sit, sit, why are you standing? (239)

Indeed, on September 20, 1990, an Israeli soldier in civilian clothes ventured into the Al-Bureij refugee camp in Gaza—by mistake or because of car trouble—and was lynched. Like the Bus 405 attack, which marks the timeframe in which Nabila reveals her secret to Karim and Sana, the Palestinians' lynching of an Israeli soldier indicates that over a year has passed since Nabila orchestrated the encounter that brought all of her offspring together.

Michael devotes an entire chapter, somewhat detached from the main plot, to illustrate the atmosphere of the dreadful days of the Palestinian popular uprising, when the Israeli-Palestinian conflict spread in all its terror and brutality to the city streets and places of recreation in Israel. The clear distinction between the home front and the battlefront, which existed when armies waged battle on the borders, became blurred. In the "intifada of stones," as the first Palestinian popular uprising was called, anyone could become a "fighter," "terrorist," or victim.

In one chapter of his novel, Michael creates a situation in which Ze'ev witnesses a dialogue between a mother and daughter in an optometrist's waiting room. The daughter refuses to participate in a birthday party for her father because the venue for the party is a restaurant. "I'll celebrate with him another time. Privately," she tells her mother. "I'm not going to restaurants that blow up. I heard that you see dead bodies with pieces of steak in their mouths. That's not for me, mother. I'm telling you, that restaurant will blow up and everyone will die" (177). "Ze'ev understood how she felt," the omnipotent narrator says. "The past 24 hours were very hard on Israel. A bomb was planted in the Carmel Market . . . and a few hours later, there was an explosion at the central bus station in Afula . . . The most sophisticated army in the Middle East stood helpless in the face of rivals who fervently sought to kill and die." The narrator sums up the deformation that occurred in war lives in Israel by stating: "Bullets and bombs capable of deterring a suicide attacker have yet to be invented" (179).

Ze'ev is therefore trapped between the chilling words of the young Israeli girl—who was scared to death by the frequent attacks that claimed the lives of civilians in restaurants, markets, and bus stations, and he understands how she feels—and his awareness of his Palestinian family's predicament, where the "most sophisticated" army in the Middle East continues to act like an army at war:

> In his office at home, the letters from Nabila piled up . . . they described the distress of the family, sitting in darkness, surrounded by the army, and cut off from the outside world. Roaring aircraft prowled the sky in search of live Palestinian targets. Heavy bombings, designed to defeat an armed military force, unleashed their wrath on rickety and dilapidated buildings. Many civilians were killed. (179)

Additional information on the incessant attacks in the cities of Israel, while the army remains powerless, is conveyed again and again in the words of Joshua Reshet, the neighbor who looms over Ze'ev at night. Ze'ev, who proudly carries his Ashkenazi name but knows that he is also an Arab named Badir, feels during that period "as if he has a hump on his back" (179). The relations of knowing and not knowing, one of the central motifs in the novel, are also present between Ze'ev and his neighbor. Ze'ev says little and serves primarily as a sympathetic ear for Joshua. "'I'm listening,' Ze'ev said in a hushed, after-midnight voice" (160), but he evades taking a stand. In response to Joshua's bellicose and hate-filled declarations, Ze'ev says "I don't know," and this infuriates the neighbor:

> "What do you mean you don't know? Just now they announced there was another attack. There was a bombing in Jerusalem. There were people killed, including children and elderly people. Brave passersby ran to

help the injured, and then another bomb exploded among those who came to offer assistance. And you tell me you don't know," he scolded Ze'ev. "Get it into your head, those Arabs are a pestilence. They not only hate life, they hate anything with a whiff of culture. I know them like the back of my hand. After all, I'm from the Middle East. They won't rest until they wipe out all of the Jews here. Their lust for murder is embedded in their blood." (181)

The neighbor's declaration that he knows the Arabs well comes in the context of his earlier assumption that "you, Mr. Epstein, you surely don't originate from here, not from the Middle East" (36). In the heat of his words, which the lonely and bitter man feels obliged to express to someone willing to listen, he does not wait for Ze'ev to confirm or refute his assumption. "Mr. Epstein, I've never met anyone as taciturn as you" (158), he declares after realizing that he is the only one stating, in a loud and deep voice, the absolute verities in which he wholeheartedly believes, and that Ze'ev may actually think differently. Indeed, Ze'ev's dual identity makes it difficult for him to agree with his neighbor, but at the same time he listens to him—out of empathy and from a need to conceal his origin: "And Ze'ev thought to himself that the grief-stricken neighbor, who was still looking for his son's severed head, would surely suffer a stroke if he uncovered his secret" (182). And in another place, after Joshua calls the Arabs "a detestable race," Ze'ev thinks: "How would Joshua react if he knew I was a member of that race. And even so, he looked at him now with great compassion, as always" (240).

The distaste and the understanding, two conflicting emotions, Ze'ev feels toward his neighbor and others help to shape the hero of *Pigeons at Trafalgar Square* as a balanced, inclusive, cultured, and benevolent person, who ostensibly has the potential for building a bridge between the two peoples.

Engineering an Identity

Sami Michael took a difficult mission upon himself when he decided to appropriate Ghassan Kanafani's heritage and continue it in his own spirit.

He had to portray a less rigid hero than the one Kanafani abandoned as a proud Jew, who—like his Palestinian father—was unwilling to relinquish any of his unequivocal affiliation to a single people and a single heritage. Kanafani constructed his story on a sharp dichotomy that leaves no room for compromise; therefore, his sole conclusion is that the conflict will be decided through war. Michael sought to combine contrasts, to create a hero who lives at peace with structured internal ambivalence. Depiction of the character according to Kanafani's criteria leads to Dov's utter rejection of the parents who abandoned him as an infant and reappear in his life twenty years later. From his perspective, this late return was impossible. Sami Michael, on the other hand, sought to fashion a different hero, an evolving one who is capable of affiliating with and embracing both heritages.

It seems that each author created a hero in his own image and character. While Kanafani gave the extremist father the right to have the last word, Michael accorded this right to the mother; after the death of her husband, Ze'ev's Palestinian mother—in her soft and feminine yet manipulative way—leads her son on a path of compromise and inclusion. In a prelude to the encounter between the two parts of her family, which Nabila arranges at Ma'ayan Harod (so that her Palestinian son and daughter will see their Jewish brother, but will be unaware of their connection with him, and her Israeli son and grandson will observe their family dynamic), Ze'ev complains resentfully: "Why play this game? I'm an Israeli Jew. I can't be a Palestinian Muslim. If I connect with Nabila's family, I'll be considered a traitor and imposter in Israel, and for them, I'll be a sort of suspicious add-on" (25). But in time, Michael's hero indeed accepts the call of "flesh and blood," as the Palestinian mother expected in Kanafani's novella. Michael's novel, in fulfilling the mother's wish in both of the literary works, portrays a relationship of genuine friendship and profound understanding, as well as an unconsummated erotic attraction between the mother and her son.

Kanafani emphasizes the unequivocal choice of a single identity by depicting his hero, Dov, as a Jew who keeps kosher and goes to synagogue. Michael, on the other hand, does not associate his hero, Ze'ev, with traditional Judaism. As a counterweight to Kanafani, Michael underlines the complete secularity of Ze'ev's Israeli family. His mother Riva and father

Ephraim, as well as his business partner and confidant Shmil, are entirely secular. In light of the budding relations between Ze'ev and his Palestinian family, Anat is the one who insists on lighting candles on Sabbath eve and other ritualistic trappings in order to strengthen his Jewish identity. At every opportunity, she reminds him where he came from and where he should be heading. For example, when he says that their neighbor Joshua Reshet "wakes up every morning surrounded by bloodthirsty enemies, real and imagined" she screams: "Imagined? . . . I might understand if someone else said this, but you? The son of a Holocaust survivor?" (239). She usually recoils from the strange neighbor, but if he provides an opportunity to reinforce her husband's affiliation with his heritage, she will grab that opportunity. In any case, from Anat's perspective, Ze'ev is the son of Riva, and no one else. Even before their marriage, Anat showed that she was not frightened about his genetic heritage, as long as it was clear to both of them where he and she stood: "I love you, but you should know that even for you, I won't be an Arab." And Ze'ev responds: "No one will force you to be what you don't want to be. We're not dealing with the engineering of identities" (80). He was speaking about her, and not about himself.

Since Michael does engage in the "engineering of identities," his hero is attentive to his Palestinian identity, though he will never abandon his Israeli identity. In his effort to belong to both sides, he concocts a territorial-business compromise solution: the Cypriot Project. Israeli and Arab partners will build in Cyprus (which is geographically close but far from the Israeli-Palestinian conflict) a huge hotel, vacation apartments, and a geriatric center attached to a large hospital, with outstanding medical personnel from Cyprus, Israel, and Palestine. Shmil, also a dreamer, is enthralled by Ze'ev's idea, but also anchors it in the solid ground of reality:

> The war isn't over yet. We're still slaughtering each other. At first we thought—Molotov cocktails here, stones there, and it would end until the next outbreak. But it hasn't ended, my son. It's an ongoing conflict—waning and waxing, but never ending. And you, Ze'evik, are building a utopia. You want to build on foreign soil what we haven't succeeded in doing here. (103)

The hero is building a utopia and the writer is creating an ideal hero. But there is no room for either in this time and place. Shmil knows that his partner, who is dear to him like a son, is trying to unite the two identities within him, and he explains to Ze'ev that this is impossible:

> You have to decide. Either one or the other. You can't sleep with the Arabs at night and live with the Jews during the day. If I were you, I'd decide one way or the other. Because, between you and me, there will never be real peace between the two sides. The Jews remember their days of glory, and the Arabs worship the glory of the past. There's no chance of reconciliation. So choose, my son. (106)

But Ze'ev, who was engineered by Sami Michael, his creator, to be a person capable of holding two identities within him, does not intend to choose. Shmil tells him that he is "just a boy that God is toying with" (109), and if we look at the writer as the God of his literary work, then Michael created an endearing child, a "gift child," an imagined superhero. In a frank and poignant conversation between Ze'ev and Shmil, the "boy" insists on keeping both of his identities, while Shmil recognizes the potential disaster in Ze'ev's dual existence. Ze'ev, as expected, attributes his ability to identify with both heritages to the two mothers who shaped his personality. As noted, Michael dedicates the novel to "all mothers, who are the promised land of the human race," and thus the hero's inclination to reconcile the opposing sides stems from his connection to the two mothers; this blending of opposites is a promised land, an impossible utopia.

> "Do you feel you're a Jew?"
> "Of course, I'm Riva's son from the day I know myself. I'm an Epstein."
> "And that Arab woman?!"
> "I can't forget that she gave birth to me."
> "And to what extent are you prepared to be loyal to her?" . . .
> "Come on, really. I couldn't think of harming Israel's security, just as I couldn't think of hurting Nabila and my brother and sister."
> "What does that mean?" Shmil pressed.

"If one of them were to do something, I'd help him get away and immediately turn myself in."

"Ah, my dear boy! I'd say you're dangling on a rope above an abyss, and both sides will fire at you with no hesitation. I wouldn't want to be in your place." (108)

Conscious of the inability of a flesh and blood hero to hold two identities in a conflictual reality rife with hatred and blood, Michael fulfills Shmil's nightmarish prophecy. He chose the First Intifada in order to bring the superhero and his mother—who both serve as an antithesis to the militant father and husband—back down to reality. The closed ending of the novel is a link to Kanafani, but also poses a challenge to him.

Bear, Wolf, Sheep in a Pen, Pigeons in the Square

Before we get to the sad denouement of the novel, let us look at the names Michael chose for his hero and his book, a name and title that were not chosen arbitrarily.

As noted, Kanafani named his hero Dov; and Michael, who sought to disconnect from the Palestinian writer's underlying text, changed the names of the heroes. He replaced the name of Dov [bear], one wild animal, with the name of another wild animal, Ze'ev [wolf]. Thus, Michael maintained a connection with Kanafani's hero while defining a distinct identity for his own hero. However, Michael's specific choice of animal, a wolf, and the change in the hero's Arab name from Khaldun to Badir are not coincidental. Michael sought to give his hero a particular symbolic meaning when choosing these two names: Ze'ev and Badir.

During one of the clandestine meetings between the Palestinian mother and her son, at a hotel in Sweden, Ze'ev mumbles his Arab name and chuckles. Nabila responds angrily: "Badir, that's your name. Why are you laughing? . . . Why are you emphasizing the letter 'd'? You're mangling the name." Ze'ev stresses the "d" and chuckles because he is thinking of what *ba-dir* means in Hebrew—"in the sheep shed." In Hebrew, *ba* means "in the" and *dir* means "sheep shed," and when joined together in *badir*, the "d" is emphasized [sounds: *baddir*]. From the Palestinian mother's perspective, *badir* is an Arabic word that means "full moon" and the first syllable *ba* is stressed. But her Hebrew son associates the name with "in the sheep shed," and thus finds it amusing. "Look how the similarity between languages can be deceiving" (87), he says—and he is right. Because if it were not deceiving, his two names—which evoke a vision of peace ("the wolf shall dwell with the lamb")—would have empowered him to unify the two hostile factions in his family. He could have even created the utopia envisioned in his Cypriot Project: to channel the knowledge and experience of all members of his family toward peacemaking.

The hero's dual name, Ze'ev-Badir, is alluded to early in the novel, but the title *Pigeons at Trafalgar Square* becomes clear only toward the end of the book. As noted, the novel begins with the picnic at Ma'ayan Harod, with the Palestinian part of the family unaware that the person they are encountering is their Jewish brother. In London, at Trafalgar Square, they already know. Kanafani wrote about returning to Haifa, while Michael brings together the Muslims and the Jew, members of the same family, in far-off London. This is apparently because the Middle East, where all of the family members live, is seething with unrest in 1990 and this type of get-together is dangerous. Another reason for choosing the distant locale is perhaps the fact that Trafalgar Square in London is teeming with pigeons that are not afraid of people, a place that might cheer the spirit of those who live in fear every day: "They came from a city that experiences siege, curfew, and closure from time to time, a city that sometimes turns into a battlefield, and they now savored the feeling of calm that enwrapped them" (203).

Ze'ev's well-intentioned choice turns out to be an unfortunate one. The pigeons, the symbol of peace [in Hebrew, the same word is used for "dove" and "pigeon"], which in London embody peace and the absence of fear, become threatening animals at Trafalgar Square: Suhail, Sana's son, whose mind and soul have been damaged by the Jewish-Palestinian conflict, recoils from the friendly pigeons that come up very close to people and are not afraid of them. The pigeons frighten him.

Pigeons also have a symbolic dimension in the context of the hero himself. These animals, which have grown accustomed to people, are an illustration of B. F. Skinner's educational-behavioral school, which Ze'ev latched onto after learning he was born to Arab parents. The American psychologist and behavioral scientist accords decisive weight and priority to a person's education and upbringing, rather than to their origin and genetics. Skinner's views developed following research on simple learning by rats and pigeons. Ze'ev Epstein, Sami Michael's Jewish-Arab hero, is thus not only a dove [pigeon] in a political sense, he is also a pigeon in the educational sense. His name is Ze'ev [wolf], but he is actually the pigeon in the square or the lamb in the sheep shed (Badir), seeking to bring together the two parts of his family in a neutral place, far from the wolves of war of the Middle East—whether in Sweden, London, or Cyprus—and hoping to elicit the best from the meeting and from each member of the family.

The Father's Curse

While Trafalgar Square only threatens, Ramallah kills. When the pigeons come too close, it is intimidating; Ze'ev the pigeon's close relations with his Muslim family are deadly. When Shmil warns Ze'ev about becoming too intimate with his family, and especially with his mother ("she's Arab and Palestinian, and you won't persuade me that they don't dream about wiping out Israel"), Ze'ev replies: "If I'm growing closer to Nabila and to my sister and to my brother, it's not at the expense of Israel and not at the expense of Adiv and not at the expense of Anat. I have room for everyone" (237). This conversation between Shmil, who repeatedly warns that Ze'ev is walking a tightrope above an abyss, and Ze'ev, who feels he has the strength to accommodate both sides within him, takes place before the next-door neighbor tells Ze'ev about the lynching of the Israeli soldier who entered the Al-Bureij refugee camp in Gaza, a real occurrence that seeps into the novel. The neighbor concludes his words with a racist epithet: "a detestable race." Ze'ev enters his home and does not feel detestable. On the contrary, he feels pride in his shapely body, his beautiful family, and his pure soul that contains "neither Jewish hatred nor Palestinian animosity" (240). He peeks into his son's room and great joy fills his heart at the sight of the boy sleeping serenely and securely in his protected home. Nonetheless, something disturbs his sense of happiness: "In a momentary flash, he suddenly pictured his nephew Suhail, Sana's son, cowering in fear of the pigeons at Trafalgar Square. He immediately tried to erase the image from his mind, but it stubbornly reappeared, hovering in front of his eyes, nagging and irritating" (240–41). The neighbor's harsh words and the image of a terrified Suhail, who unlike his peacefully sleeping son flinches even from friendly pigeons, continue to trouble him. He tries to obscure the upsetting contradictions and contrasts by approaching his wife Anat that night and asking her for a baby girl.

All this is a buildup to the dramatic ending of the novel, which tries to wrestle with the denouement of Kanafani's novella. As noted, the novella leaves the hero, who is only nineteen years old, with the father's prophetic curse: One day, on the battlefield, his Palestinian brother will rise up against him and kill him. Michael adopted the curse, aiming to contend with it at the end of his novel. But much earlier, the chapter on Ze'ev's meeting with his Palestinian parents concludes by describing the curse's impact on the hero and his Jewish mother:

> Ze'ev was shocked. A man stood before him who, without blinking an eye, inscribed the names of his two sons in the book of the dead. Fierce hatred burned in his eyes when he went on to say, "From this moment onward, you'll no longer be the man you were until now." Later, Ze'ev and Riva listened in silence to the sound of the engine awakening below. For the first time in years, they went to sleep immersed in heavy silence. (50)

Let us return to the ending of the novel. A joyous and colorful wedding precedes the confrontation with the deceased father's prophetic curse, which weighs heavily upon the shoulders of the two mothers and the son. But Riva is old and has forgotten the prophecy, leaving only the Palestinian mother and her Jewish son with this burden. A familiar literary convention is to portray a happy event and convey a convivial feeling before delivering the anticipated blow. Michael uses the precipitous fall from zenith to nadir in a very creative way.

The wedding is the climax of the rapprochement process between Ze'ev's two families. Imbued with faith that nothing bad would happen to a hybrid like himself, Ze'ev comes to Ramallah to celebrate his brother

Karim's marriage to the young and beautiful Zahwa. In London, he contributed significantly to strengthening their relationship and he feels committed toward them. He arrives in Ramallah with Anat, Adiv, and Shmil, whose large dimensions fill Ze'ev's big car. Anat, who is now pregnant, shows openness and generosity toward the host family, and charms all who see her. The inquisitive Adiv is "like someone immersed in a sea of colors and sounds" (248). The temporary illusion that good times have come is reinforced by the general situation of relative quiet in late 1990 or perhaps early 1991: "Again there was hope in the air, cautious hope. Those were days of relative calm between the two peoples. Fewer confrontations and clashes, but still innocent victims fell. But Ze'ev was not fearful on the way to the wedding. His sense of security may have come from feeling that he himself was a son of both peoples" (247). While Ze'ev draws his confidence from his dual affiliation, Anat's confidence stems from her dual existence: "Now I'm actually two, she told herself over and over" (246). From her perspective, bringing a daughter into the world, a sister for Adiv, would further anchor their father, her husband, in the Jewish-Israeli experience.

Yet even in that hour of joy and family unity, she knows that everything is transitory, that the family spirit will fade, and that the situation in the Middle East will revert to its wretchedness, with animosity toward the other its most "sustainable" characteristic. "The two scarred peoples, immersed in deep hatred, are obstinate like no others and therefore no chance of reconciliation is foreseeable" (247). Nabila also knows, and in mixed feelings of happiness in the present and fear for the future, the wedding chapter concludes: "Inhaling the sweet breath of her three grandchildren, she felt that no one was richer and happier than her. And at the same time, she also felt that no one was more threatened than her in this reality of shifting sands under stormy gusts of wind" (250–51).

The chapter describing the lynching of her Jewish son, who deluded himself into thinking that no harm would come to him in his mother's territory, also opens with the realization that took root in her—that the dreamlike happiness that appeared for a fleeting moment was only a harbinger of a nightmare that often materializes in the world of war: "During a time of war, a grandmother must not embrace all of her grandchildren at once . . . war has evil and greedy eyes. Nabila was happy that day, Karim's wedding day, yet with her life experience should have known that happiness in wartime is a sort of disastrous blindness" (252). Indeed, she should have known. Nonetheless, she asks her Jewish son to come to her after she broke her leg. His determined response echoes in her ears with unparalleled sweetness, which the narrator expresses threefold: "'**I'm coming!**' he told her immediately, and she rejoiced upon hearing his rapid response . . . '**I'm coming!**' What is more gladdening than these words . . . '**I'm coming!**' How delightful the sound of these words" (253, emphasis added). This adds another strong hint to the array of hints about Oedipal relations that developed between the mother and her son. She knew, but could not restrain herself. He did not know, but responded to the call of flesh and blood. "He got into his large and luxurious car with the Israeli license plates; he felt so secure, so immune to injury and danger" (253).

The violence between the two conflicted peoples reached a new peak of brutality at that hour. Michael masterfully describes the horror: Jewish women were murdered and dismembered. "Later, there was a bombing in a bustling pedestrian mall, body parts scattered among the store entrances, and dismembered limbs were strewn everywhere, even on the treetops." Michael criticizes his hero, who has yet to learn that "grief is thirsty for revenge, which will eventually come." Nor did the radio warn him against crossing the Green Line, red with blood, at such a time: "It was not yet permitted to broadcast the news about Israel's retaliation for the acts of terror in the streets" (253).

Just as Michael does not hesitate to describe the general atrocities, he is not reticent in describing the horror of the lynching. A pack of bloodthirsty youths block Ze'ev's way, and though he realizes that "it's either them or me" (255), he refrains from using his sturdy vehicle to slice through the human herd besieging him. In his last moments, he feels sorry for himself and for his two mothers—"how unfair if he dies when Riva and Nabila are still alive . . . but he won't run over those children. His foot pressed the brakes, the clenched fists banged on his windows, like starving children who wanted his life, not bread" (255–56). Even when facing death, Michael's "engineered" hero is contemptuous of "people who become a herd."

It turns out that Ze'ev does not die alone. His brother Karim comes to rescue him, and a "faceless" man later informs Nabila: "I've never seen such sacrifice. Karim bodily defended the Jew, his brother" (259).

In the epilogue to the novel, the mother and sister of Ze'ev and Karim, the brothers who were not separated in death, are standing on the soil of Cyprus, where Ze'ev's dream was supposed to be fulfilled, and Nabila points toward Israel and Palestine across the sea. "They were silent, the silence of survivors looking out upon the remnants of their world, reduced to ashes" (260), the narrator says. After the terrible lynching, in which the mother, who had found her lost son, loses him and his brother on a single day, a ray of hope appears. The Cypriot Project materializes after all, and Anat and Shmil are on their way for its launch, together with Ze'ev's two sons. It turns out that Ze'ev and Anat did not have a daughter as they wished, but another son. Adiv has yet to come to terms with his father's departure and his brother's arrival, but he continues his father's tradition of asking questions. Zahwa, the young wife, gave birth to Karim's second daughter; the first daughter was from a previous marriage. Nabila is now already a grandmother of five. She learns Hebrew in order to speak with her two Israeli grandsons. In her opinion, Suhail's condition is improving. Sana, as usual, is skeptical. She is also disdainful of her mother's belief that the father's curse on that night in Haifa after the 1967 war has proven to be false.

"Your father's wish," Nabila argues, "did not come true, Sana. Karim and his brother did indeed meet, but they did not kill each other. On the contrary. The complete opposite." And Sana replies: "What difference does it make? They both died" (261).

Did Sami Michael in his novel *Pigeons at Trafalgar Square* (Text B, the hypertext) succeed in countering Ghassan Kanafani's bellicose and unequivocal message in his novella "Returning to Haifa" (Text A, the hypotext)? Nabila would apparently answer in the affirmative, and Sana in the negative.

9

Soldiers in a Bubble in Ron Leshem's *Beaufort*

A Novel about an Outpost in the "Mud of Lebanon"

"Welcome. If there is a heaven, this is what it looks like, and if there is a hell, this is how it feels."

Between Truth and Imagination

In 1957, Dov Sadan wrote an introduction to the Hebrew edition of Erich Auerbach's seminal work, *Mimesis: The Representation of Reality in Western Literature* (1946). In his essay, Sadan contends that Auerbach has a very specific notion of reality, which, he argues, is the starting point for understanding the scholar's deep exploration of the complex relationship between literature and life. Sadan's words sound as though they were penned today:

> The starting point of his [Auerbach's] exploration is the fact that the earth, representing the entirety of world literature, is shrinking, and as it does so, to an ever-greater extent, it deprives us of diversity, which is the heart and soul of literature. The unification of life, the undermining of unique traditions, the convergence of lifestyles, the spread of standardization, whether by the American-European or Russian-Bolshevik edition, will, inevitably, bring about the foundation of a single culture, already forming, and the day is near in which the multiplicity of languages shall be reduced, perhaps even to a single tongue, and we shall find that the idea of world literature is both fulfilled and destroyed as one.[1]

The global village, as foreseen by Sadan—who had no way of predicting the advent of the internet and Facebook and other social media platforms that would render his vision so tangible—cannot be extended to our unique war experiences here in Israel. The internet, which introduces people to one another in a virtual reality, bridging geographic distances and synchronizing biological clocks, appears irrelevant and even ridiculous when seen in the context of a small group of soldiers engaged in military service or outright war, isolated by geography and circumstance and sequestered by necessity. The assertion regarding the culling of languages to a single dominant tongue is also stripped of relevance when paired with the reality of a group of soldiers huddled within a tight perimeter, facing the trials of proximate death, erotic longing, and a craving for the trappings of a normal life; within that perimeter, the group develops its own sub-dialect, forged under the presence of a shared will to live and a frequent, hovering fear. The collective experience of a band of warriors stationed in an outpost or a forward operating base is so fundamentally different from that of a single person situated in a sanitized environment, on a train or in the comfort of their home, updating a friend in some distant part of the world about their whereabouts. And this is done, one can assume, in a standardized and flattened form of English, which is not necessarily their mother tongue. The smell of sweat and urine and bad breath, of burnt flesh and blood and fear, are not transmitted online. Nor are unique phrases—hatched every day anew within the bubble—easily created over email. Military service is an individual and collective experience that is resistant to standardization and has, though one wishes the circumstances were otherwise, indirectly served to preserve the diversity of human experience, "the heart and soul of literature."

This is strikingly evident in Ron Leshem's *Beaufort* and Yehoshua Kenaz's *Infiltration*. The novels are different in tone and period, but provide, when viewed in tandem, a glimpse into the shifting nature of the Israeli war novel. Both depict the secluded world of soldiers. Both are relayed by a first-person narrator. Both contain dialectal flourishes unique to the novel and the insular worlds portrayed within its pages. But the similarities, which invite comparison, offer a stark and instructive glimpse into what has changed in Israeli society and how this change is reflected in the Israeli literature of war. Patriotism, for example, remains prevalent, as does ethnic strife, but the former is expanded while the latter is turned on its head. *Beaufort*, the novel set in the year 2000, has a Sephardic narrator who is not only given the reins of the story—a far cry from *Infiltration*—but also is given the privilege of doubting the patriotism and the soldierly competence of his Ashkenazi soldiers and peers. This is a sea change from the Israel of the fifties. The army, too, remains a sort of microcosm of Israeli society, a melting pot. However, forty-five years after the 1955 basic training that is the setting for *Infiltration*, the crucible of the army reflects a much-altered society.

Leshem's *Beaufort* chronicles the day-to-day lives of soldiers at the outpost during its final days under an Israeli flag. The precise details of the daily lives of the platoon of combat soldiers, all serving within the confines of a heavily reinforced outpost in South Lebanon, in advance of the May 2000 withdrawal, are delivered in colorful, slang-heavy narration by a first person protagonist, Second Lieutenant Liraz "Erez" Liberti. The commander of the fourteen-man platoon, who is a year older than his men, making him an authority figure and a friend, tells the story in his own voice, pulling no punches as he relays his and their tale in the perpetually bombarded and threatened outpost of Beaufort.

In its force and authenticity, Leshem's novel, more than any of the Israeli novels that preceded it, resembles Remarque's *All Quiet on the Western Front*, which serves as a benchmark for the martial and warlike nature of a literary work. Perhaps only Avigdor Hameiri's *The Great Madness* can compare. But in the aforementioned works the soldier-narrator is a figure without authority, who recounts the tale from a place of victimhood. Here Liraz-Erez, the junior officer, is a gung-ho soldier with full confidence in the army. He would like to see the unit assigned missions that are more significant and difficult; he would like to head out into the field, charge, and engage in combat, and not merely make do with perimeter security and stationary night-time ambushes for a faceless enemy. At the same time, Liraz-Erez concerns himself with the welfare, safety, and even happiness of his soldiers. He is a protagonist who changes slowly, remaining convinced for nearly the full length of the narrative that the Israeli presence in the Security Zone is fully justified. Even when that faith in the eighteen-year occupation is finally cracked, and when an entire country, including its soldiers, begins to doubt the necessity of the military presence in the string of fortresses north of Israel's border—Liraz-Erez ["Erez" means "cedar" in Hebrew] clings to the faith that the occupation of that part of the Land of Cedars is crucial to the safety of Israel's citizens.

The name of the real-life platoon commander who served as an inspiration to Ron Leshem in his construction of Liraz-Erez was an officer by the name of Rotem Yair, whom "everyone called Ronen, though, because Rotem is a babe's name" (*Beaufort*, 354).[2] Leshem divulges this in the afterword, which is entitled "Between Truth and Imagination" (353–57).

The manner in which Erez's name is explained in the novel is a good example of the way that a kernel of truth is masked and made into fiction. In the second chapter, the narrator introduces himself, beginning with an explication of his name:

> But anyway my name is really Liraz. In basic training, at the very first roll call, the platoon commander ran down the names and when he got to mine he stopped. He didn't like it, my name. "Wait, wait. What's that?" he asked. "What kind of name is that? Liraz? That's a chick's name. From now on you're Erez, like the cedars of Lebanon. Congratulations." Erez. That's who I am to this day. (14)

In this way, both the flesh and blood inspiration for the character and the character himself were assigned new names. Similarly, the author retained the reasoning for the name change: Liraz, like Rotem, was deemed a girlish name. Liraz becomes Erez, a name that evokes the heights of the outpost, positioned upon "the roof of the world," from which Liraz-Erez and his soldiers peer out.

"Try to imagine that they stick you high up on a mountain cliff, higher than the roof of the Azrieli Building. How could you not have a breathtaking view?" the narrator asks in the first chapter of *Beaufort*. "Here it's wide expanses of green countryside checkered with patches of brown and red, snowy mountains, frothing rivers, narrow, winding, deserted European roads, and the sweetest wind there is" (5). In *Infiltration*, there is no such vantage point, no soul-expanding view. But in both novels the soldiers are closed off from the outside world, placed in a bubble within which a unique dynamic takes hold. The characters are all young and are all forced, personally and collectively, to face trials that most of their peers around the world never have faced and never will. The jarring and demanding world of the military, the "kingdom of uncertainty," as the army is sometimes known, is portrayed in a changing light, illuminating that which endures and that which has been altered in the literature of Israeli war.

Infiltration, Beaufort—A Meeting Point

In *Infiltration*, the ugliness of the landscape is perfectly paired with the physical and spiritual incarceration of the soldiers. Set in the summer of 1955, at a training base in the center of Israel, Kenaz's novel does not unfold during a time of war. It is a story about teens, fresh from high school, and their harrowing encounter with the military. The narrator, Melabbes, is not an officer but a private; a chasm separates him from his commanders.

In *Beaufort*, the narrator, as noted, is the platoon commander; his soldiers play a supporting role, filling in the group profile of a small outfit linked by friendship and camaraderie, and divided by ideological tension and frustration.

This difference in perspective is artfully displayed by the narrators' depiction of their initial encounter with the geographic setting of the novel. At daybreak, on their first morning at Beaufort, the commanding officer tells the soldiers: "Welcome. If there is a heaven, this is what it looks like, and if there is a hell, this is how it feels," further sharpening the contrast between the stunning scenery and the stifling entrenchment within the bowels of the outpost—"This pit, called the submarine, is where my entire life will be taking place from now on," Erez says, his bitterness dipped in the knowing humor of the army veteran (7).

The privates marching into Camp Sarafand at the start of basic training have no such perspective. Melabbes relays that they are greeted by "a row of eucalyptus trees with whitewashed trunks" (*Infiltration*, 7),[3] and the base itself, "with its whitewashed paths and ugly eucalyptus trees and fences under the dusty summer sky, looking more and more like a vast desert without a single oasis that would welcome the wondering lost souls and quench their thirst for pity and forgiveness" (19). Both authors chose to lend poetic expression to the soldiers' first encounter with the place, where they will spend many months, divorced from their civilian surroundings.

In the minds of Israelis at large and more specifically in the minds of Israeli soldiers, the eucalyptus tree is a dominant feature of the army landscape, towering over the soldiers' consciousness. While Eli Amir's protagonist-narrator finds peace and quiet in the shade of a eucalyptus tree just outside Gaza in advance of the outbreak of war in 1967,[4] the revulsion that the soldiers in *Infiltration* feel for the tree seeps all the way into *Beaufort*, which is set amidst cedars, not eucalyptuses.

In both novels, the dusty eucalyptus, which is planted in many army bases, serves as a synecdoche for the sorrowful surroundings. During one of the platoon's final stretches of leave from South Lebanon, Erez and the rest of the guys descend from the high ridge of the Beaufort and head south to Israel. River, the platoon's combat medic, continues on to the Golan Heights to meet Hodaya, a young woman he once loved and has not seen for a year. The distressing feeling within him is cast upon the landscape: "He hated this place intensely without knowing why—simply hated it. Maybe it was the eucalyptus trees. There was nothing he despised more than cheap eucalyptuses, which reminded him of army bases" (263). If forty-five years have not dulled the soldiers' detestation of oppressive army bases, scenically characterized by the eucalyptus tree, then it is a sign that there are many feelings, revolting and moving, that are common to the Israeli soldier across time.

Above and beyond the encounter with the physical location, it is incumbent upon us to examine the soldiers' meeting with one another and their commanders. Yehoshua Kenaz chose a stealth take-down exercise, in which the new recruits slam one another to the ground after stopping the flow of blood to their brains, as symbolic of their first meeting. Those harshly subdued soldiers experience a semi-comatose state, "like a dream, only without the literary, sometimes baroque, ambience that accompanies dream images" (3). Melabbes slips from consciousness as he succumbs and awakens slowly to a scene in which his mates, like him, are sprawled out on the ground in a circle. "I looked around me. My waking friends gave me back my reflection as in a mirror. How ugly this awakening was, how wretched the eye rollings, the limb jerkings, the head shakings, the stupid, glassy looks from the frightened eyes, the gray faces, frozen in the terror of oblivion" (5). This ugly and violent drill, performed with almost no guiding hand—the commanders and instructors play but a minor role in this maneuver—marks the beginning of the basic training course in the summer of 1955, and it is in this way that the recruits are acquainted with one another. It serves as an illustration of the shock, estrangement, bewilderment, humiliation, and denuding forced upon the soldiers by the sharp departure from the familiar and warm civilian world and the entry into the foreign and rigid realm of the military. This surreal drill is devoid of literary ambience, baroque or poetic; it is but a nightmarish and laconic dive from the high heights to the deep depths.

In *Beaufort*, the initial meeting is chaotic but not mindless. It takes place in February 1999, when Liraz "Erez" Liberti first leads his platoon to the mountaintop. The commander has served there before, but for his soldiers, "his kids," it is the first time (32). Upon arrival, at three in the morning, they are "jammed" into the briefing room for an introductory lecture by the company commander, Naor Furman, and then sent to their quarters for a bit of sleep. Here too there is a depiction of a transitory state of consciousness, where light and darkness, dreams, arousal, and sickness all intermingle. "But where the kids sleep, in the inner rooms, the light is on all the time, and it blinds you and is really strong and it produces unnatural colors, totally psychedelic. Staring directly into the bulbs mesmerizes you for a few minutes, then you feel dizzy and want to puke" (52).

Here, though, as opposed to *Infiltration*, there is no lack of purpose, no stark aimlessness. Erez makes sure everyone is up for dawn alert, his "youngsters" standing with full battle gear on their backs, staring at the green-and-white sign on which the aim of the mission is printed: "TO DEFEND ISRAEL'S NORTHERN BORDER, FROM MOUNT DOV IN THE EAST TO ROSH HANIKRA IN THE WEST" (53, capital letters in original). The words force them into a serious state of mind, the platoon uplifted by the gravity of their mission. Eventually, doubts start to trickle into their hearts and they begin to question the necessity of their presence on the summit, where some feel they are nothing more than "cannon fodder."

The army as a scene of social integration, a melting pot, is a common theme of the war novel. In Remarque's novel, the integration is across socioeconomic lines. "By threes and fours our class was scattered over the platoons amongst Frisian fishermen, peasants, and laborers with whom we soon made friends" (*All Quiet on the Western Front*, 12, digital version). In the Israeli war novel, the divide is ethnic. Kenaz devotes ample space in *Infiltration* to the revulsion the Ashkenazi characters feel for their Sephardi peers; the ethnic divide, still unbridged, is strewn with racism. In a blunt and unflinching manner, Kenaz depicts the disgust that the "silver spoon" Ashkenazim of the leafy neighborhoods of Jerusalem feel for the songs and dances of their platoon mates, mostly immigrants from Arab lands. The cultural clash between the two groups is a sort of looking glass through which we are able to view the strained relationship between First Israel and Second Israel during the years of mass immigration.

The fear of "Levantism" and its possible takeover of the nascent country is vividly depicted in the novel, as the Ashkenazi recruits perceive the Mizrahim (Sephardim) as Arabs: "We don't want Arab songs in the army!" Hedgehog shouts. "We don't want to hear that shit here!" (90). Only Alon, the idealistic kibbutznik, beautiful in body and soul, is willing to accept the others, while his friend Micky, the cynical Ashkenazi and his verbal sparring partner, wonderfully crafted as Alon's antithesis, seems to have been given a glimpse into the future:

> "No!" cried Hedgehog. "They can go back where they came from and sing those disgusting songs there. Not here! . . ."
>
> "They've got the right to sing their songs," said Alon sadly. "It's not only our army. It's their army too."
>
> "One day it'll really be their army," said Micky. "They'll be the majority here. They have lots of kids." . . .
>
> "Their children will be just like us," promised Alon.
>
> "Or our children'll be like them," grinned Micky, "and in the end it'll be just another Arab state . . ." (90–91)

Micky's "dark" forecast that "it'll really be their army" one day already begins to take shape in *Yasmine*, a novel of the Six-Day War. Kabi, the protagonist's brother, is wounded during the war. He turns to his brother Nuri, who is visiting him in the hospital, and says: "It was our war . . . Look around you, most of the wounded are from the mass immigration, as they call us. Jews from Iraq, Romania, Morocco, Tunisia, Libya, Turkey, Iran . . . It's a revolution. From now on, the state is as much ours as theirs" (*Yasmine*, 79).[5] In *Beaufort* there is no need to point, no need to look around. The facts are clear, the situation completely natural. The majority of Erez's soldiers—himself included—are Mizrahi Jews. The standoffishness delineated across ethnic lines remains; only in this later novel, it has been inverted: The Sephardi is wary of the Ashkenazi. The two Ashkenazi characters in Leshem's novel, both of whom dare to question the necessity of Israel's presence in South Lebanon and are later killed while serving at the outpost, make Erez's ambivalence about them quite tangible. But the "impulsive *ars*,"[6] who was also "a devoted player with good intentions" (119), harbored reservations about the viewpoints, behavior, music, and appearances of the Beaufort's two Ashkenazi soldiers, Ziv Farran and Yonatan Spitzer. His preconceived notion of Ashkenazim is infinitely more playful and placated than the virulent distaste exhibited by Hedgehog and Micky and the other Ashkenazim in *Infiltration*. They are openly disdainful of their platoon mates Rahamim Ben-Hamo, Zaki, Sami, Zero-Zero, Peretz-Mental-Case, and the rest of the Mizrahi Israelis at Camp Sarafand that summer.

The first meeting between Erez and Ziv, the veteran soldier from the sappers' unit who arrives at the fort and is killed five days shy of his release from the army, is charged. The Ashkenazi "pretty boy," who "looked like he'd been parachuted in from some commercial for low-cal sour cream," "one of those TV soldiers," sits down at the Friday night dinner in the mess hall and introduces himself: "Nice to meet you, I'm Ziv Farran." Erez, pained by what eventually happened to Ziv and by his changing attitude toward him, twice relays the scene in which Ziv extends a hand to him and he recoils at the gesture. The first time, Erez says he "didn't even reply" (110). In the retelling, he says he made do with "a quick feeble handshake that made it clear how little patience I had for being friendly" (112). The episodic story of the brief period of time he spent with Ziv and the repetitive nature of the tale, with Erez telling us again and again that he cannot recall the exact date of his death—"I swore I'd never forget the date, but suddenly now I can't remember. A total disgrace" (110)—is evidence of the contradictions surging within him regarding his feelings for Ziv and the nature of his tragic death: He wants to preserve the trauma and to deflect it, and above all to plant within himself the narrative that he will stick with.

Ron Leshem describes Erez's aversion to Ashkenazim in the army as a product of an obscured appreciation, blended with an inferiority complex and topped with a general skepticism regarding their military capabilities, for "real fighters don't shine like that" (112). On that Friday night, when Ziv and two other "white-bread" soldiers from the Engineering Corps arrive at the outpost, Erez and Oshri—a sergeant of Yemenite heritage who is later wounded—promptly sit down in their spots to ensure that none of the Ashkenazi newcomers "accidentally breach custom" and sit near them. Yet later, Erez realizes that Ziv "doesn't look at me like some fuckup inferior punk from Afula who likes to play with guns . . . Maybe he even respected me." He then understands that it is "impossible not to break down barriers with the guy" (126).

Between Erez's initial reaction to ignore Ziv and belittle his military competence ("if that little white boy really knows something about bomb removal, I'll cut my dick off"), to a deep appreciation of his professionalism and heroism, which is later revealed, Ron Leshem inserts the scene in which Erez learns of Ziv's opposition to the Israeli occupation of South Lebanon. The author chose to have this knowledge revealed in the shower. Nakedness is of great significance in army and war stories. The cloth of the uniform, after all, makes the soldier resemble his peers, while in the shower the soldier is stripped of uniformity, of his military appearance, and rendered a fragile and free civilian. So it is with Remarque: "But when we go bathing and strip, suddenly we have slender legs again and slight shoulders. We are no longer soldiers but little more than boys; no one would believe that we could carry packs. It is a strange moment when we stand naked; then we become civilians, and almost feel ourselves to be so" (*All Quiet on the Western Front*, 15, digital version). Erez too reports a feeling of freedom in the shower: "First, the cloth that has been strangling your body is removed: The shirts that have been sticking to you are taken off, the socks. A winter wind strokes your skin, it's orgasmic. You die from happiness, even if you're frozen to the bone" (*Beaufort*, 119).

And in fact when the two are in the shower, liberated and equal, with the socioeconomic gap between them hinted at only by their respective toiletries bags, one decrepit, the other "looking like it belonged to a battalion commander" (121), Erez sees Ziv's white shirt, draped over the fancy toiletries kit, bearing the slogan of the Four Mothers movement: OUT OF LEBANON IN PEACE. In the interest of tracing the line between truth and imagination, it may be worth noting that according to both Ron Leshem and Noam Barnea's father (see my introduction to this book), the slogan was written on a button and not a T-shirt. The discrepancy does not change Erez's encounter with Ziv in the shower, where he learns of his identification with "that band of females, those hysterical women that stir up trouble at intersections, wailing and moaning and threatening to wear us all down" (121). The gung-ho platoon commander responds with a venomous comment: "Here's a piece of free advice you pansy piece of shit. If you don't want this entire outpost to fuck your little ass to pieces, you'd better not play the PEACE NOW activist up here" (123). But in the end these two opposites, the *ars* and the Ashkenazi, the gung-ho lieutenant and the leftist, are bound together in friendship: "Sounds stupid but I hadn't ever really had any Ashkenazi friends until then. Until him. He would laugh at everything I said, look at me with this great look, didn't make fun of me even when I said something stupid. He wasn't patronizing." In the end, they head out together on an unclear, unnecessary, and dangerous mission, during which Ziv is killed.

Ron Leshem also crafted Yonatan Spitzer, one of Erez's soldiers and a fictionalized version of Tzachi Itach, the last casualty in Lebanon before the withdrawal, as an Ashkenazi. And here too he follows the same pattern: The ethnic tension soars when Erez encounters an Ashkenazi who doubts the righteousness of the army's mission. So it was with Ziv, when Erez learned of his support for the unilateral withdrawal from Lebanon, and so it is with Spitzer, when Erez hears him say that the initial Israeli capture of the Beaufort, in 1982, was at its core a strategic error: "There was no military significance in conquering Beaufort. IDF convoys had already surrounded the whole range of hills on the first morning of the war and our troops were much deeper in Lebanese territory, on the way to Beirut. They'd left Beaufort behind and the fortress itself didn't bother anyone. It was just a little enclave" (250). In both cases, Erez's reaction is similar. He tells Ziv not to "play the PEACE NOW activist up here" unless he wanted the "entire outpost to fuck your ass to little pieces," and he tells Spitzer: "Go on, get off it. You're totally fucking wrong, you pussy . . ." (251). [A more literal translation of the Hebrew is: "Go on, Spitzer, and take your Ashkenazi ass with you."]

Erez's responses to Ziv and Spitzer are indicative of his efforts to divorce himself from the statewide quarrels, led by a group of largely Ashkenazi mothers, and to continue to believe in the justness of Israel's presence in Lebanon and in the fraternity of brothers in arms. In an internal monologue, he tells Ziv:

> We were fighters; that's what we had enlisted to be. We'd chosen to be at the outpost, surrounded by the best friends you can ever have, partners in everything. Friendships that need no interpretation and in which there were no cracks. Telling a soldier at Beaufort that he was not needed was certainly not a healthy idea, and sure wouldn't motivate anybody. It was a lie, too. A complete and total lie. Anyone who didn't understand that, anyone who didn't see that the alternative was dead children all along the northern border, was an ass, a fool. (122)

That is why Spitzer's comments about the utter uselessness of the capture of Beaufort and the price paid in blood by the six dead commandos, including the commander of the Golani Brigade's recon unit Goni Harnik, who was killed in vain, are, for Erez, a gross infidelity, a "profaning (of) the dead," and all that is holy (250). The ethnic resentment rises to the fore each time he encounters this sort of talk, encroaching on his patriotism and his blind faith in the justness of war.

Just as it was in advance of Ziv Farran's death, so too is it with Yonatan Spitzer, the platoon's last casualty in Lebanon. Erez, once the disgust subsides, is drawn toward the refined Ashkenazi soldier, a musician who wants to audition for the stage after his army service. The two develop a close bond and, after a brief leave, just before their final trip back to Beaufort, Erez opts to share a room with Spitzer in a motel in the northern Galilee. Erez steps out of the shower; here, too, the shower, which strips the soldiers of their uniformity and offers them a feeling of momentary freedom, is chosen as the location for the revelation of secrets. Erez and Spitzer flip through the TV channels and stop at the nightly news broadcast. The piece is about the protests against Israel's interminable presence in Lebanon, which has seeped from the civilian sphere to the military and the active duty soldiers:

> "It appears that something has changed, a landmark in the history of the war in Lebanon," the correspondent was saying. "Now it is no longer the parents demanding immediate withdrawal, it is the soldiers themselves. 'Bring us home,' that is the new motto spreading from unit to unit. They are saying in a clear, direct voice, 'None of us wants to be the last casualty in Lebanon. None of us wants to die for no reason.'" (275)

This news broadcast, happened upon by the two soldiers, one an enlisted man and one an officer, sparks a heart-to-heart. Yonatan Spitzer grieves for the loss of his dear friend Tomer Zitlawi, who was killed at Beaufort after the death of Ziv Farran, and he pulls a black T-shirt (again, a T-shirt) from his bag, a memorial for Zitlawi. During the course of their conversation, Spitzer also finds out Erez's real name:

> I stood up to get dressed. From the corner of his eye he caught sight of my wallet, with my army ID sitting on top of it, on the dresser. He looked at the picture, read what was written there.
> "What is it?" I asked him with a smile. I knew.
> "Nothing," he answered. "Nothing at all."
> "The name?" I asked.
> "It says 'Liraz Liberti,'" he said.
> They hadn't known, until then, didn't have a clue. Everywhere—signatures, lists, documents—I was Erez. "When I enlisted I was still called Liraz," I told him. He was stunned, I think, but he played it cool, afraid of offending me or asking too many questions. (276–77)

The name Liraz reveals the loaded complexity of the protagonist's identity crisis. Liraz is more often a girl's name and not the name of a masculine commander. On the other hand, Erez is the most macho of Israeli names, and one that manages to evoke the land of cedars with every mention. Liraz was a name bestowed by parents who had immigrated to Israel from Arab lands and sought to give their son a gentle name (it means "to me a secret") that sounded, to their ears, to be modern, en vogue, part of an effort to flee what they may have perceived as their coarse, Arab identity. And in that paradoxical way, the Mizrahi kid from the periphery made it to the gates of the army with a girl's name, a name that apparently reflects his real identity, but the army forced him to change it as soon as he joined up.

The desire to be accepted, the inferiority complex, the identity crisis, the competitiveness, and the gap between Ziv and Erez, and between Erez and Spitzer, are all fueled by ethnic strife and all offer a striking glimpse of the face of the army and the way it has changed from Goni Harnik's kibbutz-led IDF in 1982 to that of Liraz and Zitlawi in the year 2000.

In so far as Spitzer's Ashkenazi identity is concerned, Erez, as mentioned earlier, calls Ziv a "pretty boy"; Spitzer is much the same. In the motel room, on the eve of their last deployment, Erez describes him in this way: "Zitlawi used to call him the Little Prince. He was thin, tall, with huge eyes and tiny ears. And that winning, beautiful smile. The face of a genius, of a rich kid . . ." (278). Erez is also suspicious of the Ashkenazi soldier's warrior skills, just as he was with Ziv. Erez grapples with the notion that someone who was having trouble opening a pack of lemon-flavored wafers, doing it "like a nice Ashkenazi boy with his delicate hands" (276) might also be a highly competent warrior:

> He was considered one of the rising stars, right from the time he enlisted, and destined for great things. He was quiet, but a leader, had great stamina and a positive attitude. He was always singing. Everyone knew him. I actually hadn't thought much of him at the beginning. In training, and during the first tour of duty in Lebanon, he hadn't seemed enough of a killer, wasn't hot-blooded enough. He was about as opposite of me as possible. (278)

And perhaps, because Spitzer is not equipped with the killer instinct, Erez recognizes his other attributes—that he is a clear-headed and loyal soldier—and offers him the opportunity to go to an officers' training course. But Yonatan will be given no such opportunity. His tragic and dreadful death, in one of the most gruesome sections of *Beaufort*, resembles the most grisly scenes in *All Quiet on the Western Front*.

The ethnic strife portrayed in the year 2000 in *Beaufort*, when compared to that which is depicted in *Infiltration*, is restrained, forgiving, and threaded with humor. Erez, the Sephardic commander, looks down at, but also up to, his Ashkenazi soldiers, those subordinate to him and those serving beside him, and is continually in the process of growing closer to them, befriending them, valuing them, and becoming a brother to them. This is in sharp contrast to the unwavering antagonism embedded in *Infiltration*, where a sliver of distant hope is provided only at the end: The enmity-filled tension is tempered by time, lessened only in the coming generation.

Toward the end of *Infiltration*, at the very end of the new soldiers' misery, as rain falls like a blessing, cutting the heat that accompanied them throughout basic training, Zero-Zero is told that his wife has given birth to a baby boy:

> "I've got a sabra son," he said, "a sabra like them," and he pointed to a few of our number. "He'll be like the kids who grow up here from the beginning. He'll talk Hebrew like them. He won't know no foreign language, only Hebrew, and he'll sing their songs. Here it's a good place for kids to grow up. They turn out better looking, healthier, strong. I won't call my kid any of those lousy names from over there, Lupu, Shmupu, Berko, Shmerko. I'll give him a sabra name, one of those new names, not losers' names. What a crazy world, I'm telling you, that I've got a sabra kid! I'll bring him up like one of them strong, nice-looking kids, so he'll fit into this country. So he won't be shit like me." (592–93)

And yet, even in the later novel, the Sephardic-Mizrahi character, a native-born Israeli, is forced to grapple with the seeming inappropriateness of his given name; nonetheless, in *Beaufort*, he is given the privilege of narration, and, though he may be hot-blooded, the author endowed the character with a warm heart. Moreover, Lt. Liraz Liberti, masquerading as Erez in *Beaufort*, is given a sane and even-keeled voice, akin to the voice that Kenaz gave to his hero, Alon, who has a pure soul and a golden heart. Both are "die-hard" lovers of the army and the country, but Alon the Ashkenazi, the kibbutznik of Israeli lore, with the long forelock of hair and the golden sheen, was "wasted" for naught, committing suicide during basic training, for, as is revealed, he suffered from a mental illness. Erez, on the other hand, a Sephardic platoon commander from Afula, with no long forelock of hair or golden sheen, "a midget with spiky hair" (84), is willing to die only if he is certain that he will not be "wasted" in vain. In the interim, he is revealed to be a physically and mentally tough soldier who has passed all of the trials of fire that *Beaufort* could produce and all those that continued to be a part of his war life even after he descended from the mount.

"I Will Still," the epilogue to *Beaufort*, serves as a response to the eulogy-like prologue, "What He Can't Do Anymore." "I Will Still" is told five years after the withdrawal, in 2005, and Erez says: "Five years have passed so how could we not heal? A few things have changed since those times, when we were such jerks. There's no more purple rain . . . I'll still watch Hapoel bring home the trophy, I'll still take one of my little nephews to a movie, and my son, too, and maybe my grandson . . ." (351). And in this, the novels are alike: Hope resides in continuity, in the son, the grandson, the next generation.

10

The Bereaved Family in A. B. Yehoshua's *Friendly Fire*

A Novel of the Second Intifada

> "I may not be a bereaved father like you, Mr. Kidron, only a bereaved uncle, but I have insider knowledge, family knowledge, of your grief, and I respect it a great deal."

The chapter is devoted to Aviva Flekser, the mother of Erez Flekser (1981–2013), an Israeli Air Force fighter pilot killed in a helicopter crash (March 13, 2013).

A Duet

The novels of A. B. Yehoshua are characterized by structural experimentation. The author uses the Reshoot technique of multiple narration in *The Lover* and *A Late Divorce*. *Four Seasons* (*Molcho* in Hebrew) is constructed around the calendar. *Mr. Mani* consists of five conversations, in which only one voice is heard, and it is up to the reader to imagine the other. These creative structures provide a deep "dialogic" quality, in the spirit of the theorist Mikhail Bakhtin, to Yehoshua's oeuvre. His novel *Friendly Fire* (*Esh Yedidutit*, 2007),[1] subtitled "A Duet," is a prime example of his dialogic method.

On the second day of Hanukkah—the text suggests this is 2007—Daniela, a teacher of English, bids farewell at Ben-Gurion Airport to her husband Amotz Ya'ari, an engineer specializing in elevators, and sets off alone to visit her expatriate brother-in-law Yirmi (Yirmiyahu) in Tanzania, where he is known as Jeremy. Amotz stays behind in Tel Aviv. From the moment of their parting, the couple's activities are narrated separately. The novel takes place over one week, from the second day of Hanukkah through the eighth, in alternating chapters. Daniela is unaccustomed to traveling without her husband; he is uneasy with her being away from him. Their two stories, linked experientially and linguistically, constitute a duet. Seven days is a long time for this symbiotic couple to be apart. Because it is "not quite right to make a consolation visit from Asia to Africa for only three nights" (205), it has been decided that the week of Hanukkah, when the teacher is on holiday from school, will be dedicated to mourning for her sister, Shuli, who died a year earlier.

Typically, a person travels to get over his or her grief, but Daniela goes to the Morogoro Nature Reserve to "prevent the pain of her loss from diminishing" (35); to connect with the anguish and memory of her beloved sister's death in the location where she died. At the same time, she wants to understand what is happening to her brother-in-law, a bereaved father for the past seven years and a widower for one year, who has chosen to disconnect from his relatives, his countrymen, and his homeland to live in Africa.

The drama of brother-in-law and sister-in-law growing closer to one another is central to the "African chapters" of the novel. It is a long and painful road, strewn with barbs leveled by Yirmi and displays of concern, openness, and generosity from Daniela. Decades of memories testify to the connections between the two, and unresolved issues are clarified. At the heart of this process is the story of the bereaved father dealing with the death of his son. In their limited time together, Daniela manages to pry from Yirmi the story of his investigation into his son's death at the hands of his fellow soldiers. He reveals secrets he kept even from his wife. Little by little, it becomes clear that the "duet" with her husband in Israel is merely structural and external, based on wordplay and literary artifice. The true duet develops in Africa between her and her brother-in-law, whose shocking story she hears for the first time.

Yehoshua provides a visual expression of the duet that will develop between them. On the morning she arrives at Yirmi's residence in Tanzania, she finds an African dress she bought three years earlier at the market in Dar-es-Salaam, hanging "at full length alongside her brother-in-law's khaki clothing" (64). This is her second visit, having previously made the trip with Amotz to visit Shuli and Yirmi. Now she has come alone, to visit Yirmi at the colonial estate where he works as the administrator of an anthropological research project seeking traces of the ancestral apes of humanity. Here, Daniela and Yirmi "perform" the duet. It is a verbal dialogue for two performers; Yirmi laments the end of sexual relations with his wife after the death of their son. His confessional lamentation prompts a confessional response from Daniela. The theme and melody are similar, and in this case, there is an audience.

The catalyst for the confessional dialogue between Daniela and Yirmi about the loss of sexuality is the presence of an elegant, tall, Black Sudanese woman, Sijjin Kuang, a pagan by faith and an expert driver of a Land Rover, who two days earlier had brought Daniela from the airport to the base camp of the anthropological project. Sijjin's whole family was murdered in the civil war in South Sudan, and in Yirmi's opinion her driving has become a substitute for the sexuality she has lost. "He senses, from within his own soul, the soul of someone whose sexuality has faded, that the memory of a family massacred before her eyes has snuffed out her womanliness. At least this is how he feels, because this is also what happened with Shuli, Daniela's sister. The friendly fire burned out what little sexuality she still had" (164).

Yirmi's confession takes place on the fourth day of Hanukkah, while Sijjin Kuang is driving the Land Rover. The noise of the car engine is the "music" accompanying Yirmi's words and Daniela's response, producing a unique duet. Sijjin Kuang senses that the Israelis' Hebrew conversation is becoming "important" (164). She hears the tone, the melody, without understanding the words themselves. She is the audience for the intimate details Yirmi shares with Daniela about her sister Shuli and the role of her nephew Eyal in their lives after his death.

> After Eyal's death he was allowed to be with them everywhere, all the time . . . Yes, if a character in a film, or music at a concert, brought him somehow to mind, either one of them was permitted to say a word in the middle of the movie or the performance . . . They knew and agreed

that he was available at every moment, and neither of them could say, Enough pain . . . But not during sex. Here exist only two, a man and a woman, and their son, dead or alive, has no place in their bed or their bedroom. Because if the dead son slipped into the shadow of a passing thought or became embodied in a bare leg or the movement of a hand, the sex would die down at once, or else be putrid. And maybe to preserve Eyali, from the day of the funeral to the day she died, her sister resolutely put an end to her sexuality, and thereby his as well, for how could he impose himself on her when he knew that at any moment she might open the door of her mind and say, Come, my son, come back and I will grieve for you again. (164–65)

The dead-living son interferes with his parents' lovemaking; because his mother wants him everywhere all the time, his father cannot say to him: "Just a minute, son, stop, wait a bit, you came too soon . . . this too is a battleground" (165). Now Yirmi is done talking, but for Daniela the conversation is not over.

This confession of yours is so painful and understandable and natural. For weeks after he died . . . we also couldn't touch one another. And Amotz, who always wants it—in that period he was careful not to try and persuade me. Without a word of explanation, he just went celibate. Then something strange started up with him, which sometimes happens to him even now. He started crying in movies, in the dark, sometimes over silly things . . . and when I look over at him, he is self-conscious and ashamed . . . (166)

Two Adults Discuss the Bible in the Heart of Africa

Daniela's testimony that her husband became sentimental and cried for no apparent reason, although the real reason was the death of Eyal, is met with blunt disbelief by Yirmi. "Crying in the dark? Amotz? I don't believe it" (166). Yirmi has a different picture of his brother-in-law, and a deep grudge against him is slowly revealed in the chapters of the mourners' duet of Yirmi and Daniela. The names of the two men, referring to two biblical prophets—Isaiah the son of Amotz and Jeremiah the son of

Hilkiyahu—suggest their different natures: a conflict of personalities that goes back to antiquity. Daniela, who sees the heart of the matter, is a modern female version of the biblical Daniel, interpreter of dreams. It might seem that Daniela, like other women in Yehoshua's works, is spoiled, dependent, and chronically fearful of abandonment, but in fact she possesses sharp female intuition; she is kind of an intuitive psychologist who knows how to listen and spur others to go deep inside themselves. With their ability to listen and their personal charm, Yehoshua's female protagonists win the hearts of men and inspire them to reveal their secrets. Daniela is one of these. She gives Yirmi "one of her radiant looks, guaranteed to inspire trust" (278).[2]

The Hebrew Bible has a special role in *Friendly Fire*. A conversation—call it a duet—about the Bible, the prophets in particular, is sparked between Daniela and Yirmi on the sixth day of Hanukkah. It takes place in the Land Rover, an intimate space, with Yirmi at the wheel and not Sijjin Kuang. This time, no audience is listening to the complex melody of their words, but there is background music: "The dirt road is well-packed. The Land Rover's tires ride as smoothly as if it were asphalt" (279). The Bible, the very root of the Jews, the people Yirmi seeks to disconnect from, becomes a foil for the deep African roots that the anthropological team seeks to discover. The prehistoric monkey bones the researchers have unearthed are considered a national treasure: "In Africa they do not have artistic masterpieces, nor historical memories of ancient battles and wars that changed the face of the earth, nor writers and thinkers whose works have become classics, and yet, humanity originated in Africa, so why should they not take pride in what they have given to the world?" (303). After his son's death, Yirmi cut himself off from Israel and the Jews, but he is still bound—however acerbically—to the national treasure of his people.

Daniela listens with interest to Yirmi's original, if somewhat childish, survey of the Bible. He begins by asking her if she has ever taught the Bible. It turns out that she has indeed taught a story from the Bible that parallels Yirmi's choices in life, and the fact that Daniela (and Amotz on an earlier trip) came to visit him in Africa: Joseph and his brothers—"a charming tale of a whole family that settled in Africa following one brother, the administrator" (274). To this story of the administrator who rose to greatness in Egypt, far from his brethren, Yirmi adds another tale, the Binding of Isaac, known as the *Akedah*. The ram (*ayil*) caught in the thicket that Abraham sacrifices in place of his son Isaac is clearly meant to represent Yirmi's son Eyal, who was accidentally shot by comrades pursuing an escaped Palestinian. Yirmi tells of hearing a lecture by "an author or poet, who rebound the binding of Isaac, and then I saw how it's possible to find new ore in texts that have been mined over and over" (275). Yehoshua, through Yirmi, is referring to himself: He is the author who repeatedly finds a new angle on the *Akedah*. Ever since the critic Mordechai Shalev pointed out the *Akedah* theme in Yehoshua's early novella "Three Days and a Child," the motif may be found in nearly all of his works.[3] In *Friendly Fire*, Eyal is killed by his young friends, below the rooftop (an urban hill) from which he came down, and that "lecturer or poet" tried "to describe what the whole story of the captive son and the big knife looked like from down below, from the point of view of the two youths who were guarding Abraham's donkey at the foot of the mountain" (275). This entire duet about the well-known stories that touch on Yirmi's fate as a bereaved father and recent widower is a prologue to what he has to say about the prophets for whom he and his brother-in-law Amotz are named.

The Biblical prophet Isaiah, son of Amotz, enjoyed a high status in the land of Judah, as suggested by his responses to and role in the foreign policy of the kingdom, and his relationship with the kings Ahaz and Hezekiah (see Isaiah 7:12, 39:3). Isaiah was married and a father, and refers to his wife by the honorific title of "prophetess": "I was intimate with the prophetess, and she conceived and bore a son" (Isaiah 8:3). Daniela, too, is a sort of prophetess, and she and Amotz have a son and a daughter. Isaiah's prophecies of consolation are engraved in the hearts of his listeners and readers much more than his prophecies of fury. Jeremiah, by contrast, was "a man of conflict and strife" (Jeremiah 15:10), and the fury that filled his heart made him a lonely, barren individual (Jeremiah 15:17, 16:2, 5, 8). A strange and gloomy man, he lived a long time, afflicted by hatred of life and misanthropy. After the destruction of the First Temple, he went to Egypt with other survivors (Jeremiah 43). In the novel, Egypt is a synecdoche for the Dark Continent, and Yirmi, spurning his brethren, intends to live out his life in Africa.

After Yirmi tells Daniela that popular Israeli lecturers tend to focus on the Bible's "nice, clear-cut subjects" (275), such as Jacob and Esau, Samuel and Saul, Cain and Abel, and avoid the violent texts of the prophets, she says: "The prophets, I don't think I ever looked at them after my matriculation exams." To which Yirmi replies: "Me neither, until Eyal was killed. And then I reread them, prophet after prophet, and suddenly one day I saw the profound curse that has penetrated the genes of this people." In his opinion, the hypnotic rhetoric of the prophets distracts the mind from the essence of what they are really saying: "Between the lines and in the lines. Death, destruction, exile, punishment, more punishment, devastation, plague, and famine. Starving people eating their babies" (279). This is how Yirmi reads the prophetic texts, and in particular the furious words of Jeremiah, his namesake, as if the name itself had sealed his fate in advance. "Before I created you in the womb, I selected you; before you were born, I consecrated you," says God to the prophet in Jeremiah 1:5, and so too the modern Jeremiah was a prophet of rage before he became one in fact. In both cases, fate and destruction pushed their innate determinism to an extreme. "Did you also read Jeremiah?" asks Daniela, and Yirmi answers: "Of course. After all, I am his namesake, tied to him from birth. And I quickly caught on that this was the sickest and most dangerous of all the prophets. An unstable man. Exasperating. Jumping from topic to topic. A professional grouch" (280)—thereby describing himself.

However, there is one episode in the Book of Jeremiah that touches Yirmi deeply. It involves rebels who went down to Africa with him and defied him, unwilling to give up their rituals of idolatry. Yirmi, living in Africa among pagans—typified by the elegant Sijjin Kuang, who believes in spirits and stones—identifies with them. He too is a rebel. He rebels against the "holy" institutions of the state and the army that brought about the death of his son; Yirmi is consumed by hatred of the nation and of himself.

> I came upon that passage simply by chance—two or three months after we buried Eyal—and I was so moved I wanted to hug those exiles in Egypt from a distance of twenty-five hundred years. People who stood

up bravely against the cursing crybaby, the professional killjoy, who also inflicted his name on me. (282)

Apart from the mutinous exiles in the Book of Jeremiah, there is another book of the Bible that moves Yirmi. It was in the love poetry of the Song of Songs "that Eyal's death suddenly overwhelmed me, and I read this poetry drowning in tears" (280). This was because this beautiful passionate book "of love and the wondrous eroticism and descriptions of nature" represented for Yirmi all that Eyal would not live to experience.[4] Yirmi in Africa pelts Jeremiah with fire and brimstone—but how does he feel about Isaiah? The familiar conflictual pairings of the Bible—Cain and Abel, Jacob and Esau, Saul and Samuel—direct our attention to the pair at the core of the novel: Jeremiah and Isaiah. Daniela is married to the prophet of consolation, a modern counterpart to Isaiah the son of Amotz, but she travels in the heart of Africa with a prophet of doom, Jeremiah, who speaks in Biblical terms of the tension between him and his brother-in-law.

Friendly Fire according to Jeremiah

"It's true that sometimes, amid those horrible passages of rebuke phrased in such flowery language, an implausible snatch of consolation will creep in, something utopian and grandiose" (279). Yirmi has the two of them in mind: Isaiah son of Amotz in the Bible, and Amotz Ya'ari his brother-in-law, who coined the implausible, flowery, grandiose expression *esh yedidutit*, borrowing the English term "friendly fire," intending but failing to console. Friendly fire took the life of Yirmi's son, Eyal. It was after that disaster that Amotz, the uncle, used the term. Daniela did not know that Amotz was responsible for the expression taking root in their family. She hears about it for the first time in Africa, the Dark Continent, from the "prophet of hatred," the bereaved father of her nephew Eyal.

The oxymoron "friendly fire" always offended Daniela. Now she learns that it was her husband Amotz who applied it to the disaster and planted it in family parlance. The evolving dialogue between Daniela and Yirmi, situated within Yehoshua's solidly built fictional structure, encompasses multiple meanings of the phrase: the simple fact and the euphemistic, metaphoric, and ironic implications.

Daniela learns the origin of the over-used phrase "friendly fire" while hiking on a hillside with Yirmi. She enters a miserable hut to get a sense of the abject poverty and heavy stench endured by the African villagers. "In the corner, ringed with black basalt stones, burns a purplish flame" (76). Yehoshua's rare Hebrew term for this flame, *zehorit (shel esh)*, prompts us to trace its source in antiquity. In the Mishnaic tractate detailing the rituals of Yom Kippur, the word is used regarding the sacrificial scapegoat, a "sin offering" that is symbolically associated with the *Akedah* and Abraham's faith in God. Here is the shocking description of pushing the goat off the cliff to its death: "What did he do? He divided a strip of crimson cloth (*lashon shel zehorit*); one end of it he tied to the rock, and one end he tied between its two horns. He pushed it over backward and it was tumbling down. By the time it was halfway down the mountain it had broken into pieces" (Yoma 6:6). In other words, the strip of *zehorit* is tied to the horns of the scapegoat, and its death is thus connected to the death of the soldier Eyal ("deer" in Hebrew, another horned animal). The scapegoat is sacrificed to pay for the sins of the atoning community. Abraham sacrifices a ram caught by its horns in a thicket, in place of Isaac. In Israeli culture, the Binding of Isaac is a metaphor for the sacrifice of young soldiers in defense of the nation. Even the crimson or purple color of the *zehorit*, pinned between basalt rocks in the novel, and strung between the horns of the scapegoat in Tractate Yoma, ties the cloth to blood, fire, and ash.

The color red is dominant in *Friendly Fire*, as it is in Yehoshua's novel *Open Heart* (*HaShiv'a MeHodu* in Hebrew, *The Return from India*, 1996). In that novel, however, red symbolizes the color of love, passion, and shame, whereas in *Friendly Fire* it is the color of anger and fire. A phallic image of military violence, symbolized through religious ritual, may be found in a scene at the army camp where Amotz and Daniela's son Moran, a reserve soldier, has been confined for going AWOL. "On a small stage stands a Hanukkah menorah fashioned of big copper shell casings from helicopter cannons. Four thick white candles stand at attention, dominated by their commandant, a giant red *shammash*" (160). The army rabbi delivers a sermon, "waving the huge *shammash* like a torch"

(161). There is a clear link between Amotz, talking his way past the guards at Moran's base to bring him fresh underwear, and Daniela, entering an African hut uninvited, to find a *zehorit* of purple flame. Amotz exits the gate of the base, "where the Ethiopian guards have lit a holiday campfire of their own. Apparently, they have added a foreign substance to the fire, perhaps brought from home, which turns the flame from red to purple" (162). The Hebrew for purple, *segulah*, can also mean "treasure."

"They're not afraid the straw will catch fire and burn down the hut?" Daniela asks Yirmi. His answer works on two levels: literal and symbolic or connotative. "That's an eternal flame," says the bereaved father, to which Daniela replies: "Friendly fire." They have turned away from the African woman spreading dung on the roof of the hut, and are focused on their private Israeli pain. In effect, they envy the eternal African flame, which burns for the sake of life, because the eternal Israeli flame burns for the dead. The term "eternal flame" is pregnant with associations. In Judaism, it refers specifically to the light over the Ark symbolizing the presence of God and the "enlightenment" of Torah. The Jewish flame that burns for the dead is a "yahrzeit candle." But here Yirmi refers explicitly to the Israeli ethos in which the eternal flame is lit in memory of the fallen soldiers. Daniela's eyes tear up from the smoke that fills the hut, yet the reason for her tears is undoubtedly not just physical. As the coded language in their "duet" grows more complex, Yirmi wishes to emphasize that the eternal flame in the hut is "friendly fire indeed," literally *esh yedidutit amitit*, "truly friendly fire" (76). The word *amitit*, an important code word in the novel, here distinguishes between fire that is a basic element of subsistence (here in Africa) and the friendly fire that sowed death (there in Israel).

At this point, when the real (literal) friendly fire collides with the figurative expression—some would call it demagogic or hypocritical, others might say poetic or palliative—both speakers are aware of its double meaning. Yirmi informs Daniela that her husband was the first to blurt out the double-edged expression:

> Yes, back in Jerusalem, at the Foreign Ministry, when the army officer and doctor came into my office. It was Amotz who brought them, because

when Eyali filled out the forms, back in basic training, he listed you and Amotz to be informed in case of bad news. They could not conceal the fact that a soldier had been killed by our own forces, because this had already trickled into the media, and so, while I am standing there with the poisoned lance stuck in my heart, and this angel of death, in uniform, brings me the message that the gunfire came from our soldiers and he trembles as he explains what happened in the battle, as if there really had been a battle and not simply the killing of a soldier who was mistaken for the enemy, a wanted man, it somehow seemed to your Amotz, my Amotz, our Amotz, who had come from Tel Aviv with this bearer of bad news, that I didn't comprehend the explanations—or the opposite, maybe he was actually trying to console me, to loosen the rope that was wound around my neck, since being killed by our own forces is a hundred times crueler than "enemy fire"—and then he grabs my hand and hugs me tight, and says to me, Yirmi, what they mean is friendly fire. (77)

Yirmi holds these words against Amotz. Not only did he join forces with the accursed bearer of bad news, "this angel of death," but Amotz, uncle of Eyal, had the gall and insensitivity to couch the horror in a euphemism that hides the facts. Yirmi further tells Daniela that Amotz fell in love with this wretched expression and repeated it over and over. He knows that his brother-in-law did not intend to hurt him, so he offers two theories for his inflated use of these false words: Maybe it seemed to Amotz that he, a father getting news of his son's death, had not grasped what he was told, and therefore sharpened the meaning with a phrase borrowed from English, for sometimes metaphor is stronger than direct speech. Or maybe the opposite: Amotz hoped the expression would soften the harshness of "killed by our own forces."

Whatever Amotz intended, Yirmi tells Daniela that the expression had a surprising effect on him, and he suddenly saw a ray of light. He continues to relive the moment when he was hit with the terrible news and the expression "friendly fire" began to register: "Suddenly, amid all the shock and anger, I also understood that inside this stupid oxymoron, this *friendly fire*, there was something more, some small spark that would help me navigate through the great darkness that awaited me and to better identify the true sickness that afflicts all of us" (77).

How will this euphemism help Yirmi illuminate our true sickness? Daniela does not ask, and Yirmi does not say. *Friendly Fire* does not offer an explanation, but maybe the Bible does. Was it not the prophet Jeremiah, battling the false prophecies of pretenders, who cried out: "From the smallest to the greatest, they all are greedy for gain; priest and prophets alike, they all act falsely. They dress the wound of my people as though it were not serious. 'Peace, peace,' they say, when there is no peace"(Jer. 6:13–14). The two prophets of truth and fury, the biblical Jeremiah and Yehoshua's modern Yirmi, utilize polite expressions like "peace" and "friendly fire" to expose the mendacious delusions that false prophets spread among their own people.

Friendly Fire according to Amotz

Along with his fondness for analogies, A. B. Yehoshua also employs the Rashomon technique in his works—describing the same events from different points of view. Two of his novels, *The Lover* and *A Late Divorce*, are entirely written in this fashion. In *Friendly Fire*, he tells the story of Eyal's death from Amotz's standpoint as well.

Amotz's version of the terrible tidings and his euphemistic reaction are framed as follows: Nofar, Amotz's daughter, comes to his home with a friend who knows about her beloved cousin's death at the hands of Israeli forces. They have come to light Hanukkah candles with Amotz, who is alone at home; his wife is in Africa. The curious friend, who notices among the many family photos in the living room a picture of Eyal framed in black, turns to Amotz: "Nofar told me that you had to break the news to his parents." Amotz corrects the nosy friend's assumption: "To his father. I wasn't alone; an officer and a doctor were with me" (108). In other words, he was not the sole "messenger" (*mevaser*), a word spoken by Yirmi in Africa and by this friend in Tel Aviv. As the conversation progresses, the friend wonders if it was necessary to tell the bereaved father that his son was killed by mistake by his fellow soldiers. Amotz explains that the media "called it 'our own forces,' and I put it slightly differently, to soften it" (108).

It should be noted that this sort of euphemism also exists on the Palestinian side. Before Yirmi ran off to Africa, he was in a different phase of bereavement, obsessively investigating the death of his son. On one of his visits to the house in Tulkarm, where his son had stood guard on the roof and was shot by his friends who mistook him for a wanted Palestinian, a young pregnant woman tells Yirmi, in good Hebrew, that she does not remember this "work accident." Yirmi is shocked. "Work accident?" The woman explains: "That's the expression we use when they get killed by their own mistakes—for instance, while preparing a bomb" (221). It turns out that not only Amotz used an expression that offended the bereaved father—who wants to hear facts and not euphemisms—the woman on the rooftop did too.

There is no essential difference between the accounts of the two brothers-in-law of the scene of the terrible tidings. Both make it clear that Amotz came to Yirmi, together with an officer and a doctor, to tell him his son had been killed. Both versions mention that the media had already announced that a soldier had been killed "by our own forces." Both agree that it was Amotz who came up with the phrase "friendly fire" in order to soften or console. So why does Yehoshua give us the two versions? Perhaps he wanted to highlight the fundamental difference between the two men by means of the two prophets he has associated with them. Whereas Jeremiah is famous for his rebuke: "Peace, peace, there is no peace," Isaiah is known for consolation: "How beautiful on the mountains are the footsteps of the herald [*mevaser*] announcing peace, bringing good tidings, proclaiming salvation" (Isa. 52:7). The confrontation between the brothers-in-law is rooted in an ancient layer of perception and language. Yirmi, a modern incarnation of Jeremiah, rejects "friendly fire" as a cynical, baseless expression that is incapable of papering over painful truths. He regards this as artificial, euphemistic, sanitized speech, afraid of confronting unadorned horror, a symptom of the profound sickness of a society prone to "laundered language." Yirmi uses the expression to demonstrate its absurdity to listeners (in the spirit of "peace, peace, there is no peace"). Amotz, on the other hand, the modern Isaiah, sticks to his belief that language can cushion and console.

When Nofar's friend asks if these words really did help, Amotz does not answer because Nofar enters the room and the three of them light a truly friendly fire in the Hanukkah menorah. The answer, however, is implied: Nofar enters the room dressed in black; Daniela responds with great sorrow to Yirmi's account of Amotz's failure to console. The verse from Isaiah about the beautiful mountains and the bearers of good news rings ironic, as Amotz ascends to Jerusalem to tell the father that his son has been killed.

What was Amotz Ya'ari trying to do when he changed the banal "killed by our own forces" into "killed by friendly fire"? It was an attempt at what the Russian literary theorist Viktor Shklovsky called "defamiliarization": adding a poetic dimension to ordinary language, thereby turning the familiar into something strange, effecting a "de-automatization" of speech.[5] This may be fine in a different context, but not when informing a father that his son has been killed by his friends. Preceding Shklovsky, the Hebrew poet Haim Nahman Bialik, in a famous essay of 1915 entitled "Revealment and Concealment in Language," wrote about the restoration of the original freshness and vitality of overused words: "Every day, consciously and unconsciously, human beings scatter heaps of words to the wind, with all their various associations . . . Words rise to greatness, and, falling, turn profane. What is essential is that language contains no word so slight that the hour of its birth was not one of powerful and awesome self-revealment, a lofty victory of the spirit."[6]

Amotz apparently meant well when he scattered the words "friendly fire" to the winds, seeking a fresh association for the blunt phrase "killed by our own forces." However, Amotz's cosmetic coinage was monstrous to Yirmi's ears. Possibly Amotz simply felt compelled to fill the terrible void with words, to combat the nothingness with a word, for this is what humans, and not animals, can do. This impulse is given expression in Bialik's essay:

> But man dies—and his space becomes unoccupied. There is nothing to serve as a diversion—and the barrier is down. Everything suddenly becomes incomprehensible. The hidden X descends upon us in all its fearful shape—and we sit mourning on the earth before it for a moment in darkness and dumb as a stone. But for a moment only. For the Master of all life anticipates the opening with a closing. He immediately furnishes us with a new "talisman" [*segulah*] with which to divert ourselves and dissipate the fear. Before the covering stone is sealed over the dead,

the space that was emptied is again occupied with a word, whether it be one of eulogy, or solace, or philosophy, or belief in the soul's immortality, or the like. The most dangerous moment—both in speech and in life—is that between concealments, when the void looms. But such moments are very rare both in speech and in life. (Bialik, "Revealment and Concealment in Language," 171–75)

Amotz did not allow this gap between concealments to widen. When the void—*tohu* in Hebrew—was momentarily revealed, he swiftly sealed it off with words intended to console.

The Bereaved Uncle and Cousins—The Family of Grief

Several situations, some of them embarrassing, show how the angry prophet Yirmi misinterprets Amotz's empathy over the loss of his son. The bereaved father, after despairing of his quest to discover who shot Eyal, begins a "great project of forgetting." "You know very well," he tells Daniela, "I'm here [in Africa] not only to build up my pension, but also to forget him and everyone who reminds me of him" (191). He demonstrates his determination to forget with dramatic acts such as incinerating the newspapers and Hanukkah candles that Daniela has brought him from Israel. By contrast, Amotz tells everyone he encounters that he is a member of the "family" of bereaved Israelis, and embellishes himself with labels that support that self-perception. When he arrives at the army base where his son Moran has been detained, and his entry is blocked by two Israeli soldiers of Ethiopian origin (thereby perpetuating his literary "duet" with his wife in Africa), Amotz delivers a strange monologue that can be read as emotional manipulation, masquerade, or absolute truth.

> Now listen, you are new recruits, but I am a bereaved father. Seven years ago, my oldest son fell in a military action in the West Bank, in Tulkarm. So please, don't be hard on me now. It's already late, and the one son I have left is here with the reserves, a combat officer who needs warm clothing. Here, please, I'm opening the bag, so you can see for yourselves it's only undershirts and shorts and not bombs or grenades. (147)

The opening of the bag containing intimate items of clothing can be seen, perhaps, as a metaphor for opening the heart. He dares to open his heart to these strangers and speak a subjective "truth"; Amotz Ya'ari adopts Eyal as a son and sees himself as a bereaved father. The soldiers apparently sense that the man's claim is not entirely false, "and so they open the gate for the bereaved father bringing warm clothes to his remaining son" (150). But Amotz is aware that he is not who he said he was, and when the officer who has confined Moran wonders how Amotz got into the base, he invents a surprising term consistent with the objective familial relationship. We have already seen, when he first used the phrase "friendly fire," that Amotz scatters words to the wind and enriches the terminology of grief. Bialik would have regarded this expression as "powerful and awesome self-revealment":

"I told the recruits at the gate that I am a **bereaved uncle**."

"**Bereaved uncle?**" the adjutant says, marveling. "What on earth is a bereaved uncle?"

Moran, surprised by his father's words, reminds his friend about his cousin who was killed seven years before.

"**By friendly fire**," Ya'ari quietly adds. (154, emphasis added)

In this family novel, Yehoshua conveys the scope of the damage that bereavement inflicts on the extended family; not in the sense of a national collective, but in a biological sense. Bereavement in his view strikes not only parents and siblings, but also aunts and uncles and cousins. Moran shirked his reserve duty in the occupied territories because he suffers the family trauma—a cousin who was killed there by his comrades—and he is afraid, plain and simple. His sister Nofar avoided military service, choosing to serve instead as a volunteer in the trauma unit of a hospital, where she apparently believes in the resurrection of the dead (213).

In the days when Amotz is a "straw widower," with his wife off in Africa to visit a real widower, he is restless in part because his office is closed for Hanukkah. In his wanderings, he barges into his daughter's rented room in Jerusalem, like the way he invaded the army base where his son is confined. Nofar is not at home. It turns out that Eyal's photograph hangs not only in her parents' home but in hers, too, over her bed. When Nofar and her friend came to light candles, the friend saw the picture and asked Amotz about the cousin who was killed. Now, in his daughter's home, Amotz is the one who notices the photo of Eyal as a teenager, "a picture he hadn't known existed—and mumbles something about the source of his family's melancholy" (188).

Freud, in his essay "Mourning and Melancholia" (1917), treats melancholy as a reaction to the loss of a loved one. The couple from whom Nofar rents her room are both doctors and do not need the father to explain what weighs so heavily on his daughter. "Nofar talks again and again about the friendly fire—those are the words she uses," they tell her father, and wonder in the same breath: "How is it that such a story is so deeply embedded in her? How old was she at the time, anyway? Because it seems to them that she gets a bit confused about dates" (188). It turns out that despite her young age—she was thirteen years younger than Eyal, only eleven and a half when he died—she was in love with him and was certain that he loved her too. It was no surprise that she did hospital work in lieu of military service: Eyal had been a medical student, at the army's expense, but he did not work as an army doctor, insisting on combat duty instead. Nofar does the opposite, perhaps as a corrective. In any event, the disaster dominates her life, and it really is no surprise that an old photo of her cousin hangs over her bed.

Just as Yirmi doubts that Amotz shares his grief over Eyal's death, he is also suspicious of Nofar's authentic feelings of grief and loss. He alone can claim the loss, and he alone has experienced two opposing phases of reaction to it: first, discovering what truly happened, down to the last detail; and second, disconnection from everything that could remind him of his son:

> The first months of mourning are a whirlwind of absurdity. On the outside you keep your cool, and inside you lurch from fantasy to the absurd, and until I came to the final, philosophical flash of recognition, at night on the rooftop of that house in Tulkarm, I was unable to get free of all the absurdity and begin the process of forgetting. (200)

What the two phases have in common, apparently, is a sense of totality. But during the second, African phase, when he describes the earlier phase to Daniela, it becomes clear that his disconnection is an illusion.

In the first phase, when he wanted to fathom the night his son was killed, Yirmi kept replaying the video of the military funeral as it was broadcast on television. Night after night he watches "the drama of Nofar, who seemed about to throw herself in the grave after him" (200). Daniela does not immediately respond to Yirmi's skeptical words, "drama" and "seemed." At the end of that day's confession, she says: "Please, Yirmi, don't say again that Nofar only seemed as if she wanted to throw herself . . . because it was very real, Yirmi, believe me, the girl was in total despair at the funeral, and it still lingers" (201).

The family grief also touches Efrat, Moran's wife. On another trip by Amotz Ya'ari to visit the detainee in the northern army base, his daughter-in-law and two grandchildren come along. Nadi (Nadav), his younger grandchild, looks like Eyali, Amotz realizes as they spend time together on Hanukkah. On their way home from the base, Amotz hesitantly shares this observation with Efrat, and in return she hesitantly discloses an important fact about Eyali, her husband's cousin:

> Ya'ari smiles at the sight in the mirror of his grandchildren sitting behind. "You know," he says to his daughter-in-law, "yesterday, when I spent time with the children, I thought I saw a new resemblance between Nadi and Daniela."
>
> "Daniela?" Efrat turns around and peers at her son for a moment.
>
> "Maybe not Daniela herself," he backtracks a bit, "but via Daniela to Shuli and to Eyal when he was small. You, of course, can't see that similarity, but I knew Eyal when he was Nadi's age . . ."
>
> Efrat again turns her head toward the backseat. The possible resemblance to Moran's cousin excites her but is also confusing. She hesitates a moment before reacting, but finally has the courage to tell her father-in-law something that even her husband does not know. In her fifth month, when it was already known that the unborn child was a boy and not another girl, without consulting Moran she wrote to Yirmi and Shuli and asked for permission to name the baby after their son. But they refused. Politely, sympathetically, but firmly. She thought she was making a gesture of consolation, then realized that was only adding to their pain. (268)

Amotz too, when he spoke the words "friendly fire," saw that as an act of consolation, but the phrase had the opposite result. During the Hanukkah holiday, he and Efrat conduct a duet, characteristic of fathers and daughters-in-law in Yehoshua's works, which parallels the African duet between the brother-in-law and sister-in-law.

In the novel, where mysticism and rationalism vie for primacy, the names of the people are significant. The three main characters—Yirmiyahu, Amotz, and Daniela—share a magical-biblical connection, and other prophets have lent their names to characters in *Friendly Fire*: Amotz's father is named Joel, and the officer who detains Moran is called Hezi, short for Ezekiel. It could be that Efrat's participation in the family's grief has fated Nadi to resemble his father's cousin, at least in the eyes of his grandfather Amotz. The text offers an allusion linking Nadi to the Binding of Isaac: "In the rear-view mirror Ya'ari notices his grandson's mounting fury. If he were able to free himself of the straps that **bind** him, he'd climb out of the chair and start kicking the car door hard" (242, emphasis added).

Amotz commends Efrat for her desire to name her son after Eyali, revealing another hint of his own identification with the pain: "'It was good that you made the gesture, and good that you understood why it was refused. **Although, in their place'** . . . He does not continue, and even resists thinking what he had intended to say" (268, emphasis added). This is not the first time he put himself in their place. After Moran is released from the base, he and Efrat go off in the car to be alone together, but return later than planned. Waiting anxiously for them, Amotz imagines a flat tire, engine trouble, a catastrophic car wreck. He promises himself: "Even if Daniela is not at your side when you hear the terrible news, you will not run away to Africa or any other continent" (256). Amotz is not Yirmi, even if he maintains a secret, ongoing dialogue with him.

In the same spirit in which he rejects the participation of his close family, his natural partners in grief, Yirmi bears a grudge against Eyal's friends who have become "almost-family." He hoped they would help him find the soldier who shot Eyal, so that, so he claimed, he could forgive him. However, he fails to penetrate the information blackout the friends have imposed. Yirmi tells Daniela:

For you have to understand, his friends didn't abandon us. We aren't the Americans or Japanese, who send telegrams of condolence to parents in distant cities and say, Bye-bye and we won't be seeing you. With us there are established customs of bereavement, rules by which you don't abandon the soldier's family, but you maintain a connection. An institutional connection and a personal one. (200)

But instead of those new family connections bringing him closer to solving the riddle, they distance him from the solution:

[The] presumptuous, pathetic and pointless attempt to identify the shooter becomes harder and more complicated every day. The individual friendly fire is absorbed into the "fire of our own forces," a collective fire, and then slowly, slowly is transformed from army fire to civilian fire, and civilian fire to undefined fire, until the shooter himself is no longer sure whether one night he got up and shot his friend by mistake. (201)

The Kidron Family From the Tower of the Winds—Another Bereaved Family

A. B. Yehoshua, master of parallels, sets up another bereaved father, a minor character in the novel, alongside the obsessions of Yirmi and his feverish confession to his sister-in-law during the Hanukkah holiday of 2007. Yirmi searches for the soldier who shot his son, and Mr. Kidron is determined to find whoever is responsible for the winds that wail in the elevator shaft of the apartment he and his wife moved into after their son, a soldier, was killed. Mr. Kidron, whose name in Hebrew connotes "sadness" or "gloom," is in effect the "chief resident"; his complaints are in effect the collective complaint of those who bought apartments in the Pinsker Tower, whose elevators were installed by the engineer Amotz Ya'ari.

Eyal's friends "keep an eye on one another lest a careless word be spoken . . . [and] pass [their] suspicions from one to the next, back and forth, like a volleyball" (200–201). Yirmi, the bereaved father, knows that his attempt to identify the guilty party (who he declares is not to blame, only Eyal was to blame) will never be realized. So too the leader of the tenants, a bereaved father, knows he will not find out who is responsible for the moaning winds: "You are a corrupt bunch who shift the blame from one to the other so we can't catch you" (332).

The fire, the color red, and the roof invoking the Aramaic *me'igra rama lebira amikta* [from the high roof to the deep pit] are motifs that appear dozens of times in the novel, each appearance warranting its own interpretation. The wind (*ruah*) is also a motif, appearing at every turn and advancing the plot. The sincerity of Amotz's pain is tested by the fiery, critical Yirmi on the day his son was killed, when Amotz first uttered the notion of "friendly fire," and Hanukkah menorahs display many fires during the week-long holiday, the real time of the novel. The wind, too, the other foundational element, calls upon Amotz Ya'ari to prove his honesty and ability to console. His wife Daniela, a teacher of English, would doubtless know that the Hebrew *ruah* (plural *ruhot*) divides in English into several words: wind(s), spirit(s), ghost(s). The multiple meanings of *ruah* enable a wealth of literary and symbolic wordplay, a game of revealment and concealment.

Amotz Ya'ari (*ya'ar* means forest), the prophet of consolation, must prove over and over that he is not a false prophet. It is not the wind in a forest he must deal with, but rather urban winds in Tel Aviv, which wail and weep in the elevator shaft of the Pinsker apartment tower—named for Dr. Leo Pinsker, author of the inspiring Zionist tract "Auto-Emancipation" (1882)—apparently owing to a defect in construction. Daniela has gone off to Africa to bond with the spirit (*ruah*) of her dead sister, and like an ancient prophet who puts on his spiritual father's mantle to internalize his spirit, she wears her sister's windbreaker jacket (*mei'il ruah*). In Africa, she conducts a duet both material and spiritual with Yirmi, who is pursued by the ghosts (*ruhot*) of his loved ones, even as he has escaped them. As a counterweight to her caustic brother-in-law, who declares he is not a Sudanese who believes in spirits (*ruhot*), Daniela meets Sijjin Kuang, the elegant Sudanese woman, a feminist and pagan animist, who believes in sacred spirits (*ruhot*) that inhabit trees and stones. The rich resonance of *ruah*, the literal metaphor and the concrete symbolism, is epitomized by the wakened winds (*ruhot*) that blow in the shaft and make noises that imitate bitter weeping, which Mr. Kidron and his wife can no longer endure. The elevators externalize the grief they are trying to keep inside.

When Amotz first meets Mr. Kidron, the bereaved father and claimant from the new apartment tower, he sees a mirror image of Yirmi, the bereaved father, who fled to Africa. On a Friday morning, the fifth day of Hanukkah, after hearing about "strong easterly winds" on the radio, Amotz is in a good mood [*ruah*]. He goes to the "tower of winds" to listen to the "whining winds." When he opens the "fire door that separates the parking area from the elevators," it seems that "the easterly winds have worsened the roaring." It is here, near the elevators, that he meets Kidron, "an older man, with a melancholy face and sunken cheeks. He wears old khaki pants, and his shoes are covered with fresh mud, as if he were returning from a tramp through the fields" (168). But Mr. Kidron is not returning from the fields but from the cemetery. As opposed to Yirmi, who fled to Africa and does not visit his son's grave, Kidron visits his son's grave every morning. Amotz is curious where Kidron finds the time to file legal complaints about the elevator, and gets an earful:

> My work is brief, though not easy. To go every morning to the military cemetery, to my son's grave, walk around the gravestone a bit, pull a few weeds, remove an old pebble and replace it with a new one. Sometimes, if a tear comes, I also have to wipe it. All in all, not much employment. Which is why I have plenty of time to demand that others fulfill their obligations. (170)

Amotz takes the opportunity to utilize the phrase he scattered to the wind at Moran's army base, responding with "a touch of inner satisfaction": "I may not be a bereaved father like you, Mr. Kidron, only a bereaved uncle, but I have insider knowledge, family knowledge, of your grief, and I respect it a great deal" (170).

Two days have passed since then, during which the restless Amotz continued to wander around Tel Aviv and Jerusalem. On the afternoon of the seventh day of Hanukkah, he finds Mr. Kidron sitting in his office with legal papers in his hand. The secretary admitted him to Ya'ari's office out of respect for the bereaved father after he told her the whole story of his son's death a few months earlier. Mr. Kidron, whose hearing is affected by the void within him, says to Ya'ari: "You have a tree that makes a pleasant noise outside a closed window, but with us, when we get home and get near the elevator, we don't hear the wind but howls of pain" (332).

No doubt Kidron's bereavement influences Amotz's decision to carry out a thorough nighttime inspection to determine the reason for the howls of pain coming from the elevator. "You will be surprised to learn that despite my age," he tells Kidron—Amotz is sixty-one—"this is the first time I am hunting for winds at night. Like surgery or war, you know when you start, but not when you'll finish" (333). The combination of a windy night, war, and surgery suggests a vision of illness and bloodshed (*halom-mahala-milhama*), an operation undertaken on the eighth and last night of Hanukkah at the insistence of a bereaved father, in search of the reason for cries and moans in the Pinsker Tower, where he and his wife bought their flat after their son was killed. Amotz explains to himself the unconventional nocturnal project that verges between reality and fantasy:

> True, a sharp lawyer could juggle these windy complaints [*tlunat ha-ruhot*], tossing them from one party to the next till the complainant's spirit [*ruah*] broke. But here we have a bereaved father, and there is strong fellowship between him and a bereaved uncle. Amotz takes the trouble on a stormy night to instill team spirit [*ruah tzevet*] in all those responsible to determine who among them is the guilty party. (340)

Macabre episodes in Yehoshua's works take place mainly at night.[7] Here, too, the macabre motif is present to warn the tenants that the elevators are not working on this night. Mr. Kidron has posted "signs lettered with an ink marker and bordered with thick black lines . . . on the walls of the lobby and the doors of the elevators, which on first glance resemble formal death notices" (342).

The door of the Kidron apartment on the twenty-fourth floor is open this night. The apartment is brightly lit, and the dining table is filled with snacks and carafes of *black* coffee. Mrs. Kidron is dressed in *black*. The setting suggests a family sitting shiva. Mr. Kidron is "formally attired, in a **dark suit** and tie, as if dressed for battle [*ruah krav*] with the representatives of the construction company" (342, emphasis added). Nofar, we recall, was also dressed in black, a symbol of her continued mourning.

When Amotz arrives, the conversation turns to bereavement and mourning. Toward the end of the divided novel, on the last night of Hanukkah, Amotz's spirit is also divided: His attention is split between this bereaved, wind-haunted family and his wife, soon to land at the airport. A conversation takes place between him and Mrs. Kidron, as an airplane glides over the city:

> "Your son . . . the soldier," he mumbles, almost casually, his eyes still fixed on the plane, "did he get to know this new apartment?"
>
> "No. He was killed two months before we moved here. We wanted to cancel the purchase, but it was too late."
>
> "Why cancel it? Doesn't it make it a little easier, moving to a new place?"
>
> "So, we hoped, but in the autumn these winds started up, which only made us more depressed."
>
> "Depressed because of the winds? But it's purely a technical problem."
>
> She regards him with a fearful expression.
>
> "Is that what you believe?"
>
> "I don't believe it; I'm certain of it." (344)

Is this confident declaration that the fearsome winds are external, and not turbulence of the soul, another attempt by Amotz at consolation, in the spirit of the prophet Isaiah? Perhaps.

As he gets to know this new bereaved family, he asks to see a photograph of the son. It turns out that whereas his nephew Eyal's picture is on display at his home, and hangs over Nofar's bed in her rented room, the Kidrons have hidden away their son's photos deep in a closet. His parents prefer to bond with him in memory and imagination:

> Both of us, says the mother, agreed not to get stuck on a figure fixed in time. We try to go back and connect through activity, take him places he never saw and imagine how he would behave there. We want to keep him in perpetual motion, to allow him to grow and even grow old, so he will not be forever frozen in pictures from childhood or the last photos from his military service. (344–45)

This encounter brings to mind Roland Barthes's *Camera Lucida: Reflections on Photography* (1982), his last major work and a very personal one, composed after the death of his mother. Barthes states, in various ways, that the essence of photography is that it captures something in the past that cannot be restored. "Looking at a photograph, I inevitably include in my scrutiny the thought of that instant, however brief, in which a real thing happened to be motionless in front of the eye." "The photograph is literally an emanation of the referent," wrote Barthes.[8] Mr. and Mrs. Kidron are parents who have not reconciled themselves to their son as the past that cannot be restored. They do not agree with Barthes that "photography has something to do with resurrection," because they do not regard their son as being dead. By storing his photographs deep in the closet, they deliberately repress his death. These are parents who wish to preserve their son in a continuing present that does not end until he grows old and dies a natural death.

When Daniela returns from her African adventure, the bustling urban world annoys her and the abundance of possessions in her home seems unnecessary. "Even the family photos on the walls—she and her husband, children, and grandchildren, and the last picture of her nephew—seem excessive in number" (383). In other words, Daniela unknowingly adopts the approach of the Kidrons, who, despite the dark winds that blow within them and inside the elevator shaft (in the building they moved to after their son died), cling to a dynamic approach to the living and the dead, and relate to their son as if he were alive, see him in their mind's eye growing up, enjoying the beauty of nature and a world that in effect surrounds him. They reject photographs that demonstrate frozen truth, and instead embrace the living flow of imagination.

Can it be that Shuli and Yirmi would have adopted the Kidrons' form of grief if Shuli had not died and if Yirmi had not fled to Africa and obsessively read the Bible with such negativity? Could Yirmi find any consolation in reading the eternal promise of love and wondrous eroticism in the Song of Songs, or is it really his destiny, his inherent nature, to rail like Jeremiah against the vicissitudes of life that remind him of what he and Eyal "cannot do anymore"? Here Yirmi, the prophet in exile, plays that game by himself. This is the masculine bereavement he has taken upon himself, a legacy of grief that is his property alone.

11

Fighting Men, Adored by Women. Really?

The Examined Corpus through the Lens of Gender

Since the dawn of civilization, war tends to be a gendered, triumphalist, and manly tale, where women serve and adore their men. In the first song in the Bible, Lamech boasts to his wives Adah and Zillah that he has killed a man for wounding him—"Adah and Zillah, hear my voice. O wives of Lamech, give ear to my speech. I have slain a man for wounding me, and a lad for bruising me" (Genesis 4:23).[1] This song is the prototype for wars to come: Women are called to passively witness, to look on with admiration as men fight for victory and immortality.

The Hebrew etymology linking the words "man-heroism" (*gever-gvura*) and "immortality-victory" (*netzach-nitzachon*) speaks volumes on the strong traditional link between these elements. The connection between heroism, the love of women, the gaze of women, conquering women (the common metaphor is penetrating a wall or fortified city), and falling into their net (for example, when the woman is deceitful and serves the opposing side)—are all realized in the character of the heroic Samson, often compared to the Greek Heracles: Both possessed exceptional physical strength, struck down many foes, and were felled by a woman. Beating in the hearts of biblical heroes is the spirit of God, who is given titles related to the military (emphasis added to the quotes)—Lord of hosts; to war—"the Lord, **the Warrior**—Lord is His name!" (Exodus 15:3); to valiance—"the Lord, **mighty and valiant**, the Lord **valiant in battle**" (Psalms 24:8); to immortality—the Eternal One of Israel; and to greatness, might, and triumph—"Yours, Lord, are **greatness, might,** splendor, **triumph** and majesty" (I Chronicles 29:11).

The ancient myths seep into the unheroic modern literature, but with completely opposite meanings. This literature utilizes the elements of the epic poems and heroic tales of antiquity in a creative-subversive manner, redefining war and its consequences. The Jewish-Austrian satirist Karl Kraus expressed this irony when he defined war as a phenomenon that has no winners, only losers: "What is war?" he asked at the height of World War I. "First, one hopes to win; then one expects the enemy to lose. Then, one is satisfied that the enemy too is suffering. In the end, one is surprised that everyone has lost."[2]

The trajectory described by Kraus, moving from triumphalism to the unheroic realization that the price of war is heavy and meted equally to all who participate in it, is also characteristic of the history of Israeli war narratives. How then, does this trajectory manifest itself in relation to the position of women in Israeli war narratives? In her book *Barricade of Mothers*,[3] Dana Olmert suggests that women tend to gain power as the narrative of heroic war loses some of its force. Olmert studies a range of texts, from the early days of the Zionist movement to the twenty-first century. The early Israeli archetype of women in war is based on a combination of two older models: The biblical archetype of Hannah, *Em Ha'Banim*, the Mother of Sons, who sacrifices her sons willingly on the altar of religious faith, is melded with early Zionist Spartan ideals to create the Israeli archetypal mother who raises warriors and willingly sends them to military service and heroic death.[4] However, Olmert suggests that in the wake of the Six-Day War of 1967, and increasingly so in the late 1980s, representations of Israeli women change: Women, and particularly mothers, emerge as figures of protest, their position as outsiders to the patriarchal military order calling its heroic code of values fiercely into question. While Olmert is correct in noting a broad cultural shift in the representations of women in Israeli war narratives, it is nevertheless the case that when we closely examine Hebrew texts of many different periods, women tend to remain on the margins, defined mainly in relation to the experience of men—fathers and sons, living soldiers and the fallen.

Agnon, for instance, treats World War I and the myth of the fearless warrior ironically in his novel *To This Day*. When the war spins out of control, the scholar Dr. Mittel asks the narrator: "What's new in the world? Anything besides killing and being killed? First men go mad and start a war and then the war goes on by itself" (*To This Day*, 30).[5] The fighters' heroism is only apparent in the image, the picture: "My only son is fighting in it, too. **In case you've never seen him, here's a photograph**. Doesn't he look the hero in his uniform? A world conqueror!" (30, emphasis added).

In this highly charged situation, where a father refers ironically to his only son who went to battle and is destined to be killed, the role of the woman is also present, watching the fighter go to battle while her heart swells with pride. In this case, the woman is the mother. "His dear mother has good reason to be proud of him," the father asserts. The narrator, who happened to be visiting Dr. Mittel on the day his son left for the army, also notes the mother's pride in her patriotic son. "I remembered the boy's mother **scrutinizing** every item that he packed in his kitbag, her **eyes bright with joy** at the sight of her boy going off to defend the Fatherland" (30, emphasis added).

In *To This Day*, other women are represented aiding the war effort as train workers: "Since it was wartime and every able-bodied man was in the army, the trains were run by women" (37). One unique woman stands at the center of the story: Brigitta Schimmermann, an actress in a small theater, who during the war became a benevolent nurse of sorts and established a hospital for the war-wounded, while the men of her family, her husband and father-in-law, were weapon manufacturers. This vicious cycle, in which she eases the pain of the wounded while her male relatives are partially responsible for their wounds, makes a mockery of the woman at the home front enlisted to aid the war effort. Her admiration for her husband and father-in-law, who supply the army with weapons of destruction, along with the map in her room, where she pins small flags to track the advance of the German forces, are Agnon's cynical depiction of a woman taking part in a war by offering services to its victims, while she herself observes its course from a stance of empathy and support.

Women in Bartov's *The Brigade* are represented in a dichotomous way. Some provide sexual services to soldiers storming the gates of the brothel and are a disparaged, indistinguishable mass of female flesh—"It's the same with all of them, the Uzbeks, the Poles, the Italians. Exactly the same" (*The Brigade*, 31).[6] The opposite model is a unique, singular woman. She is beloved by the protagonist, who is emotionally at the mercy of her infrequent letters:

> I remind myself every day to forget Noga and her letters, and every day I whisper to myself that today they'll arrive. My hope is futile—I don't receive them simply because they're not being written any more . . . Noga won't write again . . . and we know something about love in time of war. Only an extraordinary girl can love from afar, remembering, yearning, and if someone is to blame, then it's me, who innocently believed that you, Noga, that you are that extraordinary girl. (102–3)

These two types of women embody the binary attitude toward women—either whore or saint—and both contrasting models of femininity torment the protagonist of *The Brigade*.

German women were perceived by the Brigade soldiers as collaborators of the Nazi executioners and their superiors, since they "clapped," "greeted them with flowers," "blessed their blood," and "benefited from the plunder" (120). They, along with Brigitta Schimmermann from *To This Day*, belong to the women observing war from the outside and admiring its manly array. In *To This Day*, they were German women during World War I; in *The Brigade*, they were German women during World War II. In *The Brigade*, some Jewish Brigade soldiers felt they could exact revenge on German women even if they did not take an active part in the atrocities. Their punishment would be "female": rape. Twice, in the middle of the novel and at its end, Brigade soldiers tried to hurt women associated with the Nazis, and twice they failed. Chapter 2 centers on the internal arguments in the Brigade and within the individual's soul about the morality of such vengeance.

Hanoch Bartov utilizes the convention of women observing the male fighters in another abhorrent way. When two Brigade soldiers try to assault a mother and daughter in their home, the women watch the Jewish soldiers not with admiration but with a desire to blame and degrade. They observe their men with admiration, but they watch the Jewish soldiers in order to perform a *selection*. Giladi, one of the soldiers who strongly opposed the "lineup of disgrace," expresses it as follows:

> I hereby declare that I will not participate in the lineup of disgrace . . . seventy guys, seventy Jewish soldiers will line up for identification in front of two Nazi women, whose husbands, brothers and sons . . . How could you imagine such a sight here, today . . . for me, it's enough to think that my elderly father stood like this in their lineups, while real murderers paced before them, perhaps the same men who were absent last night from the homes of those Nazi women because they're now . . ." (117)

In her article "Volunteer Women in Blue and Khaki: *Eretz-Israeli* Women in the British Army in Egypt During World War II," Nitza Priluk writes that about 4,000 female soldiers from pre-state Israel volunteered to serve in the British Army during World War II and were assigned to two armed forces: 3,155 women served in the Ground Forces and 789 in the Air Force. "In the melting pot of the British Army," Priluk writes, "women of different backgrounds met, some for the first time—native-born and new immigrants, from the city and the kibbutz, secular and religious, single and married, some who were active in the Palmach and the underground organizations and others who were distant from politics."[7] In *The Brigade* by Hanoch Bartov, there is no mention of "our heroic sisters of glory," as they were called by the national institutions that exhorted women to join the British Army.[8] Women are only mentioned in the novel through the prism of sexuality and their function in the male soldier's system of needs.

The status of women in Yehuda Amichai's dual narrative in *Not of This Time, Not of This Place* is different. Here they are the very essence of life and death. At the "Roman party" in Yitzhaq and Mina's crumbling Jerusalem home, the party of the collapsing masculine collective that opens the novel, the protagonist stands on the edge of the roof "and all his life was with him: all his memories, childhood and encounters. His wars, Little Ruth and his wife Ruth, who during the war waited for him at the mouth of a Negev wadi when he returned from the night's battles" (*Not of This Time, Not of This Place*, 14).⁹ Little Ruth and his wife Ruth are included in "all his life." They are an inseparable part of his past, and the protagonist feels immense guilt toward both. He abandoned them both: one on the eve of World War II, the other during Israel's War of Independence. When he married Big Ruth after the War of Independence, it was a marriage of commitment to the devoted woman who awaited a warrior returning from battle.

In contrast to these two Ruths of the past, who coalesce into a single woman in the protagonist's mind, Patricia, the woman of the present, embodies a relationship of equality between a man and a woman. He is not the only fighter—she is also described in militaristic terms: She enters the room "proud and standing tall, like a conquering army" (60). She conquers him just as he conquers her. Patricia, like the protagonist, also feels guilt toward her abandoned partner: "Do you still love your husband? No. I'm only connected to him. He needs me because of what happened to him in the war. Do you love your wife? We met in a wadi, in the Negev, on the day of a great war. I returned from a nighttime battle and she was there. She deserves a child from me" (458). Both lovers are tied to a wife or a husband and feel obligated to them because of the war lives they were involved in. But in the summer of 1959, when the world seemingly begins to sink around them and an atmosphere of decadence takes over, they both forget their obligations to their respective partners and cling to an all-encompassing love that makes them forget all else. They make love and try to forget the war: "Gone was the face of Patricia's husband, the taciturn and troubled man. Gone too was the face of his good wife Ruth, with whom he had seen a peaceful life since meeting that dawn in the yellow Negev, burning in the sun and war" (314–15).

Patricia's husband, who comes to Jerusalem to try and win back his wife, is likened to Orpheus. After he fails in his quest, the two lovers turn off the light and say in unison, signifying the equal nature of their relationship: "Let's play a war game! Because they did not know how to approach each other after her husband Orpheus appeared" (282). Their mutual love that makes them forget their daily commitments is perceived as a joint act of military defiance—"and they raised the flag of rebellion" (285).

In Amichai's novel, the woman is a full partner in the love that defeats the war. But when the war strikes again, and the protagonist from Jerusalem steps on a mine on Mount Scopus that had been lying in wait for him from another war—not from that time and not from that place—the woman is no longer at his side. Meanwhile, the protagonist from Weinburg returns from the city of his childhood (which he visited that same summer, while his alter ego was making grand love in Jerusalem and dying from love and a mine) and he sees the woman differently, as a piece of immortal life granted by a second chance: "For what is immortality in human life if not to see for the second time a childhood or a **woman** or a place?" (615, emphasis added).

In Kenaz's *Infiltration*, the ethos of the man in the army is idealized again and again:

- "You don't know what's happening in the army now . . . Since Dayan became chief of staff, they've started building **an army of men** in this country" (*Infiltration*, 22).[10]
- "We need two things: personal example and discipline. Otherwise, we don't stand a chance. And it has to begin from the top. **The leaders have to be men**" (25).
- "What's the matter with you? Why don't you sing **like men**?" (29).
- "You believe all that crap about how **they turn babies wet behind the ears into men**" (81).
- "This is your home now! . . . They educate you **to be men**" (98).
- "When we're young and strong, on the brink of life, **the life of men**" (150) (emphasis added to all of the quotes).

The idealization of this ethos in *Infiltration* is, in fact, meant to refute it. That is, the very choice of "grade B" or unfit recruits as the novel's protagonists is intended to undermine the heroic and "manly" image of the soldier. The novel does not center on the question of the recruits' masculinity, but rather on the education they received, which identified—and continues to identify—a man as a fighter, and assumed—and continues to assume—that the masculinity of a man in uniform stirs the admiration of women.

One of the main themes of Kenaz's novel is the relationship between the comrades Micky and Alon. "But you're sure," Micky challenges Alon, "that any girl would prefer some paratrooper or combat fighter to a grade-B recruit from Training Base Four, right?" (71). Alon wins the affection of Dafna, his beautiful, sensitive, and unique girlfriend, who is aware of his mental state but is still unquestionably faithful to him, proving that it is indeed possible for a "grade-B recruit" to win a girl's heart. It appears that the image of a woman watching and admiring the manly fighters is stronger than the reality of his life. Alon, due to his personality and biography, embodies the influence of the kibbutz education system, a microcosm of the prevalent education in all Israeli society, with regard to cultivating the legend of the manly fighter. Alon is the victim of the indoctrination spanning from his kibbutz education to his basic training. He is always willing to honor it and is always ready to defend it with all his might. And so, Kenaz describes Alon's enslavement to the myth of the fighter: "Alon knitted his brows in concentration. The captain's deliberate voice droned on monotonously, and to Alon his words sounded like the glorious verses of an ancient epic, told by the elder of the tribe to the young warriors sitting in a circle at his feet, calling silently on the spirits of their ancestors to come and inspire their hearts and empower their arms for war" (53).

"Back to the platoon at a run, and I want to see you lift your knees and hear you sing. Let Sergeant Ofra see **what kind of men you are!**" (29, emphasis added). This is how the physical training (PT) instructor encourages the recruits to sing: They need to impress the female sergeant with their masculinity. There is only one woman in the whole base—the PT instructor Ofra. However, rather than have her observe the soldiers and feel awed by their appearance, Kenaz turns the tables. The recruits see her emerge between light and darkness, like a goddess from another world, and they cannot believe their eyes:

> This vision did not belong to the time and place in which we were imprisoned. The whole squad rose to its feet and went to join Avner, who was standing in front of us at a vantage point before which the whole horizon lay open . . . and before we could reach his side, **she** entered our field of vision, running toward her dogs. At first she did not notice

us standing next to the eucalyptus trees, and her run was free and light, her feet barely touching the ground and her head flung back. The smile illuminating her face, slightly flushed from her running, was apparently not meant for strange eyes to see . . . when . . . she turned her face to lay her cheek against its [her dog's] body, her eyes were directed toward us and our presence was immediately revealed. (26, emphasis added)

This goddess appears again, this time only to the narrator, who wonders what she is really made of. One weekend, the whole platoon was kept on base despite an explicit promise of a long-awaited furlough. The sudden cancellation of the furlough was part of the series of abuses the recruits suffered. That Friday evening, the narrator wandered around the camp looking for a connection with home by meeting Arik, a friend from high school who was also in basic training at Training Base 4. On his way to the prosaic meeting with the friend, he encounters a woman of legend:

> I left the lines of the enlisted men and turned onto the dirt road leading to the staff quarters. I stood still to orient myself before making another attempt to reach Arik's company, and then I saw **her** again.
> She was coming from the end of the road. In uniform, a knapsack hanging on a strap from her shoulder, a big bag in her hand. She looked as if she were on her way home. Her dogs weren't with her. . . . I strained my eyes to examine her while she was still far away. It was definitely **her**. She walked quickly, apparently in a hurry. Perhaps the vision of her as an ancient goddess of the hunt was only a figment of my imagination? . . . I stood at the side of the road and stared at her as she came rapidly toward me. It had nothing to do with courage or provoking fortune . . . it was simply a need, stronger than fear or pain, to see her at close quarters, if only for a moment, and stand next to her face-to-face. (75–76, emphasis added)

When the "ancient goddess of the hunt" approaches, this time without her two dogs,[11] the narrator notices an owl badge hanging on her sleeve, a badge for soldiers who excel at sight and perception, also at night. But she does not give the saluting soldier even the slightest glance: "She walked past me, and I saluted without taking my eyes from her. She didn't return my salute and her eyes turned me to air, to a void in the vast spaces she surveyed" (76). In this passage, Kenaz completely upends the myth of the woman admiring the male fighter. It was he, the feeble, feminine man who looks on at the female soldier in uniform and worships her mythological image.

Avner, a lover of women who has ample sexual experience, would readily leave his married girlfriend Aliza, who risks her marriage by traveling from Jerusalem to the base, in order to win the heart of the mysterious woman with whom he has never spoken a word. The rumor that she has no interest in men is another element drawing in the adolescent soldiers, who watch her with hungry eyes. After declaring that he wants to be a gynecologist, Avner says:

> Imagine that PT instructress we saw today coming to me for an examination when I'm a gynecologist. And I say to her: "Take it off, take it all off, let's see all your secrets" . . . I want to know all the secrets of her body, all its hiding places . . . Not liking men is exactly what makes her so attractive, like a fortress you have to conquer by force. (42)

The dichotomy separating the attainable woman, the whore, from the beautiful and bad woman, a fortress to be conquered, is maintained throughout the novel.

Furthermore, the military setting maintains the distinction between "men," the ultimate compliment, and "women," the ultimate insult: "Listen, just listen to that disgusting, degenerate moaning, like a lot of **bitches in heat**" (91, emphasis added). And gossip is always seen as a female trait: "Everyone talks about everyone else here behind their backs, **like a bunch of old women**" (129, emphasis added).

Infiltration also includes representation of a homosexual man, who had no place in the army in the 1950s and was humiliated and beaten bloody. The multifaceted marginality of Rahamim Ben-Hamo, one of the novel's anti-heroes (a grade-B recruit, Mizrahi, new immigrant, and gay), makes him a scapegoat for accusations and turns him into the punching bag of the whole platoon: "I'll tell all that stuff to the instructors and they'll bring MPs and take care of you for good, like they do in the army to buggers like you" (57). When a blanket, army property, is burned, the feminine, homosexual demeanor of Rahamim Ben-Hamo makes him an easy target for framing, and he is blamed for the fire: "Suddenly you felt like a smoke, and you dunno how to smoke, do you, **'cause you're not a man**. So your fag fell on the blanket and burned it" (58, emphasis added).

In his book *David, Jonathan and Other Soldiers*, Danny Kaplan writes: "Being a combat soldier is not only associated with masculine hegemony, it is also contrasted with images of the 'other,' those who are not 'real' men. The value of a man can be raised by distancing him from insulting references to lesser masculinity, such as images of immaturity, femininity, homosexuality and also the enemy."[12] Indeed, when Rahamim Ben-Hamo announces to his tormentors—"I'm engaged, if you want to know," he is answered mockingly: "Congratulations, Ben-Hamo! Who's your fiancée? Muhammad?" (*Infiltration*, 88). Indeed, Rahamim Ben-Hamo is pitiful, as his name suggests [*rahamim* means "pity" in Hebrew], though he can also be disgusting. He cried like a baby in the arms of his big mother and beautiful sister, his two "women" who brought him home-cooked food from the transit camp, and at the same time he was ashamed of them and rejected them.

The military experience distances women from men and brings men together in an intimate, sometimes very problematic way. Kenaz represents these relationships in a complex, multifaceted manner in *Infiltration*.

Women are at the center of the novels *My Michael*, *Yasmine*, and *To the End of the Land*. These three novels revolve around two axes: a mostly masculine axis of nationality and hegemony, and a feminine axis, where women have an ambivalent attitude toward the fighter who goes off to war.

Hannah Gonen, the heroine of *My Michael*, has no interest in the war going on in 1956. She is wholly focused on her sickness and her hallucinations. The war, the sickness, and the nationalist dreams of grandeur on one side, and the romantic-feminine dreams on the other, play a transparent game of reflections in the novel. Amos Oz utilizes the stereotype of the woman attracted to men in uniform in order to underline her disdain for her husband; she looks up to strangers and looks down on her husband. He is not a combat soldier, not a paratrooper or a pilot, as he apologetically states again and again; he is just a soldier in the Signal Corps. In contrast, the fighters who are strangers but fulfill her erotic yearnings are described as follows: "In Café Allenby on King George Street, I saw four handsome French officers. They were wearing peaked caps, and purple stripes gleamed on their epaulets. Only in films had I seen such a sight before" (*My Michael*, 166).[13] "On David Yellin Street . . . I passed three paratroopers in mottled battledress. Submachine guns hung from their shoulders . . . One of them, dark and lean, called after me—'Sweetheart.' His comrades joined in his laughter. I reveled in their laughter" (166–67). What would be perceived today as sexual harassment, was welcomed in the fifties as a compliment by the woman admiring the dark man, wearing a uniform and carrying a gun.

After Israel captured East Jerusalem in 1967, two local Palestinian journalists, the Muslim Abu Nabil and the Christian Abu George, talk about their politically oriented children: Nabil is the son of the former, and Yasmine is the daughter of the latter. Their difference in gender does not affect their readiness to join the Palestinian cause, and both fathers express dissatisfaction mixed with pride about the political activities of their children:

> [Abu Nabil] looked around and leaned closer to his friend. "Two days ago, Abu Ammar [Yasser Arafat's nom de guerre] called my Nabil and inducted him into Fatah. I said to him, 'Ibni, son, why are you doing this? You've just got married, your wife is pregnant.' You know what he said? 'It's how you brought me up, Father.'"
>
> "I'm worried too, desperately afraid that my Yasmine will be stupid enough to join Abu Ammar's people in Paris," Abu George sighed. (*Yasmine*, 108)[14]

And indeed, Yasmine arrives in Israel carrying "three secret letters given to her by Fayez, the head of Fatah in Paris. When he instructed her how to conceal them and who to give them to, she felt she was fulfilling an important patriotic mission" (135). Yasmine indeed fulfills her mission. The Israeli soldier inspecting her baggage at the Allenby Bridge checkpoint does not open the suitcase containing the concealed smuggled letters.

That soldier is portrayed by Eli Amir as someone performing his duty with compassion and humor. For example, when he hears that the "Princess"—as she was introduced by her father at the checkpoint—had arrived from Paris, he hums the song of Yves Montand, trying in this way, and in other ways, to ease the tension between the occupier and the occupied. Maybe for this reason he does not insist on opening all of her luggage, and after opening two bags he skips the third. But for Yasmine, "The sight of his fingers handling her underwear made her sick" (138). This is Eli Amir's subversive interpretation of the convention of a woman looking at soldiers and being attracted to them—"the soldier who rummaged in her underwear with clumsy fingers" (166) was like all the other soldiers, inspecting papers and searching bags and cars. He and they appeared to her "older than national servicemen, bareheaded, their uniforms untidy. This was her first sight of Israeli soldiers, and she didn't know they were reservists" (135). To her, they were "low-grade, undignified conquerors" (166).

This educated Arab woman, who would not cease to resist the new reality forced upon the Palestinian people, would nonetheless fall in love with Nuri Imari—the Jewish governor. Nuri was an Israeli soldier who served in the war and was appointed to govern the occupied civilian population. His civilian clothes and sloppiness do not inspire the same antagonism that the uniforms and sloppiness of the Israeli soldiers made her feel. She wonders: "Who was that Nuri? A young man in an off-the-peg suit that was too new and already wrinkled, a cheap tie knotted carelessly, untidy hair and thick, supposedly fashionable sideburns" (165–66). Despite his problematic identity and unkempt appearance, or maybe because of them, she is swept away with him, not easily, into a relationship of tormented love. A powerful and complex dynamic develops between them, with both sides playing the roles of occupier and occupied.

"Didn't we say we'd have a few puffs of family-together time?" Ora, the heroine of Grossman's *To the End of the Land*, despairingly asks her son Ofer, who is leaving on a military operation instead of going on a nature hike they had planned together as part of his pre-discharge furlough and re-acclimation to civilian life. "Mom, it's not a game, it's war," Ofer answers. "And because of his arrogance—his, and his father's, and his brother's"—the men patronizing her, the only woman in the family, she says—"she still wasn't convinced that the male brain could tell the difference between war and games" (*To the End of the Land*, 71).[15]

This witty retort by Ora has a wide context, since her life has fluctuated between war and games ever since she met Avram and Ilan. The three met when they were only sixteen years old in a dark hospital in Jerusalem during the Six-Day War, where they all suffered from sickness, fever, and hallucinations. It is now thirty-five years later and "her Moirae gather to determine her fate, to circle her in a dance of mockery and rebuke" (142), again and again.

Ora had an emotional and spiritual bond with the short and stocky Avram, but was attracted physically to the tall Ilan. However, her marriage to Ilan instead of Avram was quite literally the result of a lottery game invented by her two lovers while they were still soldiers:

> "Take a hat," Ilan and Avram had told her cheerfully over the military phone from the base in Sinai, "and put slips of paper in it, but identical ones." Then they'd both laughed. "No, no, you don't have to know what you're drawing lots for." That laughter still rings in her ears. They haven't laughed that way since. They were twenty-two, in their last month of their regular army service. (220)

Throughout her life, Ora, the woman whose marital choice was taken from her, continues to pay the price of the lottery forced upon her by the two men who confused an arbitrary lottery with free choice.

Just as she complied with the verdict of her two "husbands" who toyed with her fate and theirs, a generation later she complies with the decree of her son, who goes to war with youthful enthusiasm in place of a nature hike with her. Just as in the last month of their army service the two men who loved her determined how her marital choice would be made, on the last day of his military service her son Ofer determines that she will be the one to take him to the war. The masculine hegemony imposes its will on the woman who gives in to its demands. And the mother Ora is indeed tormented:

What have I done?
   I took Ofer to war.
   I brought him to the war myself. (122)

In *To the End of the Land,* Grossman places the literary convention of the woman watching the drafted soldier with admiration and pride in an absurd context: The driver Ora enlists to transport her son to the war is Sami, an Arab. Unprepared, Sami is suddenly trapped between his loyalty to Ora as the "family driver" and his loyalty to his own identity, to himself. Ora forgot to mention "this one little detail" when she phoned him, that she was commissioning him to bring her son Ofer to the rendezvous point from which the Israeli soldiers would embark on military missions in Jenin or Nablus. But then she sees her son, in uniform and carrying his weapon, through Sami's eyes: "Her heart sank when she saw his [Sami's] face darken in a deadly coupling of anger and defeat. He got it all in the blink of an eye; he saw Ofer coming down the steps with his uniform and rifle, and realized that Ora was asking him to add his modest contribution to the Israeli war effort" (63).

There are three heroes in this drama: "Ofer at the top of the steps, his rifle dangling, a magazine attached with a rubber band," Sami the Arab driver who "stood without moving and looked as though someone had slapped him," and Ora, the Israeli woman. Sami looked "as though she [Ora] herself had come over and stood facing him, smiled broadly with her light-filled joy and warmth, and slapped his face as hard as she could" (63). It seems that just as her two lovers trapped her by forcing her to pull a slip of paper from a hat determining who she would marry—without her knowing the nature and consequences of this game—a generation later she trapped her friend, the Arab driver, who did not know the purpose of his services. Grossman's inclination to observe passing moments that illustrate absurdity through the lens of a camera or recording device (as discussed in chapter 7) brings him to describe Ora, Sami the driver, and Ofer, who is wearing a uniform and carrying a gun and bullets, as follows: "For one moment they were trapped, the three of them, condemned in a flash" (63).

Furthermore, a television camera captures Ora at the soldiers' rendezvous point prior to them departing on a mission. She is forced once more to succumb to the nationalist masculine hegemony and play into its hands. Dilemmas, fears, and anguish are unsuited for the camera, which is meant to convey to its audience the carnival atmosphere of those eager for battle, and the Israeli mother would not disobey the rules. She takes part in the celebration of the sacrifice.

Ofer [fawn in Hebrew] "holds her with a slight authoritarian arrogance and turns her toward the camera—his move had caught her by surprise and she'd almost tripped, then held on to him with a nervous laugh, and it was all there" (81). But in fact, it was not "all there." The camera did not capture her feeling of betrayal "when he had decided to volunteer for the operation and kept it from her. When he had given up, without much deliberation, on their trip." Grossman continues:

> An even greater treachery, and an intolerable foreignness, resided in his ability to be such a soldier-going-to-war, so able to do his job, so insolent and joyful and thirsty for battle, thereby imposing her role upon her: to be wrinkled, yet glowing with pride (a poor man's coat of arms: **Mother of Soldier**), and to be a total dimwit, blinking with ignorant charm at the men's stance in the face of death . . . "What can a son tell his mother at a moment like this," asks the reporter, all sparkling with amusement. "Keep the beer cold for me till I get back!" the son laughs, and hearty cheers come from every direction . . . "I have something else to tell her," says her son on the television, and he smiles knowingly. He puts his lips to her ears and still looks at the camera with one twinkling eye, full of life and mischief . . . and she sees the camera quickly trying to invade the space between mouth and ear, and she sees the extremely attentive expression on her own face, her pathetic supplication exposed as she displays for all to see . . . what soft and natural intimacy flows between her and Ofer. (81–82, emphasis in the Hebrew original)

Light years separate the Jewish-German mother in *To This Day*, who sends her son off to fight in World War I out of an innocent and authentic patriotic sentiment for the "German motherland," from the Israeli mother in *To the End of the Land*, set in the first decade of the twenty-first century, who is unwillingly pulled into the masculine nationalist euphoria because she lacks the strength to resist. The mother in *To This Day* collaborates fully with the war effort and is proud and at peace with her son volunteering for the war. The mother in *To the End of the Land* views her son volunteering as a betrayal and a breach of trust, but to the camera she broadcasts fidelity to the rules. She is torn between her son's wishes and the public's demands, on the one hand, and her profound understanding that this is a disaster. But when faced by the crowds and the cameras, who cannot tell games from war, she is forced to pretend, to play the role of the proud mother. She expresses her inner resistance only to herself or to Avram, the biological father of her son Ofer; Avram learned the meaning of war, firsthand, thirty years ago.

Pigeons at Trafalgar Square also deals with mothers. While *To the End of the Land* deals with a woman with two husbands and a son with two fathers, *Pigeons at Trafalgar Square* deals with a son with two mothers. Both are gentle and devoted and want what is best for their shared son. The convention of the soldier appearing before a woman and stirring her emotions is represented in a surprisingly similar way in both novels. In *To the End of the Land*, Ora watches her son Ofer in uniform and carrying a gun, and Sami the Arab, who came to her aid since she had no husband with her; she observes how Sami's face **darkened** when he saw Ofer's uniform and gun. Similarly, in *Pigeons at Trafalgar Square*, Nabila watches her lost son, dressed in an IDF uniform, and her husband Rashid, a militaristic Palestinian from Ramallah: "The handsome woman anxiously watched her husband's lips . . . the man scowled, his face **darkened** with rage" (*Pigeons at Trafalgar Square*, 50, emphasis added).[16]

The horror at her biological son becoming a soldier in the enemy's military is obviously not lost on Nabila, the Palestinian mother in Sami Michael's *Pigeons at Trafalgar Square*, but while her husband, his biological father, seems ready to explode and curses his son, "the mother Nabila's eyes never left her son . . . her two eyes were pools of longing and sorrow" (49). Michael added deeper layers to the traditional classical-mythical role of the mother in this novel, portraying both the biological and adoptive mothers as "the promised land of the human race"—the motto of his novel.

In many of the war novels, the women at home, far from war experiences, are the focus of the soldiers' longings at nights before falling asleep, of their dreams, of their intimate conversations during guard duty, at rest, or in moments of danger. This pattern appears in S. Yizhar's *Days of Ziklag*, Hanoch Bartov's *The Brigade*, Yehoshua Kenaz's *Infiltration*, Ron Leshem's *Beaufort*, and other novels regarding military service and war. This motif appears powerfully in *To the End of the Land*, when Avram returns from captivity and tells of a Cochin guy from Bat Yam, a short and gaunt reservist, who in the Abbasiya Prison in Egypt would cry at nights, not because of the torture, but "out of jealousy for his girlfriend, because he could sense that she was being unfaithful" (*To the End of the Land*, 170).

The women in these novels, who meet soldiers on their short furloughs from their outposts or bases, or from the war, also have a face and a voice. In *Infiltration*, the recruits go on furlough twice, and the description of the occurrences in those few days spans many pages. In fact, Part Two of the novel, entitled "A Night of Atonement" (*Infiltration*, 215–343), deals with the recruits' first such vacation and their encounters with girls—some had stayed at home and others were also on leave from the army. Some of Part Four, entitled "The Cannons' Roar" (505–93), also recounts a furlough, when Micky arrives at Alon's kibbutz and meets Dafna, Alon's unique girlfriend, an ideal character who understands Alon and protects him, and Micky cannot decipher the secret of their relationship.

As opposed to the strong bond between Alon and Dafna in *Infiltration*, which the furlough only accentuates, furloughs from the army are described in many novels, including *Infiltration*, as frustrating and stressful. Following a long wait filled with expectation and much planning by the recruits or fighters closed off in an outpost, a base, or any other form of "out there," the actual homecoming exposes the disconnect between the woman who remained on the home front and the soldier living an intense military life that the woman is unable to comprehend.

"That same evening I had a fight with Lila." This is how chapter 10 of *Beaufort* begins, when the protagonist Erez goes home on furlough (168). Lila tells him of her friend who got tired of her boyfriend after his injury: "She wanted someone to go to the beach with, not some gimp" (169). Erez's reaction is scathing: "You all pick up and leave. In the history of our company, in all of the neighboring outposts, in every story I'd ever heard, they always left, sooner or later" (169). After this blanket accusation of all women, he also breaks up with Lila "because there was no place for her in my life. I needed to concentrate on carrying out my job without the burden of a girlfriend. She was so preoccupied with totally unimportant things. She could spend ages trying to pick out the colors of sheets and blankets, or where to hang pictures" (171). His world of war is very distant from hers, both geographically and mentally: "She didn't understand . . . But how could she? How could she reach out and talk to me in my own language when she wasn't up there [at Beaufort] with me to know how it felt?" (171–72).

Rotem Yair, whom everyone called Ronen, is the prototype for the literary character Liraz-Erez Liberti, whom everyone calls Erez. Rotem Yair married Lipaz Azulai, the prototype for Erez's girlfriend Lila. Their argument and separation turn out to be a temporary crisis. It was meant to convey the disconnect between the war front, populated by men, and the home front, populated by women; there are no women in Beaufort. It is quite literally the fortress of men. It is also meant to discredit the myth of women's loyalty to fighters, their supposed compassion that stems from love and admiration. In *Not of This Time, Not of This Place*, Yehuda Amichai cultivates this myth. Throughout the novel a fundamental image recurs: The woman Ruth is waiting for the protagonist Joel at the edge of the wadi when he returns exhausted from the night battles of the War of Independence. In return, he marries her. Liraz-Erez (Rotem-Ronen) also eventually marries Lila (Lipaz), even though her wait for her loved one and his trust in her were not mythological in nature and were instead quite prosaic. His innermost secrets from Beaufort would forever remain hidden to her: "She has never read the dozens of letters he wrote her from the hill because he destroyed them, afraid to send them, fearing that she'd be disgusted and alarmed and that she'd leave him" (356).

The furlough—going home—is not the only situation where soldiers can interact with women. Sometimes women come alone or as part of a family visit to see their soldier. This tradition has a heartbreaking representation in *Infiltration*. Rahamim Ben-Hamo, the platoon's punching bag, does not go home on furlough; he is confined to the base as punishment for allegedly burning a blanket—something he did not in fact do. His mother and sister come to visit him, and the usual mockery and abuse he suffers now turns toward the women who appear at the gate of the army base.

> After handing out the passes. Benny called Rahamim. "Mommy's come to see you," he said, "and she brought your sister too. I don't know how the hell they got past the main gate. But that's not my affair. Go and find them and tell them that this isn't a kindergarten or a vacation camp. I don't want anything like this to happen again. The MP at the gate of the base has instructions to let you through. For fifteen minutes and not a second more. Is that clear?" (*Infiltration*, 203)

The recruits exiting the gate gaped at the two women. The tall, shapely sister was "ignoring the stares of the soldiers standing on the other side of the road" (204). Ben-Hamo, who feared the leers that might intrude upon the meeting between him and the two women, who arrived bearing bags of food, tells his mother and sister to go away. The sister tries to understand why he is not approaching them and ends up starting a conversation with her spectators. During this conversation, it becomes apparent that she has served in the army and is still serving: "We brought him some treats for the holiday. We were lucky they let us through the main gate. I did my service in the military police and I do my reserve duty here, I know the guys here and the officers. They did us a big favor and let us in. So what's the matter with him now?" (205).

Ben-Hamo's sister's beauty and assertive conduct immediately make her a sudden center of attraction for the soldiers, who want to see how things pan out. Rahamim finally approaches the two women, and furiously kicks the pots, spilling their contents. He doubtlessly acted this way because of the looks fixed on him and on the women who came to comfort him in his solitude, because the moment he thought his comrades had left, the narrator, who cannot resist his voyeuristic impulses, witnesses a scene that displays just how important these women—especially the "big mother"—are to the soldier-child. She was and would remain a womb he would long for, a bulwark of support for the soldier who suffers buckets of insults and humiliation from everyone he encounters:

We began walking away, and after ten or twenty paces, I turned around and stood still. Rahamim was kneeling in front of his mother, embracing her thick waist and burying his head in her belly . . . Rahamim's mother stroked his head, murmuring something in their language, and tried to make him stand up, but she couldn't detach him from her body. His shoulders shook. His sister picked up his beret, which had fallen on the ground, shook off the dust, and looked at it and at the recruit's badge attached to it. His mother went on murmuring to him, and he raised his head slightly, shook it from side to side as if to say, *No, no*, and let it fall onto her belly again. (208)

The world of families visiting soldiers is described as a colorful carnival in *Friendly Fire*, whose setting is fifty years after *Infiltration*. Corporal Benny's statement from *Infiltration* that "this isn't a kindergarten or a vacation camp" is no longer relevant. This is how "Parents' Day" is described, with the gender-based interests of mothers and fathers at their children's event still distinct and unchanging:

The Israeli din gains volume. The bluish smoke pollutes the winter air. Recruits, stuffed full with meats and sweets, improvise a mini-soccer match at the edge of the visiting area, or walk arm-in-arm with their girlfriends within the perimeter set by their commanding officers. Fathers laugh heartily, sharing memories of their own army days, and mothers exchange phone numbers, so that together they will be able to keep track of special events during the months of training . . .

Parents' visiting day loosens the disciplinary leash, and many recruits walk around without their berets or weapons; some have even traded in their army boots for civilian shoes. A few assertive mothers have succeeded in penetrating the base to inspect their children's living conditions. (*Friendly Fire*, 294–95)

Moran, who was confined to the base, stands out from his peers: He is older, has a wife and children, and is suffering a punishment unbefitting his status. The split structure of the novel allows A. B. Yehoshua to "send" Moran's mother, the "big mother" to Africa, and only his father Amotz Ya'ari, his wife Efrat, their son Nadi, and their daughter Neta arrive to visit him. Efrat is dissatisfied with her husband's appearance, once more breaking the convention of the woman swooning over a soldier in uniform: Moran's unruly work uniform smells of gun oil and he is unshaven, "'Sexy like Arafat,' Efrat says maliciously, looking at her husband" (293).

Interestingly, the traditional gender difference with regard to the army also applies to Moran's two little children in *Friendly Fire*: His son Nadi is excited by the base and his daughter misses her parents when they drive off in the grandfather's car to work out the tension in their relationship. While the parents are away, the grandfather takes his two grandchildren to see a Syrian tank from the Yom Kippur War, placed in the base as a reminder of past heroism. The children's behavior described by A. B. Yehoshua reinforces the gender-oriented perception of them:

> Come, children, let's see this tank, says Ya'ari to the dismay of his granddaughter, who **has had more than enough of this military tour** and wants very much to return to her parents, having sensed the tension between them. But Nadi's **manly spirit** pleases Ya'ari, and he wants to satisfy the boy's **military curiosity**, and so, as they stand before the tank, an obsolete Soviet model whose camouflage paint was designed for the basalt terrain of the Golan Heights, he complies with his grandson's request to lift him on top of the turret. (299–300, emphasis added)

In the overview presented in this chapter, we see almost no literary representation of women's basic training, operations, or command in the Israeli army. Women always appear on the sidelines of the military array: observing, supporting, waiting at home, visiting army bases, bringing their fighters to the war. One exception is the PT instructress, Sergeant Ofra from *Infiltration*, who has a position of command in the base. Unfortunately, however, she is not described as a woman of flesh and blood, but as an ineffable goddess. Another exception is Rahamim Ben-Hamo's beautiful sister, who stands like a beggar at the base's gate, draws curious looks from recruits, and randomly mentions that she serves in the army. Otherwise, the military service of women is ignored in Israeli prose.

The seeds of change, of a departure from the traditional gender roles with regard to the army, appear in *To the End of the Land*. A military base populated by women is described in the novel, and when the male soldier arrives, he sees a vibrant, dynamic, feminine military world that forces him to sheepishly lower his eyes:

> How happy she used to be, Avram thinks and glances at her face. She used to be such a giggler. He remembers how he came to visit her when she was in basic training, at Bahad [Training Base] 12. He walked along the edge of the parade ground, suddenly finding it difficult to stand proudly upright in front of all these hundreds of girls—in his fantasies, the legendary city of girls had a constant soundtrack of sighs and damp moans and longing gazes . . . and suddenly, from afar, a tall, crumpled soldier draped in a sack-like uniform, with red bouncy curls cascading under a crooked cap and cherry lips, ran toward him with open arms, legs slightly askew, laughing joyfully and calling from one end of the camp to the other, "So very very much Avram!" (*To the End of the Land*, 201–2)

Here the tables have turned: A male soldier comes to visit an army of female soldiers, and he is the admirer standing in awe of the sight, the sound, and the lively place that brought the women together. He, the man, enters the gate of the female military base, Training Base 12—"the legendary city of girls" in his eyes. He comes to visit his female soldier, whose defining feature is not her uniform, but her run toward him, since he is a whole world to her—"So very very much Avram." Training Base 12, a women's basic training base, is mentioned once in *Infiltration* as well, which otherwise focuses on the basic training of men with limited physical capabilities in Training Base 4. These two training bases, 12 and 4, were adjacent to each other. "Once on our morning run our platoon met a girls' platoon running opposite us on the road . . . We saw each other and waved . . . You can't imagine how happy I was" (*Infiltration*, 80).

After Tiki Vidas' autobiographical book, *Voices That Never Leave Me*, which describes the experiences of a female Signal Corps soldier during the Yom Kippur War, Shani Boianjiu was one of the first women to write about women's experiences in the army, in her novel *The People of Forever Are Not Afraid*. There is now also a wonderful movie on this topic,

Zero Motivation. If more voices like these emerge, the army will no longer be portrayed as an exclusively masculine narrative. The military lingo, the army's lexicon of abbreviations, and the perception of war will have a feminine side as well, perhaps leading to an outstretched hand for peace.

Conclusion

In my opinion, the image "Cold Blood" by the artist Hila Lulu-Lin provides an accurate portrayal of our lives in the shadow of war.

The bottom part of the image shows the routine-Israeli-hedonistic reality of a Tel Aviv summer. Tel Aviv has one of the prettiest and most colorful beaches in the world. The line of hotels, some rising to the sky and some sprawling heavily on the ground, were built some distance from the sea, preserving a decent strip of sand for vacationers. Mild waves and warm waters await those wishing to take a dip in the sea. The hotels represent vacation, relaxation, tourism, recreation—the good life. Yet these careless days of summer are threatened. The top part of the image is deceiving. At first glance, it seems to be a serene sunset. However, it is incongruous with the bright daylight filling the bottom part of the image: The sea and the bathers are not basking in the last rays of afternoon, but rather in the bright blue light of midday. A second glance at the red skies reveals to the observer's amazement that these are not skies, this is not a sunset, not even a gathering of dark clouds, but a slice of uncooked meat—large, juicy, and raw—stretching like a canvas above the joyful bathers in the illuminated blue sea. This dissonance becomes apparent to the observer in stages, and the last stage—the sudden stage of realization—shocks us to our core.

What does this image have to do with the novels chosen to represent our lives under the constant threat of war?

The Yom Kippur War, which is defined both in life and literature as a calamity that occurred "out of the blue," is not the only event that corresponds to this image. Even a war novel such as *Beaufort*, describing events in the secluded Beaufort base, dwells on the motif of normal city life undisturbed by the war being waged somewhere up north. In

Conclusion • 335

"Cold Blood" by Hila Lulu-Lin

one crazy operation, the combat soldiers—the protagonists of the novel—descend by foot from the mountain along with cooks, soldiers from the Signal Corps and Ordnance Corps, and administrative personnel ("pencil pushers"), and sneak toward the border in order to get home in this "creative" way. Since it is dangerous to send these troops home on furloughs by car or helicopter, the soldiers march in a long line through the underbrush, along a steep rocky slope, forging a new path that is still part of the war zone, surrounded by green-black darkness like in a dream, until the pickup point where Safari trucks suddenly appear to transport them home. And when the border opens and they cross into Israel, they "can see the first light in the sky . . . a new day" (*Beaufort*, 153)[1]—not a dim twilight, but a reassuring sunrise, symbolizing a new beginning, hope. The routine morning rising over the northern city Kiryat Shmona demonstrates to the soldiers that the home front, so close physically, is mentally so distant.

This is how the new day is described through the eyes of the exhausted, dusty fighters, weary from crossing the fields on the other side of the border:

> Milk trucks unload their wares at Itzik Zagouri's grocery . . . the bakery puts out its first tray of croissants and the paperboys deliver their newspapers . . . people are out jogging, waving hello to you. It's **a different planet**. Such sweet moments, like from a movie, and at first glance everything seems so innocent. Just a village filled with calm people smiling at one another, unaware of what's happening a few feet away from their lives, right under their noses. (153–54, emphasis added)

The phrase "a different planet" was coined by Ka-Tsetnik (Yehiel De-Nur) as a name for Auschwitz in his dramatic testimony during the Eichmann trial. This phrase takes on the opposite meaning in *Beaufort*: The soldiers, coming from the realm of fear and death, observe the city awakening to a life of activity and contentment; they understand that after one night of walking they had reached a golden morning, a different planet.

Another example describing a repressed consciousness of war appears in *The Brigade* by Hanoch Bartov, when celebrations are held on Tel Aviv rooftops while World War II rages on and Jews are being murdered in Europe. The sixteen-year-old protagonist-narrator, about to join the Jewish Brigade, cries out: "Why don't you all enlist? Why aren't you all fighting? Why aren't you all at the front? Why are you conducting weddings on the roof, with sandwiches, with salami, with beer, with wine? How can you be so happy here?" (*The Brigade*, Hebrew, 54.)

For comparison, here is another description of a city during World War II. Mario Fortunato describes fascist Rome in *The Innocent Days of War*:

Rome is gray and filthy in the rain. The streets are empty, no longer lined by fine shops. Although the regime tries to conceal its consequences, the war has descended upon the city like a dry easterly wind, leaving behind painful desolation and both material and moral destitution.[2]

In the "State of Tel Aviv," however, vacationers crowd the beaches, frolic in the sea, or celebrate on the rooftops. Even in Kiryat Shmona, so close to a war that has gone on for decades, routine daily life continues. The residents eat and drink, even jog and wave hello, while the consciousness of war is distant from them or repressed within them.

The blood-red sky—that slab of cold meat—is distant, both present and absent, and foreboding. The red color dominating *Friendly Fire* also supposedly represents the glowing candles of Hanukkah—when the narrative takes place—or the red traffic light refusing to change while the protagonist is in a rush. However, the dream depicted in the glow of the red traffic light clarifies that this color represents the deeply repressed fears of the protagonist, who lost a nephew in the army and whose son is currently mobilized as a reservist. In his dream, the elevator operator is supposed to bring him up to the third floor to view the city from above, but presses the button for the basement instead and tells him: "be prepared for an endless descent; in Turkish times this was a deep cistern." (*Friendly Fire*, 247).[3] The red in the novel is the color of rage, danger, and grief.

Even *Days of Ziklag* by S. Yizhar, often considered the definitive epic of Israel's War of Independence, is not a novel about blood, fire, and pillars of smoke. Instead, the novel deals with a group of adolescents in that magical stage between childhood and adulthood, who are therefore trapped inside themselves, even more than in the fortress. Yizhar also wrote the novellas "Khirbet Khizeh" and "The Prisoner," which began the tradition of anti-war prose in Israeli literature. More than fifty years after *Days of Ziklag*, we find the young and lively protagonists of *Beaufort* similarly living in a detached reality on a solitary Lebanese mountaintop, and the complexity of their relationships and the intensity of their emotions pale in light of the prevailing state of war. Most of these protagonists are patriots, but they are no longer the iconic blue-eyed pioneers; they are the darker-skinned sons of more recent immigrants, the Second and Third

Israel, slowly achieving an honorable place in the army. These soldiers yearn to be accepted into the center of Israeli culture and consciousness, and the army is a means toward that end. However, their patriotic fervor also weakens as the war stretches on and the losses are perceived to be a "waste."

None of the novels mentioned in *War Lives* include a hero's death. And if there is one, such as Ziv's death in *Beaufort* while disarming a mine on the mountain slope, it would be considered a "waste" in Beaufort lingo because it occurred just days before his scheduled discharge from the IDF. In *To This Day*, the death of only sons sacrificing themselves on the altar of Germany during World War I is treated ironically by Agnon. In *The Brigade*, a soldier's suicide just hours before the declaration of the end of World War II is an unnecessary death that cries to the heavens. Hanoch Bartov specifically chose to start his novel with this meaningless death to emphasize its anti-heroic nature. Later in the novel, another unnecessary death occurs when a soldier of the Jewish Brigade goes to search for his parents who were lost in the Holocaust and is murdered by Nazis on one of the trains still running in Europe after the war. In *Not of This Time, Not of This Place*, Yehuda Amichai's dual narrative, the death of one of the conflicted protagonist's friends takes on meaning that resonates with the spirit of the novel. While six of the friends returned from the War of Independence battles confused and with tormented souls, the one who died in the war did not die a hero's death but "remained at peace with everything" (*Not of This Time, Not of This Place*, Hebrew, 347). The protagonist who returns in 1959 from Jerusalem to his childhood city, Weinburg, witnesses the joyfulness and revelry of the place, the same city that murdered its Jews several years earlier, and is pained by the hedonism filling this sinful city. At the same time, he weeps for those who were murdered (those "burning," in his words). Their smoke blends with the smoke of the trains still arriving in droves to the city of wine and pleasure. None of those burned had the chance to die a hero's death, although Little Ruth actually was a hero. But she, along with all the others, was taken and reduced to ashes.

In this lyrical novel, which takes place about a decade and a half after the Holocaust, there is one image that corresponds to the illustration, where the sky is red from raw meat. Here, the skies are already black from seared meat: "The clouds of the smoke of the burning are cast over the world, each cloud shaped like a person burning and all his features burning" (276).

There are additional examples of unglorified death in the novels chosen in *War Lives* to reflect Israeli war literature. In *Infiltration*, Yehoshua Kenaz creates an iconic protagonist, a kibbutznik ready to sacrifice his life for his country. But as the novel develops, this model character's latent mental illness emerges, until finally he shoots himself and fails to die a heroic death like those he idolized. In *My Michael* by Amos Oz, the protagonist makes an anti-heroic declaration, stating again and again that he is not a tank commander or a pilot, but a Signal Corps soldier. Though deployed in a (military) communications role, he is unable to communicate with his wife, who grows more and more detached from him; he is a soldier who fails on the battlefield of family life too. In *Yasmine* by Eli Amir, the protagonist's war on the battlefield is short and fragmented. The main part of his war is after the Six-Day War, when he tries to help and save those under occupation in post-war Jerusalem, with very limited success. In *To the End of the Land* by David Grossman, one of the three protagonists, Ilan, follows the voice of his friend Avram, heard on the two-way radio when the line of fortifications on the Suez Canal collapsed during the Yom Kippur War. His pursuit did not help Avram, who was captured and later returned from Egyptian captivity a bleeding, pus-ridden lump of meat, a total wreck. Thirty years later, Ora, the third side of the eternal friendship triangle, is still trying to help Avram rebuild his life. In *Pigeons at Trafalgar Square* by Sami Michael, two blood brothers are lynched and murdered, one of them Jewish and the other an Arab; the Arab brother is killed while trying to shield his Jewish brother with his own body.

In *Friendly Fire*, the unheroic death is especially degrading and humiliating. The soldier was killed by friendly fire while going down from the roof to wash a bucket that contained his feces.

The unnecessary death, common to many of the novels, is closely connected to the image of the bathers in the blue sea of Tel Aviv, while a red canvas of meat looms above them. Unnecessary death, the image tells us, is not only the fate of soldiers in Training Base 4 of 1955, in the Suez

Canal fortifications of 1973, in Beaufort of 2000, in the occupied territories and at the checkpoints. The yet unseared meat also threatens the city of pleasures, threatens us all. And in the meantime, under the bleeding meat's shadow, we live our lives. Lives of war and peace.

Appendix:
Novels Analyzed in War Lives

Notes

Bibliography

Appendix
Novels Analyzed in War Lives

Agnon, Shmuel Yosef. *To This Day*. Translated by Hillel Halkin. London: Toby Press, 2009.

Amichai, Yehuda. *Lo Meakhshav, Lo Mikkan* [Not of This Time, Not of This Place]. Tel Aviv: Schocken, 1963 [Hebrew].

Amir, Eli. *Yasmine*. Translated by Yael Lotan. London: Halban, 2012.

Bartov, Hanoch. *The Brigade*. Translated by D. S. Segal. Philadelphia, PA: Jewish Publication Society, 1968.

Grossman, David. *To the End of the Land*. Translated by Jessica Cohen. New York: Vintage International, 2010.

Kenaz, Yehoshua. *Infiltration*. Translated by Dalya Bilu. South Royalton, VT: Steerforth Press, 2003.

Leshem, Ron. *Beaufort*. Translated by Evan Fallenberg. New York: Bantam Dell, 2008.

Michael, Sami. *Yonim Be-Trafalgar* [Pigeons at Trafalgar Square]. Tel Aviv: Am Oved, 2005. [Hebrew].

Oz, Amos. *My Michael*. Translated by Nicholas de Lange in collaboration with the author. London: Vintage, 1991.

Yehoshua, Abraham B. *Friendly Fire: A Duet*. Translated by Stuart Schoffman. London: Halban, 2008.

Notes

Introduction

1. Ron Leshem, *Beaufort*, trans. Evan Fallenberg (New York: Bantam Dell, 2008).

2. Ron Leshem, "Paper Soldier," [Hebrew] *Steimatzky Magazine*, Spring 2007, 8. The Yom Kippur War is the common Hebrew title for the October 1973 conflict between Israel and an Arab coalition of neighboring states, directed by Egypt and Syria. The Lebanon War began in June 1982. Both events are considered turning points in Israeli history and public perception of war, signaling the end of post-1967 triumphalism.

3. Hanoch Bartov, *The Brigade*, trans. D. S. Segal (Philadelphia, PA: Jewish Publication Society, 1968); S. Yizhar, *Yemei Ziklag* [Hebrew], [Days of Ziklag], (Tel Aviv: Am Oved, 1958); Yehoshua Kenaz, *Infiltration*, trans. Dalya Bilu (South Royalton, VT: Steerforth Press, 2003); Amos Oz, *My Michael*, trans. Nicholas de Lange in collaboration with the author (London: Vintage, 1991); Eli Amir, *Yasmine*, trans. Yael Lotan (London: Halban, 2012); Sami Michael, *Refuge: A Novel*, trans. Edward Grossman (Philadelphia, PA: Jewish Publication Society, 1988); David Grossman, *To the End of the Land*, trans. Jessica Cohen (New York: Vintage International, 2010); Eshkol Nevo, *Neuland*, trans. Sondra Silverstone (London: Vintage, 2016).

4. David Grossman, *See Under: Love*, trans. Betsy Rosenberg (London: J. Cape, 1990), 458. Translation altered.

5. Yoram Eshet-Alkalai, *A Soldier Returns Home*, trans. Jessica Cohen (eBookPro Publishing, 2019).

6. Sami Michael, *Pigeons at Trafalgar Square* [Hebrew] (Tel Aviv: Am Oved, 2005). Cited translations by Orr Scharf.

7. The English version of this novel—*Not of This Time, Not of This Place*, trans. Shlomo Katz (New York: Harper and Row, 1968)—is extensively abridged. Therefore, *War Lives* contains adaptations and translations from Amichai's Hebrew original: *Lo Meakhshav, Lo Mikkan* (Tel Aviv: Schocken, 1963). Page numbers refer to the Hebrew edition.

8. Dana Olmert, *A Barricade of Mothers: Mothers of Soldiers in Israeli Zionist Culture and Literature* [Hebrew] (Tel Aviv: Hakibbutz Hameuchad, 2018).

9. Olmert, *Barricade of Mothers*, 179.

10. Adia Mendelson-Maoz, *Borders, Territories, Ethics: Hebrew Literature in the Shadow of the Intifada* (West Lafayette, IN: Purdue Univ. Press, 2018).

11. Ranen Omer-Sherman and Rachel Harris, eds., *Narratives of Dissent: War in Contemporary Israeli Arts and Culture* (Detroit, MI: Wayne State, 2012).

12. Mendelson-Maoz, *Borders, Territories, Ethics*, 20.

13. Erich Maria Remarque, *All Quiet on the Western Front*, trans. A. W. Wheen (London: G. P. Putnam's Sons, 1929).

14. Avigdor Hameiri, *The Great Madness: The Notes of a Hebraic Officer in the Great War*, trans. Yael Lotan (Haifa: Or-Ron, 1984).

15. Avner Holtzman, *Avigdor Hameiri and War Literature* [Hebrew] (Tel Aviv: Ma'arachot, 1986), 92–94.

16. Holtzman, *Avigdor Hameiri*, 20.

17. Irène Némirovsky, *Suite Française*, trans. Sandra Smith (New York, Vintage, 2007). In her preface to the French edition, author, biographer, and Némirovsky's close friend Denise Epstein stresses that the novel is a masterpiece showcasing in real time France's acceptance of humiliation, persecution, and massacre (Némirovsky, *Suite Française*, 427).

18. Antoine de Saint-Exupéry, *Flight to Arras*, trans. Lewis Galantiere (New York: Harcourt, 1942).

19. Giddon Ticotsky, "Afterword," in Antoine de Saint-Exupéry, *Flight to Arras / Letter to a Hostage*, trans. Giddon Ticotsky (Tel Aviv: Sifriyat Poalim, 2009), 190.

20. Nitza Priluk, "A Jewish Soldier in the Kaiser's Army Writes from the Front 1914–1916" [Hebrew] in *Yedda-Am: A Stage for Jewish Folklore* 40–41, no. 75–76 (2015): 149–67.

21. The work was published in 1929 and by the end of that year it reached the shelves of about a million readers in Germany and another million in the United States, Britain, and France. Close to the Great War's centenary, the novel was republished in revised editions around the world, including in Israel.

22. S. Y. Agnon, *To This Day*, trans. Hillel Halkin (London: The Toby Press, 2009).

23. Yoram Kaniuk, *1948*, trans. Anthony Borris (New York: NYRB Lit, 2012).

24. Kaniuk, *1948*.

25. On "The Covering of the Blood, or At the Same Time," see the third chapter of Nitza Ben-Dov, *And It Is Your Praise: Studies in the Works of S. Y. Agnon, A. B. Yehoshua and Amos Oz* [Hebrew: *Ve-Hi Tehilatekha*] (Tel Aviv: Schocken, 2006).

26. Yehudit Hendel, *The Mountain of Losses* [Hebrew] (Tel Aviv: New Library, 1991). Cited translations by Orr Scharf.

27. A. B. Yehoshua, *Mr. Mani*, trans. Hillel Halkin (San Diego, CA: Harcourt, Brace and Company, 1993).

28. Zeruya Shalev, *Pain* (Jerusalem: Keter, 2015). English translations courtesy of the author. Page numbers refer to Hebrew edition.

29. All translations of Biblical verses are by Robert Alter, here from *The Wisdom Books: Job, Proverbs and Ecclesiastes. Translation with Commentary* (New York: W. W. Norton, 2011).

30. Robert Alter, *Ancient Israel. The Former Prophets: Joshua, Judges, Samuel and Kings: A Translation with Commentary* (New York: W. W. Norton, 2014).

31. A. B. Yehoshua, *Friendly Fire: A Duet*, trans. Stuart Schoffman (Orlando, FL: Harcourt, Inc., 2008).

32. William Whiston's 1736 translation of Josephus's works was hailed as the most popular book after the Bible (Old and New Testaments) in Protestant England. See Lisa Ullmann, "Foreword," [Hebrew] in Flavius Josephus, *History of the Jewish War against the Romans*, trans. Lisa Ullmann, ed. Israel Shatzmann (Jerusalem: Carmel, 2009), 17.

33. "But if anyone makes an unjust accusation against us, when we speak so passionately about the tyrants, or the robbers, or sorely bewail the misfortunes of our country, let him indulge my affections herein, though it be against the rules for writing history . . ." Flavius Josephus, "Preface," *War of the Jews* 4:11, in *The New Complete Works of Josephus*, trans. William Whiston (Grand Rapids, MI: Kregel, 1999), 668. In addition, the ornate speeches made by some of Josephus's protagonists, including the speech of King Agrippa at the eve of the war and the speeches of Eleazar Ben Yair on Masada, were inventions of Josephus the historian (Jonathan Price, "Introduction," in Flavius Josephus, *History of the Jewish War against the Romans*, trans. Lisa Ullmann, ed. Israel Shatzmann (Jerusalem: Carmel, 2009), 59). This rhetorical-literary device attests to the added artistic-psychological dimension of historical works.

34. Ullman, "Foreword," 15.

35. Ullman, "Foreword," 7.

36. Price, "Introduction," 58.

37. Sigmund Freud, *Introductory Lectures on Psychoanalysis*, trans. James Strachey, eds. James Strachey and Angela Richards (London: Penguin, 1991), 179.

38. Agnon, *To This Day*.

39. On Agnon's dream about returning from the war and encountering himself, see Nitza Ben-Dov, *Agnon's Art of Indirection: Uncovering Latent Content in the Fiction of S. Y. Agnon* (Leiden: E. J. Brill, 1993), 43–49. See also Nitza Ben-Dov, *Unhappy/Unapproved Loves: Erotic Frustration, Art, and Death in Agnon's Fiction* [Hebrew] (Tel Aviv: Am Oved, 1997), 57–70. On the reordering of letters to create the words "dream" (*halom*), bread (*lehem*), war (*milhamah*) before falling asleep, see Ben-Dov, *Unhappy/Unapproved Loves*, 109–11.

40. Remarque, *All Quiet on the Western Front*.

41. A. B. Yehoshua, *The Lover*, trans. Philip Simpson (Orlando, FL: Harcourt, 1993).

42. Hendel, *Mountain of Losses*, 77.

43. Leshem, *Beaufort*.

44. Holtzman, *Avigdor Hameiri*, 7.

45. Holtzman, *Avigdor Hameiri*, 39. Indeed, Hameiri's *The Great Madness* was published in 1929 concurrently with Remarque's *All Quiet on the Western Front*. For his part, however, Hameiri firmly insisted that he wrote his book long before his German counterpart. See Holtzman, *Avigdor Hameiri*, 43–46.

46. Reuveni enjoyed a brief wave of renewed appreciation in the wake of a revised edition of his trilogy *All the Way to Jerusalem*, edited by Yigal Schwartz, who also wrote an afterword. See Chamutal Bar Yosef, *The Heksherim Lexicon of Israeli Authors* [Hebrew], ed. Zissi Stavi and Yigal Schwartz (Beersheba: Ben-Gurion University, 2014), 833.

47. In his article "The Jewish Author Who Dipped His Pen in His Own Blood" [Hebrew] (*Odyssey Magazine* July 2014, an issue dedicated to the First World War centenary), Assaf Mond writes: "Thanks to *All Quiet on the Western Front*, the war had transformed from an event that begs repression into an alluringly marketable product—and the ripples of the wave that had washed over Europe had reached the Mediterranean shores of Palestine. As Ya'akov Horowitz set to work on a Hebrew version of Remarque's bestseller for the Stybel publishing house, while international interest in combat soldier war memories was at its peak, Hameiri submitted his manuscript to Mitzpe Publishers." In his article, Mond cites journalist Uri Keisari's comparison of the two pacifist bestselling novels: "In May–July 1929, I was in Europe. On ships at sea, on trains on land; at French, Belgian, Swiss border crossings; in offices, halls, bars, restaurants, cafés, everywhere, on every corner, in every hand: *All Quiet on the Western Front*. Fatalistically, this book would appear wherever one went, like the plague, a ghost that moves from one place to another. Eight people sitting in a train car. Seven of them are reading a book. All seven books are *All Quiet on the Western Front*. On a smaller scale, the same is happening to us here, now. *The Great Madness* is in every hand. On the beach, in damsels' hands. In school corridors, in students' hands. On the train, in workers' hands. In the city, rural community, village. At home, out and about—*The Great Madness*."

48. Shlomo Pappirblat, *Kavim Shel Aysh* [Lines of Fire], *Galleria* supplement [Hebrew], *Haaretz*, July 8, 2015.

49. Bartov, *The Brigade*.

50. From "Dew of Vengeance," (composed late 1944), in Amir Gilboa, *Hineh Yamim Ba'im: Shirim 1942–1946* [Hebrew], eds. Hagit Halperin and Ilan Berkovich (Tel Aviv: Hakibbutz Hameuchad, 2007), 146. Translated here by Orr Scharf.

51. Yehuda Amichai, "Bifurcated Soul" [Hebrew], *Yedioth Ahronoth*, Friday, December 26, 1997. Poem translation: "Rain Falls on the Faces of My Friends," trans. Robert Alter, in Robert Alter, ed., *The Poetry of Yehuda Amichai* (New York: Farrar, Straus and Giroux, 2015), 10.

52. Amichai, "Bifurcated Soul."

53. Alter, "Introduction," *Poetry of Yehuda Amichai*, xvii.

54. Motti Golani, *Wars Don't Just Happen: On Memory, Force, and Choice* [Hebrew] (Ben Shemen: Modan, 2002), 171.

55. See the chapter "Farewell to Uri" in Golani, *Wars Don't Just Happen*, especially page 77.

56. Alan Paton, *Cry, the Beloved Country* (Middlesex, UK: Penguin Books, 1959), 72.

57. Oz, *My Michael*.

58. Amir Oren, "David's Sling," [Hebrew] *Haaretz*, March 16, 2014. Motti Golani writes about the initiative to start the 1956 war in his two books (both published in Hebrew): *There Will be War Next Summer: Israel on the Road to the Sinai Campaign—The Path to War* (Tel Aviv: Ma'arachot, 1997); and *Wars Don't Just Happen*, 173–84.

59. See Nitza Ben-Dov, *Written Lives: On Israeli Literary Autobiographies* (Tel Aviv: Schocken, 2011), in the chapter "This Is an Illusion, Not a City: City and Woman in *My Michael*," 109–19, especially 111.

60. For example: in one of the novel's most sarcastic passages, Michael's four aunts, who had raised him after his mother's death, come from Tel Aviv to visit him in Jerusalem. Mesmerized by their nephew's academic success, the aunts praise his decision to give up kibbutz life in favor of an academic career, telling his wife: "You should be glowing with pride at his success. I still remember how Micha's friends made fun of him after the War of Independence for not going off with them like a numbskull to some kibbutz in the Negev. Instead, he sensibly chose to go to Jerusalem to study at the university, and to serve his people and his country with his brains, with his talents, and not with his muscles like a beast of burden" (112–13). Upon hearing the aunts' chatter, Hannah is not filled with pride, but rather with contempt.

61. Eli Amir, *Yasmine*, trans. Yael Lotan (London: Halban, 2012).

62. *Ma'ariv*, June 16, 1967. The article was included in Natan Alterman, *The Triangular Thread: Essays 1967–1970* [Hebrew], redacted by Menachem Dorman (Tel Aviv: Hakibbutz Hameuchad, 1971), 38–43. The essay is available online.

63. Yehoshua, *The Lover*.

64. Yitzhak Ben-Ner, *Rustic Sunset and Other Stories*, trans. Robert Whitehill (Boulder, CO: Lynne Rienner, 1998).

65. Amos Oz, *To Know a Woman*, trans. Nicholas de Lange (New York: Harcourt Brace Jovanovich, 1991).

66. Avner Holtzman, "Scars of Fire: Forty Years of Writing on the Yom Kippur War," *OT: A Journal of Literary Criticism and Theory* 4 [Hebrew] (2014): 43–74.

67. Holtzman, "Scars of Fire," 60.

68. Gideon Avital-Eppstein, *The Yom Kippur War, 1973: A Battle Over the Collective Memory—A Never-Ending War* [Hebrew] (Jerusalem: Schocken, 2013), 124.

69. An exceptional representation of the war is found in Tiki Vidas, *Voices that Never Leave Me* [Hebrew] (Tel Aviv: Ma'ariv, 2004). And see Gideon Avital-Eppstein's analysis of this work, 130–33.

70. Avital-Eppstein, *Yom Kippur War*, 26.

71. An email Shalev wrote to me on December 12, 2014, in reply to my email of the same date.

72. I keep the correspondence with Prof. Gabriela Shalev and David Grossman. Grossman's letter is handwritten, a rare commodity in the age of email and the internet. After telling me that Shaul's bravery had found its way into the pages of Grossman's novel and became literary material, Shalev gave me a copy of Shaul's commemorative book, which contains moving documentation of the "beautiful, short life" of her husband.

73. Michael, *Pigeons at Trafalgar Square*. Cited translations by Orr Scharf.

74. Ron Leshem, "Life on Paper" [Hebrew], *Steimatzky Magazine*, Spring 2007.

75. On the stream of consciousness in *Days of Ziklag* and on the novel's realism and other matters, see Gidi Nevo, *Seven Days in the Negev: S. Yitzhar's Days of Ziklag* [Hebrew] (Tel Aviv: Hakibbutz Hameuchad and the Ben-Gurion Research Institute for the Study of Israel and Zionism, 2005).

76. Baxtin argues that in the literary and artistic chronotopes, the outlines of time and space merge to perfection. The chronotopes include those of "path," "castle," "drawing room," etc. Mikhail Baxtin and Wendy Rosslyn, "The Forms of Time and the Chronotopes in the Novel," *PTL: A Journal for Descriptive Poetics and Theory* 3 (1978): 493–528.

77. Avi Ma'apil, *The Shaping of Reality in S. Yizhar's Prose* [Hebrew] (Hebrew University of Jerusalem: Doctoral Dissertation, 1988).

78. *Days of Ziklag* was first published in 1958 by Am Oved in two volumes. In 1989, it was published by Zmora Bitan in two volumes and contained 1,156 pages. In 1996, Ohad Zmora published at his own initiative a festive edition in honor of Yizhar's eightieth birthday, of which five hundred numbered copies were printed. In this special edition, *Days of Ziklag* spreads across three volumes and 1,555 pages.

79. Aristotle, *Poetics*, 1451b [opening of Chapter IX], *Aristotle in 23 Volumes, Vol. 23*, trans. W. H. Fyfe (Cambridge, MA: Harvard Univ. Press, 1932).

80. Gidi Nevo, *Seven Days in the Negev: S. Yitzhar's Days of Ziklag* (Tel Aviv: Hakibbutz Hameuchad and the Ben-Gurion Research Institute for the Study of Israel and Zionism, 2005), 173–84.

81. The phrase "accursed mountain" (*har haqlala* in Hebrew) is fraught with meaning, not least because of its origin in Deuteronomy 11:29 ("I shall set the blessing on Mount Gerizim and the curse on Mount Ebal"). The English translation of *Beaufort* omits the line containing this phrase in the Hebrew novel. Leshem used this phrase for the title of his first foray into the story of Beaufort in the weekend supplement of the *Yedioth Ahronoth* daily (May 11, 2001), but the phrase was also used in reference to the *Gladiola* outpost on Mount Dov (Amir Buhbut, "A Peek at the IDF's Most Dangerous Outpost" [Hebrew], *Walla! News*, September 5, 2013, https://news.walla.co.il/item/2681163, accessed June 25, 2022.

82. See his article "Negating the Akedah by Actualizing It" in *In the Opposite Direction: A Collection of Studies on Mr. Mani by A. B. Yehoshua*, edited with an introduction by Nitza Ben-Dov [Hebrew] (Tel Aviv: Hakibbutz Hameuchad, 1995), 394–98.

83. Virginia Woolf, *Three Guineas* (Oxford: Blackwell, 2012), 6.

1. Only Sons and Bereavement in S. Y. Agnon's *To This Day*

1. Quotes from Agnon's novel are taken from S. Y. Agnon, *To This Day*, trans. Hillel Halkin (London: The Toby Press, 2009).

2. Haim Be'er, who discusses *To This Day* in his book *Rooms Full of Books* [*Hadarim Meleim Sefarim*] (published in Hebrew in 2016), suggests that Mittel's character is based on the bibliographer William Ze'ev Zeitlin (1850–1921). Be'er, 67–76.

3. I have slightly amended the translation here. Halkin's translation does not include some of the references to "war"—which are significant for my interpretation.

4. Schimmermann, a wealthy and boastful arms dealer, serves in *To This Day* as the prototype of the militaristic Germans of World War I: "Schimmermann senior was known to me only by hearsay and from the photographs and caricatures of him in the newspapers. That evening I was introduced to him in person. A quick mind and ready conversationalist, he was also a big eater, drinker and smoker whose cigar never left his mouth after dinner. At first he talked about the 1870 Franco-Prussian War, which was an idyll compared to the current war" (63).

5. "In a certain sense," Haim Be'er writes in his book (see note 2) on *To This Day*, "Agnon not only examines the experience of the First World War from a post-WWII perspective, but the opposite: He examines the Second World War experience through the First [World War]."

2. Vengeance or Salvation? The Tragic Dilemma in Hanoch Bartov's *The Brigade*

1. Hanoch Bartov, *The Brigade* (Tel Aviv: Am Oved, 1965, and Hakibbutz Hameuchad, 2011). Citations from the novel are from the English translation, *The Brigade*, trans. D. S. Segal (Philadelphia, PA: Jewish Publication Society, 1968).

2. Avner Holtzman, "Afterword," [Hebrew], in *The Brigade* (Tel Aviv: Hakibbutz Hameuchad, 2011), 250. Republished in his *Hanoch Bartov's Art of the Narrative*, chapter 6: "Write That We Remained Jews" [Hebrew] (Jerusalem: Bialik Institute, 2015), 121–39.

3. On autobiographical novels, see Ben-Dov, *Written Lives*. Quite a few novels can belong to both genres at the same time: Yoram Kaniuk's *1948*; Sami Michael's *Refuge* (which details the first three days of the Yom Kippur War and more; see *Written Lives*, 145–56); Amos Oz's *My Michael* (discussed here, chapter 5, and in *Written Lives*, 109–19),

a novel that takes place against the backdrop of the Sinai War; *Infiltration*, a novel about boot camp at Training Camp 4 of the IDF in 1955, whose linkage to the life of its author, Yehoshua Kenaz, is well known (here, chapter 4); and Eli Amir's *Yasmine*, a novel focusing on the encounter between Jews and Arabs in East Jerusalem after the Six-Day War (here, chapter 6). The autobiographical elements of *Yasmine* are conspicuous: Even the protagonist's last name, Amar, is almost the same as the author's last name: Amir. Army and wars, it turns out, are an inseparable part of every Israeli, including the writers who tend to write about themselves.

4. In the section "Story Time and Narrative Time," I address the perspective Bartov acquired in the twenty years that lapsed between the time of the novel's events ("story time"), the summer months of 1945, and the time of recording them in writing, 1965, and how this narration time finds its way into the novel itself.

5. In the chapter "A Hebrew Youth in the Land of the Holocaust" in his *Roots on the Treetop* [Hebrew] (Tel Aviv: Aleph Publishers Ltd., 1969), Mordechai Avishai devotes six pages to the novel (137–42), but only a single sentence to the subject of vengeance (141–42). In contrast, Moshe Gil, who published a relatively comprehensive critical study of *The Brigade* shortly after the novel's publication (*Moznayim* Vol. 23, Iyar 1965, republished in his *Selected Essays*, Jerusalem: Rubin Mass, 1970, 200–7), devotes one and a half pages to vengeance (206–7), considering it a major theme in the work. According to Gil, vengeance led Elisha Kruk, the narrator-protagonist, to suffer "one of the most severe and agonizing growing pains. All of the ambivalence that marks many notions of man, the phenomenon of 'opposites' and 'conflicts,' the rift between spontaneous drive and rational consideration—all are expressed in the problematic nature of vengeance, its meaning, its possibility, its purpose" (206). In his *Hurban: Responses to Catastrophe in Hebrew Literature* (New York: Columbia Univ. Press, 1985), Alan Mintz devotes four pages (244–48) to *The Brigade*, noting that "Bartov makes the dramatic kernel of his novel the debates among the soldiers about the ethics of revenge" (246). I elaborate on this later.

6. Ziva Shamir, in her article on *Whose Little Boy Are You?* ("Truth from the Land of Israel," *Gag: Magazine of Literature* 22 (Summer 2010) [Hebrew]: 90–95), argues that contrary to American-Jewish literature, where the "Jewish mother" plays a starring role, ad nauseam, she receives scant mention in Hebrew literature of the 1948 generation. Bartov was the first to give this character a place of honor, paving the way for younger authors like Haim Be'er and David Grossman.

7. Hanoch Bartov, *Whose Little Boy Are You?* trans. Hillel Halkin (Philadelphia, PA: Jewish Publication Society, 1978).

8. Hanoch Bartov, *Halfway Out* [Hebrew: *Regel Ahat Bahutz*] (Tel Aviv: Am Oved, 1999), 175.

9. Holtzman, "Afterword," *The Brigade*, 251.

10. Eli Eshed, "The Ultimate Hebrew Stalag" [Hebrew], *Time Out—Tel Aviv*, issue 388, April 12, 2010, 115.

11. Eli Eshed, *From Tarzan to Zbeng: The Story of Hebrew Pulp Literature* [Hebrew] (Tel Aviv: Bavel Publishing, 2002), from 226 on.

12. See Nitza Ben-Dov, "Sparta's Lost Children: On the Role of Place in the Work of Yehoshua Kenaz and in *Infiltration*" [Hebrew], *Alei Siach* 33 (1993), 113–19.

13. In *Written Lives*, I discuss the psychological-archetypal burden that Amos Oz carries, instilled in him by his parents. Therefore, forests, snow, and meadows in his work are a synecdoche for Europe (see the chapter "Amos Oz—Landscapes of his Soul," 97–108). While Oz "dresses" the Land of Israel with European landscapes, Hanoch Bartov reaches the heart of those very vistas in the flesh, feeling that he is walking in a dream.

14. A soldier's ID number is significant in army and war literature. The number is identity. In *Infiltration*, there is an anti-hero nicknamed Zero-Zero because his military ID number ends in two zeroes. The fact that only one digit separates Hershler and the narrator represents their psychological or ideological affinity.

15. During a visit to Hanoch Bartov at Ichilov Hospital on October 7, 2013, after he broke his hip and suffered many other ailments, but was completely lucid; as usual, an indomitable repository of memories, humorous and open to discuss anything, he told me he named this character Bubi because of his good looks—he had a "baby face."

16. In that same conversation (see previous note), Bartov told me that Tamari is Mordechai (Motke) Hadash, the son of one of the founding families of the Kinneret commune.

17. Mikhail Bakhtin, "Discourse in the Novel," *The Dialogic Imagination*, trans. Caryl Emerson and Michael Holquist, ed. Michael Holquist (Austin: Univ. of Texas Press, 1981, italics in Bakhtin's essay), 332.

18. Carl G. Jung, *Dreams*, trans. R. F. C. Hull (London: Routledge, 2002), 65.

19. Jung, *Dreams*, 40. It is important to note, however, that while Jung accepts Freud's observation as "basically correct," he criticizes it for being too narrow.

3. The Vengeance of the Skull in Yehuda Amichai's *Not of This Time, Not of This Place*

1. The term *Wirtschaftswunder* ("economic miracle"), also known as the miracle on the Rhine, describes the rapid reconstruction and development of the economies of West Germany and Austria after World War II (adopting an ordoliberal social market economy).

2. There is an abridged English version of this novel, *Not of This Time, Not of This Place*, trans. Shlomo Katz (New York: Harper and Row, 1968), but the translations here are by Robert Alter (who translated this chapter of *War Lives*). The page numbers refer to the Hebrew edition of Amichai's book: *Lo Meakhshav, Lo Mikkan* (Tel Aviv: Schocken, 1963).

3. Nili Scharf Gold, *Yehuda Amichai: The Making of Israel's National Poet* (Waltham, MA: Brandeis Univ. Press, 2008), 62–88.

4. S. Y. Agnon, *A Guest for the Night*, trans. Misha Louvish (New York: Schocken, 1968). The novel was originally published in 1939.

4. Abjection, Camaraderie, and Passion in Yehoshua Kenaz's *Infiltration*

1. Yehoshua Kenaz, *Infiltration*, trans. Dalya Bilu (South Royalton, VT: Steerforth Press, 2003).

2. Michael Gluzman, in a chapter entitled "Forced Masculinity in *Infiltration*," in his book *The Zionist Body: Nationalism, Gender, and Sexuality in Modern Hebrew Literature* [Hebrew] (Tel Aviv: Hakibbutz Hameuchad, 2007), 222, notes two perspectives through which the military experience is described in the novel: from the perspective of the early 1960s, when younger writers who came of age in sovereign Israel treated the militaristic ideals of the Palmach generation with skepticism, alienation, and parody; and from the perspective of the 1980s, a period when the melting pot gave way to the politics of identities.

3. The four stories in the collection are: "The Three-Legged Chicken," on early childhood; "Henrik's Secret," on later childhood; "Musical Moment" (also the name of the collection), where the narrator is on the threshold of adolescence; and "Between Night and Dawn," in which the Kenazi "self" is in the last year of high school, setting off with his friends to a Gadna camp for pre-army training.

4. See Ben-Dov, *Written Lives*.

5. Hanna Herzig, in her book *The Voice Saying I: Trends in Israeli Prose Fiction of the 1980s* [Hebrew] (Ra'anana: Open University, 1998), 51, argues that Kenaz's choice of the "unchosen" as the representatives of young Israeliness brings into sharper focus the unresolved problems of the military and social ethos. Herzig writes (205): "The choice of basic training and the army—among the cornerstones of the Israeli ethos—allows us to examine the individuals within the togetherness, from both the social side and the personal-psychological side, in conditions of ordeals, crowdedness, and a need to survive."

6. Julia Kristeva, *Powers of Horror: An Essay on Abjection*, trans. Leon S. Roudiez (New York: Columbia Univ. Press, 1982), 140.

7. Kristeva, *Powers of Horror*, 140–41.

8. On Kenaz's extended family, see Nitza Ben-Dov, "Sparta's Lost Children: On the Role of Place in the Work of Yehoshua Kenaz and in *Infiltration*," *Alei Siah* 33 (1993), 113–19 [Hebrew].

9. Amos Harel, *Every Hebrew Mother Should Know: A Portrait of the New IDF* [Hebrew] (Or Yehuda: Kinneret, Zmora-Bitan, 2013), 23.

10. Harel, *Every Hebrew Mother Should Know*, 84.

11. Dan Margalit, *Commando Unit 101* [Hebrew] (Tel Aviv: Moked, 1968), 25, 29.

12. Margalit, *Commando Unit 101*, 32.

13. I would not call the first chapter of *Infiltration* an exposition or prologue. In my opinion, the novel starts with a distinct scene—that is, with an incident (silencing a sentry) in which most of the basic trainees, the heroes of the novel, are introduced; some of them will become central protagonists, while others will remain secondary or marginal. In this chapter, we also find an initial description of the abusive instructor, the one who ultimately defeats Alon, who watches the basic trainees in the platoon with an "impatient, scornful expression on his face" (19).

14. Flavius Josephus, *The Jewish War* (London: Penguin Books, 1959), 362.

15. Josephus, *The Jewish War*, 362.

16. Amikam Elad writes in his article "The Coastal Cities of Palestine During the Early Middle Ages" (*The Jerusalem Cathedra*, Vol. II, 1982, 146–67) that Muslim traditions developed around the year 690 extolling the coastal cities of the Land of Israel. The Islamic praise literature (*fada'il*) promises paradise to those who settle in these cities. Acre and Caesarea are among the cities mentioned, but the primary emphasis and highest praise is reserved for Asqalan (Ashkelon).

5. Dream and Illness in Amos Oz's *My Michael*

1. Amos Oz, *My Michael*, trans. Nicholas de Lange in collaboration with the author (London: Vintage, 1991). All quotations from the novel are from the English translation by Nicholas de Lange in collaboration with the author, first published in London by Chatto and Windus in 1972, and in paperback in New York by Bantam Books in 1976. Oz completed writing *My Michael* in May 1967, about one month before the Six-Day War, and the novel debuted in Hebrew in 1968.

2. The civil war between North and South Korea broke out in June 1950 and ended in a stalemate and armistice in July 1953. Following the Israeli-Arab armistice in 1949, Arab infiltrators from Egypt and the Gaza Strip attacked Israeli settlements in the Negev.

3. Nurit Gertz, *Israeli Prose Fiction in the 1960s*, Units 4–5 (Tel Aviv: The Open University, 1982), 20 [Hebrew].

4. Kadishman's prophecy is indeed fulfilled, but only eleven years later, in the 1967 Six-Day War.

5. For Oz's readers, the great loss of life in the Korean War (about 1.2 million people) and the partitioning of the Korean peninsula, which is still a source of conflict, recall Israel's War of Independence, armistice line, and ongoing conflict with the Arabs.

6. Matzah is replaced by "cookies" in the English translation.

7. Yehoshua Kenaz, in his novel *Infiltration* set in 1955 (chapter 4 in this book), describes how prestigious it was for men of that generation to serve in the paratroops. Israel launched the Sinai War on October 29, 1956, in coordination with the British and the French, while the Americans were caught up in the presidential election, and the Soviet Union had just invaded Hungary to suppress a rebellion.

8. In the aftermath of the Sinai War, the reelected president, Dwight D. Eisenhower, and his secretary of state, John Foster Dulles, humiliated Britain and France, and demanded that Israeli forces leave the conquered territory in the Sinai.

9. Michael Strogoff is the hero in Jules Verne's novel, *Michael Strogoff: The Courier of the Czar* (1876), a romantic-thriller. In his novel, Verne transforms historical figures into figures engaged in fantastical adventures as "romantic" heroes.

6. Language Barriers, Roadblocks, and Frustrated Love in Eli Amir's *Yasmine*

1. Originally published in Hebrew under the title *Yasmine* (Tel Aviv: Am Oved Publishers, 2005). Copyright © 2005 by Eli Amir. Translation Copyright © 2012 by the Estate of Yael Lotan.

2. Nuri describes the "minister in charge" as a cabinet minister, who did not have a specific portfolio but was an adviser to the prime minister. Eli Amir, *Yasmine*, trans. Yael Lotan (London: Halban, 2012), 54; based on *Yasmine* [Hebrew edition] (Tel Aviv: Am Oved, 2005), 60. All English translations, unless otherwise noted, are from the above edition. Hereafter, page numbers for the English translation are noted in parentheses in the body of the chapter. Amir mentions a few public leaders who served during the Six-Day War, and we may assume that Yisrael Galili, the influential "minister without portfolio," was in his mind when he designed the character of Nuri's superior.

3. It is important to note that throughout the novel, the War of Independence is referred to as the '48 War, a testament to Amir's effort to alternate between the Israeli and the Arab point of view. Even the Western Wall, the conquest of which is described from a two-sided Arab perspective (see below) is called by Amir the "Jews' Wall."

4. In giving his novel a woman's name, Eli Amir seems to be following Gustave Flaubert in *Emma Bovary* (1856), Leo Tolstoy in *Anna Karenina* (1873–77), and Theodor Fontane in *Effi Briest* (1895). In these novels, the heroine aspires to find a romantic and powerful man to enrich her life, but her quest is frustrated and ends in suicide. Amos Oz, in *My Michael*, creates Hannah Gonen as his narrator-protagonist as a similar aspirant, but entitles his novel after her husband, the source of her frustration. However, Amir's *Yasmine* is the antithesis of these suicidal women. She is an educated woman, an opinionated fighter, who would sooner put an end to her love than to her life.

5. The actual quotation is from Frantz Fanon, *Black Skin, White Masks* (1952), ed. Charles L. Markmann (London: Pluto Press, 2008), 8: "To speak means to be in a position to use a certain syntax, to grasp the morphology of this or that language, but it means above all to assume a culture, to support the weight of a civilization." Fanon (1925–61) was an Afro-Caribbean psychiatrist, philosopher, and revolutionary writer, who had been a member of the National Liberation Front (FLN) of Algeria, and who resided in Paris during the same period as Amir's fictional character Yasmine, prior to her return home to her family.

6. Intertextuality in this novel focuses on "strong texts," both ancient and modern. Sometimes the allusion is quiet and subversive; other times, it is open and declarative. The reader plays an important role in realizing and interpreting these two-way intertextual processes. See Chana Kronfeld, "Intertextual Agency" in *Intertextuality in Literature and Culture: A Festschrift for Ziva Ben-Porat*, Michael Gluzman and Orly Lubin, eds. [Hebrew] (Tel Aviv: Porter Institute for Poetics and Semiotics and Hakibbutz Hameuchad Press, 2011), 11–57.

7. Haim Nahman Bialik, "Yehi Helki Imakhem," 1905. http://benyehuda.org/bialik/bia089.html.

8. The Hebrew original is *"mesahek berogez im ha'ivrit,"* literally: plays angrily with Hebrew.

9. Natan Alterman, "The Silver Platter," trans. Ami Isseroff. http://zionism-israel.com/hdoc/Silver_Platter.htm.

10. The soldiers of the Iraqi delegation, who had begun to arrive in Jordan on the eve of the Six-Day War, never actually participated in the fighting. See Shimshon Yitzhaki, *Through the Eyes of the Arabs: The Six-Day War and Aftermath* [Hebrew] (Tel Aviv: Misrad Habitahon, 1969), 11–57.

11. A. B. Yehoshua, *The Liberated Bride* (Tel Aviv: Hakibbutz Hameuchad Press, 2001); trans. Hillel Halkin (London: Peter Halban Publishers Ltd., 2003).

12. Benjamin Harshav's monumental writings on the modern Jewish revolution deal with the multilingualism of Eastern European Jews, many of whom spoke six or seven languages—and in some exceptional cases, as many as thirteen. Harshav's insights can also help us understand the multilingualism of Mizrahi writers in particular and Israeli writers in general, given that the new universal language of English penetrates their writing in various ways. See Harshav, *The Bellybutton and the Globe: Multilingualism in Jewish History and in the Global Village* [Hebrew] (Tel Aviv: Hakibbutz Hameuchad and the Porter Institute for Poetics and Semiotics, 2012), 423–50.

13. During Nuri's trip back from the war, he hitches a ride to Jerusalem with a taxi driver who is ironically described quoting verses from the Bible, recounting a midrash about our exceptionalism as a people, singing, and bragging. An atmosphere of "me and no one else" arises from the words on the radio as well. Throughout the entire novel, Nuri's pain focuses on the blindness of those with official roles. Here he reflects on the words of his boss, the "minister in charge," himself a bereaved father, his son having fallen in the Sinai War: "I disliked his patronizing attitude toward the Arab population, and felt uneasy when he indulged in his grand pathos-filled visions while refusing to face reality. I wasn't willing to view the Arabs as 'our cousins who work for us,' as inferior people without ideology and dreams. I wanted to help this post-occupation population as if they were regular immigrants, destined to be our neighbors for the rest of our lives" (212).

14. The historical date and details of Nasser's speech and the Israeli response are accurate.

15. Yitzhaki, *Through the Eyes of the Arabs*, 94–97. http://www.sixdaywar.org/content/docs.asp.

16. Yehuda Amichai's novel *Not of This Time, Not of This Place* (see chapter 3) begins as follows: "The evening breeze pushed the window open and the aroma of eucalyptus in bloom flooded the room. The eucalyptus was very late blossoming in this hot summer. It had a heavy oppressive smell, the aroma of alien trees whose ancestors had been brought from Australia" (Yehuda Amichai, *Not of This Time, Not of This Place*, trans. Shlomo Katz [Tel Aviv: Schocken, 1963], 1). Amichai employs the alien eucalyptus, which was adopted by the Zionist pioneers and which lent the landscape an indigenous look, as a metonymy for the Israeli heroes who came from all parts of the world, but who pretended that they were native Israelis.

17. On the eve of the Six-Day War, the Jordanian-Egyptian defense pact was signed, and King Hussein was forced to allow Ahmed Shukeiry, his sworn enemy, and his organization, the PLO, a free hand to conduct organizational activities in Jordan. Despite his promise that he would not appear in public, Shukeiry hurried to the Old City of Jerusalem the very day he arrived in Jordan from Egypt and gave a speech before a fired-up crowd that was already celebrating their soon-to-be "victory" over Israel. Shukeiry's incendiary rhetoric amplified the tension and impatience of the crowd, to the point where it was feared that they would burst out into rioting right then and there. To Hussein's good fortune, Shukeiry did not have enough time to carry out his entire plan; the Six-Day War broke out before the PLO had completed its reorganization campaign. Shukeiry, the leader of the Palestinians, fled Jerusalem back to Jordan on the very first day of the war (Yitzhaki, *Through the Eyes of the Arabs*, 56). In *Yasmine*, the protagonist, Nuri Imari, inherits his office. At first, his lover Yasmine refuses to set foot in the office. Slowly but surely, however, she becomes accustomed to the presence of Israeli rule over a Palestinian stronghold. In this office, which essentially is Shukeiry's house, a conversation of great meaning will unfold between Nuri's proud father and Senator Antoine, who despite initial hesitation has reached the point where his enemy has become his friend.

18. Golani, *Wars Don't Just Happen*, 194.

19. In Genesis (22:1–18), Abraham was commanded by God to sacrifice his son Isaac, but that sacrifice was a test of Abraham's willingness to obey God, and the sacrifice was canceled. In Mosaic law, human sacrifices were forbidden as idolatrous Canaanite rituals. Thus, Jephthah's vow would be considered blasphemous. In the play *Agamemnon* by the Greek tragedian Aeschylus, based on the legendary curse on the House of Atreus, Agamemnon must sacrifice his daughter Iphigeneia to appease the goddess Artemis so that the Greek army can sail to Troy. This sacrifice is responsible for his own death when he returns home.

20. Agnon, *To This Day*, 86. For an analysis of this dream, see Ben-Dov, *Agnon's Art of Indirection*, 45–49. Agnon's reflective dream of the vow and the sacrifice, in which the protagonist goes out to greet himself, is surprisingly similar to Rebbe Nachman of

Bratslav's "Yom Kippur Dream." See Zvi Mark, *The Revealed and Hidden Writings of Rabbi Nachman of Bratslav* (Berlin: De Gruyter Oldenbourg, 2015), 303.

21. Albert Camus, *The Stranger*, trans. Stuart Gilbert (New York: Vintage Books, Random House, 1954), 74–76; Joseph Conrad, *Heart of Darkness*, (London: Penguin, 1995), 32.

22. In Akira Kurosawa's famous film *Rashomon* (1950), thinking about, knowing, remembering, and understanding a complex event are given contrary subjective and objective interpretations. See Robert Anderson, "The Rashomon Effect and Communication" in *Canadian Journal of Communication* 41, no. 2 (2016): 250–65.

23. In the same way that the War of Independence is not called by that name in the novel, the Farhud is not named. The Farhud was a pogrom carried out against the Jews of Baghdad on June 1–2, 1941, immediately following the British victory in the Anglo-Iraqi War and the collapse of the pro-Nazi government of Rashid Ali.

24. These words do not appear in the published English translation. See the Hebrew edition of *Yasmine*, 56.

25. Nuri is obsessed with a primitive notion of reincarnation. As a boy, he hears from an old man that when a person dies, his soul leaves his body, circles around the family, and reincarnates itself in the form of a new baby. His maternal uncle, Nuri Elias Nassah, died before he was thirty and Nuri is named for him. During the waiting period before the war, the protagonist had not yet turned thirty and as he waits, he fears that his own fate will resemble that of his uncle; this personal fear merges with the general fear of the unknown (28). Two months after the war, when he is already serving in his demanding new role, the members of the office of the Minister in Charge throw him a surprise thirtieth birthday party. Nuri is embarrassed; since his bar mitzvah, seventeen years earlier, no one had celebrated his birthday (294). The number thirty has additional significance: The lands of *Dir al-Arnab* were expropriated from Ghadir's Galilean family for thirty liras a dunam—an allusion to Judas Iscariot's betrayal of Jesus for thirty shekels.

26. After the War of Independence, Mount Scopus remained an Israeli enclave that one could only reach in a military convoy.

27. See Nitza Ben-Dov, "And She Did Not Know a Man—On the Story of Jephthah's Daughter, On the Ending of the Book of Judges, On the Ending of the Story of Saul's Daughter and Other Endings" [Hebrew], *Alei Siah* 48 (December 2002): 7–16.

28. Nine lines from Bialik's *Yehi Helki Imakhem* [Let My Lot Be With You] appear in *Yasmine*.

29. Jacqueline Amati-Mehler, Simona Argentieri, and Jorge Canestri, *The Babel of the Unconscious: Mother Tongue and Foreign Languages in the Psychoanalytic Dimension*, trans. Jill Whitelaw Cucco (Madison, CT: International Universities Press, 1993).

30. Even though the name and description of the kibbutz point to Beit Oren—"I could see Kiryat Oranim, my old kibbutz, from afar, clinging to the hillside, hugging the boulders

and the woods, firm and prosperous" (408)—Amir seems to be invoking Mishmar Ha'emek, the kibbutz where he was educated and where his Israeli identity crystalized.

31. See Ezekiel 16:1–8. [In a land filled with its enemies]: " . . . And when I [God] passed by thee [Israel] and saw thee wallowing in thy blood, I said unto thee: In thy blood, live; yea, I said unto thee: In thy blood, live; I cause thee to increase, even as the growth of the field . . . Now when I passed by thee, and looked upon thee, and behold, thy time was the time of love, I spread my skirt over thee, and covered thy nakedness; yea, I swore unto thee, and entered into a covenant with thee, saith the Lord God, and thou becamest Mine." *Tanakh: The Holy Scriptures* (Philadelphia, PA: Jewish Publication Society of America, 1985), 658.

7. The Human Voice in Inhumane Wars in David Grossman's *To the End of the Land*

1. Regarding the end of *The Disassembler*, Holtzman (2014) writes: "So, in one fell swoop, the hero's life journey as a Jew wandering the world was severed, and the reader wonders about the meaning of this ending and the special weight accorded to the war as a real and symbolic conclusion to the tortuous life story" (51).

2. Yuval Neria, *Fire* [Hebrew: *Esh*], (Tel Aviv: Zmora Bitan, 1989), 143. Neria's *Esh* is his only work of fiction. Translation mine.

3. Ben-Ner, "Nicole," 164.

4. Ben-Ner, "Nicole," 176.

5. Oz, *To Know a Woman*, 90.

6. On *To Know a Woman* by Oz, see chapter 11 in Ben-Dov, *And It Is Your Praise*, 253–66.

7. In *Written Lives*, in the chapter entitled "Haim Be'er: Strands of His Life" (120–41), I discuss the scramble of times in Be'er's autobiographical novels, *Feathers and The Pure Element of Time*, as part of his poetics (the beginning and the ending latch onto each other) and of the awareness of death infused in his work. On the novel *Feathers* and the Yom Kippur War, see 129–32.

8. Haim Be'er, *Feathers* [Hebrew: *Notzot*] (Tel Aviv: Am Oved, 2005), 247.

9. Be'er, *Feathers*, 294.

10. The IDF published a special issue of its *Bamahane* magazine to mark the twenty-fifth anniversary of the Yom Kippur War. On the cover, spread across the entire page, the following text appears in bold letters: "2,233 soldiers were killed in the Yom Kippur War. 7,251 soldiers were injured. 17 soldiers remain missing." The format itself reflects the terrible bereavement and calamity.

11. *Ethics of the Fathers* [*Pirkei Avot*] 3:15.

12. Be'er, *Feathers*, 283.

13. David Grossman, *To the End of the Land*, trans. Jessica Cohen (New York: Vintage International, 2010). 3.

14. Grossman, *To the End of the Land*, 3.

15. 1 Kings 19:12.

16. Grossman, *To the End of the Land*, 3. The tension between the signifier and the signified during the conversations is one of the novel's achievements. This tension may be described according to the theory of Ferdinand de Saussure, who distinguished between the material dimension of the linguistic sign and its meaning: Signifier is the name given to the phonic dimension of the word, or, more precisely, to the mental image of the word's sounds, for the purpose of separating it from the signified, which is the word's meaning. A signifier is, therefore, the (tonal) representation of the word without the meaning attached to it. The combination of the signifier and the signified creates the linguistic sign. See E. F. K. Koerner, *Ferdinand de Saussure: Origin and Development of His Linguistic Thought in Western Studies of Language*. Braunschweig: Friedrich Vieweg & Sohn, 1973, 1–14.

17. Some parts of the text to which I refer were cut from the final published translation. The translator, Jessica Cohen, was kind enough to provide me with her translations of the passages that did not appear in the English edition. Quotes from the unpublished translation appear here in italics.

18. As noted earlier, Ora means "light" in Hebrew.

19. The italicized lines in this paragraph do not appear in the English translation. (For the Hebrew source text, see David Grossman, *Isha Borahat Mibsora* (Tel Aviv: Hakibbutz Hameuchad, 2008), 62.

20. In his article "The Gospel of Avram" [Hebrew] (*Iton 77*, no. 332, 2008: 30–34), Amos Levitan argues that Avram is the central character, and not Ora. Levitan contends that by choosing to begin the story during the Six-Day War, Grossman "already plants the roots of the calamity in the successful war" (Levitan, 30), noting that fear for the existence of the State of Israel appears in the novel's initial pages with mention of the rumors of the Arab victory and conquest of Tel Aviv. The existential fear that is an integral part of Israel's wars continues to accompany the characters in the Yom Kippur War, as Avram asks on the two-way radio before falling captive: "Hello, Israel, homeland? Do you even exist anymore?" (*To the End of the Land*, 574).

8. Brothers in Blood in Sami Michael's *Pigeons at Trafalgar Square*

1. Ghassan Kanafani, "Returning to Haifa," in *Palestine's Children: Returning to Haifa and Other Stories*, trans. (from Arabic) Barbara Harlow and Karen E. Riley (Boulder, CO: Lynne Rienner, 2000).

2. Gérard Genette, *Palimpsests: Literature in the Second Degree*, trans. (from French) Channa Newman and Claude Doubinsky (Lincoln, NB: Univ. of Nebraska Press, 1997), 5.

3. In *Haaretz's* English edition, translated and abridged from the Hebrew, the headline read "With thanks to Ghassan Kanafani."

4. *Pigeons at Trafalgar Square* has not been published in English. The quotations here were translated by Ira Moskowitz. The page references are to the Hebrew original (*Yonim Be-Trafalgar*, Tel Aviv: Am Oved, 2005).

5. The American psychologist B. F. Skinner (1904–90) pioneered the school of radical behaviorism.

9. Soldiers in a Bubble in Ron Leshem's *Beaufort*

1. Dov Sadan, Introduction to Auerbach's Hebrew edition of *Mimesis: The Representation of Reality in Western Literature*, trans Baruch Kroh (Jerusalem: Bialik Institute, 1969), 17.

2. Quotes from Leshem's novel are taken from Ron Leshem, *Beaufort*, trans. Evan Fallenberg (New York: Bantam Dell, 2008). Excerpt(s) from *Beaufort: A Novel* by Ron Leshem, copyright © 2007 by Ron Leshem. Used by permission of Dell Publishing, an imprint of Random House, a division of Penguin Random House LLC. All rights reserved. Reprinted by permission of SLL/Sterling Lord Literistic, Inc. Copyright by Ron Leshem.

3. Quotes from Kenaz's novel are taken from Yehoshua Kenaz, *Infiltration*, trans. Dalya Bilu (South Royalton, VT: Steerforth Press, 2003).

4. Moreover, as noted in chapter 6, Abu George, the journalist and father of Yasmine, goes up to the roof in the beginning of *Yasmine* to see how far the Israelis have advanced in East Jerusalem and his view is blocked, Eli Amir writes, "by a spreading *shajarat al-yahud*, a Jews' tree—the eucalyptus."

5. Quotes from *Yasmine* are taken from Eli Amir, *Yasmine*, trans. Yael Lotan (London: Halban, 2012).

6. The English translation generally sidesteps this racially loaded word, meaning pimp in Arabic and conveying a veritable rainbow of connotations in Hebrew, mostly pejorative.

10. The Bereaved Family in A. B. Yehoshua's *Friendly Fire*

1. A. B. Yehoshua, *Friendly Fire: A Duet*, trans. Stuart Schoffman (Orlando, FL: Harcourt, Inc., 2008). Excerpts from *Friendly Fire* by A. B. Yehoshua. Copyright © 2007 by Abraham B. Yehoshua. English translation copyright © 2008 by Stuart Schoffman. Used by permission of HarperCollins Publishers.

2. On this unique breed of women in Yehoshua's late works, who are essentially variations on Mrs. Ashtor from his first short story, "The Old Man's Death," see Ben-Dov, *And It Is Your Praise*, chapters 5, 6, and 8.

3. Mordechai Shalev published his essay on "Three Days and a Child" in *Haaretz* in 1988 and continued to research the theme of the *Akedah* in later works by Yehoshua. His work was included in the volume *In the Opposite Direction (BaKivun HaNegdi): A Collection of Studies on Mr. Mani by A. B. Yehoshua*, edited by Nitza Ben-Dov [Hebrew] (Tel Aviv: Hakibbutz Hameuchad, 1995). On the *Akedah* element in Yehoshua's novel *A Journey to the End of the Millennium*, see Ben-Dov, *And It Is Your Praise*, 199–211.

4. In Ron Leshem's novel, *Beaufort* (2008), dealing with Israel's second Lebanese war, the friends of a fallen comrade play a game called: "What He Can't Do Anymore."

5. Viktor Shklovsky, "Art as a Technique" in *Literary Theory: An Anthology*, eds. Julie Rivkin and Michael Ryan (Malden: Blackwell Publishing Ltd., 1998), 16, 19.

6. Haim Nahman Bialik, "Revealment and Concealment in Language," trans. Jacob Sloan, *Commentary* 9, no. 2 (February 1950): 171–75.

7. The old man from the first floor in Yehoshua's first story, "Death of the Old Man," is buried in darkness, and the train from the early story "The Yatir Evening Express" is wrecked in a wadi on a cold night. The open-heart surgery during which Lazar, the hospital administrator in *Open Heart*, dies, is scheduled for late afternoon, a quiet time, with the intention of continuing into the evening. In *The Liberated Bride*, Prof. Carlo Tedeschi dies at night, and his funeral takes place at night. His wife reads her eulogy by the light of a small flashlight in the Sanhedria cemetery in Jerusalem. On this macabre motif, see Ben-Dov, *And It Is Your Praise*, chapter 5.

8. Roland Barthes, *Camera Lucida: Reflections on Photography*, trans. (from French) by Richard Howard (New York: Hill and Wang, 1982), 77–82.

11. Fighting Men, Adored by Women. Really?

1. In this chapter, translations of biblical verses are taken from *Tanakh: The Holy Scriptures* (Philadelphia, PA: Jewish Publication Society, 1985).

2. Karl Kraus, *Die Fackel*, no. 46, October 9, 1917 (English translation from Wikiquote).

3. Olmert, *Barricade of Mothers*.

4. Olmert, *Barricade of Mothers*, 32.

5. Quotes from Agnon's novel are taken from Agnon, *To This Day*.

6. In this chapter, the pages cited for *The Brigade* refer to the Hebrew original: Hanoch Bartov, *Pitzei Bagrut* (Tel Aviv: Hakibbutz Hameuchad, 2011).

7. Nitza Priluk, "Volunteer Women in Blue and Khaki: *Eretz-Israeli* Women in the British Army in Egypt During World War II," [Hebrew] *Et-mol* 1 (177), published by Yad Ben Zvi Institute (September 2004), 16–20.

8. Priluk, "Volunteer Women in Blue and Khaki," 17.

9. The pages cited for *Not of This Time, Not of This Place* refer to the Hebrew original.

10. Quotes from Kenaz's novel are taken from Yehoshua Kenaz, *Infiltration*, trans. Dalya Bilu (South Royalton, VT: Steerforth Press, 2003).

11. For Agnon, and not only for him, dogs have a sexual context. Tirza from *In the Prime of Her Life* gets closer to Akavia Mazal by fabricating a story about being bit by a dog, and the man called Sweet Foot from *Only Yesterday* controls and plays with dogs and women.

12. Danny Kaplan, *David, Jonathan and Other Soldiers: Identity, Masculinity and Sexuality in IDF Combat Units* [Hebrew] (Tel Aviv: Hakibbutz Hameuchad, 1999), 159.

13. Quotes from Oz's novel are taken from Amos Oz, *My Michael*, trans. Nicholas de Lange (Orlando, FL: Harcourt, 2005).

14. Quotes from Amir's novel are taken from Eli Amir, *Yasmine*, trans. Yael Lotan (London: Halban, 2012).

15. Quotes from Grossman's novel are taken from David Grossman, *To the End of the Land*, trans. Jessica Cohen (New York: Vintage Books, 2011).

16. The pages cited for *Pigeons at Trafalgar Square* refer to the Hebrew original.

Conclusion

1. Quotes from Leshem's novel are taken from Ron Leshem, *Beaufort*, trans. Evan Fallenberg (New York: Bantam Dell, 2008).

2. Mario Fortunato, *The Innocent Days of War* [Hebrew], trans. (from Italian) Saviona Mane (Tel Aviv: Matar, 2010), 41.

3. Quotes from Yehoshua's novel are taken from A. B. Yehoshua, *Friendly Fire*, trans. Stuart Schoffman (Orlando, FL: Harcourt, Inc., 2008).

Bibliography

Agnon, Shmuel Yosef. *A Guest for the Night*. Translated by Misha Louvish. New York: Schocken, 1968.
Alter, Robert. *The Poetry of Yehuda Amichai*. New York: Farrar, Straus, and Giroux, 2015.
Alter, Robert. *The Wisdom Books: Job, Proverbs and Ecclesiastes*. Translation with Commentary. New York: W. W. Norton, 2011.
Alter, Robert. *Ancient Israel. The Former Prophets: Joshua, Judges, Samuel and Kings: A Translation with Commentary*. New York: W. W. Norton, 2014.
Amati-Mehler, Jacqueline, Simona Argentieri, and Jorge Canestri. *The Babel of the Unconscious: Mother Tongue and Foreign Languages in the Psychoanalytic Dimension*. Translated by Jill Whitelaw Cucco. Madison, CT: International Universities Press, 1993.
Anderson, Robert. "The Rashomon Effect and Communication." *Canadian Journal of Communication* 41, no. 2 (2016): 250–65.
Aristotle. *Aristotle in 23 Volumes*. Vol. 23, *Poetics*. Translated by W. H. Fyfe. Cambridge, MA: Harvard Univ. Press, 1932.
Bakhtin, Mikhail. "Discourse in the Novel." In *The Dialogic Imagination: Four Essays*. Translated by Caryl Emerson and Michael Holquist. Edited by Michael Holquist, 259–422. Austin: Univ. of Texas Press, 1981.
Barthes, Roland. *Camera Lucida: Reflections on Photography*. Translated by Richard Howard. New York: Hill and Wang, 1982.
Bartov, Hanoch. *Whose Little Boy Are You?* Translated by Hillel Halkin. Philadelphia, PA: Jewish Publication Society of America, 1978.
Baxtin, M. M., and Rosslyn, Wendy. "The Forms of Time and the Chronotopos in the Novel: From the Greek Novel to Modern Fiction." *PTL: A Journal for Descriptive Poetics and Theory* 3, no. 3 (1978): 493–528.
Ben-Dov, Nitza. *Agnon's Art of Indirection: Uncovering Latent Content in the Fiction of S. Y. Agnon*. Leiden: E. J. Brill, 1993.

Ben-Dov, Nitza. "And She Did Not Know a Man—On the Story of Jephthah's Daughter, On the Ending of the Book of Judges, On the Ending of the Story of Saul's Daughter and Other Endings." *Alei Siah* 48 (December 2002): 7–16.

Ben-Dov, Nitza. "My Imaginary Offspring: Reality and Fantasy in *Days of Ziklag* by S. Yizhar and in *If There is a Heaven* by Ron Leshem." *Hebrew Studies* 50 (2009): 185–94.

Ben-Ner, Yitzhak. *Rustic Sunset & Other Stories*. Translated by Robert Whitehill. Boulder, CO: Lynne Rienner, 1998.

Bialik, Haim Nahman. "Revealment and Concealment in Language: Reflections on the Nature of Literature." Translated by Jacob Sloan. *Commentary* 9, no. 2 (February 1950): 171–75.

Camus, Albert. *The Stranger*. Translated by Stuart Gilbert. New York: Vintage Books, Random House, 1954.

Conrad, Joseph. *Heart of Darkness*. London: Penguin, 1995.

de Saint Exupery, Antoine. *Flight to Arras*. Translated by Lewis Galantiere. New York: Harcourt, 1942.

Elad, Amikam. "The Coastal Cities of Palestine During the Early Middle Ages." *The Jerusalem Cathedra*, vol. 2 (1982): 146–67.

Eshet-Alkalai, Yoram. *A Soldier Returns Home*. Translated by Jessica Cohen. [No Place of Publication]: eBookPro Publishing, 2019.

Fanon, Frantz. *Black Skin, White Masks*. Edited by Charles L. Markmann. London: Pluto Press, 2008.

Freud, Sigmund. *Introductory Lectures on Psychoanalysis*. Translated by James Strachey. Edited by James Strachey and Angela Richards. London: Penguin, 1991.

Gennete, Gérard. *Palimpsests: Literature in the Second Degree*. Translated by Channa Newman and Claude Doubinsky. Lincoln, NB: Univ. of Nebraska Press, 1977.

Gold, Nili Scharf. *Yehuda Amichai: The Making of Israel's National Poet*. Waltham, MA: Brandeis Univ. Press, 2008.

Grossman, David. *See Under: Love*. Translated by Betsy Rosenberg. London: J. Cape, 1990.

Hameiri, Avigdor. *The Great Madness: The Notes of a Hebraic Officer in the Great War*. Translated by Yael Lotan. Haifa: Or-Ron, 1984.

Josephus, Flavius. *The New Complete Works of Josephus*. Translated by William Whiston. Grand Rapids, MI: Kregel, 1999.

Josephus, Flavius. *The Jewish War.* London: Penguin Books, 1959.
Jung, Carl G. *Dreams.* Translated by R. F. C. Hull. London: Routledge, 2002.
Kanafani, Ghassan. "Returning to Haifa." In *Palestine's Children: Returning to Haifa & Other Stories.* Translated by Barbara Harlow and Karen E. Riley, 149–96. Boulder, CO: Lynne Rienner Publishers, 2000.
Kaniuk, Yoram. *1948.* Translated by Anthony Borris. New York: NYRB Lit, 2012.
Kenaz, Yehoshua. *Musical Moment.* Translated by Dalya Bilu and Betsy Rosenberg. South Royalton, VT: Steerforth Press, 1995.
Koerner, E. F. K. *Ferdinand de Saussure: Origin and Development of His Linguistic Thought in Western Studies of Language.* Braunschweig: Friedrich Vieweg & Sohn, 1973.
Kristeva, Julia. *Powers of Horror: An Essay on Abjection.* Translated by Leon S. Roudiez. New York: Columbia Univ. Press, 1982.
Mark, Zvi. *The Revealed and Hidden Writings of Rabbi Nachman of Bratslav.* Berlin: De Gruyter Oldenbourg, 2015.
Mendelson-Maoz, Adia. *Borders, Territories, Ethics: Hebrew Literature in the Shadow of the Intifada.* West Lafayette, IN: Purdue Univ. Press, 2018.
Michael, Sami. *Refuge: A Novel.* Translated by Edward Grossman. Philadelphia, PA: Jewish Publication Society, 1988.
Mintz, Alan. *Hurban: Responses to Catastrophe in Hebrew Literature.* New York: Columbia Univ. Press, 1985.
Némirovsky, Irène. *Suite Française.* Translated by Sandra Smith. New York, Vintage, 2007.
Nevo, Eshkol. *Neuland.* Translated by Sondra Silverstone. London: Vintage, 2016.
Omer-Sherman, Ranen, and Rachel Harris, eds. *Narratives of Dissent: War in Contemporary Israeli Arts and Culture.* Detroit, MI: Wayne State, 2012.
Oz, Amos. *To Know a Woman.* Translated by Nicholas de Lange. New York: Harcourt Brace Jovanovich. 1991.
Paton, Alan. *Cry, the Beloved Country.* Middlesex, UK: Penguin Books, 1959.
Remarque, Erich Maria. *All Quiet on the Western Front.* Translated by A. W. Wheen. London: G. P. Putnam's Sons, 1929.
Shklovsky, Victor. "Art, as Device." *Poetics Today* 36, no. 3 (2015): 151–74.
Shklovsky, Viktor. "Art as a Technique." In *Literary Theory: An Anthology*, edited by Julie Rivkin and Michael Ryan, 8–14. Malden: Blackwell Publishing Ltd., 1998.
Tanakh: The Holy Scriptures, Philadelphia, PA: Jewish Publication Society, 1985.

Woolf, Virginia. *Three Guineas*. Oxford: Blackwell, 2012.
Yehoshua, Abraham B. *Mr. Mani*. Translated by Hillel Halkin. San Diego, CA: Harcourt, Brace & Company, 1993.
Yehoshua, Abraham B. *The Lover*. Translated by Philip Simpson. Orlando, FL: Harcourt, 1993.
Yehoshua, A. B. *The Liberated Bride*. Tel Aviv: Hakibbutz Hameuchad Press, 2001, trans. Hillel Halkin. London: Peter Halban Publishers Ltd., 2003.
Yitzhaki, Shimshon. *Through the Eyes of the Arabs: The Six-Day War and Aftermath*. Tel Aviv: Misrad Habitahon, 1969. http://www.sixdaywar.org/content/docs.asp.

Hebrew sources

Alterman, Natan. *Hahute Hamishulash* [The Triangular Thread: Essays 1967–1970]. Redacted by Menachem Dorman. Tel Aviv: Hakibbutz Hameuchad, 1971.
Amichai, Yehuda. "*Nefesh Mifutzelet*" [Bifurcated Soul]. *Yedioth Ahronoth* (December 26, 1997).
Amir, Eli. *Yasmine*. Tel Aviv: Am Oved, 2005.
Avishai, Mordechai. *Shorashim Bitzameret* [Roots on the Treetop]. Tel Aviv: Aleph Publishers Ltd., 1969.
Avital-Eppstein, Gideon. *1973: Hakrav Al Hazikaron* [The Yom Kippur War, 1973: A Battle Over the Collective Memory—A Never-Ending War]. Jerusalem and Tel Aviv: Schocken, 2013.
Bartov, Hanoch. *Pitzei Bagrut* [The Brigade]. Tel Aviv: Hakibbutz Hameuchad, 2011.
Bartov, Hanoch. *Regel Ahat Bahutz* [Halfway Out]. Tel Aviv: Am Oved, 1999.
Bar-Yosef, Chamutal. "Reuveni Aharon (1886–1971)." In *Lexicon Heksherim* [The Heksherim Lexicon of Israeli Authors]. Edited by Zissi Stavi and Yigal Schwartz. Beersheba: Ben-Gurion Univ., 2014.
Be'er, Haim. *Notzot* [Feathers]. Tel Aviv: Am Oved, 2005.
Be'er, Haim. *Hadarim Meleim Sefarim* [Rooms Full of Books]. Jerusalem: Mineged, 2016.
Ben-Dov, Nitza. *Ve-Hi Tehilatekha* [And It Is Your Praise: Studies in the Works of S. Y. Agnon, A. B. Yehoshua and Amos Oz]. Tel Aviv: Schocken, 2006.
Ben-Dov, Nitza. *Haim Ktuvim: Al Autobiographiot Sifritiyot Yisraeliot* [Written Lives: On Israeli Literary Autobiographies]. Tel Aviv: Schocken, 2011.

Ben-Dov, Nitza. *Ahavot Lo Miusharote* [Unhappy/Unapproved Loves: Erotic Frustration, Art, and Death in Agnon's Fiction]. Tel Aviv: Am Oved, 1997.

Ben-Dov, Nitza. "*Yaldai Hadimyon Sheli*" [My Imaginary Offspring]. *Keshet Hahadasha* 23 (Spring 2008).

Ben-Dov, Nitza. "Yiladeiha Ha'avudim Shel Sparta" [Sparta's Lost Children: On the Role of Place in the Work of Yehoshua Kenaz and in *Infiltration*]. *Alei Siach* 33 (1993).

Ben-Dov, Nitza. *Bakivun Hanegdi* [In the Opposite Direction: A Collection of Studies on Mr. Mani by A. B. Yehoshua]. Edited by Nitza Ben-Dov. Tel Aviv: Hakibbutz Hameuchad, 1995.

Buhbut, Amir. "Hatzatza Lamutzav Hamisukan Biyoter Shel Tzahal" [A Peek at the IDF's Most Dangerous Outpost]. *Walla! News* https://news.walla.co.il /item/2681163 (September 5, 2013).

Eshed, Eli. "Hastalag Haivri Haultimativi" [The Ultimate Hebrew Stalag]. *Time Out-Tel Aviv* 388 (April 12, 2010).

Eshed, Eli. *Mitarzan Ad Zbeng* [From Tarzan to Zbeng: The Story of Hebrew Pulp Literature]. Tel Aviv: Bavel Publishing, 2002.

Esterkin, Y. "Hayal Al Niyar" [Paper Soldier]. *Steimatzky Magazine* (Spring 2007).

Fortunato, Mario. *Yemei Hamilhama Hatmimim* [The Innocent Days of War]. Translated by Saviona Mane. Tel Aviv: Matar, 2010.

Gertz, Nurit. *Hasiporet Hayisraelit Bishnote Hashishim* [Israeli Prose Fiction in the 1960s], Units 4–5. Tel Aviv: The Open University, 1982.

Gil, Moshe. *Katavim Nivharim* [Selected Essays]. Jerusalem: Rubin Mass, 1970.

Gilboa, Amir. "*Tal Nekamot*" [Dew of Vengeance]. In Amir Gilboa, *Hineh Yamim Ba'im: Shirim 1942–1946* [The Days Are Coming: Poems 1942–1946]. Edited by Hagit Halperin and Ilan Berkovich. Tel Aviv: Hakibbutz Hameuchad, 2007.

Golani, Motti. *Tehiye Milhama Bakayitz* [There Will be War Next Summer: Israel on the Road to the Sinai Campaign—The Path to War]. Tel Aviv: Ma'arachot, 1997.

Golani, Motti. *Milhamot Lo Korot Me'atzman* [Wars Don't Just Happen: On Memory, Force, and Choice]. Ben Shemen: Modan, 2002.

Gluzman, Michael. "Gavriyut Kfuya Bihitganvut Yihidim" [Forced Masculinity in *Infiltration*]. In his *Haguf Hatziyoni* [The Zionist Body: Nationalism, Gender, and Sexuality in Modern Hebrew Literature]. Tel Aviv: Hakibbutz Hameuchad, 2007.

Grossman, David. *Isha Borahat Mibsora* [To the End of the Land]. Tel Aviv: Hakibbutz Hameuchad, 2008.

Harel, Amos. *Teda Kol Em Ivriya* [Every Hebrew Mother Should Know: A Portrait of the New IDF]. Or Yehuda: Kinneret, Zmora-Bitan, 2013.

Harshav, Benjamin. *Hapupik Vehaglobus* [The Bellybutton and the Globe: Multilingualism in Jewish History and in the Global Village]. Tel Aviv: Hakibbutz Hameuchad and the Porter Institute for Poetics and Semiotics, 2012.

Hendel, Yehudit. *Har Hato'im* [The Mountain of Losses]. Tel Aviv: New Library, 1991.

Holtzman, Avner. *Avigdor Hameiri Vesifrut Hamilḥamah* [Avigdor Hameiri and War Literature]. Tel Aviv: Ma'arachot, 1986.

Holtzman, Avner. "*Michvot Aish: Arba'im Shnot Ktiva Al Milhemet Yom Hakippurim*" [Scars of Fire: Forty Years of Writing on the Yom Kippur War]. *OT: A Journal of Literary Criticism and Theory* 4 (Summer 2014).

Holtzman, Avner. "Aharit Davar" [Afterword]. In *Pitzei Bagrut* [The Brigade]. Tel Aviv: Hakibbutz Hameuchad, 2011.

Herzig, Hanna. *Hakol Haomer Ani* [The Voice Saying I: Trends in Israeli Prose Fiction of the 1980s]. Ra'anana: Open University, 1998.

Kaplan, Danny. *David, Yehonatan Vehayalim Aherim* [David, Jonathan and Other Soldiers: Identity, Masculinity and Sexuality in IDF Combat Units]. Tel Aviv: Hakibbutz Hameuchad, 1999.

Kronfeld, Chana. "Sochnut Intertextualit" [Intertextual Agency]. In *Intertextiyaliyut Bisifrut Ubitarbut* [Intertextuality in Literature and Culture: A Festschrift for Ziva Ben-Porat]. Edited by Michael Gluzman and Orly Lubin. Tel Aviv: Porter Institute for Poetics and Semiotics and Hakibbutz Hameuchad Press, 2011.

Leshem, Ron. "Life on Paper" [Hebrew], *Steimatzky Magazine* (Spring 2007).

Levitan, Amos. "Habisora Al Pi Avram" [The Gospel of Avram]. *Iton 77*, no. 332 (2008).

Ma'apil, Avi. *Itzuv Hamitziyut Bisiporet Shel S. Yizhar* [The Shaping of Reality in S. Yizhar's Prose]. Hebrew University of Jerusalem: Doctoral Dissertation, 1988.

Margalit, Dan. *Yehidat Commando 101* [Commando Unit 101]. Tel Aviv: Moked, 1968.

Michael, Sami. *Yonim Be-Trafalgar* [Pigeons at Trafalgar Square]. Tel Aviv: Am Oved, 2005.

Mond, Assaf. "Hasofer Hayehudi Shetaval Et Ayto Bidamo" [The Jewish Author Who Dipped His Pen in His Own Blood]. *Odyssey Magazine* (July 2014).

Neria, Yuval. *Esh* [Fire]. Tel Aviv: Zmora Bitan, 1989.

Nevo, Gidi. *Shiva Yamim Binegev* [Seven Days in the Negev: S. Yitzhar's Days of Ziklag]. Tel Aviv: Hakibbutz Hameuchad and the Ben-Gurion Research Institute for the Study of Israel and Zionism, 2005.

Olmert, Dana. *Kihoma Amodna: Imahot Lalohamim Besifrut Ha'ivrit* [A Barricade of Mothers: Mothers of Soldiers in Israeli Zionist Culture and Literature]. Tel Aviv: Hakibbutz Hameuchad, 2018.

Oren, Amir. "Kela David" [David's Sling]. *Haaretz* (March 16, 2014).

Pappirblat, Shlomo. *"Kavim Shel Aish"* [Lines of Fire]. *Galleria* supplement, *Haaretz* (July 8, 2015).

Price, Jonathan. "Mavo" [Introduction]. In Flavius Josephus, *Milhamot Hayehudim Beroma'im* [History of the Jewish War against the Romans]. Translated by Lisa Ullmann. Edited by Israel Shatzmann. Jerusalem: Carmel, 2009.

Priluk, Nitza. "Hayal Yehudi Betzva Hakaiser Kotav Mehahazit 1914–1916" [A Jewish Soldier in the Kaiser's Army Writes from the Front 1914–1916]. *Yedda-Am: Bama Lefolklore Yehudi* 40–41, no. 75–76 (2015).

Priluk, Nitza. "Mitnadvote Bikachol Ubikhaki" [Volunteer Women in Blue and Khaki: *Eretz-Israeli* Women in the British Army in Egypt During World War II]. *Et-mol* 1 (177), Yad Ben Zvi Institute (September 2004).

Reuveni, Aharon. *Ad Yerushalayim* [All the Way to Jerusalem: A First World War Trilogy]. Tel Aviv: Hakibbutz Hameuchad, 1987.

Sadan, Dov. "Mavo" [Introduction]. In Erich Auerbach, *Mimesa: Hitgalmut Hamitziyut Bisifrut Hama'arav* [Mimesis: The Representation of Reality in Western Literature]. Translated by Baruch Kroh. Jerusalem: Bialik Institute, 1969.

Shalev, Mordechai. "Hotem Ha'akedah" [The Stamp of the *Akedah* in *Three Days and a Child*, in *Early Summer 1970* and in *Mr. Mani*]. In *Bakivun Hanegdi* [In the Opposite Direction: A Collection of Studies on Mr. Mani by A. B. Yehoshua]. Edited by Nitza Ben-Dov. Tel Aviv: Hakibbutz Hameuchad, 1995.

Shalev, Zeruya. *Ke'ev* [Pain]. Jerusalem: Keter, 2015.

Shamir, Ziva. "Emet Mieretz Yisrael" [Truth from the Land of Israel]. *Gag: Magazine of Literature* 22 (Summer 2010).

Ticotsky, Giddon. "Aharit Davar" [Afterword]. In Antoine de Saint-Exupéry, *Tayas Krav | Michtav Leben Aruba* [Flight to Arras | Letter to a Hostage]. Translated by Giddon Ticotsky. Tel Aviv: Sifriyat Poalim, 2009.

Ullmann, Lisa. "Hakdama" [Foreword]. In Flavius Josephus, *Milhamot Hayehudim Beroma'im* [History of the Jewish War against the Romans]. Translated by Lisa Ullmann. Edited by Israel Shatzmann. Jerusalem: Carmel, 2009.

Vidas, Tiki. *Kolot Shetamid Eti* [Voices that Never Leave Me]. Tel Aviv: Ma'ariv, 2004.

Yehoshua, Abraham B. "Levatel Et Ha'akedah Al Yidei Mimusha" [Negating the Akedah by Actualizing It]. In *Bakivun Hanegdi* [In the Opposite Direction: A Collection of Studies on Mr. Mani by A. B. Yehoshua]. Edited by Nitza Ben-Dov. Tel Aviv: Hakibbutz Hameuchad, 1995.

Yizhar, S. *Yemei Ziklag* [Days of Ziklag]. Tel Aviv: Am Oved, 1958.

Index

Italic page number denotes illustration.

Abbasiya Prison (Egypt), 327
"abjection" literature, 138, 140, 144
Academy Awards, 1
"accursed mountain," 350n81
Aeschylus, 358n19
Agamemnon (Aeschylus), 358n19
Agnon, S. Y., 15–16, 24–25, 27–29, 51, 66, 67, 69, 71–81, 117, 186, 200, 312, 338, 347n39, 351n5, 358n20, 364n11. See also *To This Day*
Agnon's Art of Indirection: Uncovering Latent Content in the Fiction of S. Y. Agnon (Ben-Dov), 29, 358n20
Agrippa (King), 347n33
Akedah (binding of Isaac), 68–69, 290, 293, 363n3
Al Wardah al Baidha (film), 196
Aliyat Hano'ar, 93
All Quiet on the Western Front (Remarque), 11, 12, 15, 29, 34, 36, 51, 271, 276, 278, 283, 348n45, 348n47
All the Way to Jerusalem: A First World War Trilogy (Reuveni), 28, 348n46
allegories, 35; social, 189
Allenby Bridge, 202–4, 208, 209, 217, 321
alliteration, 25, 27, 237
allusions, 10, 249; language of, 103; literary, 32

Alter, Robert (Uri), 34, 347n29, 353n2
Alterman, Natan, 40, 185, 186–87, 188
Amalekites, 56, 91
Amati-Mehler, Jacqueline, 214
American-Jewish literature, 352n6
Amichai, Yehuda, 5, 31–34, 51, 66, 73, 84, 107, 109–35, 147, 314, 316, 328, 338. See also *Not This Time, Not of This Place*
Amir, Eli, 2, 16, 39–41, 51, 135, 183–219, 183–219, 222, 223, 243, 274, 322, 339, 351–52n5, 356n2, 356n3, 356n4, 356n5, 362n4. See also Six-Day War; *Yasmine*
Ammunition Hill (Jerusalem), 186
Amonites, 24
"Amos Oz—Landscapes of His Soul" (chapter, Ben-Dov), 353n13
analogies, 10, 115, 296; historical, 114
And It Is Your Praise (Ben-Dov), 346n25, 362n2, 363n3, 363n7
Anderson, Hans Christian, 189
Anna Karenina (Tolstoy), 174, 356n4
Arab Revolt, 71, 72
Argentieri, Simone, 214
Aristotle, 57–58, 60, 61
Ashkenazi, 5, 53, 60, 64, 137, 138, 205–6, 257, 271, 276, 277, 278, 279, 280, 282, 283, 284

Auerbach, Erich, 269
Auschwitz, 336
autobiographical novels and details, 4, 9, 10–12, 32, 35, 51–52, 66, 360n7
Auto-Emancipation (Pinsker), 305
Avidan, David, 52, 237
Avigdor Hameiri and War Literature (Holtzman), 12
Avital-Eppstein, Gideon, 42, 44–45, 46, 349n69

Babel of the Unconscious: Mother Tongue and Foreign Languages in the Psychoanalytic Dimension, The (Amati-Mehler, Argentieri, Canestri), 214
Bamahane (IDF magazine), 360n10
Barnea, Aharon, 54, 62–63, 279
Barnea, Noam, 54, 63, 65, 279
Barricade of Mothers: Mothers of Soldiers in Israeli Zionist Culture and Literature (Olmert), 6–7, 31
Barthes, Roland, 309
Bartov, Hanoch, 2, 15, 29–31, 33, 43, 44, 51, 82–108, 221–22, 224, 312, 313, 314, 327, 336, 338, 352n4, 352n5, 352n6, 353n13, 353n15, 353n16. See also *The Brigade*
basic training, 35, 51, 66, 136–74, 271, 272, 273, 275, 283, 284, 295, 317, 318, 331, 332, 354n5. See also *Infiltration* (Kenaz); training bases
Baxtin, Mikhail, 56, 350n76
Beaufort (historic crusader fortress), 1, 53, 54–55, 57–60, 61, 62, 63, 64, 65, 271, 273, 274, 277, 279–80, 281, 328, 334, 338, 340, 350n81
Beaufort (Leshem), 1, 27, 50–66, 273–84, 327, 334, 336, 337, 338, 350n81, 363n4. See also First Lebanon War

Be'er, Haim, 45, 55, 225, 227, 351n2, 352n6, 360n7
Ben-Gurion Airport, 285
Ben-Gurion, David, 37, 148, 164
Ben-Ner, Yitzhak, 42, 44, 223
Ben-Yehuda, Eleazer, 41
bereavement, 17, 29, 43, 44, 52, 66, 67, 68, 71–81, 224, 297, 300, 304, 307, 308, 309, 360n10. See also grief
Bertelsmann Publishing House, 174
"Between Night and Dawn"(Kenaz), 354n3
Bialik, Haim Nahman, 48, 186, 210, 212–13, 298–99, 300, 359n28
bidirectional intertextual links, 32
Biram, Arthur, 28
Black Skin, White Masks (Fanon), 356
Boianjiu, Shani, 332
Book of Jeremiah (Biblical book), 291, 292
Book of Judges (Biblical book), 24
Book of Proverbs (Biblical book), 20
Borders, Territories, Ethics (Mendelson-Maor), 7
Brigade Juive, La (Van Oppen), 30
Brigade, The (Bartov) 2, 15, 29–31, 51, 70, 82–108, 312–14, 327, 336, 338, 352n5
Brigade, Jewish (in the British Army), 2, 29–31, 32, 51
British Army, 2, 15, 29–31, 37, 70, 82, 85, 88, 93, 314
British mandate, 37
Bus 405 (terror attack, July 6, 1989), 251, 255, 256

Café Allenby, 177, 321
calamity, 158, 334, 360n10, 361n20
camaraderie, 3, 6, 35, 59, 70, 153, 155, 273

Index • 375

Camera Lucida: Reflections on Photography (Barthes), 309
Camp Sarafand (Tzrifin IDF military base), 273, 277
Canestri, Jorge, 214
"Cannons' Roar, The" (chapter and song in Kenaz's *Infiltration*), 154, 170, 172, 327
Catch-22 (in Hebrew, *Milkud-22*) (Heller), 52, 87, 237
Céline, Louis-Ferdinand, 138
chronotope, 56, 236, 350n76
Church of the Redeemer (Jerusalem), 189, 190, 191
close reading, 6, 8
"Coastal Cities of Palestine During the Early Middle Ages, The" (article, Elad), 355n16
Cohen, Jessica, 361n17
"Cold Blood" (image, Hila Lulu Lin), 334, 335
collective memory, 30, 42, 45
Commando Unit 101 (Margalit), 35, 37, 136, 150, 151
"confessional narrative," 174, 287
confusion, 21, 22, 32, 43, 94, 139, 188, 206, 229, 252
Conrad, Joseph, 202
consciousness, 66, 109, 110, 126, 136, 144, 175, 191, 208, 233, 275; Amichai's, 32; Israeli, 8, 152, 338; Jewish, 29; loss of, 139, 145, 274; political, 183, 189; repressed, 336, 337; soldier's, 274; stream of, 55, 57, 350n75
"Covering of the Blood, or At the Same Time, The" (Agnon), 15–16, 346n25
Criminal Investigations Unit (CID), 167
Cry, the Beloved Country (Paton), 36–37
cultural semiotics, 41
Cypriot Project, 260, 263, 268

Dado: 48 years and 20 Days (Bartov), 44, 222, 224
David (King), 56–57
David Yellin Street (Jerusalem), 177, 321
David, Jonathan and Other Soldiers: Identity, Masculinity and Sexuality in IDF Combat Units (Kaplan), 320
Dayan, Moshe, 37, 316
Days of Ziklag (Yizhar) 2, 54, 350n75, 350n78
"Dead of the Desert, The" (poem-Bialik), 48
death, unglorified (in vain) 11–12, 19, 53, 60, 61, 67, 280, 284, 338–40
defamiliarization, 298
"Dew of Vengeance" (poem, Gilboa), 31
diegetic and metadiegetic time, 8–9, 12–13
"different planet, A" (phrase, Ka-Tsetnik), 336
Dissembler, The (Bartov), 221–22, 360n1
"Divided Soul, A" (article, Amichai), 33–34
"Doctor's Divorce, The" (Agnon), 186
dogs, 317, 318, 364n11
dreams, 2, 23, 25, 27, 59–60, 88, 101, 104, 105, 113, 114, 133, 176–77, 181–82, 201, 202, 212, 215, 217, 275, 289, 320, 327, 353n19, 357n13
Dulles, John Foster, 356n8

Earth, mother 36–37, 148, 159–64. See also "mother of soldiers"
Effi Briest (Fontane), 174, 356n4
Eichman trial, 33, 89, 336
Eisenhower, Dwight D., 356n8
Elad, Amikam, 355n16
Elazar, David ("Dado"), 224
El-Balad (Jerusalem Old City), 189

Eleazar Ben Yair, 158, 347n33
Eliel, Yossie, 58
"elimination" or "ten little Indians" (literary pattern), 12
Emma Bovary (Flaubert), 174, 356n4
"Emperor's New Clothes, The" (social allegory, Anderson), 189–90
Encyclopedia Hebraica, 175
End to End (Bartov), 82
Epstein, Denise, 346n17
escapism, portraying of author's, 2, 3, 5, 6, 49, 70, 87–88, 305
Eshed, Eli, 89
Eshet-Alkalai, Yoram, 4, 12
Eshkol, Levi, 198–200
Ethics of the Fathers (Pirkei Avot), 118, 119, 120, 122
ethos, Israeli, 6–7, 20, 139, 294, 316, 354n5; Zionist, 197
eucalyptus trees, 190, 197–98, 273, 274, 318, 358n16, 362n4. *See also* "Jews' tree"
euphemisms, 297

fabula and syuzhet, 191–92
Facebook, 270
Fanon, Frantz, 356n5
fantasy, 11, 32, 58, 181, 301; rape, 181; reality and, 232, 307; retributive, 104; surrealism and, 27; vengeance, 106
Farhud (pogrom against Baghdad Jewry), 359n23
Fayid (a former military airfield in Egypt), 226
Feathers (Be'er), 45, 55, 225–27, 360n7
Fire (Neria), 44, 222–24
First Lebanon War (1982), 2, 17, 18, 27, 50–66. See also *Beaufort* (Leshem);

"Operation Peace for Galilee"; Second Lebanon War
First World War (1914–1918), 11–14, 16, 23–24, 27, 28, 51, 53, 67, 68, 69, 71–81, 200, 348n47, 351n5. *See also* "Great War, The"; *To This Day* (Agnon); World War I
Flaubert, Gustav, 174, 356n4
Flavius Josephus, 22, 347n32, 347n33
Flekser, Aviva, 285
Flekser, Erez, 285
Flight to Arras (de Saint-Exupéry), 14–15
"Following Her Path: Feminism Legacies" (lecture series), 46
Fontane, Theodor, 174, 356n4
"forbidden magazines," 90
"Forced Masculinity in *Infiltration*" (Gluzman), 354n2
Fortunato, Mario, 336
Four Mother's movement, 61, 62, 279
Four Seasons (Yehoshua), 285
France, 13–14, 346n17
Franco-Prussian War (1870), 351n4
Freud, Sigmund, 23–24, 205, 301, 353n19
friendly fire, 67–68, 287, 292–99, 300, 301, 303, 304, 305, 339
Friendly Fire (Yehoshua), 22, 52, 66–69, 285–309, 330, 331, 337, 339. *See also* Second Intifada
Friends Tell About Jimmy (memorial book), 149

Galili, Yisrael, 356n2
"Garden, The" (Kiryat Shaul cemetery), 43
Garden of Eden, 127
Gaza City, 16, 40, 192, 194, 196
gender, 38, 236, 310–40
Genette, Gérard, 241

German Jews, 24, 28, 72, 76, 77, 78, 80; psychological state of, 74–75
Germans of the Mosaic Faith, 28, 74–79
Gil, Moshe, 352n5
Gilboa, Amir, 31
Glickman, Uri, 64
global village, 270
Gluzman, Michael, 354n2
Golani Brigade, 58, 280
Golani, Motti, 199, 349n58
Gold, Nili Scharf, 112–13
Goren, Shlomo, 189
"Gospel of Avram, The" (article, Levitan), 361n20
Gouri, Haim, 140–41
Great Bitter Lake, The (Egypt), 225
Great Madness: Notes of a Hebraic Officer in the Great War, The (Hameiri), 12, 29, 52, 271, 348n45, 348n47
Great War, The (1914–1918), 24, 25, 27–29, 51, 53, 71, 72, 76, 346n21. *See also* First World War; *To This Day* (Agnon); World War I
Green Line, 49, 267
grief, 67, 68, 73, 81, 258, 267, 285, 286, 300, 301, 302, 303, 305, 306, 309, 337. *See also* bereavement
Grossman, David, 2, 3, 4, 7, 16, 20, 42–48, 52, 69, 220–39, 322, 324–25, 339, 350n72, 352n6, 361n16, 361n20. *See also To the End of the Land*; Yom Kippur War
Guest for the Night, A (Agnon), 115–17
Guterman, Raz, 58

Haaretz (daily newspaper), 241–42, 363n3
Hadash, Mordechai (Motke), 353n16
"Haim Be'er: Strands of His Life" (chapter, Ben Dov), 360n7
Halfway Out (Bartov), 82, 85
hallucination, 32, 120, 323
Hameiri, Avigdor, 12, 13, 27, 28, 51, 229, 271, 348n45, 348n47
Hanukkah, 68, 285–86, 287, 289, 293, 296, 297, 299, 300, 302–3, 304, 305, 306, 307, 308, 337
Harel, Amos, 142, 143
Harnick, Goni, 58, 64
Harris, Rachel, 7, 8
Harshav, Benjamin, 41, 357n12
Har-Zion, Meir, 37, 150–51
He Walked Through the Fields (Shamir), 36, 58
"Heart Murmur" (chapter, Kenaz), 154
Heart of Darkness (Conrad), 202
heaven, 69, 91, 162, 195, 269, 273, 338
Hebrew Bible, 68, 289. *See also* Books of: Judges; Jeremiah; Proverbs; Song of Songs
Hebrew literature, 2, 4, 6, 10, 15, 20, 25, 36, 57, 61, 108, 185, 221, 352n6, 354n2. *See also* American-Jewish literature; world literature
Hebrew University of Jerusalem, 71, 110, 175
Hehalutz (Hebrew periodical), 79
Heletz oil field (Israel), 143, 144, 146
Heller, Joseph, 87, 237
Hendel, Yehudit, 17, 27, 43, 44
"Henrik's Secret" (Kenaz), 354n3
"Here Lie Our Bodies" (poem, Gouri), 140–41
Herzig, Hanna, 354n5
Hezbollah, 1, 59
historical fact and fiction, relationship between, 8–12, 16, 33, 42, 43, 46, 51–52, 55, 56–64. *See also* testimony and fiction

historiography, 33; Arab, 71; Jewish, 71; literary, 10, 54

history and memory, 9–20

Holocaust, 1, 3, 5, 28, 29–34, 35, 51, 71, 83, 89, 100, 104, 106, 243, 244, 245, 260, 338, 352n5; and War of Independence, 31–34, 109–35

Holtzman, Avner, 12, 13, 27, 44, 82–83, 84, 87, 348n45, 360n1

homosexuality, 93, 319–20

Horowitz, Ya'akov, 348n47

Hurban: Responses to Catastrophe in Hebrew Literature (Mintz), 352n5

hypertext and hypotext (intertextuality), 241–42, 243–44, 268

identity, 49–50; hybrid, 41, 50, 197, 216, 265

If There Is a Heaven (the Hebrew title of *Beaufort*), 269, 273

Illan, Uri, 148–49, 152, 157

imaginary worlds, 10

immigration, 72, 138; mass, 35, 137, 216, 276, 277; second wave, 71; Zionist, 32

"immortality-victory," 310

improvised explosive devices (IEDs), 1

In the Opposite Direction: A Collection of Studies on Mr. Mani by A. B. Yehoshua (Ben-Dov), 351n82, 363n3

"In the Prime of Her Life" (novella, Agnon), 364n11

In This Terrible Wind (Amichai), 31–32

"Inferno: Forty Years of Writing on the Yom Kippur War"(article, Holtzman), 44

Infiltration (Kenaz), 2, 35–37, 51, 66, 86, 87, 92, 136–73, 270, 271, 272, 273–84, 316, 319, 320, 327, 328, 329, 330, 331, 332, 339, 351n3, 353n14, 354n2, 354n8, 355n7, 355n13

Innocent Days of War (Fortunato), 336–37

internet, 270, 350n72

intertextuality, 40, 50, 240, 242, 357n6. See also hyper- and hypotext

intifada (Palestinian uprising), 7, 8, 67; First Intifada, 48, 50, 240, 242, 250, 255, 262, 287; intifada of stones (early name of the First Intifada), 256; Second Intifada, 2, 27, 48–49, 66, 67, 69, 242, 255. See also *Pigeons at Trafalgar Square* (Michael); *Friendly Fire* (Yehoshua)

Introduction to Psychoanalysis (Freud), 23–24

irony, 28, 40, 74, 76, 77, 114, 116, 178, 180, 186, 188, 254, 311

Isaiah (prophet), 288–89, 290, 292, 297–98, 308

Islamic praise literature (*fada'il*), 355

Israel Defence Forces (IDF): Military Intelligence Directorate, 51, 58; Ordnance Corps, 335; Paratroops Corps, 37; Rabbinate, 196, 225; Signal Corp, 37, 178, 320, 332, 335, 339. See also YAEL (IDF elite bomb squad)

"Israeli at the UN: One Against Many, An" (lecture, Gabriela Shalev), 46

Israeli war narratives, ambivalent relationship with war and military life, 8; women in, 311

Israeli war novel, 3, 7–8, 311; ethnic divide within, 276; shifting nature of, 270

Itach, Tzachi, 279

Jabel Scubus, 212. See also Mount Scopus

Jephthah (Yiftach) the Giladite (Judge), 22, 24, 200–202, 208, 209, 210, 212, 218, 358n19
"Jews' tree," (eucalyptus) 190, 197–98, 362n4. *See also* eucalyptus trees
"Jewish Author Who Dipped His Pen in His Own Blood" (article, Mond), 348n7
Jewish Brigade (in the British Army), 2, 30–31, 32, 51. See also *Brigade, The* (Bartov)
"Jewish mother," 352n6
Jewish War, The (Josephus), 22–23
Jibli, Yitzhak, 35, 151, 152, 154, 157, 158–59, 160
Jotapata (Yodfat), cave of, 23
Journey to the End of the Millenium, A (Yehoshua), 363n3
Journey to the End of the Night (Céline), 138
Jung, Carl G., 104, 105, 353n19

Kanafani, Ghassan, 49–50, 240–48, 252, 258–59, 262–63, 265, 268. *See also* Michael, Sami
Kaniuk, Yoram, 15, 351–52n3
Kaplan, Danny, 320
Karpel, Dalia, 241–42
Ka-Tsetnik (Yehiel De-Nur), 336
Keisari, Uri, 348n47
Kenaz, Yehoshua, 2, 35–37, 51, 66, 86–87, 92, 136–73, 270, 273, 274, 276, 283–84, 316–17, 319, 320, 327, 339, 351–52n3, 354n3, 354n5, 354n8, 355n7. See also *Infiltration*
Keshet Hahadasha (Hebrew literary journal), 54–55
Keshet, Sylvie, 62
"Khirbet Khizeh" (novella, Yizhar), 337

kibbutz (kibbutzim), 17–18, 19, 136, 139, 142–51, 163, 164, 165, 167, 170, 172, 205, 206, 215–18, 276, 282, 284, 314, 317, 327, 339, 349n60, 359–60n30; Beit Oren, 359–60n30; Mash'abei Sadeh, 19; Rosh Hanikra, 18; Yehi'am, 17
Kilometer 101 (landmark), 225
King George Street (Tel Aviv), 177, 321
Kiryat Oranim, 215, 216, 217, 359–60n30
Kiryat Shaul Cemetery, 43
Kiryat Shmona, 336, 337
Kiryat Ya'arim, 251
Kochav Hayarden, 151
Kol Yisrael (The Voice of Israel), 193
Kraus, Karl, 311
Kristallnacht, 126
Kristeva, Julia, 138, 140
Kurosawa, Akira, 359n22

Lamed Heh disaster (January 16, 1948), 140–41
Land of Israel/Eretz Yisrael/Mandatory Palestine, 22, 28, 30, 32, 83, 114, 161–62, 163, 197, 207, 353n13, 355n16
Late Divorce, A (Yehoshua), 285, 298
Lebanon War. *See* First Lebanon War; Second Lebanon War
"leftist Tourette's Syndrome," 7
Leo, Christian, 113
Leshem, Ron, 1–2, 3, 5, 27, 50–66, 269–84, 350n81, 363n4
"Let My Lot Be With You" (poem, Bialik), 183, 213, 359n28
Letter to a Hostage (de Saint-Exupéry), 14
Levantism, 276
Levitan, Amos, 361n20

Liberated Bride, The (Yehoshua), 188, 363n7
literary fiction, 12, 223, 224–25
"literature of defeat," 14
"Lo Meakhshav, Lo Mikkam" (Hebrew title of *Not of This Time, Not of This Place*, Amichai), 345n7, 353n2
Lover, The (Yehoshua), 27, 42, 43, 285, 296
Lulu-Lin, Hila, 334, 335
Lunenfeld (village near Leipzig), 78

Ma'apil, Avi, 56
Ma'ayan Harod National Park, 250, 259, 263
"make love, not war" (slogan) 40, 202, 217
"man-heroism," 310
Man Walks Home, A (Eshet-Alkalai), 12
Margalit, Dan, 150
Masada (historical site), 158, 347n33
masochisim, 157, 200. *See also* sadism
melancholy, 29, 124, 301, 306
melting pot, 35, 137, 138, 272, 276, 314, 354n2; literary, 83
Mendelson-Maor, Adia, 7–8
Michael, Sami, 2, 4, 48–50, 55, 240–68, 326, 339, 351n3. See also *Pigeons at Trafalgar Square*
Michael Strogoff: The Courier of the Stars (Verne), 182, 356n9
Mimesis: The Representation of Reality in Western Literature (Auerbach), 362n1
Mintz, Alan, 352n5
Mizrahim, 137, 163, 184, 198, 205, 206, 216, 276, 277, 282, 283, 319, 357n12
Mond, Assaf, 348n47
Montaigne, Michel de, 144, 148
Montand, Yves, 203, 322

Morogoro Nature Reserve, 286
Mossad (intelligence agency), 249
Mount Scopus 135, 209, 210, 211, 213, 214, 316, 359n26. *See also* Jabel Scubus
Mountain of Losses, The (Hendel), 17, 27, 43–44
mourning, 6, 61, 67–68, 80, 141, 208, 286, 298, 307–8. *See also* bereavement, grief
Mourning and Melancholia, (Freud), 301
Mr. Mani (Yehoshua), 17–18, 19, 68–69, 203, 285
multiculturalism, 40, 41, 43, 206
multilingualism, 40, 41, 43, 188, 202, 206, 357n12
"Musical Moment" (Kenaz), 137, 354n3
"My Imaginary Offspring: Reality and Fantasy in Days of Ziklag" (Ben-Dov), 54–55
My Michael (Oz), 2, 37–39, 40, 55, 174–82, 320, 321, 339, 351–52n3, 355n1, 356n4. *See also* Sinai War

Nachman of Bratslav (Rebbe, Rabbi), 358–59n20
Narratives of Dissent (Omer-Sherman and Harris), 7
Nasser, Gamel Abdul, 191, 192, 193, 194, 195, 357n14; and Eshkol, 198–200
National Liberation Front (FLN, Algeria), 356n5
"Negating the Akedah by Actualizing It" (article, Yehoshua), 351n82
Negev 18–19, 55, 110, 119, 143, 163, 164, 176, 315
Negev Brigade, Palmach 32, 34, 51
Némirovski, Irène, 13–15, 346n17

Neria, Yuval, 43, 222, 223–24
Neuland (Eshkol Nevo), 2
Nevo, Eshkol, 2
Nevo, Gidi, 350n75
"Nicole" (short story, Ben-Ner), 42, 44, 223, 224
"Night of Atonement, A" (Kenaz), 327
1948 (Kaniuk), 15
North Korea, 355n2
Not of This Time, Not of This Place (Amichai), 5, 31–34, 51, 66, 70, 73, 109–34, 147, 148, 314–15, 328, 338, 358n16
Nutrition Army, 225, 226, 327

Oedipal, 245, 250, 253, 267
Old Man's Death, The (short story, Yehoshua), 362n2
Olmert, Dana, 6–8, 311
Omer-Sherman, Ranen, 7–8
On Friendship (de Montaigne), 144
Only Yesterday (Agnon), 364n11
Open Heart (Yehoshua), 293, 363n7
Operation Kadesh, 37, 39–40, 246. *See also* Sinai War
"Operation Peace for Galilee," 53. *See also Beaufort* (Leshem); First Lebanon War
Oren, Amir, 37, 125
oxymorons, 53, 68, 121, 125, 221, 292, 295
Oz, Amos, 2, 37–39, 42, 55, 174–82, 224–25, 320, 339, 353n13, 355n1, 355n5, 356n4. *See also My Michael*; Sinai War

Pain (Zeruya Shalev), 18–19
Palestinian Liberation Organization (PLO), 358n17
Palestinians, 183, 184, 188, 206, 207, 241, 243, 245, 250, 254–56, 358n17
Palmach, 32, 34, 37, 124, 153, 314, 354n2. *See also* Negev Brigade
"Paper Soldier" (article, Leshem), 345n2
Paratrooper Unit 101, 136
Paratrooper's Brigade, 143, 151, 153, 190
Pardes Hanna (town), 215
Passionsspiele, 101
Paton, Alan, 36–37
Peace Now (movement), 279–80
peacetime, 4, 6, 35
People of Forever Are Not Afraid, The (Boianjiu), 332
pigeons, 263–64, 265
Pigeons at Trafalgar Square (Michael), 4, 48–50, 240–68, 326, 339
Pinsker, Leo, 305
Pinsker Tower, 304–5, 307
Poetry of Yehuda Amichai, The (Alter, ed.), 34
Popper-Lynkeus, Josef, 224
Popular Front for the Liberation of Palestine, 245–46
Powers of Horror: An Essay on Abjection (Kristeva), 138
Price, Jonathan, 23
Priluk, Nitza, 14–15, 28, 314
"Prisoner, The" (novella, Yizhar), 337
protagonists (theoretical development in literature), 2, 6, 9–10, 22, 32, 33–34, 70, 174, 186, 248
Publius Flavius Vegetius, 5
Pure Element of Time, The (Be'er), 360n7
"Purple rain" (vernacular for incoming fire and the whistle of mortar shells), 1, 284

Rabin, Yitzhak, 34
radio and television broadcasts, 38, 42, 178, 183, 184, 192
"Rain Falls on the Faces of My Friends" (poem, Amichai), 32, 34
rape-fantasy, 181
Rashomon (film, Kurosawa), 359n22
rashomon technique, 12, 206, 296
recurring patterns, 10
red (color), 68, 293, 305, 337
Refuge (Michael), 55, 243
reincarnation, 359n25
Remarque, Erich Maria, 11, 12, 15, 25, 34, 36–37, 51, 271, 276, 278, 348n45
Return from India (Yehoshua), 293
Returning to Haifa (Kanafani), 240, 241–42, 243, 244, 256, 268
Reuveni, Aharon, 28, 348n46
"Revealment and Concealment in Language" (essay, Bialik), 298, 299, 363n6
rhetorical-literary device, 347n33
Rooms Full of Books (Be'er), 351n2
Roots on the Treetop (Avishai), 352n5
Rosenberg, Isaac, 28
Rustic Sunset and Other Stories (Ben-Ner), 223

Sadan, Dov, 269, 270
sadism, 141, 155, 157, 209. *See also* masochism
Saint-Exupéry, Antoine de, 14
Sapir Prize, 1, 63
Sassoon, Siegfried, 28
Saussure, Ferdinand de, 361n16
Scrolls of Fire (Kovner), 149
Second Aliyah, 28, 71

Second Lebanon War (2006), 53, 69. *See also* First Lebanon War
Security Zone (South Lebanon), 27, 50–51, 53, 59, 271
See Under: Love (Grossman), 3
Selected Essays (Gil), 352n5
self-sacrifice, 8, 148
Seven Days in the Negev (Gidi Nevo), 350n75
Shalev, Gabriela, 46–48, 350n71, 350n72
Shalev, Mordechai, 290, 363n3
Shalev, Shaul, 46–48, 350n72
Shalev, Zeruya, 16–19
Shamir, Moshe, 36, 58
Shamir, Ziva, 352n6
Sharm el-Sheikh (Egypt), 193
Sheikh Jarrah (neighborhood in Jerusalem), 184, 186
Shklovsky, Victor, 298
Shukeiry, Ahmed, 197, 202, 207, 358n17
"Silver Platter, The" (Alterman), 185, 186, 187, 188, 189
Sinai Peninsula, 39, 40, 54
Sinai War (1956), 2, 18, 19, 33, 35, 37, 39, 49, 136, 174, 176, 180, 194, 246, 349n58, 351–52n3, 355n7, 356n8, 357n13. See also *My Michael* (Oz); Operation Kadesh
Six-Day War (1967), 2, 16, 17, 18, 19, 39–41, 42, 48, 51, 69, 181, 183–219, 220–21, 223, 228, 229, 232, 233, 235, 236, 237, 276–77, 311, 323, 339, 351–52n3, 355n1, 355n4, 356n2, 357n10, 358n17, 361n20. See also *Yasmine*
Skinner, B. F., 245, 248, 263–64, 362n5
skulls, 93, 109–35

social integration, army as a scene of, 276
Soldier Returns Home, A (Eshet-Alkalai), 4; entitled also *A Man Walks Home*, 12
Song of Songs (Biblical scroll), 52, 292, 309
South Korea, 176, 355n2
South Lebanon, 1, 27, 50, 53, 59, 60, 271, 274, 277, 278. *See also* Security Zone.
"Sparta's Lost Children: On the Role of Place in the Work of Yehoshua Kenaz and in *Infiltration*" (article, Ben-Dov), 353n12, 354n8
"stalag fiction," 89, 90
Star of David, 95
"State of Tel Aviv," 337
Steidele, Hans, 113
"Storm in June" (Némirovski), 13–14
Straits of Tiran, 39, 192, 193, 194
stream of consciousness 55, 350n75
structural tensions, 9
Suite Française (Némirovski), 13–15, 29, 346n17
symbolism, 58, 124, 305
symbols, 30, 32, 40, 104, 115, 122, 129
synecdoche, 126, 274, 290, 353n13
Szenes, Hannah, 29

Tanzania (a country in East Africa), 66, 68, 285–87
tarab (Arabic music), 197, 198
Terra Sancta College, 175
testimony and fiction, 83, 120, 124, 196, 222, 336; as a literary ploy, 9–20. *See also* historical fact and fiction, relationship between

thesis and antithesis, 35, 48, 146, 152, 153, 154, 163, 170, 176, 221, 244, 254, 263, 276, 356n4
"This Is an Illusion, Not a City: City and Woman in *My Michael*" (chapter, Ben-Dov), 349n59
Thomas, Dylan, 237, 238
"Three Days and a Child" (Yehoshua), 68, 290, 363n3
Three Guineas (Woolf), 69
"Three-Legged Chicken, The" (Kenaz), 354n3
Through Arab Eyes: The Six-Day War and Its Aftermath (Yitzhaki), 193
Ticotsky, Giddon, 14
"time of the troubles," (1935–1939) 71
Tiran and Sanafir (islands), 193
To Know a Woman (Oz), 42, 224
To the End of the Land (Grossman), 2, 3, 16, 20, 42–48, 52, 69, 220–39, 320, 322–27, 331–32, 339, 361n16, 361n20. *See also* Yom Kippur War
To This Day (Agnon), 15, 24, 67, 71–81, 312, 313, 325–26, 338, 351n2, 351n4
Tolstoy, Leo, 174, 356n4
training bases, 4, 12, 137, 138, 168, 171, 317, 318, 332, 339. *See also* basic training; *Infiltration* (Kenaz)
Trumpeldor, Joseph, 148
Trumpet in the Wadi, A (Michael), 245
"Truth from the Land of Israel" (article, Shamir, Ziva), 352n6
"Twentieth Century's One Hundred Greatest Novels" (list), 174

Ullmann, Lisa, 22, 347n32, 347n33
"Under Milk Wood" (Thomas), 52, 237

Unhappy/Unapproved Loves: Erotic Frustration, Art, and Death in Agnon's Fiction (Ben-Dov), 347n39
University of California, Berkeley, 34
"Unparallel Reality" (article, Alterman), 40

Van Oppen, Mark (Marvano), 30
Verne, Jules, 356n9
Vidas, Tiki, 332, 349n69
Voice Saying I: Trends in Israeli Prose Fiction of the 1980's, The (Herzig), 354n5
Voices that Never Leave Me (Vidas), 349n69, 332
"Volunteer Women in Blue and Khaki: *Eretz*-Israeli Women in the British Army in Egypt During World War II" (article, Priluk), 314

Wallach, Yona, 52, 237
war (*milhamah*), illness (*mahalah*), dream (*halom*), and bread (*lehem*), thematic and tonal link between, 20, 22–23, 347n39
war (*milhamah*) and folly (*helma'ut*), alliterative (tonal) link between, 27
"war of choice," 7
War of Independence (1947–1948), 2, 5, 16, 17, 35, 37, 39, 51, 54, 55, 56, 70, 109–35, 136, 153, 162–63, 181, 206, 315, 328, 337, 338, 355n5, 356n3, 359n23, 359n26; Holocaust and, 31–34. See also *Not of This Time, Not of This Place* (Amichai)
war, repressed consciousness of, 336
Weil, Hermann, 14, 28

"What He Can't Do Anymore" (post-mortem game), 51, 52, 53, 54, 284
Whiston, William, 347n32
Whose Little Boy Are You? (Bartov), 82, 84–85, 352n6
wind (as a motif), 305–6
Wirtschaftswunder ("economical miracle"), 353n1
With His Own Hands (Shamir), 36
Woolf, Virginia, 69
world literature, 10, 15, 269. See also Hebrew literature
World War I (1914–1918), 28, 29, 71–81, 115–16, 311, 312, 313, 325, 338, 351n4 See also First World War; "Great War;" *To This Day* (Agnon)
World War II (1935–1945), 2, 3, 72, 80, 82, 83, 84, 85, 88, 102, 109, 115, 313, 314, 315, 336–37, 338, 353n1. See also *Not of This Time, Not of This Place* (Amichai)
Written Lives: On Israeli Literary Autobiographies (Ben-Dov), 349n59, 351n3, 353n13, 360n7
Würzburg, Germany, 32, 33, 66, 109, 113

YAEL (IDF elite bomb squad) 54, 60
Yasmine (Amir), 2, 16–17, 39–41, 51, 135, 183–219, 243, 276–77, 320–22, 339, 351–52n3, 356n2, 356n4, 356n5, 358n17, 359n24, 362n4. See also Six-Day War
"Yatir Evening Express, The" (Yehoshua), 363n7
Yehoshua, A. B., 5, 31–34, 51, 73, 84, 107, 109, 112, 147, 285–309, 314, 328, 338, 362n2, 363n3, 363n7

Yehuda Amichai: The Making of Israel's National Poet (Gold), 112
Yishuv, 28, 29–34
Yitzhaki, Shimshon, 193–94
Yizhar, S., 2, 54, 56–57, 58–59, 327, 337, 350n77, 350n78
"Yom Kippur Dream" (Rebbe Nachman of Brestlav), 358–59n20
Yom Kippur War (1973), 2–3, 4, 16, 17, 27, 42–48, 69, 220–39, 331, 332, 334, 339, 345n2, 351n3, 360n10, 361n20. See also *To the End of the Land* (Grossman)
Yom Kippur War, 1973: A Battle Over the Collective Memory—A Never-Ending War, The (Avital-Eppstein), 42, 45

Zero Motivation (film, 2014), 332–33
Zionist Body: Nationalism, Gender, and Sexuality in Modern Hebrew Literature, The (Gluzman), 354n2

After four years as assistant professor in the department of Near Eastern Studies at Princeton University, **Nitza Ben-Dov** joined the faculty of the University of Haifa, where she is a professor of Hebrew and Comparative Literature. A literary critic and a scholar, Ben-Dov has written numerous articles and is the author of several books, published in Hebrew and in English, including *Agnon's Art of Indirection* (in English); *Unhappy/Unapproved Loves*; *Ve-Hi Tehilatekha: Studies in the Works of S. Y. Agnon, A. B. Yehoshua and Amos Oz* (in Hebrew); and *Written Lives: On Israeli Literary Autobiographies*. Ben-Dov is the 2021 Laureate of the Israel Prize for Literature.

Printed in the USA
CPSIA information can be obtained
at www.ICGtesting.com
CBHW020512151024
15716CB00012B/31